D1739104

International and Multicultural Organizational Communication

George Cheney, editor
University of Utah and The University of Waikato

George A. Barnett, editor
University of Buffalo, State University of New York

HAMPTON PRESS, INC.
CRESSKILL, NJ 07626

Library of Congress Cataloging-in-Publication Data

International and multicultural organizational communication /
    George Cheney, editor, George A. Barnett, editor
        p. cm.
    Includes bibliographic references and indexes.
    ISBN 1-57273-549-X (cl) -- ISBN 1-57273-550-3 (pb)
        1. Communication in organizations. 2. Intercultural communication.
    3. Diversity in the workplace--Management. I. Cheney, George.
    II. Barnett, George A.

    HD30.3.I559
    658.4'5--dc22

                                                        2004060642

Hampton Press, Inc.
23 Broadway
Cresskill, NJ 07626

CONTENTS

INTRODUCTION

George Cheney and George A. Barnett

As we enter the 21st century, the world is indeed becoming a smaller place. This is now a truism from the standpoint of our sheer interconnectedness, at least for the segment of the world's population that has access to computers and international travel. It is also true in terms of the "global" purviews not only of the United Nations, Exxon-Mobil, The IMF (International Monetary Fund) and World Bank, and Greenpeace, but also of antiglobalization social movement organizing, professional conferences, and terrorist organizations such as Al-Qaeda (yes—the last should be considered as network forms of organization; see Stohl & Stohl, 2002). But, the world is also a larger place, in terms of population, the complexity of social systems, and the sheer magnitude of events.

Communication and information technologies, as well as improvements in transportation, have compressed time and space the world over, creating what McLuhan (1966) long ago labeled *the global village*. But, his confident vision blurred distinctions between positive and negative trends in globalization, just as it overlooked the fact that various kinds of local interests would inevitably be reasserted within the giant village (as we are witnessing in areas from the former Yugoslavia to Indonesia). Still, McLuhan did focus our attention on that fact that communication technology, the media, and now computers have recreated the world such that an event in one place reverberates in others in a faster, more direct way than in the past. Also, just physically getting from one place to another can be achieved in a fraction of the time thought possible even two generations back due to the development of the global transportation infrastructure.

    The process of strengthening the ties among distant localities in such a way that local events are shaped by circumstances at other places in the world is known as *globalization* (Giddens, 1990). This is a helpful, if generic, definition. It is neutral in its description, but it does allow for probing about the *types* of ties between people and places. Of course, the processes of globalization are anything but neutral, in that despite appeals to the "ocean wave" metaphor, globalization does not "just happen." Certainly, ancient empires, medieval-to-modern colonialism, and early state-run enterprises (such as the Dutch East Indies and West Indies Companies in the 17th century) provided powerful and disturbing introductions to globalization. And, although it is convenient to relegate those kinds of institutions and state forms to the past, we must recognize that each of those formations has its descendants today (as is painfully evident in the controversy over Nike's activities in Southeast Asia). From the standpoint of power and equality, then, one of the first questions we must ask is: "Globalization on *whose* terms? (see e.g., Townsley & Stohl, 2003).

    This increase in international communication has led to the worldwide diffusion of values, ideas, opinions, and technologies. A rosy vision of this trend highlights greater interdependence, unity, and collaboration, not to mention the sheer ease of communication and the exchange of ideas. From a more critical stance, of course, we may raise concerns about cultural imperialism, cultural homogenization, and even cultural and social genocide. From the quarters of sociology, economics, and political science, cautions about and critiques of globalization have been growing in number, depth of analysis, and sense of urgency (e.g., Gray, 1998; Stiglitz, 2002). Within communication studies, such critical questions have been raised for some time by scholars in cultural studies as well as in media (e.g., Grossberg, 2001) and very recently in organizational communication (e.g., Cheney, 2000; Stohl, 2005, Zoller, in press).

    For communication scholars in general, and for those in organizational communication in particular, the relationships of technological advances to what we might call "cognitive geography," to various types of human relationships, and to organizational boundaries are of particular importance. Increases in trans-border communication not only reflect our changing conceptions of time and space but also serve to alter further those conceptions. According to Giddens (1990), technologies such as computer-mediated communication (CMC) facilitate the process of time–space "distanciation," in which physical distance becomes increasingly less important in social relations. Thus, globalization stretches the boundaries of social interaction such that the connections between different social contexts become networked across the earth as a whole (Barnett, 2001; Barnett & Lee, 2001). "Place" becomes in this sense less important as a foundation for communication, just as, from a postmodernist standpoint, the author becomes less important than the message itself and its possibilities for being played out in individual and collective consciousness.

Although the term *globalization* has taken on a number of different meanings in recent years (Sklair, 1999), it commonly refers to changes in technology and the expansion of the economic environment to the world as a whole. The global economy today is based on some new systems of production (the celebrated but often exaggerated transition from an industrial to information-based economy), finance, and consumption—all of which are all facilitated by the adoption of computer technologies (Monge & Fulk, 1999). Ironically, however, the very terms in a constellation with globalization—*information age, E-economy*, and so on—direct attention away from the fact that the world still does necessarily produce manufactured products; that smokestacks stand used and unused; that sweatshops persist although they may have changed location; and that the exhaust fumes we breathe are testimony to a not-so-completely-*post*-industrial age. We bring up this point as one where the material and the symbolic have an interesting interplay. And, we emphasize that organizing terms such as *globalization* and *diversity* can be employed in a variety of ways, sometimes to exalt, sometimes to promote, sometimes to cover up, sometimes to divert (Cheney, 2001; Cheney,2004; Cheney, Christensen, Zorn, & Ganesh, 2004).

Importantly, Chase-Dunn (1999) identified five dimensions of globalization. They include the following:

1. Common ecological constraints.
2. Cultural globalization.
3. Political globalization, consisting of institutionalization of international political structures.
4. Globalization of communication.
5. Economic globalization: the worldwide interrelationships of markets and finance, good and services, and networks created by transnational corporations.

This is a reasonably complete list, reminding us of the multiple facets or dimensions of globalization. By the late 1990s, however, economic and technological senses of globalization had overcome cultural, social, and even political meanings—at least in terms of how the trend is most commonly discussed in popular discourse. In fact, this narrowing of the concept was already evident in 1992, when the European Union dropped many of its barriers to the free flow of capital and labor (Cheney & Stohl, 1991). That is to say, globalization gradually became equated with widespread access to new technologies and with the spread of neo-liberal market capitalism. Countering this "hegemony of perspective," groups and networks advocating local economic concerns as well as global environmental ones have made their voices known, often quite loudly, at Seattle, Genoa, Quebec, Miami, and Washington, DC.

The study of "global culture" focuses on the homogenizing effects of the media, consumer products, and transnational organizations, their impact on local or national culture and the emergence of global consciousness with its implications for the global community. Such trends may be seen from either positive or negative viewpoints, of course. One aspect of the emerging global culture has been the change in individual identity for some citizens from one that is strongly grounded in territory to another that is part of a more general global identity. However, in witnessing regional and ethnic conflicts around the world we have to conclude that the attachment to place is still very much a part of the global cultural landscape and that the idea of a "global citizen" may be relevant to a much smaller segment of the population that had been recently imagined.

Certainly, some forms of religious fundamentalism—and we mean to include those of Judaism, Christianity, and Hinduism, as well as examples from the Islamic world—have expressed themselves in ways that are fiercely protective of their geographic as well as social boundaries.

A more nuanced claim might then be that for certain classes of people, place has become less important than their interconnections with other kinds of people in that same class, regardless of the specific countries from which those people come. Indeed, George Cheney witnessed just this phenomenon on a recent visit to Monterrey Tec (ITSEM), in Mexico, where some of the students explained how they identified more with a technologically savvy elite around the world than with the majority of their fellow Mexicans. In this sense, then, certain "global cultures" exist, and they are present at airports, at conferences, at expensive hotels, and of course through the Internet. Add this kind of global culture to the list of global cultures that already includes rampant consumerism, pop music, cinema, and television. In terms of organizational studies, we should acknowledge also the international diffusion of managerial knowledge and the fact that western rationalist modes of organizing work, with efficiency as their hallmark, are in ascendancy along with neo-liberal multinational market capitalism (Munshi & Cheney, 2003).

Communication, the central organizing term of our discipline, is even more polysemic than is *organization*, *globalization*, or *diversity*. *Communication* is not only ambiguous but it is also a contested term. How we conceive of it—for example, "What we have here is a failure to communicate," as one expression of misunderstanding—helps shape our goals in trying to improve it. For purposes of clarifying our own discussion and hinting at some ways to look at communication in the global context, we find it helpful to use sub-terms to capture the complexities of communication and also to suggest different angles on the problem of communication and globalization. A list of such terms would include the following:

- symbol
- message

- information
- interaction
- influence
- persuasion
- relationship
- narrative
- performance
- network
- campaign
- discourse

As is seen here, each of our authors would tend to emphasize one, two, or several of these terms, just as we would ourselves employ different key terms for the analysis of communication. Think, then, about your own perspective on the issue.

Choosing one term or another to "represent" communication has real practical consequences for our research. For instance, we have already commented on how the broad "discourses" of globalization have shifted in recent years so as to emphasize the technological and the economic over the cultural, social, and political. But we could just as well examine under the umbrella of "discourse" the diffusion of managerial knowledge internationally: how certain trends or programs or techniques become the accepted "way to do things" and then are adopted on a worldwide basis (Cheney, 1999). For example, consider how some programs of organizational change (Total Quality Management, etc.) and the imperative for change itself have been embraced almost unthinkingly by many organizations and industries around the world (Zorn, Christensen, & Cheney, 1999).

A focus on "information" and "information flows" directs our attention to how the world works today in terms of the transmission of bits of information that in turn represent stock prices, consumer confidence, or the value of the dollar (Salisbury & Barnett, 1999). Within this discursive context, "The Market" becomes an agent that has voice, desire, temperament, and design (Cheney, 1998, 2004). We try to "read" the market and its direction through decoding bits of information. At the same time, we recognize that persuasion and information intermingle here, as when announced fears of a recession actually contribute to that outcome. The conception of communication as information thus plays an important role in popular awareness, including the idea that a person can be a "message" to be decoded, as when a highly skilled computer analyst moves from one corporation to another.

The metaphor of the "network" is very appealing today, not only in social scientific investigations but also in everyday talk (Barnett & Lee, 2001). Barnett and colleagues, for example, conducted extensive research on the globalization of communication, focusing on such channels as telecommunication (Barnett,

1999, 2001; Barnett, Jacobson, Choi, & Sun-Miller, 1996; Barnett & Salisbury, 1996), the Internet (Barnett, Chon, & Rosen, 2001), monetary flows (Barnett & Salisbury, 1996); trade (Barnett, Salisbury, Kim, & Langhorne, 1999), education (Barnett & Wu, 1995; Chen & Barnett, 2000), air traffic (Barnett, 1996), and international news flow (Kim & Barnett, 1996). To a great extent, these studies have been influenced by the assumptions of Systems Theory and have adopted a network conception of communication and relationships. Barnett et al.'s research indicates that the international communications networks in some respects are becoming denser, more highly interconnected, more highly integrated, and more centralized around the United States, western Europe, and East Asia.

In terms of communication-as-interaction, we are compelled to understand the nature of workplace interchanges, especially where organizations are transformed through the diversification of their workforce. Because many organizations today operate worldwide, they necessarily have social interactions with people from other cultures. They must negotiate business relations in order to coordinate activities and accomplish their goals. Often managers come from a different culture than their subordinates, who are typically from local or sometimes indigenous cultures (Lee & Barnett, 1997). As a result, the culturally governed rules for communicating task directives may differ considerably between the host culture and the visiting manager. When differences in culture accompany power differentials—as they almost easy seem to do in the organizations with which we are familiar—there will be concealed if not visible effects. Additionally, there are differences in the wider culture of work: with implications for everyday practices, for individual and corporate identity, and for power and resistance, as well as for organizational performance (Graham, 1995).

Popular usage of the term *globalization* implies that recent developments in communication and information technology have created a context in which the global market rather than separate national or regional markets has become the relevant arena for economic competition (Chase-Dunn, 1999). Thus, even college graduates today are urged to "think globally" as they plan their careers and prepare for the effects of international competition on the specific industry or organization in which they will work. Sometimes, this imperative is issued rather mindlessly, without attention to the specific points of relevance—for example, obscuring the fact that most of the economies of the world are still overwhelmingly domestic. Again, information technologies have provided the mechanisms for the acceleration of trade and investments through the ability to move money across international borders (Barnett & Salisbury, 1996). And, free trade agreements in Europe, Asia, and the Americas have allowed for greater movement of capital and information although not always labor (Fuentes-Batista & Barnett, 2000).

In certain ways, globalization has facilitated the internationalization of the world's labor market. Despite rising protectionist responses to the flow of people across international borders, skilled as well as unskilled workers migrate from poorer countries on the periphery of the world's economic system to industrialized nations in order to escape the cycle of poverty (Barnett, Rosen, & Chon, 2000; Massey et al., 1993). But, when the immigrants arrive in western Europe, North America, or Australasia, they frequently take jobs at the bottom of the socioeconomic scale, such as in food processing or menial service work. Because these individuals come from the world over, their presence creates a multicultural, although usually far from integrated workplace. (Of course, we cannot ignore the fact that one result of the internationalization of many industries and the implementation of various free trade agreements is that firms themselves are allowed easily to migrate.)

Diversity itself becomes an important and contested term within this context, as seen in recent writings on management trends. The term at once signals a concern for a multicultural workforce and an attempt to contain that diversity such that it can be employed predictably in the service of a firm. Diversity management in this way becomes framed within the context of organizational socialization and managerial control, and much of this emphasis is not surprising, even when the initiative stops short of racism. As we asked earlier with respect to globalization, we must question in any particular case: "Whose vision of diversity?" (e.g., Ashcraft & Allen, 2003).

This book focuses on the implications of globalization for social organizations and the study of organizational communication. It does not provide a comprehensive review of the communication process associated with increasing globalization and cultural variability in multinational organizations; rather, it presents a series of chapters that provide a few examples of current research on the topic. The reader is directed to Stohl (2001) for an excellent overall review of this literature in which she considers trends of divergence (e.g., the reassertion or emergence of local identities) together with trends of convergence (e.g., cultural imperialism).

This book deals with the implications of globalization and diversity for contemporary organizational life. The chapters presented here are wide ranging in terms of how they approach international and intercultural issues. For example, two of the chapters (Hafen; Munshi) consider critically what we mean by "diversity management" and explore implications for management practice and organizational training. Two chapters (Becker; Houston & McPhail) concern how intercultural and international issues are manifested in various kinds of organizations within the United States. Houston and McPhail assess the implications of the Million Man March for intercultural communication within an ad hoc, social movement organizing context. And, Becker offers a multidimensional model of cross-cultural training. One chapter offers detailed cross-cultural comparisons of the U.S., China, and Taiwan (Cai and Hung) In the third section of the book, two chapters (Díaz-Sáenz & Witherspoon; Pérez) focus on Mexican organizations, addressing issues of community within the workplace and the projection of an international image externally. Finally, two chapters deal broadly with international contexts for organizing: in terms of refugee assistance (Ngai & Koehn) and technological development (Ganesh).

With this collection, we seek to push the boundaries of organizational communication beyond its current confines. The authors represented here draw on a wide array of literatures, including those of international development, international migration and demographics, postcolonialism, and social movements. The organizations studied represent all major sectors and a variety of national and ethnic contexts. The chapters appropriately blur the distinction between "internal" and "external" organizational communication (see Cheney & Christensen, 2001) as they treat phenomena that cross those borders as well. The chapters feature empirical, interpretive, and critical postures toward research. They engage practical as well as theoretical issues. Above all, the authors lead us to reflect on the changing shapes of organizations and institutions in today's world.

REFERENCES

Ashcraft, K. L., & Allen, B. J. (2003). The racial foundations of organizational communication. *Communication Theory, 13*(1), 5-38

Barnett, G.A. (1996). Multilingualism in telecommunication and transportation. In H. Goebl, P.H. Nelde, Z. Stary, & W. Wolck (Eds.), *Contact linguistics: An international handbook of contemporary research* (pp. 431-438). New York: Walter de Gruyter.

Barnett, G.A. (1999). The social structure of international telecommunications. In H. Sawhney & G.A. Barnett (Eds.), *Progress in communication sciences. Vol. XV: Advances in telecommunications* (pp. 151-186). Stamford, CT: Ablex.

Barnett, G.A. (2001). A longitudinal analysis of the international telecommunication network: 1978-1996. *American Behavioral Scientist, 44*(10), 1638-1655.

Barnett, G.A., Chon, B., & Rosen, D. (2001). The structure of internet flows in cyberspace, *NETCOM, 15*(1-2), 61-80.

Barnett, G.A., Jacobson, T.L., Choi, Y., & Sun-Miller, S. (1996). An examination of the international telecommunications network. *The Journal of International Communication, 3*, 19-43.

Barnett, G.A., & Lee, M. (2001). Issues in cross-cultural communication research. In W.B. Gudykunst & B. Mody (Eds.), *Handbook of international and intercultural communication* (pp. 275-290). Thousand Oaks, CA: Sage.

Barnett, G.A., Rosen, D., & Chon, B.S. (2000, April). *A network analysis of international migration.* Presented at the Sunbelt Social Networks Conference, Vancouver, BC.

Barnett, G.A., & Salisbury, J.G.T. (1996). Communication and globalization: A longitudinal analysis of the international telecommunications network. *Journal of World Systems Research, 2*(16), 1-17.

Barnett, G.A., Salisbury, J.G.T., Kim, C., & Langhorne, A. (1999). Globalization and international communication: An examination of monetary, telecommunications and trade networks. *The Journal of International Communication, 6,* 7-49.

Barnett, G.A., & Wu, R.Y. (1995). The international student exchange network: 1970 & 1989. *Higher Education, 30*, 353-368.

Chase-Dunn, C. (1999). Globalization: A world-systems perspective. *Journal of World-Systems Research, 5*(2), 187-215.

Chen, T., & Barnett, G.A. (2000). Research on international student flows from a macro perspective: A network analysis of 1985, 1989 and 1995. *Higher Education, 39*, 435-453.

Cheney, G. (1998). It's the economy, stupid! A rhetorical-communicative perspective on today's market. *Australian Journal of Communication* (Special issue).

Cheney, G. (1999). *Values at work: Employee participation meets market pressure at Mondragón*. Ithaca, NY & London: Cornell University Press.

Cheney, G. (2000). Thinking "differently" about organizational communication: Why, how and where? *Management Communication Quarterly, 14*, 132-141.

Cheney, G. (2001). *The local and the global: Trends in tension*. Unpublished paper, The University of Montana-Missoula.

Cheney, G. (2004). Arguing about the "place" of ethics in market-oriented discourses. In S. Goldzwig & P. Sullivan (Eds.), *New directions in rhetorical criticism* (pp. 61-88). Thousand Oaks, CA: Sage.

Cheney, G., & Christensen, L.T. (2001). Organizational identity: Linkages between internal and external organizational communication. In F.M. Jablin & L.L. Putnam (Eds.), *The new handbook of organizational communication* (pp. 231-269). Thousand Oaks, CA: Sage.

Cheney, G., Christensen, L.T., Zorn, T.E., and Ganesh, S. (2004). *Organizational communication in an age of globalization: Issues, reflections, and practices*. Prospect Heights, IL: Waveland Press.

Cheney, G., & Stohl, C. (1991). European transformations and their implications for communication research. *Journal of Applied Communication Research, 19*, 330-339.

Fuentes-Bautista, M., & Barnett, G.A. (2000, June). *Telecommunication in the era of trading blocs: A longitudinal network analysis of the Americas*. Paper presented to the International Communication Association, Acapulco, Mexico.

Giddens, A. (1990). *The consequences of modernity*. Stanford, CA: Stanford University Press.

Graham, L. (1995). *On the line at Subaru-Isuzu*. Ithaca, NY & London: Cornell University Press.

Gray, J. (1998). *False dawn: The delusions of global capitalism*. London: Granta Books.

Grossberg, L. (2001). *Why does neo-liberalism hate kids? The attack on youth and the culture of politics*. Unpublished manuscript, The University of North Carolina at Chapel Hill.

Kim, K., & Barnett, G.A. (1996). The determinants of international news flow: A network analysis, *Communication Research, 23*, 323-352.

Lee, M., & Barnett, G.A. (1997). A symbols-and-meaning approach to the organizational culture of banks in the United States, Japan, and Taiwan. *Communication Research, 24*, 394-412.

McLuhan, H.M. (1966). *Understanding media: The extensions of man*. New York: Beacon.

Massey, D.S., Arango, J., Hugo, G., Kouaouci, A., Pellegrino, A., & Taylor, J.E. (1993). Theories of international migration: A review and appraisal. *Population and Development Review, 19*(3), 431-466.

Monge, P.R., & Fulk, J. (1999). Communication technologies for global network organizations. In G. DeSantis & J. Fulk (Eds.), *Communication technologies and organizational form* (pp. 71-100). Thousand Oaks, CA: Sage.

Munshi, D., & Cheney, G. *"Diversity" management and organizational control.* Unpublished manuscript, The University of Waikato.

Salisbury, J.G.T., & Barnett, G.A. (1999). The world system of international monetary flows: A network analysis. *The Information Society, 15*(1), 31-50.

Salisbury, J.G.T., & Barnett, G.A. (1999). A network analysis of international monetary flows. *The Information Society, 15*(1), 31-50.

Sklair, L. (1999). Competing conceptions of globalization. *Journal of World-Systems Research, 5*(2), 143-163.

Stiglitz, J. (2002). *Globalization and its discontents.* London: Penguin.

Stohl, C. (2001). Globalizing organizational communication. In L.L. Putnam & F. Jablin (Eds.), *The new handbook of organizational communication* (pp. 323-375). Thousand Oaks, CA: Sage.

Stohl, C. (2005). Globalization theory. In S.K. May & D.K. Mumby (Eds.), *Engaging organizational theory and research: Multiple perspectives* (pp. 223-262). Thousand Oaks, CA: Sage.

Stohl, C., & Stohl, M. (2002, November). *Organizational communication and terrorist networks.* Paper presented at the annual meeting of the National Communication Association, New Orleans.

Townsley, N., & Stohl, C. (2003). Contracting corporate social responsibility: Swedish expansions in global temporary work. *Management Communication Quarterly, 16*(4), 599-605.

Zoller, H.M. (in press). Dialogue as global issue managment: Legitimizing corporate influence in the transatlantic business dialogue. *Management Communication Quarterly.*

Zorn, T., Christensen, L.T., & Cheney, G. (1999). *Do we really want constant change?* (No. 2 in booklet series). San Francisco: Berrett-Koehler.

ACKNOWLEDGMENTS

The editors would like to thank the contributors to this book for their patience. We would also like to thank the following colleagues for their help in reviewing the manuscripts submitted to this volume.

Brenda J. Allen, The University of Colorado, Denver
Donal Carbaugh, The University of Massachusetts, Amherst
Lars Thøger Christensen, The University of Southern Denmark, Odense
Noshir Contractor, The University of Illinois, Urbana-Champaign
James A. Danowski, The University of Illinois, Chicago
Stanley A. Deetz, The University of Colorado, Boulder
Gail Fairhurst, The University of Cincinnati, Cincinnati, Ohio
Kristine Fitch, The University of Iowa, Iowa City
Howard Giles, The University of California, Santa Barbara
Shiv Ganesh, The University of Montana, Missoula
Alberto González, Bowling Green State University, Bowling Green, Ohio
Loril Gossett, The University of Texas, Austin
Teresa Harrison, The State University of New York, Albany
Michael Hecht, The Pennsylvania State University, State College
Susan Hellweg, San Diego State University, San Diego, California
Fredric M. Jablin, The University of Richmond, Virginia
Kathy Krone, The University of Nebraska, Lincoln

Debashish Munshi, The University of Waikato, Hamilton, New Zealand
Patricia Riley, The University of Southern California, Los Angeles
Marshall Scott Poole, Texas A&M University, College Station
Linda L. Putnam, Texas A&M University, College Station
William D. Richards, Simon Fraser University, Buraby, British Columbia
David R. Seibold, The University of California, Santa Barbara
William J. Starosta, Howard University, Washington, DC
Dolores Tanno, The University of Nevada, Las Vegas
James R. Taylor, Université de Montréal, Québec
Frederico Varona, San José State University, San José, California
Rolf T. Wigand, University of Arkansas, Little Rock
Theodore Zorn, The University of Waikato, Hamilton, New Zealand

In addition, the editors express appreciation to Anne Bialowas, Andrew Gilla, and Daniel J. Lair for proofreading.

Finally, this book would not have been possible without the timely support of Barbara Bernstein at Hampton Press.

This book is dedicated to all those who work for global peace with justice.

George Cheney,
Salt Lake City, Utah USA

George A. Barnett
Buffalo, New York USA

October 2004

SECTION A

Meanings of
Diversity Management

1

CULTURAL DIVERSITY TRAINING

A Critical (Ironic) Cartography of Advocacy and Oppositional Silences

Susan Hafen
Weber State University

The banner of cultural diversity *waves over educational programs, training workshops, project grants, and funding. Although it is the rare voice (either in business echelons or academe) that speaks out* against *cultural diversity, many of its advocates nevertheless question the benefits of such training and whom it really serves. Some of those voices are opponents of any diversity initiatives in organizations; others are simply critical of what changes training does (and does not) produce. This chapter maps out not only the voices but the silences—what advocates and opponents don't say—in a cartography of the organizational "ice-floe splits" we straddle as our organizations grapple with the ironies of finding common ground while celebrating our differences.*

Although the expressed goal of much intercultural education and cultural diversity training is to create an ongoing conversation about our growing organizational multiculturalism—that is, our cultural differences (and, more often, commonalities)—the entire terrain is a field of uncertain and dangerous silences. In

Adrienne Rich's (1978) *The Dream of A Common Language*, she writes of "Cartographies of Silence":

> A conversation begins / with a lie. And each /
> speaker of the so-called common language feels /
> the ice-floe split, the drift apart / as if powerless /
> as if up against / a force of nature. (p. 16)

In many organizations, the members can feel that ice-floe split, the drift apart of cultural differences. The goal of the cultural diversity training program they attend is to stop the drift apart and mend the split—or to at least begin the process. But from the standpoint of trainees, the training conversations too often "begins with a lie." The lie(s) are different from the perspectives of diversity advocates versus diversity opponents; what the participants share is an increasing frustration with the smoke and mirrors of diversity training initiatives. Diversity advocates are disillusioned with the promises of organizational multi-culturalism—where equality abides, difference is valued, and diversity is embraced. The opponents are maddened by what they consider to be an organizational knee-jerk reaction to "political correctness." The only uniformly and unequivocally positive voices about diversity training seems to come from those who benefit the most: training consultants (or their executive clients, at least publicly).

The purpose of this chapter is to map the problematics of cultural diversity training within U.S. organizations (vs. cross-cultural training for expatriate managers of international organizations) in a cartography of silences from the perspectives of both advocates and opponents. My own critical standpoint is the jaded positionality of an ex-human resources (HR) manager, now teaching diversity training classes to organizational communication seniors who struggle with valuing diversity while hating affirmative action and reverse discrimination. These students are little different from past employees: They want to embrace difference, but they don't want to change their own work styles or personal interactions; they reject racism, but "American" in Wisconsin and Minnesota (or Iowa or Utah or wherever whiteness remains largely uncontested) does not signify a person of color. Many students, like their local employers, believe that diversity training may be needed in a big company in a big city that has a lot of diversity (read, "people who aren't White"), but not in their towns. My goal each semester for students—and here for readers—is not to herald diversity training, but to deconstruct both pro and con positions. Advocacy and oppositional rhetorics are not merely mirror opposites (one the antithesis of the other); rather, each includes its own sets of omissions, silences that refuse other ways of seeing, that avoid rather than refute.

The arguments that follow are grouped into what advocates say—and do not say—and what antagonists say—and remain silent about. Before critically reviewing (and editorializing) their arguments regarding diversity training, I provide a brief historical background and definitions salient to discussions of cultural diversity within organizations. I conclude with examples of ironic dialogue among proponents of all positions, problematizing each position as only partially true and necessarily open-ended. After all is said and done, a diversity equilibrium can never be truly achieved because the marginalized voices today might be mainstreamed tomorrow and must then be ready to welcome diverse, new (and challenging) voices in ongoing organizational transformation. What is essential is that those who teach, train, or facilitate dialogue remember that they too are situated by their own cultural capital. Ironically, this is never more difficult than when the topic itself is cultural diversity, and we are confused/conflicted about when/how to recognize our similarities and our differences.

BACKGROUND AND DEFINITIONS

After Title VII of the Civil Rights Act of 1964, the 1970s was the beginning era of government-required affirmative action programs to assure equal opportunity for racial minorities and women. Not until the 1987 Hudson Institute's widely (mis)quoted and much misrepresented *Workforce 2000 Report* did organizations feel any urgency to voluntarily attempt to match the diversity of their organizations with that of their community and customer base. Although the report described with detailed statistics the influx of minorities, immigrants, and women into the job market, what people visualized was an immediate, feminized, browning of the workplace. That wasn't what the report said, and, in a follow-up report *Workforce 2020*, the authors acknowledged that their earlier study was misunderstood and exploited by "diversity entrepreneurs" (cited in Lubove, 1997, p. 125). It is still true, however, that non-Hispanic White Americans are the only racioethnic group whose percentage of the U.S. population is predicted to continue to decrease from 75% in 1990 to 53% in 2050 (Parrillo, 1996). The U.S. Department of Labor predicts that in 2010, the civilian labor force will be approximately 69% White, 13% Hispanic, 12% Black, and 6% Asian/Other (Fullerton & Toossi, 2001). Also predicted is that the percentage distribution of women in the workforce will continue to increase from 43% in 1980 to 48% by 2010, due to a projected annual growth rate for women in the labor force from 2000 to 2010 of 1.4%, compared to men's projected growth rate of only .9%.

This increasing, visible diversity of the labor pool is just one reason for the focus on cultural diversity; the second is the globalization of multinational corporations and global marketing of national corporations. Add to this the recent international pressure for the United States to shift from focusing on human rights violations in other countries to racism in its own, culminating in the first analysis of *U.S. Compliance with the United Nations Convention on the Elimination of All Forms of Racial Discrimination,* released September 21, 2000. The report addressed the "subtle and elusive" racist practices today ("Racial discrimination," 2000). Also compelling are the legal incentives of being in compliance with the 1990 Americans with Disabilities Act and federal anti-discrimination and harassment laws. The federal mandates of Affirmative Action (AA) and Equal Employment Opportunity (EEO) still drive many cultural diversity initiatives, although this conflation confuses their distinctly different goals.

Alverson (1998) differentiates between EEO/AA and what has come to be known as "managing diversity" by emphasizing that diversity is not just about hiring and retention goals to reflect the community or national demographics, which is the focus of EEO mandates or AA. Bond and Pyle (1998) noted that the popularity of diversity programs arose at precisely the time when EEO/AA programs were the most challenged. They explain the apparent contradiction by pointing to the "overall ideological shifts in the 1980s toward more market solutions and fewer government interventions" (p. 253). However, whether training is focused on EEO/AA or managing diversity, reduction of potential discrimination lawsuits is a common long-term training goal. In 2001 alone, the Equal Employment Opportunity Commission (EEOC) reported 80,840 new cases filed with 36% of them citing racial discrimination and 32% citing sex discrimination (United States EEOC, n.d.). Reverse discrimination lawsuits have also appeared, with the EEOC reporting 10,000 cases filed from 1987 to 1994 (Bond & Pyle, 1998). (Currently the EEOC does not separate reverse discrimination lawsuits from its statistics on race/sex discrimination lawsuits.) However, although EEOC discrimination cases are down from a 1994 high of 91,189 new cases, in the federal courts discrimination lawsuits have increased more than 300% in the last decade. And only 1.6% of all civil rights actions in 1998 were even cases filed by the federal government. Furthermore, only 5% of all 1998 cases went through a jury trial to a verdict, which means they were settled out of court (Fox, Glenn, Jacobs, & Karamchandani, 2000). Although these statistics provide one justification for diversity training, the distinction between diversity and EEO/AA training still needs emphasis.

Perhaps the greatest difference between EEO/AA and diversity initiatives is the shifting definition of diversity. EEO/AA is based on legal definitions of protected groups. Diversity initiatives have moved beyond race and gender to a wide (and ever expanding) range of ways people in organizations differ—and therein lies the problem and/or the solution, depending on one's perspective. Diversity can include religion, age, national origin, physical appearance and abilities, sexual orientation, mental abilities, education, personality attributes, work style, organizational department, family size, political affiliation and ideas, lifestyle, and many other factors. Diversity conflict begins with the lack of consensus about which diversities are most cogent and need to be addressed and with the inconsistencies in how they are addressed (Carter, 2000; Day-Overmeyer, 1995; Mueller, 1996). West and Fenstermaker (1995) believe that categorical diversity is too limiting, given the accomplishment of diversity across a multiplicity of differences. And by "accomplishment," they mean intersubjective understandings that occur through communication in ongoing, everyday interactions.

How organizations define diversity depends, in part, on their perceived diversity goals, which Day-Overmeyer (1995) suggested fit into three categories: (a) to reflect markets (internal and external "customers") and improve products, (b) to protect the company from lawsuits, and (c) to make employees more sensitive. The third rationale, which Cox (1994, p. 11) called a "moral imperative" and R. Thomas (1991, p. 16) framed as "humanitarianism," is today overshadowed by business and legal imperatives, which have resulted in an explosion of diversity training programs. One survey of human resource professionals at 785 companies showed that 75% of them provide diversity training or are planning to do so (Rynes & Rosen, 1995). Another survey of the top Fortune 50 corporations by A. T. Kearney Executive Search found that 70% had formal diversity management programs in place and 16% were developing them or had scattered programs (Lynch, 1997). According to *HR Focus* ("Diversity drainage," 1999), companies spend upward of $300 million annually on diversity training. A recent report in *HR Magazine* (Leonard, 2002) states that even when overall corporate training budgets were slashed by 30% in 2001, diversity training was dropped only 15%.

Unlike businesses' profit-driven motives for diversity goals, the goals of higher education should have diversity interests at their core in order to educate citizens for a pluralistic society (Smith, 1995). However, universities' diversity efforts are not solely altruistic. Universities too have federal mandates as well as profit motives. For example, universities invest in diversity to attract international students as well as ethnic minority students. International students (about 500,000 in 1998), most of whom pay full tuition, and their dependents contribute about $9.9 billion to the U.S. economy (Wingert, Babwin, & Kwon, 1998). Although another important benefit is a more culturally diverse campus, that benefit is not acknowledged by all university members; hence, the need for campus cultural diversity training programs. Whether or not diversity training is good for business, clearly it is a good business for trainers, who are often at the forefront of its advocacy.

ADVOCATES OF DIVERSITY TRAINING

The concept of valuing differences was first introduced by Barbara Walker, who became Digital Corporation's first vice president for diversity in the 1980s (Lynch, 1997, p. 44). In the video, *Champions of Diversity*, Walker talks about diversity in terms of the "personal journey, working beyond race and gender, to sexual orientation, disability, even styles of bonding, intimacy, love, forgiveness, taking risks" (p. 56). Other videos in the series created by Copeland and Griggs (a husband and wife team), profile scenes of diversity training programs, such as employees at Hewlett-Packard "gaining insights into disabilities by pretending to be disabled for a day" (p. 57), or diversity task force meetings, such as U.S. West's pluralism council. Corporate leaders in diversity, at least as profiled by R. Thomas in his "doing diversity" (1991, 1996) books include Avon, with its Women and Minority Taskforce organized in the 1970s; BellSouth, with its work-family efforts; Goodyear Tire and Rubber, which established recognition and measurement systems for managing diversity; and General Motors, which has recruited senior executives to serve as diversity champions and published a diversity brochure for all employees. Another "how to do diversity" book is *Managing Workforce 2000* (Jamieson & O'Mara, 1991), which presents "inspirational" accounts of companies' successes with "valuing diversity" training, including Merck, Procter & Gamble, Hewlett-Packard, and Hallmark.

R. Thomas (1991), like most advocates of diversity training, suggests that training be tailored to the needs of the diverse populations (employees and/or customers), which are determined by the organizational culture(s) and surfaced in an organizational culture "audit." How-to manuals (e.g., Arredondo, 1996; Gardenswartz & Rowe, 1993; Keller, Young, & Riley, 1996; Leach & George, 1995) with a variety of instruments for employee interviews, focus groups, and written surveys have proliferated for companies who do not want to pay up to $100,000 for a cultural audit—the price tag demanded by top consultants (Rynes & Rosen, 1995). Loden's (1996) how-to textbook emphasizes the importance of an implementation plan, as well as ongoing and completion assessments. The implementation plan includes diversity training programs, which means hiring trainers at an average of $2,000 per day (Rynes & Rosen, 1995) or using another how-to training textbook (see e.g., Clements & Jones, 2002; Cox & Beale, 1997; Singelis, 1998).

Universities as well as businesses are breeding grounds for assessments and training programs conducted by diversity consultants and trainers (see, e.g., Tan, Morris, & Romero, 1996; also the reports of diversity training initiatives compiled by S. Jackson & Associates, 1992). Besides their contributions to these lucrative avenues of applied education, diversity scholars have also developed theories of diversity training, such as Ramsey's (1996) model of diversity identity development training and Garcia's (1995) anthropological approach to multicultural diversity training. Diversity practitioners and communication academics could still benefit from a cross-pollination of applied organizational training research using communication theories addressing rhetorical sensitivity, self-disclosure, communicator style, interpersonal attraction, relational dimensions, and so on (Arai, Wanda-Thibaut, & Shockley-Zalabak, 2001). What, however, has been gained as a result of all these diversity audits, training programs, and theoretical models?

Black Enterprise Magazine decided to challenge some of the companies that had been touting their diversity programs, putting them up for scrutiny for outsiders to judge who the diversity programs were truly serving (Caudron & Hayes, 1997). Many companies declined to provide any more additional information than their diversity press kits contained. Other firms such as Levi Strauss and Federal Express were initially enthusiastic, but later backed out for various reasons. Six companies finally agreed to be analyzed: SC Johnson Wax, TIAA-CREF, Texas Instruments, Ameritech, JC Penney, and Pacific Gas & Electric. Due to lack of space, only the first four were actually analyzed for the magazine's article. All four companies were given high marks for progress in some areas, albeit not all areas. SC Johnson Wax has an African American Business Council, which focuses on issues relating to the hiring and retention of African Americans and has a direct line to top management decision makers. TIAA-CREF's former chairman and CEO was the first African American to head a Fortune 100 financial services company; the current vice chairman, president, and CEO is also African American. Texas Instruments developed an incentive compensation program in 1995 that rewarded managers for excelling in diversity. Ameritech has created partnerships between employees and senior managers through employee advocacy groups, such as the Black and Hispanic Advisory Panels, the Corporate Executive Leadership Program, and Gay, Lesbian and Bisexual Employees of Ameritech, and it awards bonuses to organizational teams that contributed to diversity.

Lynch (1997) provided other corporate examples: NYNEX Corporation gives "Diversity Salute" awards to employees who foster an environment of inclusiveness; Procter & Gamble won the U.S. Labor Department's Opportunity 2000 Award for its comprehensive affirmative action program; Hughes Aircraft has long had formal mentoring and minority outreach programs. Insiders at Bell Atlantic (Williams & Moyer, 1995) describe the creation of an Accelerating Leadership Diversity (ALD) process to identify and develop diverse leaders. Wisconsin Power and Light created a diversity steering team to identify company-wide issues that affect diversity (Mueller, 1996). Florida-based public warehouse giant GATX offers English and Spanish classes to its employees, hoping to create a more bilingual workforce (Loudin, 2000).

Jackson and Associates' (1992) volume of diversity case studies written by consultants or internal human resources professionals describes their successes with strategic diversity initiatives at Xerox, Pacific Bell, Digital, Harris SemiConductor, Electric Solid State, American Express, Pepsi Cola, and others. The editors emphasize that, whatever diversity initiatives an organization might undertake—and those vary across organizations—the essential principles are to "work closely with customers, anticipate problems, and institutionalize what is learned along the way" (p. 338). The author of one landmark case study, disguised as XYZ Corporation, admits a report bias in its understatement of the struggle and its emphasis on the change that occurred rather than what did not change (Alderfer, 1992). He quoted a senior Black member of the Race Relations Advisory Group: "I see it on paper, and it looks good. Why don't I feel good?"

Since the early 1990s, diversity advocates have become more critical as they attempt to publicize the problems—the struggles and the changes that do not occur—not to hammer down all organizational diversity efforts, but to revise "window dressing" programs that conceal problems instead of resolving them. These critics do not oppose diversity training; they just want to see the visible *effects* of organizational diversity, not its co-optation and patronization. Some of the problems they see with current diversity training programs are included in the subsections that follow: a revisionist stereotyping and exotification of culture, training in lieu of systemic changes, the primacy of a public relations agenda, impression management to maintain status quo, increased organizational conflict after training, lawsuits resulting from diversity training, material interests carving the diversity pie, and the (thinly) veiled interests of diversity trainers.

SILENCES:
WHAT ADVOCATES DON'T SAY

What many diversity training advocates don't often say—at least, not publicly—are the inevitable problematics of organizational initiatives, which benefit (or disadvantage) various groups and persons differently. Indeed, cultural group membership is itself contested. A cover article in *Newsweek* on race (Cose, 2000) is entitled "What's White Anyway?" and describes today's multicultural families where children with "the option of being white—those with, say, one Mexican parent or Cherokee grandfather [or both]—are more than ever inclined to think of themselves as something else" (p. 65). Responding to multigroup membership, the 2000 Census for the first time instructed respondents to check one or more boxes to indicate what they considered themselves to be. R. Jackson (2000) ended an essay on exploring race in the academy by stating that the 21st century will be influenced primarily by identity. The status of race today problematizes Ferdman's (1995) belief that one purpose of diversity training is to teach about cultural identity that "learning that individual uniqueness is not compromised by group memberships" (p. 57). The question inevitably arises of who determines the characteristics of a culture and what it means to identify (or not) with that culture.

Ethnic/Cultural Stereotyping and Exotification

Hoffman (1997) is concerned that essentialist and static notions of cultures can hurt the transformative potential of diversity training, which too often fetishes and categorizes culture, inhibiting members of that culture from constructing their own identities. Much diversity training is aligned with "multiculturalism," which Rattansi (1992) described as premised on "sympathetic teaching of 'other cultures' in order to dispel the ignorance that is seen to be at the root of prejudice and intolerance" (p. 25). Learning about other cultures is too often an exercise in replacing one stereotype with another; the trick to cultural sensitivity is to be able to categorize without appearing to stereotype. Mexican Americans are not lazy, they have a strong social orientation. African Americans are not hostile, they are direct; Asian Americans are not submissive, they are cooperative and collectivistic. Stereotyping is okay, depending upon the stereotype. It is even "laudable, given the often grotesque caricatures of African, Asian, and Arab histories and cultures," explained Rattansi, who nonetheless laments the "unacknowledged disingenuity involved in replacing one lot of selective images with another set of partial representations" (p. 34).

Multicultural programs are too often over simplistic formulas about other lifestyles, religions, holidays, customs, and worldviews, celebrated with festivals of "native" costumes, dances, and foods and discussed through ethnic literature (Goodwin, 2000; Rattansi, 1992). Not only is there rarely discussion of the differences within cultures for competing "cultural representations, knowledges and practices" (Rattansi, 1992, p. 39), but multicultural education too often is premised on learning how race/culture resides in other visual racial groups, not within the learners themselves (Wang, 2000). Paskoff (1996) complained that such programs also fail to recommend how cultural differences should then guide management practices:

> How should a worker who is Jewish and Russian be treated? An older American Indian? A disabled Hispanic female? A person whose mother is Swedish and whose father is Jamaican? How should a manager measure the blend of characteristics of an individual employee to determine which cultural strains are important so that she may adapt her interpersonal behavior accordingly? (p. 44)

Furthermore, little evidence exists that multicultural education is effective, at least not in teacher education (Goodwin, 2000) or medical education (Wang, 2000). Valli (1995) urged educators to cease reifying the essentialist construct of race (and, it might be added, ethnicity). When races are essentialized, so is the "prejudiced individual," who then "becomes the target for pedagogies that are supposed to cure them of this pathology" (Rattansi, 1992, p. 25). Individuals, no less than races and cultures, cannot be so readily simplified.

Intercultural encounters are not only racialized, but also sexualized and inter-laced with class assumptions: The result is an entangled web of ambivalence that can combine admiration, distaste, fear, and confusion.

If the multiculturalist is problematic, the antiracist is no less so. The antiracist wants to dismantle "the institutionalized practices of racism," whether in education, employment, housing, or immigration, and directly confront "racist ideologies," in part by presenting historical accounts of groups' struggles against racist oppression (Rattansi, 1992, p. 29). Ironically, Rattansi observes, while the multiculturalist essentializes ethnicity, the anti-racist essentializes cul-ture (i.e., lived experiences of members of the same race), overemphasizing similarity in order to unify marginalized communities. The result is that, by denying issues of ethnic, class, and gender differences, antiracists let their "fear of cultural differences" create more division. The problem with a focus on *cul-tural* differences, asserted Appiah (1998), is that "it's not black culture that the racist disdains, but blacks. . . . Culture is not the problem, and it is not the solu-tion" (p. 27). Ironically, their resistance to cultural differences puts antiracists in bed with conservatives who believe in assimilation as the American way and view advocates for the celebration of difference as "renegades and disrupting social harmony" (Choi, 1997, p. 123).

What the antiracists and multiculturalists share, however, is rejecting the admonition for "color blindness," corporate-speak for getting beyond race rela-tions. Alderfer (2000) deconstructed this rhetoric of color blindness that will ostensibly bring justice to organizational hiring and promotions. His analysis follows: Outside of racial interactions, color blindness is a disability. To deny the color you see is to deny the reality around you—to not see the association between race and discrimination, for example. Branch (2000), writing about the Denver Municipal Court, said that color and culture blindness "means keeping things the ways they have always been" (p. 177).

As a reaction to the rhetoric of color blindness, the new antiracist discourse advocates the study of "whiteness" as way to analyze White privilege and the integration of race with class and gender (Nakayama & Martin, 1999). Within diversity training programs, both White trainers and their client managers need to see also themselves as racialized (Johnson, 2000; see also McIntosh, 1998, for "White Privilege" activity). Educators and trainers need to understand the way that institutions "white out" their members as part of their career develop-ment, how they are socialized to "professionalism" (Fine, 2000). Cheney (2000) referred to the same idea, without calling it "whiting out," in his critique of organizational communication scholars ("we") who avoid studies or rhetoric that smacks of Marxism, aligning ourselves instead "with the 'professional' and resource rich segments of society" (p. 137). Talking about whiteness and White privilege is far more threatening to the status quo than multicultural discussions. In 1996, the first academic whiteness conference was held at the University of California at Berkeley, and the following year, a course in whiteness was offered at Macalester College, Minnesota. When a newspaper spotlighted the college course, subsequent letters (both male) to the editor expressed readers' outrage. One disputed the idea of a unified White culture of privilege, and another complained that it was time to get over "this silly obsession with race, blame, and guilt" (Burson, 1997, p. A1).

It is doubtful that these writers see themselves as racist; they are simply anti-antiracist, believing that racism, since the abolishment of slavery, has been largely eliminated. What they don't want to acknowledge is institutionalized discrimination and how they may benefit from it. Johnson (2000) used the cases of The Citadel and Texaco to illustrate the denial common among White male leaders, who meet the letter of the law rather than the spirit of the law. Denial can take the form of believing that the problem is in a few *other* individuals, who may need training, but not in the organizational structures and systemic practices.

Training in Lieu of Organizational/Structural/Systemic Changes

Experienced diversity consultants do not promote training as the ready solution when the organizational diversity problem/need appears to be institutional, rather than individual (Chung, 1997; Cox, 1994; Fine, 1995; Gallagher, 2000; Golembiewski, 1995; T. Harris, 1997; S. Jackson & Associates, 1992; Jamieson & O'Mara, 1991; Jordan, 1998; Lindsley, 1998b; R. Thomas, 1991; Watts & Evans, 2000). Institutional cultural changes emerge from changes in organizational policies and practices—the everyday assumptions and interactions that seem "natural" but that can create a climate of exclusion and/or pressured assimilation. While advocating diversity training in the form of valuing differences, R. Thomas (1991) reiterated the need for multilevel efforts to locate and change deeply rooted practices based on unconscious assumptions—what he called "changing the cultural roots that are hindrances" (p. 14; see also Chung, 1997). Those roots include tracking women and minorities into staff support departments with less power and short career ladders (Raggins, 1995).

One possibility for changing cultural roots is to make middle management accountable for managing diversity. After interviewing 16 HR practitioners and 9 consultants, and facilitating two mixed focus groups, Jordan (1998) reported that although the majority agreed on the need for management accountability, less than half received any incentives or rewards for their diversity efforts, and very few have those efforts tied to performance reviews. If internal HR practitioners cannot accomplish structural/systemic changes, external consultants with handcrafted (or borrowed) diversity training programs are even less likely to accomplish lasting change. Rose, a consultant who works with the California State University and Community College Systems, is quite aware that her diversity training sessions are merely window dressing and "another notch on the organizational belt" (cited in Lynch, 1997, p. 70). Henderson (1994) warned against training as a quick fix because there is little evidence that prodiversity attitudes are created by "logical-information inputs"—instead, a great amount of information on controversial topics can actually "harden or freeze antidiversity attitudes" (p. 137).

Window Dressing and Public Relations

Not only is the training used as window dressing, so are the trainers—or anyone involved in diversity initiatives as a person of color. And non-White organizational members are frequently pressured to "help the organization deal with diversity," as Allen (1995, p. 150) explained from her own experience as a Black faculty member expected to provide the "minority perspective." Essed (2000), a Black Dutch academic who has taught in the United States, also described this "request to represent 'colour' at forums and other formal events" (p. 890; see also Essed, 1996). Racial/ethnic identities are not only foregrounded but heightened for some scholars and professionals in what Grande (2000) termed "strategic essentialism," when, for example, Native American scholars "feel compelled to perform a hyperauthentic or racialized self to gain or retain legitimacy within their own communities" (p. 485). On the other hand, in a 1999 lecture at the University of Wisconsin-Eau Claire, novelist/filmmaker Sherman Alexie (film, *Smoke Signals*) humorously described the pressure in public and professional settings to perform as an authentic Indian by talking about his "sacred" Native American traditions.

For visibly diverse organizational members who "dress up" the organization, this becomes a Catch 22: Not only do these requests for guest lectures, panels, faculty and student advice, committee membership, and so on, consume the time needed for their own work, it also leaves them vulnerable to charges of not fulfilling their own organizational role. Furthermore, their roles in the diversity projects that sidetrack them are then viewed by resistant members (who are more likely to be White, according to Kossek & Zonia, 1994) as transparent efforts to further the trainers' own best interests. Although these academics struggle with additional diversity assignments, business professionals struggle with being sidetracked permanently (rather than as an additional burden) into support jobs often related to diversity. The case of one New York ad agency (Meyerson & Fletcher, 2000) is not unusual: Women tended to be offered HR related jobs—"positions women were thought to be particularly well suited for" (p. 134), but that disadvantaged them in their long term careers.

In a *Black Enterprise's* career roundtable of the top 50 Blacks in corporate America, this same problem surfaced: the role-slotting of African Americans for certain support-type positions (Clarke, 2000). One African-American college graduate spoke candidly in her job interviews, "Don't think about how many diversity committees I can head up or how many admissions fairs I can go to or how many times you can stick me in your yearbook to make yourself look diverse" (Bowen, Bok, & Burkhart, 1999, p. 144). This tendency to use employees as window dressing is simply another variation of employees as expendable resources to be used (and used up), according to Kirby and Harter (2001), who critique the "managing diversity" metaphor as being instituted primarily to "control diversity." That is, a profit-driven approach to diversity means controlling potential loss of profitability from harassment and discrimination without necessarily working toward "valuing differences" (p. 123). This kind of metaphor is typical organizational discourse, said Cheney and Carroll (1997), for much of "what passes for employee empowerment, employee participation, or workplace democracy in organizations . . . conducted within the context of controlled, prescribed, and carefully circumscribed activities, involving extensive monitoring and correction through tight feedback loops" (p. 594). Sounds like some diversity initiatives.

That diversity training is merely a public relations move is also no surprise to Verespej (1997), who pointed out that discrimination and harassment suits don't seem to have decreased despite the proliferation of diversity training programs. He calls for companies to announce their "zero tolerance" of discrimination and harassment, but he acknowledges that most CEOs don't see these as compelling business issues. The attitudes of these CEOs and top executives give a message to the employees who are required to attend diversity training workshops: This is just for public relations, so make a good impression and everything will be business as usual.

Impression Management to Maintain Status Quo

According to Workman (1996), a Boston-based diversity consultant, training participants use impression management skills to communicate their alignment with diversity goals, thereby denying "the possibility of guilt for any non-appropriate attitudes or behaviors discussed through the workshop" (p. 17). He concluded that with the implicit moral judgment of much diversity training, employees have a greater need to save face than to discuss and modify their own problematic attitudes and actions. Ironic that programs designed to help employees "value differences" and reduce covert pressures for diverse employees to assimilate function instead to pressure majority employees to assimilate into "politically correct" rhetoric to maintain the organization's image. Instead, many (male, White) employees who (correctly) perceive that the training is for them and about Others (female, non-White) resist this co-optation. Cargile and Giles (1996) tied trainee resistance to Festinger's theory of cognitive dissonance, citing studies indicating that counterattitudinal information is evaluated negatively. Thus, although trainee heads might nod in outward agreement, negative attitudes might actually be strengthened inwardly, rather than diminished. The struggle is between the trainees' desire for status quo and desire to not be perceived by supervisors and co-workers as "obstructionists" (Henderson, 1994, p. 147). This impression management strategy is called *ingratiation*; and it, along with the strategy of "exemplification," are the top impression management strategies used by leaders as well as trainees (Gardner & Cleavenger, 1998).

Several of the HR practitioners interviewed by Jordan (1998) wanted training to "talk tough on issues" rather than conforming to the participants' desire for a "feel good" experience (p. 63). Day-Overmeyer (1995) suggested that one problem is the lack of certification for diversity trainers; he recommended that trainers value all participants, including White males. Cross-cultural consultant Rose tries to do both things—talk tough and empathize with White males, understanding that "what white males feel is their dehumanization, the walking on eggshells, the rationalization, the apologies, the guilt. That's the price of a nontarget [referring to EEO target populations]" (cited in Lynch, 1997, p. 69). In the college setting, Karp and Sammour (2000) go for the velvet glove approach, trying for empathy versus guilt: "Try to get the SWAMs [straight, white, American males] to remember a time when they were discriminated against, e.g., too short for the basketball team, excluded from a fraternity, or maybe simply not invited to an event that others were" (p. 454).

Another kind of impression management that can occur in training is communication that is guarded and self-protective, as illustrated in the case of investment company employees who were part of a university-led action research project to "improve the quality of life for mid level professionals" (D. Thomas & Proudford, 2000, pp. 57-58). White participants described promotions as highly political and not based primarily on merits. That is, until the researchers mentioned that black employees appeared to be the most disadvantaged in the organization; the interviewees then switched tracks, saying that promotions were based on those who "do high quality work" (i.e., merit). This type of denial and ambivalence is pervasive in organizations when leadership is in denial about institutional responsibilities (Johnson, 2000). The result is that when diversity trainers are visible racial/ethnic minority group members, the content of training programs can be emotionally denied, whatever outward appearance White trainees present. The ideal co-trainers would be a combination of one SWAM and one minority female (Karp & Sammour, 2000).

The need to manage impressions and maintain the status quo can lead to the kinds of illogical thinking and emotional denial that trainers who "talk tough" make visible, thereby increasing conflicts historically pushed under the surface.

Increased Organizational Conflict After Training

Training that focuses on shaming individuals as representatives of groups creates an emotionally laden atmosphere where feelings of guilt can easily erupt into anger (anger at being made to feel guilty or anger at being made the object of others' guilt). Caudron (1993) blamed part of the problem on inexperienced, unskilled diversity trainers whose ineffective programs actually harm organizations' diversity efforts. Whatever the cause, Karp and Sutton (1993) believe that guilt-driven diversity training programs are:

> problematic because on a moral level, nobody in the training program is personally responsible for the Holocaust or the enslavement of Africans. On a functional level, when people assume global responsibility for everything, they don't have to take personal responsibility for anything . . . a focus on injustice and guilt tends to polarize the different groups into victims and oppressors. This polarization increases resentment among groups, when the goal of diversity training ought to be to reduce it. (p. 33)

That trainees made to feel guilty and silenced would become resentful is no surprise. Rage at being made to feel shamed frequently follows the initial feelings of shame, conveniently pushing them aside. (See Planalp, 1999; Planalp, Hafen, & Adkins, 2000, for a discussion of the shame-rage cycle and its effects on interpersonal and organizational messages, particularly when the shame is not acknowledged. Guilt-anger reactions in diversity training are described at length by Fine, 1995; Loden, 1996; and Lynch, 1997.)

Diversity-induced conflict may be, ironically, an inevitable result of trying to codify diversity through "compliance goals" (whether in response to Affirmative Action or mission-driven, managerial annual objectives), particularly if these goals are pigeon holed in personnel departments (T. Harris, 1997). The anthology, *Conflict and Diversity* (Brown, Snedeker, & Sykes, 1997), highlights the many nuances and complexities of conflicts arising from group, organizational, and societal diversities. There are, for example, pockets of resistance from particular groups within an organization, such as those at Krupar's (1997) university where the business school's resistance took the form of unending requests for additional data with questions like "What is the business case for diversity?" (p. 237). Another pocket of conflict can arise from especially controversial diversity topics like sexual orientation (Caudron, 1995; Loden, 1996), which Lynch (1997) called "the gay-lesbian time bomb," creating conflict among the diversity consultants themselves, because it is "off-putting to conservative corporate CEOs" (p. 161). However off-putting it might be, a 1992 U.S. Census Bureau survey showed 1.5 million self-identified households as homosexual domestic partnerships, an economic fact companies have begun to appreciate by including sexual orientation in the diversity menu (Winfield & Spielman, 1995).

Besides conflict disguised with impression management strategies, there is sometimes unspoken conflict residing in the very people volunteered to be "diversity managers"—often without staff, budgets, or real decision-making power (Brown, 1997). Silent conflict or resistance shows itself when the diversity training programs were suggested in 1998 but were still under review in 2001, or when attendance at diversity training is voluntary and no executive has yet attended (Brown, 1997). However, not all conflict leads to silence, disguised resistance, anger, or denial. Some White males, according to Henderson (1994), are swept by guilt into becoming "pro-minority" (at least temporarily— although, interestingly, they are much less likely to become "pro-feminist"); however, they too often "retreat to whiteness," returning to the comforts and shelter of their racial privileges.

Another response to conflict, similar to denial, is "splitting and projective identification" (D. Thomas & Proudford, 2000), whereby racial tensions are localized in a specific group or within particular persons, in effect absolving the system of responsibility and creating scapegoats who could be labeled "resident racists" or "confrontational people" or "groups you can't satisfy" (p. 63). An understanding of this phenomenon is important when conducting any kind of diversity audit. Another phenomenon to be alert to is the potential for diversity training programs to result in the lawsuits that they were initially designed to avoid.

Lawsuits Resulting from Diversity Training

When Texaco was hit with a landmark settlement, one of the plaintiffs' attorneys justified it by stating, "What we're trying to do is change the corporate culture to make it much more open for people of different backgrounds," which included "sensitivity training" (Lubove, 1997, p. 123). Ironically, the lawsuit was generated from an executive's infamous remark comparing African Americans to black jellybeans at the bottom of the jar, an analogy that the executive heard at a diversity workshop for Texaco employees (Von Bergen, Soper, & Foster, 2002). The media's reaction to the record-breaking lawsuit settlement was immediate and fierce. *Newsweek*'s report was dominated by accounts of diversity training critics who "say the very heart of many programs—highlighting group differences to create awareness—ends up alienating and offending employees" (Reibstein, 1996, p. 50). The same article described a U.S. Department of Transportation 1993 training program "in which participants were addressed as 'jerks and jerkettes'" (p. 50). In my own local newspaper, conservative Shelby Steele was quoted saying that "diversity training poisons the atmosphere of companies" (M. Jackson, 1997, p. D2). The newspaper further illustrated Steele's comment with the story of a training program at Texaco after the lawsuit, when a training consultant promised that the participants would not have to "walk out singing Kumbaya" (an African slave spiritual), infuriating one participant who described the whole program as "insensitive" (p. D1). (For a rhetorical analysis of Texaco's public response to the racial discrimination suit, see Brinson & Benoit, 1999). Lubove (1997) complained that these diversity training programs—touted as a remedy—merely compound the problems.

In another example, a racial discrimination lawsuit against R. R. Donnelley & Sons was instigated by a Black man who was forced to sit through a movie of lynchings and a questionnaire that described Black stereotypes (e.g., having a less pleasant body odor; Lubove, 1997). Although intended to sensitize White employees, the activities understandably upset Black employees. In another case, a consultant for the Federal Aviation Administration (FAA) used a training activity requiring men to "run the gauntlet" and be subjected to aggressive groping by women, in order to understand women's feelings about sexual harassment, resulting in a lawsuit by one unhappy man (Seligman & deLlosa, 1994). In the same training program, Black employees were encouraged to verbally assault individual White male employees. A lawsuit against Lucky Stores, a California-based grocery chain, followed a diversity workshop in which store managers were asked to write down their stereotypes about women; the managers' handwritten notes were later used by the court in a class action suit by female employees as evidence of managers' personal discriminatory attitudes toward women (Delikat, 1995). Diversity audits prepared for companies by diversity consultants can also be used against those same companies in discrimination lawsuits, as New York News, Inc., and Merrill Lynch & Company learned (Delikat, 1995).

Religion as well as sex and race can be a source of contention, as when the *New York Times* (E. Harris, 1998) reported a controversy resulting from a diversity training program held by *Saint Louis Post-Dispatch*; the reporter was the only Jew at the workshop that concluded with all its participants praying to Jesus. MacDonald (1993) described how diversity trainers sometimes make an example of one of the trainees, such as a sensitivity session at the University of Cincinnati, where a female academic was asked to stand in front of her colleagues as the trainer stated: "We all know who the most beautiful woman in the room is. . . . It's the woman with the three private [school] degrees and the blond hair and the blue eyes. Let's have her stand up so everybody can look at her. Look at the pearls she's wearing, her clothes, her shoes" (p. 24). These all exemplify the many mistakes that can create legal dangers during diversity training (see Delikat, 1995, for a more extensive list of mistakes).

Finally, besides the potential for lawsuits and the conflicts among participants or between trainers and trainees—whether disguised, silent, and projected, or loud and vocalized—conflicts among trainers and consultants at diversity conferences showcase their ideological diversity. In particular, Lynch (1997) noted the "tensions between civil rights moralists and business-based pragmatists" (p. 109): Moralists deny the possibility of reverse discrimination by counterarguing White male privilege; business pragmatists acknowledge Whites' feelings and include them as a category in diversity training. Both of them have interests in why and how they carve the diversity pie.

Whose Interests Carve the Diversity Pie?

The inclusion of White males in diversity training by business pragmatists is similar to the discursive move by university administrators to turn women's studies into gender studies. Fraiman (1997), similar to the business moralists, fears that the new term neglects women and Blacks and the need to redress the wrongs that continue to be perpetuated against them, with a new "cheerful cosmopolitan" discourse of inclusiveness as White men become "gendered and ethnicked" along with everyone else (p. 40). (Her fears are synonymous with fears about Affirmative Action, reframed as diversity, diluting the redress that the former provided.) As a case in point, she describes a brainstorming session by the University of Virginia's Women's Center, in which the term diversity was frequently invoked by women arguing that the center needed to change its alternative image to appeal to White heterosexuals and reach out to the mainstream. Fraiman feels frustrated with the co-optation of "diversity" and "the doggy readiness of this term to go home with whoever feeds it" (p. 42).

Another diversity issue for Fraiman is "spicing up the admittedly homogenous university population with members of the 'international' community" (p. 40). Although she is quick to acknowledge that anti-immigrant feelings run high and need to be addressed within the university population, she nevertheless resists the conflation of (particularly) Native American and African-American racial issues with the postcolonial concerns of non-Western internationals. Her point is that postcolonial studies "displace racial struggle away from our own backyard and onto spheres in which the players are reassuringly remote" (p. 41). Writing in response to Fraiman, Samantrai (1997) warned against the "paradoxical alignment of black and white Americans against ethnic minorities, along the divide of national belonging" (p. 50). She argued that Fraiman's oppositions are "false and divisive," particularly in a global economy where "borders are porous, and national and international concerns continually leak into each other on both micro and macro levels" (p. 52). Samantrai believes anti-imperialism should be added to diversity's agenda of antiracism and antisexism. Their arguments are an example of Hoffman's (1997) criticism of trait-based or fixed approaches to diversity, which obscure the necessity for "encountering the self's role in perceiving and constructing difference" (p. 378).

Both Fraiman (African American/Asian American) and Samantrai (South Asian) have positionalities vested in their own genealogy. Hoffman (1997) argued that diversity educators/trainers must focus on critical inquiry, training people how to question their own culture-based, taken-for-granted frames of reference. Locating oneself within a network of power that includes one's social identity, organizational role, and politics is an essential standpoint to understand one's potential impact (Holvino, 2000). As a consultant, Holvino found that her social identities as Puerto Rican, mixed race, professional, and female could be used to "interpret and offer a social perspective on what I was doing" (p. 226). Not only do trainers need to examine their own positionality, they need to be mindful of the perceptions of trainees that the trainers have their own political agendas, which they push via the training program (Mobley & Payne, 1992). Those perceptions might be a very good reason to use an external consultant for diversity training (Henderson, 1994).

Whether American ethnic minorities or internationals, Hadden, an employee-relations consultant in Jacksonville, Florida, said that expecting only women or minorities to conduct diversity training is a bad idea: "Most of the time, diversity training is done by very articulate, competent professionals who happen to be minorities or females. When you do that, someone who's initially resistant to begin with is going to [see that person] as someone with an ax to grind" (cited in Flynn, 1999, p. 53). Having only women or minority trainers exacerbates the fear of minority participants that they will be viewed as the sole beneficiaries of diversity programs. However, some participants are equally worried that expanding the definition of diversity (e.g., including Whites) negates the power differences in those categories, thus trivializing the realities of harassment and discrimination. The diversity trainer's challenge is to relate group differences to the struggles of groups over material conditions in everyday life as well as the workplace, one of the tasks that Aronowitz and Giroux (1993) established for any multicultural curriculum.

Teaching for diversity in an international setting can be even more challenging, due to very different social constructions and interpretations of morality and (un)acceptable material conditions. Blanks (1998), who teaches at American University in Cairo, Egypt, is sensitive to charges of imperialism reasonably levied at a professor for hoisting Western values on his Eastern students. He asks whether "liberal education itself is a form of cultural imperialism?" To illustrate his point, he describes the different values his Egyptian versus American students bring to issues such as veiling, female circumcision, inheritance laws that penalize women, arranged marriages, and divorce. On these topics his American students are predisposed to take a stance for an individual freedom, but his Egyptian students are more likely to value tradition, continuity, and solidarity. Blanks suggests that from their worldview, teaching and thus privileging Kant exemplifies Western cultural elitism.

Whatever their ideological impulses and biased positionalities, the previous examples are of trainers who are genuinely concerned with the disparate impact that organizations have on diverse individuals. However, opponents of diversity training do not view diversity trainers as so well intentioned. Lubove (1997) likes to typify them as "armies of quacks . . . actors who'd otherwise be working the dinner theater circuit [and instead] are cashing in on the diversity racket" (pp. 123-124).

OPPONENTS OF DIVERSITY TRAINING

Frederick Lynch, who wrote *Invisible Victims: White Males and the Crisis of Affirmative Action* (1991) prior to The *Diversity Machine: The Drive to Change the "White Male Workplace"* (1997), is no friend of diversity. His books do not begin with critical inquiry; they originate from an agenda of protectionism and with a tirade against political correctness. What the most recent book offers the diversity trainer, however, is an up close and personal look at diversity training programs from someone who has attended scores of conventions, conferences, and workshops and interviewed over a hundred consultants, personnel experts, and rank-and-file employees. On occasions he was one of few White males— and oppositional to boot. Surprisingly, he was not rejected; he was instead welcomed—"not only as a rare white male specimen, but as a valuable resource," and soon became a participant panelist on "white male blues" (p. 13). The details he recounted are not often read in diversity literature: training activities viewed by an opponent to diversity, from the standpoint of all those others (and they are legion) who have also groaned at a training mandate—what Lynch coined a "diversity penance."

Diversity training is a minor penance compared to other punishments levied at organizations and individuals found guilty of harassment and/or discrimination. For example, in 1997 Major League Soccer fined a White midfielder who slurred a Black midfielder $20,000 and penalized him by suspending him for the first two games (McCallum, 1998). Sports is rich in examples of diversity penance, due, said Hruby (2000), to the importance of public goodwill toward "lucrative sports franchises" leading in "tremendous pressure to punish players who make inappropriate remarks to the press" (p. 32). He cited the occasions when the National Basketball Association fined Dennis Rodman of the Chicago Bulls $50,000 for anti-Mormon rhetoric in 1997, and the fine and suspension of Cincinnati Reds owner Marge Schott in 1993 for her inflammatory language about Blacks and Jews.

In the corporate world, two departments at Hughes Aircraft lost 10% of their bonus pay when they did not hire or promote minorities (MacDonald, 1993). (The next year they received their bonuses after managing to hire people they had previously sworn did not exist.) Home Depot was ordered to pay $65 million to women denied promotions, $22.5 million in attorney fees, and institute company-wide diversity training (Lubove, 1997). Denny's restaurant chain suffered a $54 million settlement as a result of a class action suit on behalf of thousands of Black customers subjected to anti-Black prejudice from employees (Goleman, 1995). In 1999, Coca-Cola Co. beat Texaco's record of $176.1 million and Shoney's record of $132.5 million settlements in race discrimination lawsuits with their own, $192.5 million: $113 million to the aggrieved African-American workers, $43.5 million to boost the Blacks' salaries, $36 million for employment practices monitoring programs, and $20 million for the plaintiffs' legal fees (Curry, 2000). Although denying any wrongdoing, CBS paid $8 million to settle sex discrimination lawsuits on behalf of female employees at six affiliated TV stations, who alleged that "they were denied promotions, overtime and training and were subjected to sexual harassment and retaliation if they complained" (Goldsmith, 2000, p. 4). After settling a $36 million class-action lawsuit in behalf of female employees and female applicants, Rent-A-Center grudgingly agreed to fill up to 10% of its job vacancies with females in the next 15 months and to add females to its all-male board of directors ("Rent-a-Center," 2002).

These lawsuits and resulting settlements are never discussed by diversity critics such as Lynch or his admirer, Lasch-Quinn (2001), who wrote her own book lynching diversity trainers, *Race Experts: How Racial Etiquette, Sensitivity Training, and New Age Therapy Hijacked the Civil Rights Revolution*. She purported to expose the diversity movement as "ethnotherapy," grounded in the therapeutic sensibility of the 1960s. Like Lynch, she debunked popular diversity training programs, particularly diversity films such as the (in)famous *Blue-Eyed* film and training group experiments conducted by Jane Elliott (see also Lynch, 1997), which Lasch-Quinn viewed as ritualized therapy to build the self-esteem of people of color by humiliating White people. She also ridiculed Freire's (1970) critical "pedagogy of the oppressed" and hooks' (1994) "'holistic' pedagogy'" In yet another book deriding diversity training, *Discrimination, Harassment, and the Failure of Diversity Training* (Hemphill & Haines, 1997), the authors make the case that the problem with diversity training programs is that they focus on changing attitudes rather than behaviors. However, unlike Lynch and Lasch-Quinn, Hemphill and Haines legitimized the very real and massive problem of workplace discrimination and harassment. They also (not surprisingly, as management consultants themselves) have their own program to offer—"Managing MindTalk"—which Lasch-Quinn (2001) derided as yet another "quick cure" whose primary aim is to boost the income of the race experts.

Diversity opponent Flynn (1999) suggested that the special interests programs directed toward minorities and/or women skirt illegality. She said that White males need to talk too; they also have issues to communicate, such as why they are *all* (including those with stalled careers) assumed to be advantaged. They resent having to go through training usually because one White male made a mistake; and they take offense at being collapsed into one, unified "White-male culture," as if the 60-year-old with an MBA is no different from the 20-year-old high school graduate. Flynn's solution is to learn from DuPont, which has introduced a "Men's Forum," a 3-day meeting of White males, to talk about "their interactions with their fathers and other men, cross-racial relations between men, intergender relations and how the workplace is changing for men" (p. 55). Although Flynn had nothing positive to say about diversity training programs for minority populations, she made good points about the importance of not using diversity training to discriminate against any group and of keeping all communication lines open. With an increasing White underclass, many White men feel frustrated at being presumed to be privileged and rhetorically cast as top executives rather than as guys barely holding onto their jobs (Lindsley, 1998a).

SILENCES:
WHAT OPPONENTS DON'T SAY

What Lynch, Steele, Labove, Lasch-Quinn, Hemphill and Haines, Flynn, and other opponents of diversity training don't say is that, for all of its very real problems, the rubric of diversity training gives some hope to the historically disempowered as corporations, universities, and community organizations jump aboard what Lynch (1997) disparaged as the *diversity machine*. Some of the benefits of diversity training/initiatives are included in the subsections that follow: Educated employees can become empowered employees; mission-driven diversity statements can legitimate programs, initiatives, and even Affirmative Action (as a temporary plan to increase structural diversity for profit motives); homogenous group solidarity can be promoted; heterogeneous group conflict can result in increased understanding and creativity; and dialogical communication can destabilize unnecessary hierarchy that hurts productivity. Common ground, according to Watts and Evans (2000), is about organizational climate and the settings, events, and transactions that produce a supportive environment common to all of its members. Although each of the potential positive outcomes described here are illustrated with examples in the sections that follow, even these advocacy positions have imbedded silences, the absences of what is not said, that can and should be challenged.

Empowerment Through Education

Heuberger and Gerber (1999) described diversity activities in an interdisciplinary course they designed at Miami University-Ohio and the positive assessments students gave the course for teaching "cultural competence," the understanding of how one's gender, race, and economic background influence how things are done in various cultures. "Awareness" is the "soul of a training program on managing diversity," according to Geber (1990, p. 30), who described the skills provided by diversity training as simply good situational management plus "3%" cultural awareness. Caproni and Arias (1997) also focus on managerial skills training, but from a critical perspective that would provide the trainees with skills in self-reflexivity and cultural critique. The first set of skills will "help managers understand how their cultures and their status in those cultures shape their views of themselves, others, and relationships," and the second set of skills enables managers to understand "the means by which managerial knowledge is created and disseminated" (p. 294).

In a collaborative venture between the University of Oklahoma and the FAA to train 739 managers and supervisors in several states, pre- and posttests showed significant differences in participants' knowledge and attitudes (Tan et al., 1996). Valli (1995) provided examples of diversity training for White student teachers in Black schools, emphasizing the need to learn that race is a trope, not a scientific category. Darling-Hammond (2000) wrote about how successful teachers of students of color are able to connect them with their own community, using culturally familiar communication patterns, such as the African-American call-and-response and the Hawaiian "talk story." In a personal essay describing her own growing awareness of her cultural heritage as an Asian American, Talbot (1999) wrote about a multicultural counseling class that taught her about minority identity and how "it felt as if someone, some academic source, was talking about me and my life" (p. 42). A White male student quoted in a newspaper article highlighting a new class on "whiteness," said that he decided three things: "to live in an integrated neighborhood, to send his children to integrated schools, and to continue to talk about race" (Burson, 1997, p. A1).

Mission-Driven Legitimation

What the student just cited may learn is that talking about race is much easier in a class than over the fence with one's neighbors. The reason: A class on whiteness legitimates discussions on a subject people avoid everywhere else. Most experts agree that organizational diversity efforts need approval from the top to succeed—or, rather, they need approval for initiation; they need commitment to succeed (Chung, 1997; Cox, 1994; McEnrue, 1993; Rynes & Rosen, 1995; R. Thomas, 1991). If organizational diversity is about establishing a "common ground," then, according to Watts and Evans (2000), "the mission, goals, and objectives of the organization [should] address diversity directly or acknowledge its importance implicitly" (p. 209). One advantage for organizations to publicize their mission-driven diversity goals is the potential to have their commitment recognized by a publication like *Hispanic* magazine, which lists the 100 companies providing the most opportunities for Latinos ("Two thousand Hispanic corporate," 2000). Texas-based SBC Communications hit the jackpot when it received awards both from the U.S. Hispanic Education Foundation and from the U.S. Department of Labor for its "walk-the-talk" diversity programs (Loudin, 2000).

A subsidiary of American Express, Travel Related Services (TRS) is a classic example of top-down commitment to diversity as a response to high turnover costs; that commitment was then used to justify an employee survey to ascertain what their diverse needs were (Morrison & Herlihy, 1992). The results included child care, part-time benefits, sabbaticals, and more flexible work hours. Dependent (vs. child) care assistance is an example of how companies with a mission-driven commitment are increasingly responsive to diverse needs for flexible work scheduling, job sharing, and family leave in situations other than child care, such as caring for a sick spouse, parent, parent-in-law, or adopted or foster child. (See Jamieson & O'Mara, 1991, for numerous examples of companies who provide dependent care assistance.) Hewlitt-Packard's mission emphasizes flexibility, informality, and unstructured norms, all of which encourage pluralistic approaches (Cox, 1994). Lotus provides same-sex partner benefits, along with spouse benefits, and expresses its commitment to unbiased performance appraisals and promotions (Fine, 1995). Some companies— FleetBoston, General Mills, Hewlett-Packard, Kodak, and Prudential Financial—go even further by advocating legislation to ban workplace discrimination based on sexual orientation. But, although American Airlines is breaking new ground by including transgendered employees in their definition of diversity, the merged ExxonMobil is going backward by refusing to reinstate the nondiscrimination policy covering sexual orientation that had been in force at Mobil (Koonce, 2001).

In reviewing the up and down sides of diversity programs, Gottfredson (1992) reported that despite their potential for resentment, dissatisfaction, and polarization, they have also resulted in "major improvements in broader management practice" (p. 288). The best way to make the workplace fair and equitable is to make management accountable for auditing their policies for fairness—and making them responsible for the effects of unfair policies. Diversity management focused on fairness can have unexpectedly happy results. In 1993, after the riots in Los Angeles, which resulted in 1,600 severely damaged businesses, McEnrue (1993) contacted 15 companies he had surveyed the previous year about their diversity efforts to see if they now planned to do anything differently. Sadly, those that had done nothing to manage diversity previously still had no plans to initiate any programs or reviews. However, those companies with proactive diversity results were the same companies that received little or no damage, despite buildings burning next door—McDonald's, known for its diversity programs, was one of the businesses relatively unscathed.

McEnrue's 1992-1993 survey of companies in Los Angeles also inquired about managerial incentives or rewards for diversity efforts—and found few offered by the companies. Jordan's (1998) survey also did not find any of 16 companies surveyed that tied diversity results to performance reviews. Nevertheless, a few companies do. After Texaco's race discrimination settlement, they agreed to tie 10% to 20% of senior executives' compensation to diversity (M. Jackson, 1997). Xerox Corporation and Hughes Aircraft both link managerial compensation to diversity goals with bonus pay incentive programs (Lindsley, 1998b). Pepsi-Cola International, although not linking performance pay directly to diversity, does link it to people management in a way that assures diversity will be taken into consideration (Fulkerson & Schuler, 1992). For example, a manager's personal compensation is not only based on conducting performance appraisals, but on doing so "in a culturally neutral manner" (p. 265). Being culturally aware is so important to Pepsi-Cola that it created an international management institute that analyzes its programs to make certain that they are delivered in "cultural style that is appropriate at the local level" (p. 268).

The government sector has also had to reconsider its "cultural style." In 1997, Army Secretary Togo West made a commitment to the nation, live on CBS, that the sexual harassment and discrimination charges published in an Army report would be resolved by leadership solutions (Reardon & Reardon, 1999). The resulting recommendations included both training and system changes:

> adoption of more thorough and uniform screening processes to reduce perceptions of female inferiority; better preparation of male instructors who train female recruits; increased numbers of female trainers; increased sophistication in determining when males and females should be trained together; and improved instruction regarding how males and females should relate to each other professionally. (p. 601)

Because the government enforces nondiscrimination standards, it must also conform to those standards. Indeed, governmental protocols against abuse, neglect, and mistreatment in nursing homes and long-term care settings has instigated calls for diversity training for nursing home staff who are unprepared to care for elderly immigrants with language barriers or residents who are ethnically different from the staff members. Impink (2002) advocated "culturally advisory committees" made up of residents, family members, and staff. Long-term care facilities can offer language classes, traditional foods, reading rooms with multicultural books, magazines, and videotapes, and guest speakers.

From education's front, it was the 1983 publication of A *Nation at Risk* by the National Commission on Excellence in Education that spotlighted key educational issues for the U.S. public and began national reform efforts, which "revitalized the multicultural teacher education movement" (Goodwin, 2000, p.107). More recently, Lauter (1997), a professor at the University of Wisconsin-Oshkosh's College of Education, explained how the political weight of diversity rhetoric helped to secure approval for African-American and Native American courses on campus and revived the African-American Studies minor. The New Jersey School Counselor Association uses a pamphlet as a guide for teachers and students to celebrate Human Rights Week each year and advocates that schools who follow this model begin by drafting a mission statement based on assessing the specific needs of that particular school (Giaridina,

1998). From my own experiences working at several universities, I can testify that once an organization has prioritized diversity into its mission or goals, for whatever public relations strategies, the power of converting rhetoric to official, written statements can open doors for minority guest lectureships and 1-year appointments, student scholarships, new courses and materials, and so on, which can in turn draw minority group members together to provide some solidarity.

Solidarity Within Homogenous Groups

One common diversity initiative that can emerge from training is the impetus for minority interest caucus groups to meet to discuss career-related concerns, as well as simply to decrease their sense of isolation. At Xerox, the first grassroots caucus group was African American; the second was Hispanic (Sessa, 1992). Because of the success of these groups in the 1970s, management held roundtables to begin a women's caucus. It was unsuccessful. Not until the mid-1980s, when women themselves started a caucus group, did it take root. Sessa surmised that one reason might be the heterogeneity of the initial group; the later groups were comprised of homogenous racial and ethnic groups. (According to Lavole, 1996, Xerox today is a leader in diversity, in 1995 winning the first award given by the federal Glass Ceiling Commission for commitment to diversity, marketing diversity training and consulting to other companies.)

Other organizations that have used identity-based support groups include Avon, Digital Equipment (called *constituency groups*) and U.S. West (called *resource groups*), which can be sources for input on diversity strategies, as well as advice for the best approaches for customers, as well as employees, who belong to that minority group (Cox, 1994). IBM's executive-led diversity task forces (women, Asian, Black, Hispanic, Native American, White male, and People with Disabilities) were charged with a threefold purpose: to welcome group members, to maximize their group's productivity, and to increase the market share from that group's community (Lynch, 1997). At Caterpillar's Joliet plant in Illinois, a representative group of disgruntled African-American employees met with management over a recent plant reorganization that resulted in many promotions, but none of them were African Americans (Simonsen & Wells, 1994). The group had gathered statistical evidence and considered a class-action lawsuit. Instead, they collaborated with management on a solution; the result was a new, management-sponsored, African-American organization, Trust and Teamwork (TNT), which later evolved into an organization with a formal career development process, mentoring program, and community outreach program to minority youth. During this process they used an outside consultant and an internal trainer (who was also African American), who helped them first develop a TNT mission statement.

From the nonprofit sector, The Ridgeland Group (TRIG), a coalition of agencies, community-based organizations, and constituent groups, formed to develop violence prevention programming (Watts & Evans, 2000). Its success is due primarily to its youth groups (many of color), who educated TRIG about racial/cultural aspects of violence. From academe, a book entitled *Lesbians in Academia: Degrees of Freedom* tells various coming-out stories that revolve around the importance of support groups. One story in particular describes the first gay, lesbian support group formed at Phillips University in Oklahoma, an event that was reported by the local newspaper and resulted in a flurry of responses from the director of public relations, faculty, students, and community members—including a backlash campus meeting called "A Day to Reaffirm Romans I:24-27" (McDonald, 1997). After several months of contention during which time the university publicly supported the group's existence, reactionary responses died down, the group began to flourish, the faculty narrator of the story received tenure, and her office became a safe haven for gay and lesbian students to talk and find support for their very existence.

This type of social support group typifies the "group representation" necessary for democracy and social justice, for without it organizations have no way of hearing the voices and needs of all its members or of maximizing "the social knowledge expressed in discussion, and thus furthers practical wisdom" (Young, 1990, p. 186). R. Thomas (1991) pointed out that the establishment of what he called "councils for minority groups" is important less for their existence than why they were established. If their purpose is to establish acceptance and tolerance, the groups function as a "valuing difference" initiative. If their purpose is to establish a liaison mechanism with management in order to increase their visibility and promotability, then the groups function as an "affirmative action" initiative. If, on the other hand, their purpose is, as illustrated by U.S. West and IBM, to give advice to management about diverse employee/customer needs, the groups function as a longer term, committed "managing diversity" initiative. Support groups also function to provide informal mentoring (Fine, 1995). But, whatever their purpose, the support groups do provide psychological support for individual members, and their "absence could be a devastating loss to minority groups" (Cox, 1994, p. 255). What support groups can contribute for these organizational members is the sense of belonging that they do not always have in heterogenous groups.

Understanding from Conflict Within Heterogenous Groups

"Good" diversity in research models is associated with creativity and a wide range of perspectives; "bad" diversity is based on a group's need for common values and beliefs to have consensus and cohesiveness (McGrath, Berdahl, & Arrow, 1995). However, although heterogenous groups with few commonalities are more likely to experience interpersonal discomfort conflict when

solving problems and making decisions (Cox, 1994; Gottfredson, 1992), intergroup conflict based on "diversity in identities as a 'problem' that cannot
be avoided" has been overgeneralized (Cox, 1995; Nkomo, 1995; Nkomo &
Cox, 1996). Conflicts are less likely when the group members share goals, find
similarities, and, importantly, are encouraged in their interaction by organizational authorities (Triandis, Kurowski, & Gelfand, 1994; see also Triandis,
1995).

The last condition gives hope to heterogenous diversity training groups
charged with learning to negotiate both candor and sensitivity when discussing
controversial issues. Henderson (1994) emphasized the importance of providing
managers with conflict resolution skills so that they can, when appropriate,
make a managerial intervention that is "culturally proactive" (p. 203). Another
type of "authority" is the church, which, as Orbe and Harris (2001) described in
their chapter on interracial communication in the context of organizations, has
certainly had experience bringing about some social and political changes in
communities. However, as they point out, church members brought together by
shared values and beliefs, may still be separated by race. Churches that take as
their mission to not only be "a witness for justice and an advocate for the poor"
but also to "resolve racial tensions in their own bodies" (p. 211)—with pastors,
priests, ministers, bishops, and rabbis trained in handling conflict—can do an
enormous amount of good because of the authority vested in them.

The very notion of controversial discussions makes some individuals—particularly from certain cultural groups—anxious, whereas controversy and argument is valued in other cultures as a sign of closeness. Americans who live for a
time in Germany, France, Italy, or Greece are surprised at the relish with which
argument is enjoyed (Tannen, 1998). Within the United States, families with a
Jewish tradition or Italian heritage may also enjoy a "friendly contentiousness"
(p. 209). Although Tannen values dialogue over debate, she does not advocate
relinquishing conflict and criticism entirely; instead, she suggested that we learn
from other cultures how to vary the way we approach "battling" each other—
beginning by eliminating such war metaphors and then widening our vision
beyond two, polarized sides.

Controversies that cause conflict can lead to dialogue resulting in greater
understanding, not greater conflict. Thought-provoking (although *not* deliberately provocative and combative) diversity training activities may initially produce participant discomfort and, at the least, create internal conflict and
employee resistance to the activities—but some of this may occur simply as a
result of desegregating groups for training (Henderson, 1994). However, conflict can be turned into positive problem solving and reflection by locating the
problem in the institution/environment, making gender and race (or any individ-
ual/group difference, given the expanded definition of diversity) the "stimulus,
not background variables" (Smith, 1995, p. 228). Ely (1995) provided an example from her own consulting/training with a small, nonprofit feminist organiza-

tion, interviewing 12 professional women, whose jobs were segregated by race. During the feedback session after the interviews, both groups of women were surprised at how they were all complicit in the job segregation, based on their collective assumption that the women of color were needed for programming and community outreach activities, reserving the management positions for the White women. Through the discussion they were able to understand the stakes that all had in maintaining that dichotomy, even though it did not serve them well. Training activities can be opportunities to encourage "multiple perspectives, holistic thinking, and complex rather than dichotomous understanding of issues" (Smith, 1995, p. 232).

A typical kind of example in a nonprofit organization is when the conflict is over how to run a program: One group advocates a system of care designed as a "drop-in program" where needs are met one at a time; another group wants a structured, "appointment-based program" that permits more predictable scheduling of resources (Watts & Evans, 2000, p. 205). From this scenario, conflict can be resolved by compromise or, ideally, by creative synthesizing and integrating of ideas. Surfacing conflict does not, however, mean escalating it with war metaphors, exemplified by the mass media's creation of "the gender war," "battle of the sexes," or "the war on affirmative action" (see Lindsley, 1998a, for an in-depth discussion of how tolerance and social movements have been trivialized by war metaphors). Dichotomizing race, gender, lifestyles—even ideas—is ingrained into our "argument culture," which Tannen (1998) pleads in her book, *Argument Culture,* for us to reformulate from debate to dialogue.

Dialogical Communication to Destabilize Hierarchy

Dialogue does not erase those tensions; what it can do is minimize the potential for aggression, oppression, and violence. Gergen (1999) called this "transformative dialogue" and gave an example from the 1989 Public Conversations Project in Watertown, Massachusetts, whereby participants were all asked to respond to the following three questions: What is your personal history/involvement with the issue? What is at the heart of the matter for you? What pockets of uncertainty or mixed feelings do you have regarding the issue? This framework gave the participants a common understanding of how they were to talk to each other in a way that promoted "relational responsibility." A common framework for talking to and learning from one another (vs. win-lose models of debate and argumentation) can lead to common understandings and a common language for those understandings.

Examples from organizations dedicated to a common framework of shared values are perhaps more readily found in nonprofits. Judkins and Lahurd (1999) enumerated the benefits to an entire North Carolina community of a series of diversity training sessions that led to facilitated conversations among members of 125 organizations, including workplaces, schools, churches, and community groups. Wallace (2000) gave examples from the mental health field of professionals engaging in a dialogue with diverse clients based on the practice of "empathic mirroring" and "motivational interviewing." Holvino (2000) reported a critical incident in a small social change organization, where one man shared his personal immigration story, convincing the board to financially assist the immigration assistance program.

One way to facilitate a common understanding or "language" is by establishing *how* organizational members in a diversity training class or working together on a diversity initiative talk to each other. A potential example might be the use of Orbe's (1998) model of the "Outsider Within Communication Orientations" to understand how what Orbe called "assertive separation" communication style is a way for outside insiders to "counter hegemonic messages" (p. 258). Understanding different communication styles can be helped by what Kikoski and Kikoski (1999) described in their textbook, *Reflexive Communication in the Culturally Diverse Workplace*, as a "process of sharing information . . . in recursive loops by which we clarify and reduce the uncertainties we all have about each other" (p. 200). They call this practice the "missing link of diversity training" (p. 201), which can establish nonhierarchical, collaborative relationships on the premise that employees are "democratically capable of learning from each other" (p. 202). A *democracy* of dialogue is key here. The importance of openness, self-reflexivity, and nonhierarchical relationships is also key to the editors of *Teaching Diversity* (Gallos, Ramsay, & Associates, 1997).

The purpose of training oriented to valuing differences is *not* to eradicate the differences, nor even resolve the conflicts over differences, but rather to create a dialogue about how we view those differences and to promote compromises. Said (1993) urged scholars to think "contrapuntally" in concrete and sympathetic ways about other persons and peoples besides ourselves because, in his words, "No one today is purely one thing. Labels like Indian, or woman, or Muslim, or American are not more than starting points, which if followed into actual experience for only a moment are quickly left behind" (p. 336). Nevertheless, those starting-points of the very existence of visible, expressed differences can be a positive sign of a more democratic workplace. Prasad and Elmes (1997) concluded their anthology, *Managing the Organizational Melting Pot*, by suggesting that "the persistence of organizational tensions that exist around race and gender, among others, might represent a hopeful sign" (p. 373). Hopeful in the sense that all organizational members have not been colonized by the management line.

Finding—and learning how to create—democratic workplaces, uncolonized by managerial hegemonic practices, is precisely what Cheney (1995) hoped for in his studies of alternative organizations, whereby the companies themselves function as diverse minorities from mainstream, traditional corporations. Although his research is not explicitly focused on "issues of multi-cultural or multi-ethnic diversity" (p. 171), he pointed to the similarities relevant to diversity issues. Both need to make use of multiple, varied "ad hoc groups with diverse membership . . . to keep the organization together, increase participation, broaden involvement in decisions about specific programs and their implementation, and decrease both the felt and the actual distance between worker-members and the 'cúpula'" (p. 171). The expansion of valuing organizational diversity to instigating democracy in the workplace can be broadened yet further. Goodall (1995) has hopes for a dialogue that will cut across organizations and national boundaries and connect us with our human spirituality and idealism so that "work" means "work of life" (p. 118). He asked how one can love the people with whom one works when one is consumed with hate for the work (job) itself.

Talking about *love* is easy and socially rewarded; perhaps talking about *hate* in order to understand how and why hate gets socially constructed is the kind of dialogue that will bring us back to the real work of caring for each other, our organizations, and the whole planet. After all, it is the hating (based on fear) of difference that is the problem; acts of hate and *the emotion itself* are such powerful societal taboos that children are taught never to say they *hate* anyone, although hate stratagems and appeals are used widely in political campaigns (Whillock, 1995). They are used not just in political campaigns, but in many competitive events where strong emotions can be tapped for adrenaline: football games, sales meetings, military training. If love can be energizing, so can hate. Publicly, nationally, we do not personally talk *about* hate, and we do not talk *about* race. Quindlen (2000) noted that we might talk about a particular racially driven event wherein we can focus our feelings on police brutality, affirmative action, and so on, but we do not talk about our racial assumptions and attitudes. She quoted Cornell West (1993) from his essay, *Race Matters*: "Our truncated public discussions of race suppress the best of who we are and what we are as a people because they fail to confront the complexity of the issue in a candid and critical manner" (p. 76). Isn't it ironic that this color line, what DuBois called in 1903 the "problem of the 20th century," is part of what we develop diversity training programs to discuss and then attempt to "manage" precisely by avoiding any real discussion.

Concluding with Irony

Re-reading this chapter, which includes a (partial) review of literature on diversity training, I was struck by how many times I used the word *irony*. Ironic that diversity training is about difference, but too often focuses on similarities; ironic that antiracists who are pro-diversity but critical of diversity training find themselves in bed with opponents of diversity in criticizing multiculturalism. Ironic that we essentialize race in order to talk about cultural differences, or culture in order to talk about differences across races. Ironic too that, in an effort to avoid organizational pressure for cultural assimilation at the expense of difference, we pressure cultural conservatives to assimilate to what they view as "political correctness" and attempt to silence their dissenting difference. Ironic that the diversity movement, which is partially a response to affirmative action, advocates racial consciousness while also ignoring race; while affirmative action, which came out of the Civil Rights movement of color blind politics, advocates color based actions.

Skrentny (1996) ended his book, *The Ironies of Affirmative Action,* with the remark that one of those ironies is "the emotion aroused not on a passion for meritocratic hiring but on the meaning of race" (and, I might add, gender and sexuality). T. Harris (1997), writing on the "importance, ironies, and pathways of diversity," found it ironic that education has become too "political" to help organizations value diversity; he advocates strategies that force behavioral change ("their attitudes will eventually fall into line") (p. 29). More hopefully, Trethaway (1999) entitled her case study of a women's social service organiza- tion, "Isn't it Ironic: Using Irony to Explore Contradictions of Organizational Life." She advocated using irony as an approach to differences, not in an attempt to resolve what might be irresolvable, but in recognition of the paradox- es, incompatibilities, and tensions of life.

An ironic stance allows one to be "simultaneously sympathetic and critical, accepting and interventionist, passionately involved and dramatically distanced" (Pearce, 1989, p. 203, cited in Trethaway, 1999, p. 163). An ironic stance is also one that permits a rueful smile, an acknowledgment of the comic linked to the tragic, and a saving sense of humor when confronting the tensions of diversity. Workman (1999) used Burke's comic frame to suggest that organizational dis- course can better achieve cooperation through "ambivalence" than "polemical debunking" (p. 9). Irony is key to this frame of mind, because, as Workman pointed out, "there is obvious irony in the existence of a united pluralist state, where unity and diversity offer a constant tension" (p. 17). A Burkean dialogue, suggested Workman, "offers ambivalence that stays off conflict." In the pres- ence of humor and ambivalence—admitting to a world where absolutes and cer- tainties are ever challenged by uncertainties and mystery—the participants in a diversity training class might feel free to voice what they have silenced: their hopes, their fears, their anger, their guilt and shame, their *emotions.* In the absence of right-wrong polarities, perhaps we can map a cartography of the felt silences in diversity training programs, created by the "lies" we perpetuate by pretending we are more similar than we are, by minimizing our differences, even to our selves.

> A conversation begins / with a lie. And each /
> speaker of the so-called common language feels /
> the ice-floe split, the drift apart / as if powerless /
> as if up against / a force of nature. (Rich, 1978, p. 67)

Ironically, "the common language" may be the vocalized understanding that we do not and will not have a common language, not entirely. We have, in our organizational diversity efforts, too often sought common ground by exploring superficial, fluid differences—while ignoring institutionalized differences that matter, creating what Rich called "the ice-floe split, the drift apart . . . as if up against a force of nature." We are only powerless, however, if we are silent. If we lie. It is the job of educators, trainers, and facilitators, who understand the (mixed) interpersonal and organizational messages surrounding diversity, to facilitate a dialogue. However, that dialogue must first occur within ourselves as we struggle to acknowledge our sympathies and our self-protectionism; our desire for, first, our own inclusiveness; our economic interests; our personal moral standpoints; and our race. We need to confront our own silences that emanate from a fear of our own differences and differing opinions, perhaps even at odds with the organization we are shoring up through training. Celebrating diversity does not just mean welcoming different races, genders, and lifestyles—but also world views, even those who question celebrating diversity. It means letting all voices, on and (arguably) off key, into the choir, without flinching at discordant notes, without wishing that they would just be silent.

REFERENCES

Allen, B. J. (1995). "Diversity" and organizational communication. *Journal of Applied Communication Research, 23*, 143-155.

Alderfer, C. P. (1992). Changing race relations embedded in organizations: Report on long-term project with XYZ Corporation. In S. E. Jackson & Associates (Eds.), *Diversity in the workplace: Human resources initiatives* (pp. 138-166). New York: Guilford.

Aldefer, C. P. (2000). National culture and the new corporate language for race relations. In R. T. Carter (Ed.), *Addressing cultural issues in organizations: Beyond the corporate context* (pp. 19-34). New York: Guilford.

Alverson, M. (1998, July-August). The call to manage diversity. *Women in Business, 50*(4), 34-35.

Appiah, K. A. (1998, January-February). The multicultural mistake. *Utne Reader, 85*, 24-26.

Arai, M., Wanda-Thibaut, M., & Shockley-Zalabak, P. (2001). Communication theory and training approaches for multiculturally diverse organizations: Have academics and practitioners missed the connection? *Public Personnel Management, 30*(4), 445-455.

Arredondo, P. (1996). *Successful diversity management initiatives: A blueprint for planning and implementation.* Thousand Oaks, CA: Sage.

Aronowitz, S., & Giroux, H. A. (1993). *Education still under siege.* Westport, CT: Bergin & Garvey.

Blanks, D. R. (1998). Cultural diversity or cultural imperialism: Liberal education in Egypt. *Liberal Education, 84*, 30-36.

Bond, M. A., & Pyle, J. L. (1998). Diversity dilemmas at work. *Journal of Management Inquiry, 7*(3), 252-269.

Bowen, W. G., Bok, D., & Burkhart, G. (1999, January-February). A report card on diversity: Lessons for business from higher education. *Harvard Business Review, 77*(1), 138-150.

Branch, C. W. (2000). And justice is blind (to race and ethnicity): That is not good! In R. T. Carter (Ed.), *Addressing cultural issues in organizations: Beyond the corporate context* (pp. 131-146). New York: Guilford.

Brinson, S. L., & Benoit, W. L. (1999). The tarnished star: Restoring Texaco's damaged public image. *Management Communication Quarterly, 12*, 483-510.

Brown, C. D. (1997). An essay: Diversity and unspoken conflicts. In C. D. Brown, C. C. Snedeker, & B. Sykes (Eds.), *Conflict and diversity* (pp. 217-226). Cresskill, NJ: Hampton Press.

Brown, C. D., Snedeker, C. C., & Sykes, B. (Eds.). (1997). *Conflict and diversity.* Cresskill, NJ: Hampton Press.

Burson, P. (1997, May 19). Examining white "privilege." *Saint Paul Pioneer Press,* p. A1.

Caproni, P. J., & Arias, M. E. (1997). Managerial skills training from a critical perspective. *Journal of Management Education, 21*(3), 292-308.

Cargile, A. C., & Giles, H. (1996). Intercultural communication training: Review, critique, and a new theoretical framework. *Communication Yearbook, 19*, 385-423.

Carter, R. T. (2000). Perspectives on addressing cultural issues in organizations. In R. T. Carter (Ed.), *Addressing cultural issues in organizations: Beyond the corporate context* (pp. 3-18). New York: Guilford.

Caudron, S. (1993, April). Training can damage diversity efforts. *Personnel Journal, 72*(4), 51-62.

Caudron, S. (1995, August). Open the closet door to sexual orientation issues. *Personnel Journal, 74*(8), 42-55.

Caudron, S., & Hayes, C. (1997, February). Are diversity programs benefitting African Americans? *Black Enterprise, 27*(7), 121-128.

Cheney, G. (1995). Democracy in the workplace: Theory and practice from the perspective of communication. *Journal of Applied Communication, 23*, 167-200.

Cheney, G. (2000). Thinking differently about organizational communication: Why, how, and where? *Management Communication Quarterly, 14*, 132-141.

Cheney, G., & Carroll, C. (1997). The persons as object in discourses in and around organizations. *Communication Research, 24*(6), 593-630.

Choi, J. M. (1997). Racist ontology, inferiorization, and assimilation. In E. M. Kramer (Ed.), *Postmodernism and race* (pp. 115-128). Westport, CT: Praeger.

Chung, W. V. (1997). Auditing the organizational culture for diversity: A conceptual framework. In C. D. Brown, C. C. Snedeker, & B. Sykes (Eds.), *Conflict and diversity* (pp. 63-84). Cresskill, NJ: Hampton Press.

Clarke, R. D. (2000, February). Has the glass ceiling really been shattered. *Black Enterprise, 30*(7), 145-152.

Clements, P., & Jones, J. (2002). *The diversity training handbook.* London: Kogan Page.

Cose, E. (2000, September 18). What's white anyway. *Newsweek, 136*(12), 64-65.

Cox, T., Jr. (1994). *Cultural diversity in organizations: Theory, research, and practice.* San Francisco: Berrett-Koehler.

Cox, T., Jr. (1995). The complexity of diversity: Challenges and directions. In S. E. Jackson & M. N. Ruderman (Eds.), *Diversity in work teams: Research paradigms for a changing workplace* (pp. 235-246). Washington, DC: American Psychological Association.

Cox, T., Jr., & Beale, R. L. (1997). *Developing competency to manage diversity: Readings, cases, and activities.* San Francisco: Berrett-Koehler.

Curry, G. E. (2000, December 7). Racism costs corporate America. *New York Amsterdam News, 91*(49), 13-14.

Darling-Hammond, L. (2000). School contexts and learning: Organizational influences on the achievements of students of color. In R. T. Carter (Ed.), *Addressing cultural issues in organizations: Beyond the corporate context* (pp. 69-86). New York: Guilford.

Day-Overmeyer, L. E. (1995). The pitfalls of diversity training. *Training & Development, 49*(12), 24-30.

Delikat, M. (1995, March/April). The legal dangers in diversity. *Corporate Board, 169*, 11-17.

Diversity drainage. (1999, March). *HR Focus, 75*(3), 2.

Ely, R. J. (1995). The role of dominant identity and experience in organizational work on diversity. In S. E. Jackson & M. N. Ruderman (Eds.), *Diversity in work teams: Research paradigms for a changing workplace* (pp. 161-186). Washington, DC: American Psychological Association.

Essed, P. (1996). *Diversity: Gender, color, and culture.* Amherst: University of Massachusetts Press.

Essed, P. (2000). Dilemmas in leadership: Women of colour in the Academy. *Ethnic and Racial Studies, 23*(5), 888-904.

Ferdman, B. M. (1995). Cultural identity and diversity in organizations: Bridging the gap between group differences and individual uniqueness. In M. M. Chemers, S. Oskamp, & M. A. Costanzo (Eds.), *Diversity in organizations: New perspectives for a changing workplace* (pp. 37-61). Thousand Oaks, CA: Sage. .

Fine, M. (2000). "Whiting out" social justice. In R. T. Carter (Ed.), *Addressing cultural issues in organizations: Beyond the corporate context* (pp. 35-50). New York: Guilford.

Fine, M. G. (1995). *Building successful multicultural organizations: Challenges and opportunities.* Westport, CT: Quorum Books.

Fox, E., Glenn, J., Jacobs, M., & Karamchandani, S. (2000, February 14). Government reports a 300+ percent increase in discrimination lawsuits. *HR Watch*, provided by the law office of D'Ancona & Pflaum, LLD, Archive. Retrieved January 12, 2003, from http://hr.monster.com/hrwatch/2000/02/14/.

Fraiman, S. (1997). Diversity in action: The retreat from affirmative action. *National Women's Studies Association Journal, 9*(1), 39-43.

Freire, P. (1970). *Pedagogy of the oppressed.* New York: Continuum.

Fulkerson, J. R., & Schuler, R. S. (1992). Managing worldwide diversity at Pepsi-Cola International. In S. E. Jackson & Associates (Eds.), *Diversity in the workplace: Human resources initiatives* (pp. 248-278). New York: Guilford.

Fullerton, H. N., Jr., & Toossi, M. (2001, November). Labor force projections to 2010: Steady growth and changing composition [Electronic version]. *Monthly Labor Review Online, 124*(11), 21-38.

Flynn, G. (1999, February). White males see diversity's other side, *Workforce, 78*(1), 52-56.

Gallagher, T. J. (2000). Building institutional capacity to address cultural differences. In R. T. Carter (Ed.), *Addressing cultural issues in organizations: Beyond the corporate context* (pp. 229-240). New York: Guilford.

Gallos, J. V., Ramsey, J. V., & Associates. (1997). *Teaching diversity: Listening to the soul, speaking from the heart*. San Francisco: Jossey-Bass.

Garcia, M. (1995). An anthropological approach to multicultural diversity training. *Journal of Applied Behavioral Science, 31*(4), 490-504.

Gardner, W. L., & Cleavenger, D. (1998). The impression management strategies associated with transformational leadership at the world-class level: A psychohistorical assessment. *Management Communication Quarterly, 12*, 3-41.

Gardenswartz, L., & Rowe, A. (1993). *Managing diversity: A complete desk reference.* Chicago: Irwin.

Geber, B. (1990, July). Managing diversity. *Training, 27*(7), 23-30.

Gergen, K. J. (1999). *An invitation to social construction*. Thousand Oaks, CA: Sage.

Giaridina, J. C. (1998). A program to celebrate human diversity. *Education Digest, 63*(7), 9-14.

Golembiewski, R. T. (1995). *Managing diversity in organizations*. Tuscaloosa: The University of Alabama Press.

Goldsmith, J. (2000, October 26). CBS to settle sex lawsuits. *Daily Variety, 269*(39), 4.

Goleman, D. (1995). *Emotional intelligence.* New York: Bantam Books.

Goodall, H. L., Jr. (1995). Work-hate: Narratives about mismanaged transitions in times of organizational transformation and change. In R. K. Whillock & D. Slayden (Eds.), *Hate speech* (pp. 80-121). Thousand Oaks, CA: Sage.

Goodwin, A. L. (2000). Teachers as (multi)cultural agents in schools. In R. T. Carter (Ed.), *Addressing cultural issues in organizations: Beyond the corporate context* (pp. 101-114). New York: Guilford.

Gottfredson, L. S. (1992). Dilemmas in developing diversity programs. In S. E. Jackson & Associates (Eds.), *Diversity in the workplace: Human resources initiatives* (pp. 279-305). New York: Guilford.

Grande, S. M. A. (2000). American Indian geographies of identity and power: At the crossroads of indígena and mestizaje. *Harvard Educational Review, 70*, 467-498.

Harris, E. (1998, September 14). *The New York Times*, p. C9.

Harris, T. E. (1997). Diversity: Importance, ironies, and pathways. In C. D. Brown, C. C. Snedeker, & B. Sykes (Eds.), *Conflict and diversity* (pp. 17-34). Cresskill, NJ: Hampton Press.

Hemphill, H., & Haines, R. (1997). *Discrimination, harassment, and the failure of diversity training.* Westport, CT: Quorum Books.

Henderson, G. (1994). *Cultural diversity in the workplace: Issues and strategies.* Westport, CT: Quorum Books.

Heuberger, B., & Gerber, D. (1999). Strength through cultural diversity: Developing and teaching a diversity course. *College Teaching, 47*(3), 107-114.

Hoffman, D. M. (1997). Diversity in practice: Perspectives on concept, context, and policy. *Educational Policy, 11*(3), 375-393.

Holvino, E. (2000). Social diversity in social change organizations: Standpoint learnings for organizational consulting. In R. T. Carter (Ed.), *Addressing cultural issues in organizations: Beyond the corporate context* (pp. 211-228). New York: Guilford.

hooks, b. (1994). *Teaching to transgress: Education as the practice of freedom.* New York: Routledge.

Hruby, P. (2000, February 28). Overdefensive of offensive speech? *Insight on the News, 16*(8), 32-33.

Impink, A. (2002, November). Cultural sensitivity as a means of survival. *Nursing Homes Long Term Care Management, 51*(11), 14-19.

Jackson, M. (1997, November 30). Sense and sensitivity: Texaco under microscope after bias suit. *Leader-Telegram*, pp. D1-2.

Jackson, R. L., II. (2000). So real illusions of black intellectualism: Exploring race, roles, and gender in the academy. *Communication Theory, 10*, 48-63.

Jackson, S. E., & Associates. (1992). *Diversity in the workplace: Human resources initiatives.* New York: Guilford.

Jamieson, D., & O'Mara, J. (1991). *Managing workforce 2000: Gaining the diversity advantage.* San Francisco: Jossey-Bass.

Johnson, S. D. (2000). Classic defenses: A critical assessment of ambivalence and denial in organizational leaders' response to diversity. In R. T. Carter (Ed.), *Addressing cultural issues in organizations: Beyond the corporate context* (pp. 181-192). New York: Guilford.

Jordan, K. (1998). Diversity training in the workplace today: A status report. *Journal of Career Planning and Employment, 59*(1), 46-51, 61-63.

Judkins, B. M., & Lahurd, R. A. (1999). Building community from diversity. *American Behavioral Scientist, 42*(5), 786-800.

Karp, H. B., & Sammour, H. Y. (2000, September). Workforce diversity: Choices in diversity training programs and dealing with resistance to diversity. *College Student Journal, 34*(3), 451-458.

Karp, H. B., & Sutton, N. (1993, July). Where diversity training goes wrong. *Training, 30*, 30-32.

Keller, J. M., Young, A., & Riley, M. (1996). *Evaluating diversity training: 17 ready-to-use tools* . San Diego, CA: Pfeiffer.

Kikoski, J. F., & Kikoski, C. K. (1999). *Reflexive communication in the culturally diverse workplace.* Westport, CT: Praeger.

Kirby, E. L., & Harter, L. M. (2001). Discourses of diversity and the quality of work life: The character and costs of the managerial metaphor. *Management Communication Quarterly, 15*(1), 121-127.

Koonce, R. (2001, December). Refining diversity. *T+D, 55*(12), 22-28.

Kossek, E. E., & Zonia, S. D. (1994). The effects of race and ethnicity on perceptions of human resource policies and climate regarding diversity. *Journal of Business and Technical Communication, 8*, 319-334.

Krupar, K. R. (1997). A diversity and conflict perspective. In C. D. Brown, C. C. Snedeker, & B. Sykes (Eds.), *Conflict and diversity* (pp. 227-242). Cresskill, NJ: Hampton Press.

Lasch-Quinn, E. (2001). *Race experts: How racial etiquette, sensitivity training, and new age therapy hijacked the civil rights revolution.* New York: Norton

Lauter, E. (1997). Toward diversity. *National Women's Studies Association Journal, 9*(1), 44-48.

Lavole, D. (1996, November 30). Xerox diversity effort copied. *The Leader-Telegram*, p. D2.

Leach, J., & George, B. (1995). *A practical guide to working with diversity: The processes, the tools, the resources.* New York: American Management Association.

Leonard, B. (2002, April). Not all training programs have felt the full squeeze of corporate belt-tightening. *HR Magazine, 47*(4), 25.

Lindsley, S. L. (1998a). Communicating prejudice in organizations. In M. L. Hecht (Ed.), *Communicating prejudice* (pp. 187-205). Thousand Oaks, CA: Sage.

Lindsley, S. L. (1998b). Organizational interventions to prejudice. In M. L. Hecht (Ed.), *Communicating prejudice* (pp. 302-310). Thousand Oaks, CA: Sage.

Loden, M. (1996). *Implementing diversity.* New York: McGraw-Hill.

Loudin, A. (2000, April). Diversity pays. *Warehousing Management, 7*(3), 30-33.

Lubove, S. (1997, December 15). Damned if you do, damned if you don't. *Forbes, 160*(13), 122-126.

Lynch, F. R. (1991). *Invisible victims: White males and the crisis of affirmative action.* New York: Praeger.

Lynch, F. R. (1997). *The diversity machine: The drive to change the white male workplace.* New York: The Free Press.

McCallum, J. (1998, October 19). MLS takes the offensive. *Sports Illustrated*, pp. 28-29.

MacDonald, H. (1993, July 5). The diversity industry. *New Republic, 209*(1), 22-25.

McDonald, J. (1997). Being out in academia: A year of my life in Enid, America. In B. Mintz & E. Rothblum (Eds.), *Lesbians in academia: Degrees of freedom* (pp. 120-125). New York: Routledge.

McEnrue, M. P. (1993). Managing diversity: Los Angeles before and after the riots. *Organizational Dynamics, 22*(3), 18-29.

McGrath, J. E., Berdahl, J. L., & Arrow, H. (1995). Traits, expectations, culture and clout: The dynamics of diversity in work groups. In S. E. Jackson & M. N. Ruderman (Eds.), *Diversity in work teams: Research paradigms for a changing workplace* (pp. 17-46). Washington, DC: American Psychological Association.

McIntosh, P. (1998). White privilege: Unpacking the invisible knapsack. In P. S. Rothenberg (Ed.), *Race, class, and gender in the United States* (pp. 165-169). New York: St. Martin's Press.

Meyerson, D. E., & Fletcher, J. K. (2000, January-February). A modest manifesto for shattering the class ceiling. *Harvard Business Review, 78*(1), 126-136.

Mobley, M., & Payne, T. (1992, December). Backlash! The challenge to diversity training. *Training & Development, 46*(2), 45-52.

Morrison, E. W., & Herlihy, J. M. (1992). Managing diversity: A strategic "grass roots" approach. In S. E. Jackson & Associates (Eds.), *Diversity in the workplace: Human resources initiatives* (pp. 203-226). New York: Guilford.

Mueller, N. L. (1996, March). Wisconsin Power and Light's model diversity program. *Training & Development, 50*(3), 57-60.

Nakayama, T. K., & Martin, J. N. (1999). *Whiteness: The communication of social identity.* Thousand Oaks, CA: Sage.

Nkomo, S. M. (1995). Identities and the complexity of diversity. In S. E. Jackson & M. N. Ruderman (Eds.), *Diversity in work teams: Research paradigms for a changing workplace* (pp. 247-256). Washington, DC: American Psychological Association.

Nkomo, S. M., & Cox, T., Jr. (1996). Diverse identities in organization. In S. R. Clegg, C. Hardy, & W. R. Nord (Eds.), *Handbook of organization studies* (pp. 338-356). Thousand Oaks, CA: Sage.

Orbe, M. P. (1998). An outsider within perspective to organizational communication: Explicating the communicative practices of co-cultural group members. *Management Communication Quarterly, 12*, 230-279.

Orbe, M. P., & Harris, T. M. (2001). *Interracial communication: Theory into practice.* Belmont, CA: Wadsworth/Thomson Learning.

Parrillo, V. N. (1996). *Diversity in America.* Thousand Oaks, CA: Pine Forge Press.

Paskoff, S. M. (1996). Ending the workplace diversity wars. *Training, 33*(8), 42-47.

Pearce, W. B. (1989). *Communication and the human condition.* Carbondale: Southern Illinois University Press.

Planalp, S. (1999). *Communicating emotion: Social, moral, and cultural processes.* Cambridge, UK: Cambridge University Press.

Planalp, S., Hafen, S., & Adkins, D. (2000). Messages of shame and guilt. *Communication Yearbook, 23*, 1-64.

Prasad, A., & Elmes, M. (1997). Issues in the management of workplace diversity. In P. Prasad, A. J. Mills, M. Elmes, & A. Prasad (Eds.), *Managing the organizational melting pot: Dilemmas of workplace diversity* (pp. 367-376). Thousand Oaks, CA: Sage.

Quindlen, A. (2000, March 13). The problem of the color line. *Newsweek*, p. 76.

Racial discrimination in U.S. remains a stubborn problem, report says. (2000, September 22). *Saint Paul Pioneer Press*, p. A5.

Raggins, B. R. (1995). Diversity, power, and membership in organizations: A cultural, structural, and behavioral perspective. In M. M. Chemers, S. Oskamp, & M. A. Costanzo (Eds.), *Diversity in organizations: New perspectives for a changing workplace* (pp. 91-132). Thousand Oaks, CA: Sage.

Ramsey, M. (1996). Diversity identity development training: Theory informs practice. *Journal of Multicultural Counseling & Development, 24*(4), 229-240.

Rattansi, A. (1992). Changing the subject? Racism, culture, and education. In J. Donald & A. Rattansi (Eds.), *"Race," culture, and difference* (pp. 11-48). Newbury Park, CA: Sage.

Reardon, K. K., & Reardon, K. J. (1999). "All that we can be": Leading the U.S. Army's gender integration effort. *Management Communication Quarterly, 12*, 600-617.

Reibstein, L. (1996, November 25). Managing diversity. *Newsweek, 128*(22), 50.

Rent-A-Center settles discrimination suits. (2002, March 18). *Furniture/Today, 26*(28), 14.

Rich, A. (1978). *The dream of a common language.* New York: Norton.

Rynes, S., & Rosen, B. (1995). A field survey of factors affecting the adoption and perceived success of diversity training. *Personnel Psychology, 48*, 247-270.

Said, E. W. (1993). *Culture and imperialism.* New York: Knopf.

Samantrai, R. (1997). On being the object of concern. *National Women's Studies Association Journal, 9*(1), 49-53.

Seligman, D., & deLlosa, P. (1994, October 17). Thinking about the gauntlet. *Fortune, 130*(8), 214.

Sessa, V. I. (1992). Managing diversity at the Xerox Corporation: Balanced workforce goals and caucus groups. In S. E. Jackson & Associates (Eds.), *Diversity in the workplace: Human resources initiatives* (pp. 37-64). New York: Guilford.

Simonsen, P., & Wells, C. (1994). African Americans take control of their careers. *Personnel Journal, 73*(4), 99-104.

Singelis, T. M. (1998). *Teaching about culture, ethnicity, and diversity.* Thousand Oaks, CA: Sage.

Skrentny, J. D. (1996). *The ironies of affirmative action: Politics, culture, and justice in America*. Chicago: University of Chicago Press.

Smith, D. G. (1995). Organizational implications of diversity in higher education. In M. M. Chemers, S. Oskamp, & M. A. Costanzo (Eds.), *Diversity in organizations: New perspectives for a changing workplace* (pp. 220-224). Thousand Oaks, CA: Sage.

Talbot, D. M. (1999). Personal narrative of an Asian American's experience with racism. *Journal of Counseling & Development, 77*(1), 42-45.

Tan, D. L., Morris, L., & Romero, J. (1996, September). Changes in attitude after diversity training. *Training & Development, 50*(2), 54-55.

Tannen, D. (1998). *The argument culture: Moving from debate to dialogue*. New York: Random House.

Thomas, D. A., & Proudford, K. A. (2000). Making sense of race relations in organizations: Theories for practice. In R. T. Carter (Ed.), *Addressing cultural issues in organizations: Beyond the corporate context* (pp. 51-68). New York: Guilford.

Thomas, R. R., Jr. (1991). *Beyond race and gender: Unleashing the power of your total work force by managing diversity*. New York: American Management Association.

Thomas, R. R., Jr. (1996). *Redefining diversity*. New York: American Management Association.

Trethaway, A. (1999). Isn't it ironic? Using irony to explore the contradictions of organizational life. *Western Journal of Communication, 93*, 140-167.

Triandis, H. C. (1995). A theoretical framework for the study of diversity. In M. M. Chemers, S. Oskamp, & M. A. Costanzo (Eds.), *Diversity in organizations: New perspectives for a changing workplace* (pp. 11-36). Thousand Oaks, CA: Sage.

Triandis, H. C., Kurowski, L. L, & Gelfand, M. J. (1994). Workplace diversity. In H. C. Triandis, M. D. Dunnette, & L. M. Hough (Eds.), *Handbook of industrial and organizational psychology* (Vol. 4, pp. 769-827). Palo Alto, CA: Consulting Psychologists Press.

United States Equal Employment Opportunity Commission. (n.d.). Charge statistics FY 1992 through FY 2001. Retrieved January 12, 2002, from http://www.eeoc.gov/stats/charges.html.

Two thousand Hispanic corporate. (2000, January/February). *Hispanic, 13*(1), 48-56.

Valli, L. (1995). The dilemma of race: Learning to be color blind and color conscious. *Journal of Teacher Education, 46*(2), 120-129.

Verespej, M. A. (1997, January 6). Zero tolerance. *Industry Week, 246*(1), 24-27.

Von Bergen, C. W., Soper, B., & Foster, T. (2002). Unintended negative effects of diversity management. *Public Personnel Management 31*(2), 239-251.

Wallace, B. C. (2000). Mental health: The influence of culture on the development of theory and practice. In R. T. Carter (Ed.), *Addressing cultural issues in organizations: Beyond the corporate context* (pp. 131-146). New York: Guilford.

Wang, V. O. (2000). The house of god: The fallacy of neutral universalism in medicine. In R. T. Carter (Ed.), *Addressing cultural issues in organizations: Beyond the corporate context* (pp. 147-164). New York: Guilford.

Watts, R. J., & Evans, A. (2000). Enhancing diversity climate in community organizations. In R. T. Carter (Ed.), *Addressing cultural issues in organizations: Beyond the corporate context* (pp. 193-210). New York: Guilford.

West, C. (1993). *Race matters*. Boston: Beacon Press.

West, C., & Fenstermaker, S. (1995). Doing difference. *Gender & Society, 9*, 8-37.

Whillock, R. K. (1995). The use of hate as a stratagem for achieving political and social goals. In R. K. Whillock & D. Slayden (Eds.), *Hate speech* (pp. 28-54). Thousand Oaks, CA: Sage.

Williams, Y., & Moyer, J. (1995). Leadership diversity: A business necessity for Bell Atlantic. *Journal of Education for Business, 71*(1), 14-16.

Winfield, L., & Spielman, S. (1995, April). Making sexual orientation part of diversity. *Training & Development, 5*(4), 50-51.

Wingert, P., Babwin, D., & Kwon, B. (1998, January 26). Should I pack my bags? *Newsweek*, p. 37.

Workman, T. (1996, November). *And the heads kept nodding: Politically correct resistance to diversity training*. Paper presented at the Instructional Development Division, National Communication Association, San Diego, CA.

Workman, T. (1999, November). *"Framing" difference: Employing Burke's frames to "accept" barriers to diversity*. Paper presented at the Intercultural Division, National Communication Association, Chicago, IL.

Young, I. M. (1990). *Justice and the politics of difference*. Princeton, NJ: Princeton University Press.

2

THROUGH THE SUBJECT'S EYE

Situating the Other in Discourses of Diversity

Debashish Munshi
The University of Waikato

The growing interest in issues of diversity in organizations is note-worthy in acknowledging the need to achieve equality. But dis-courses of diversity management, shaped as they are by Western and West-trained managers, effectively feed into neocolonialism's agenda of controlling the Other.[1] This chapter analyses the dis-courses of managing diversity and observes hierarchies of power that are geared to exercise controlling influence on those outside the dominant frame. The analysis interweaves personal narratives with scholarly research and draws on a range of theoretical per-spectives from a number of fields including postcolonial studies, feminist critiques of neo-classical economics, and indigenous/abo-riginal studies.

---

[1]In postcolonial theory, the word other with a small "o" refers to the "colonized others who are marginalized by imperial discourse" (Ashcroft et al., 1998, p. 170).

The hymns of a borderless world sung by the minstrels of globalization may sound melodious to many. But, for those of us who come from the shadow zones outside the periphery of a western[2] worldview, transcending the barriers of nation, race, and class is too often fraught with difficulties. Yet such difficulties are rarely acknowledged because of an implicit belief in the larger society that equality of opportunity is there for those who seek it. The plight of the doctors from India, China, and the former Yugoslavia who were forced to retrain as nurses in New Zealand because their qualifications were not seen to be good enough (Quaintance, 1996) is only one of the many tales of woe that frustrated immigrant professionals have.

Like these immigrants, my qualifications and work experience, too, were never good enough to translate into job interviews. Unable to find employment, I decided to become a student once again. As someone situated at the margins of power in a western setting, I chose to do a doctoral research project on how the non-western other is constructed and positioned at the peripheries of power circles, initially in media but more substantially in management. In particular, I decided to examine media and management discourses of plurality, track levels of power imbalances in them, and observe patterns of conflation between the narratives of colonialism and neo-colonialism. This chapter, which in a large part condenses the introductory chapters of my doctorate thesis (completed in 2000), attempts to expose some of the affinities between old imperial colonialism and current neo-colonial globalism. In particular, it seeks to push out the layers of romantic rhetoric in discourses of diversity in the age of globalization and examine their core function of control in relation to the other.

Imperial discourses characterize subjects as the other "as a means of establishing the binary separation of the colonizer and the colonized and asserting the naturalness and primacy of the colonizing culture and world view" (Ashcroft, Griffiths, & Tiffin, 1998, p. 169). This process of constructing the other, I argue, continues in contemporary neo-colonial discourses under redesigned strategies of western control.

The purpose of this chapter is not to demonize the west but to examine western discourses of management in the context of the hegemonic worldview of the west. The terms *west* and *western* are used to denote the neo-colonial thought processes that shape institutions driven by Eurocentric visions of science, culture, business, and development. I recognize that just as there are significant others in the geographical west, there are western models in place in the east as well. Additionally, there exists a huge diversity of perspectives within

---

[2] I use the terms west and western with a small "w" for two reasons: First, I wish to emphasize that these terms reflect ideological concepts rather than geographical locations and, second, I seek to suppress the grandeur associated with the capitalization of the terms in colonial and neo-colonial discourses.

the west. I readily acknowledge that many of the scholars whose works I use for my critique of western neo-colonialism live and work in western locations.

Following one of them, Hall (1992), I examine the west as a "concept" (p. 277) and acknowledge that the use of an apparently unified and homogeneous term like the west can be seen as an oversimplification. But, as Hall (1992) convincingly argued, this simplification itself "can be used to make a point about discourse" (p. 280) in general, and the discourses of media and management in particular. Hall (1992) explained that

> the discourse, as a "system of representation," represents the world as divided according to a simple dichotomy—the West/the Rest. That is what makes the discourse of "the West and the Rest" so destructive—it draws crude and simplistic distinctions and constructs an over-simplified conception of "difference." (p. 280)

In talking of the west, particularly western business institutions and managerial thought processes, I concentrate on neo-colonial discourses that rely on an oversimplified conception of difference to consolidate the power of western elites. These elites, in most cases, consist of western, or west-trained, leaders of organizations who dictate global trade, economy, and politics. This dictation rides on a carefully crafted strategy of constructing and controlling the other.

BARBED WIRES IN A BORDERLESS WORLD: MEDIA, POLITICS, AND THE IMMIGRANT OTHER

My first step in documenting the shape, direction, and magnitude of the neo-colonial process of constructing the other was toward charting the media coverage of the highly volatile immigration issue in New Zealand in 1996 (see Munshi, 1998, 1999). Immigration surfaced as a major issue of public concern in 1996, the year I came to New Zealand. But, interestingly, the topic discussed in public fora was never immigration but *Asian* immigration. Evidently, immigration was the norm but Asian immigration was different. Although Britain continued to be the top source country for immigrants ("Fewer given residence," 1996; "Residence approvals," 1996), the media, in particular, continued to highlight the pluses and minuses of Asian immigration (see, e.g., Riordan, 1996; Roger, 1996). One question that remained unanswered was why Asians were grouped together when Europeans were not. After all, an Asian from Afghanistan had as little in common with an Asian from Korea as a European from Ireland had with a European from Spain. One possible explanation was that all Asians, no matter where they were from, were seen to be farthest from the perceived norm of an average New Zealander.

For Asians in New Zealand, 1996 was a particularly traumatic year. As politicians debated the immigration issue, racist skinheads spewed venom on hapless new immigrants. As I walked home from the university, in the Hamilton suburb of Hillcrest, one night, I was followed by a group of boys yelling anti-Asian epithets. Another night, a car nearly mounted the pavement to run me down. Even as I grappled with racism for the first time in my life, I was assured by many otherwise well-informed New Zealanders that racism was a new phenomenon in New Zealand. They suggested that I should not pay too much attention to isolated incidents. I wondered if indeed I was making too much of it until I delved deep into the history of racism against other non-western immigrants in the country.

Research soon revealed that immigration legislation in New Zealand had a history of institutionalized racism (Chen, 1993) and it was not until 1964 that racially based laws were repealed in the country. Before the turn of the century, prominent politicians such as Richard Seddon and William Pember Reeves were responsible for pushing through legislation aimed at restricting immigrants who were not of European, or more specifically British, stock (Brooking & Rabel, 1995). Although the Asiatic Restriction Act, promoted by Seddon in 1896, was officially described as "an act to prevent the influx into New Zealand of persons of alien race who are likely to be hurtful to the public welfare" (Brooking & Rabel, 1995, p. 25), Reeves tried to exclude Asians and colored persons, along with the disabled and the mentally ill, in his Undesirable Immigrants Bill of 1894 (Brooking & Rabel, 1995). Even after racially discriminatory laws were done away with in New Zealand under the Immigration Amendment Act of 1964, politicians sustained disharmony among the people by playing on racial prejudices still in existence in society. Given this background, the physical and emotional attack on Asians and Africans during the election campaign-driven immigration debate of 1996 was hardly surprising. According to the race relations conciliator, Dr. Rajen Prasad, "reports of letter boxes being attacked, children being accosted and recent arrivals being harassed had risen with the debate on immigration" ("Conciliator sees," 1996, p. 2).

In the midst of the great debate, my wife and I met with extraordinary hostility for challenging, in a newspaper article, a columnist's call to "recolonise Africa" (Hames, 1996, p. A13). All we did was to point out that the "images of horror" (Hames, 1996, p. A13) from Black Africa that baulked the columnist were, in large part, a legacy of the colonial destruction of the physical, cultural, and spiritual wealth of that formerly colonized world. We also reminded the commentator that western self-righteousness at the "long line of grisly spectres to be thrown up by black Africa" (Hames, 1996, p. A13) was hypocritical, given the history of the genocide of Native Americans in the American continents, the enslavement of Africans by European powers, and the marginalization and deprivations faced by aboriginal peoples in the Australian continent (Munshi & Kurian, 1996). Instead of responding directly to the editor, a large number of people attacked us with a volley of personal hate mail, some even asking us to get out of the country. The racist attacks on us and other others in 1996 were compounded by the fact that there was very little acknowledgment of a race problem in New Zealand. As Pountney (1999) pointed out, "individual prejudice against others who are different . . . is much more common in New Zealand than we like to admit" (p. A13). *Marking out the other is a key practice in consolidating such prejudice.*

With the Asianisation of the immigration debate in 1996, the discourse had, of course, been injected with a lethal dose of race. But, ironic as it may seem, by accepting the terms of reference for the debate, those tolerant of Asian migrants contributed to this racist discourse as well as those who were openly xenophobic. By marking out Asians as a category different from the norm, Asians were clearly situated as alien.

WALLS OF DIFFERENCE: STRUCTURING THE "NORM" TO SHUT OUT THE OTHER

This framework of difference was highlighted to me during a conversation I had with a librarian at the Hamilton Public Library in late 1996. In the middle of our conversation, the librarian interrupted me with an exclamation: "Oh, you speak such good English don't you?" "So do *you*," I replied politely. The library official was taken aback. "But I have spoken English all my life," he protested. "So have I," I said, and went on to ask him why he was so surprised at my ability to speak the language. He responded by saying that foreigners were usually not very good with English.

Not in a mood to call it quits, I asked him what made him think I was a foreigner. "Well, you look like one," he told me. "What are foreigners supposed to look like?" I persisted. "Well, different . . . you know." The operative word, quite clearly, was "different." I was *different* from what he saw as the *norm*. But what is the norm? And who gets to shape this norm?

Shortly after I arrived in New Zealand in February 1996, the immigration officials wanted me to sit for an elementary English test despite the fact that I had grown up speaking, reading, and writing English. It didn't matter to the officials that I had a degree in English literature or that I had worked all my life for a major English language daily. Neither did it matter to the officials that I was speaking to them not in Hindi, Bengali, or Swahili but in English. What did matter to them was that I was an Asian, and, therefore, a person earmarked to sit for this test. In the eyes of the policymakers, I was the *other*, a person who was *different* from the presumed *norm* and I had to officially prove myself to be normal.

Such framing was not just a personal matter. The highly polarized immigration debate in New Zealand was itself ethnocentric because it put ethnic minori-

ties outside the realm of the norm as Blommaert and Verschueren (1998) pointed out in their critique of debating diversity in the context of Belgium. In following the discourse of the immigration debate through the local media, I noted
how Asians were consistently slotted into the category of the other by those
who were for immigration as well as those who were against it (see Munshi,
1998, 1999).

EXTENDING RESEARCH: SOURCES OF OTHERING

For me, scrutinizing media texts on the immigration debate turned out to be a
pilot for a larger project on an examination of the discourses of diversity not
just in the media but also in the larger areas of business communication and
management. The study of the print media coverage of the immigration issue in
New Zealand turned out to be too limited to provide answers to my fundamental
question: Whose norms or standards are followed in framing the terms of reference for discussions on diversity? Accordingly, I extended my search to a wide
range of texts spread across media and management. My four-pronged inquiry
into the business of the other involved examining a selection of reports on the
other in the business media, theoretical work on the concept of requisite variety
in public relations, texts on intercultural communication, and the literature on
"managing diversity" in organizations. To carry out this examination, I borrowed tools from "other" fields such as postcolonial studies, subaltern historiography, feminist critiques of neoclassical economics, and indigenous/aboriginal
studies.

   While I document in detail all four lines of my inquiry into the construction
and control of the other in media and management in my doctoral thesis (see
Munshi, 2000), this chapter looks more specifically on the mechanism of control in the concept of managing diversity in organizations. As Prasad (1997)
showed in a path-breaking piece, the "discourse of workplace diversity is inex-
tricably (and fatally) linked with the discourse of colonialism" (p. 305). As in
the colonial enterprise, he pointed out that "immigrants and people of color . . .
provide one of the principal dimensions of the diversity phenomenon" (pp. 286-
287) and that their treatment resembles that of the colonized others in the hands
of colonizers. In A. Prasad's (1997) terms, most diversity management scholars
and practitioners overlook the power dynamics in motion in the industry when
they ignore "colonialism as a sense-making framework" (p. 286).

   In studying the diverse range of texts on diversity, I not only use colonialism as a "sense-making framework," but also go beyond it to train the spotlight
on the strategies of managerialism as a covert, and often overt, tool of neo-colonialism. In doing so, I argue that the neo-colonial biases of dominant elites that
direct diversity management align with the managerial and administrative biases
of the same elites.

The literature on managing diversity revolves around the strategies a "senior manager" needs to adopt to solve "the new challenges (read: problems) associated with an increasingly diverse workforce" (Orbe, 1998, p. 230). According to those seeking to manage diversity in public relations, "the diversity of ideas and viewpoints within a manager's self-regulating system should equal diversity of the environment" (Culbertson, Jeffers, Stone, & Terrell, 1993, p. 23). This emphasis on "the managerial processes of control and coordination" that "can direct the inputs of diverse people toward a common goal" (Walck, 1995, p. 119) cements the colonial approach to issues of diversity inside the walls of workplaces.

DIVERSITY MANAGEMENT
AND MANAGING THE OTHER

In an increasingly multicultural world, diversity is a major organizational issue (see e.g., Carr-Ruffino, 1996; Gardenswartz & Rowe, 1998; Kossek & Lobel, 1996; Thomas, 1991; Weiss, 1996). The sing-along celebration of a multiplicity of voices in the orchestra of diversity management is, of course, well meaning. However, although the plurality is formally validated by the presence of a range of musicians, the baton remains in the hands of a western conductor.

Despite the decreasing population ratio of the west, the subject of diversity remains, more often than not, constructed through western eyes. For this dominant faction, diversity is viewed as something that needs to be managed. "Management is always in the hands of the powerful," Blommaert and Verschueren (1998) said, and "the management of diversity is not an exception" (p. 15). The theory and practices of the management of diversity are guided by the terms of reference framed by powerful Anglo-American and other Eurocentric policymakers to keep the non-western other under control. Within this context, discussions on diversity become manifestations of neo-colonial attempts to construct and control the other.

Neo-colonialism, as the Ghanaian leader Kwame Nkrumah articulated in 1965, involves power and clout that former colonial powers, as well as new economic powers, wield over the rest of the world through lending regimes of international financial institutions, price-fixing mechanisms of world markets, and policies of multinational corporations as well as educational institutions (cited in Ashcroft et al., 1998). This overwhelming exercise of control by a largely Euro-American elite is reflected in approaches to issues of diversity.

The act of "managing" diversity has a distinct power hierarchy in which the one who manages is superior to the one managed. This, of course, gives rise to several questions: First, who are the managers? Second, what is it that gives the managers the authority to "manage" others? Third, whose norms or standards are followed in this management? Answers to these questions suggest that a system of domination is at work. As in most large organizations, as Hamel and Prahalad (1994) pointed out in their much-cited work, Competing for the *Future*, there is a "dominant managerial frame" that puts into place an administrative system that reinforces "certain perspectives and biases" at the cost of others (pp. 54-55).

The dominant managerial frame parallels the dominant ethnic frame and both set the agenda for discussions on diversity. As a result, the agenda foregrounds debate on what to do about people who are outside the dominant frame. In this debate, there are two main opposing camps. One is the overtly insular and racist camp that opposes the presence of ethnic minorities in predominantly White societies. This camp is variously represented in different countries: In the United States, champions of Proposition 187 sought to bar so-called illegal immigrants in California from receiving welfare, education, or health benefits in 1994 (van Dijk, 1995); in Europe, French authorities broke into the church of St. Bernard de la Chapelle in Paris in 1996 to round up immigrants from former French colonies in Africa (see e.g., "Shadow of Dreyfus," 1996); and in Australia, followers of politician Pauline Hanson propped up their anti-immigration campaign by hitting out not only at Asians but the first peoples of the land, the aborigines, as well (see e.g., Fitzgerald, 1996).

The other camp includes those who preach tolerance. On the surface, this camp appears democratic and progressive. But, as Blommaert and Verschueren (1998) argued, this group is no less damaging because of its drive for a re-homogenisation based on the integration, or the removal, of disturbing differences. This group, too, creates what van Dijk (1995) called "majority discourses about minorities" (p. 147). What binds the two opposing groups is their common approach to marking difference, a process described by postcolonial scholars as *othering*, a "term coined by Gayatri Spivak for the process by which imperial discourse creates its 'others'" (Ashcroft et al., 1998, p. 171). Irrespective of the monocultural or multicultural positions taken by people on issues of diversity, what remains static are dominant assumptions constructed around neo-colonial, Eurocentric norms.

Much of the orientation of diversity management is geared, according to scholars in the field, to encouraging managers to view managing diversity as a means to achieving "organizational objectives" (Kossek & Lobel, 1996, p. 10). This orientation privileges the position of managers. As organizational ends invariably reflect the demands and needs of managers who are western or west-trained, diversity management maintains the gap between western elites and the other.

In New Zealand, for example, bicultural goals of organizations have remained "unrealised for years and little progress towards them has been achieved" (Tremaine, 1997, p. 286). As both Pakeha (New Zealanders of European origin) and Maori cultures "(in all their diverse modes of expression) belong in New Zealand," organizations need to "understand the importance of both cultures as part of their broader cultural environment" (Tremaine, 1997, pp. 287-288). Despite this context, the structures of opportunity, for development and advancement, are different for the Pakeha and the Maori. The Pakeha culture of most New Zealand organizations "contrasts and conflicts with the values of Maori culture" (Nilakant, 1995, p. 402).

The field of diversity management does espouse the cause of a plural world through expressed needs to build "multicultural work teams" (Gardenswartz & Rowe, 1998, p. 129), to evolve a "consensus for change" (Carr-Ruffino, 1996, p. 550), and to "motivate a heterogeneous workforce" (Kossek & Lobel, 1996, p. 17). But, this apparent benevolence notwithstanding, the field does little to catalyze a shift in the power base in line with the changing demographics of the world. Instead, the composers of managing diversity tend to reinforce elitist control over the shift by promoting a synthetic equality that ignores the lopsidedness of existing power structures.

UNEQUAL EQUALITY
AND AN IMBALANCE IN POWER

Equality is one of the primary values in the idealized texts on managing diversity:

> Politically, we're a pluralistic society. Our diverse groups get to have a say through individual members' votes and whatever influence their interest groups can wield within the political system. Another of our key values is *equality and fairness for all*, and minority groups have always struggled toward that ideal value. (Carr-Ruffino, 1996, p. 53)

Working toward the "ideal value" of equality does sound harmonious. But, as the Nobel Prize-winning welfare economist, Amartya Sen (1992) pointed out, a closer examination of the "warm glow" (p. 30) of the rhetoric reveals how the concept of equality is often unequal. The rhetoric assumes a uniformity of the plane along which equality among people is measured. But, "human heterogeneities," as Sen (1992) observed, "make equality in one space diverge from equality in another" (p. 4). He asserts that the rhetoric of equality in income distribution conceals the "substantive inequalities in, say, well-being and freedom arising out of such a distribution given the disparate personal and social circumstances of each individual" (p. 30). In other words, the championing of a unitary notion of "equality" only consolidates the position of those who are already more equal than others.

Diversity managers promote the belief that educational parity can bring about equality of job opportunities. In line with this belief, *Workforce 2020*

(Judy & D'Amico, 1997), a much-cited think-tank approach to issues of diversity in the workplace, concludes that "the relatively modest educational gains of Hispanics have prevented them from being hired to fill many good jobs" (p. 65) in the United States. From a value-neutral equality perspective, *Workforce 2020* may be justified in its analysis. But its concern about the "sharply rising numbers of Hispanics without a completed high school education" (p. 64) does not take into consideration the sociopolitical constraints that contribute to the relatively lower educational achievement by Hispanics, many of whom are immigrants from neighboring Mexico. These constraints include policy interventions such as Proposition 187 of 1994 in the state of California "which denied so-called illegal immigrants virtually all social services, especially public education and non-emergency medical care" (Haraway, 1997, pp. 189-190). This proposition is only one of the many ways in which racism and ethnocentrism find their way into seemingly benign structures of public policy. As Haraway (1997) asserted, "despite the denial of its backers, Proposition 187 was widely understood to have fundamental racial, ethnic, class, and national targets, especially working-class Latinos of color coming across the Mexican-U.S. border" (p. 190).

The consignment of working-class Latinos to the margins fits in with the larger scheme of global business. The business motor continues to be powered by neo-classical economic principles, which divide the labor force into a powerful core and a less powerful periphery (Clegg, 1992; Humphries & Grice, 1995). In such an obviously divisive setting, discourses of harmony and equality can act, at best, as a tranquilizer to numb any sense of injustice among those on the periphery. In fact, in Humphries and Grice's (1995) analysis, more and more employees are now being "conditioned to accept, or at least tolerate, the notion that this new division of labor is not only the most efficient and effective in the face of global competition, but is also inevitable and fair" (p. 29).

This conditioning of people's minds lies at the core of the strategies of diversity management. One major strategy is to create a perception of idealized equality:

> It is well known that behavior is driven by perceptions of reality. Therefore, what people believe about their opportunities in the work environment is of vital importance regardless of whether or not these beliefs are consistent with the facts. (Cox, 1993, pp. 14-15)

This perceived equality based on grand rhetoric may be useful for some but "misleading for others" (Sen, 1992, p. 30). In fact, the image of a mythical equality only privileges "the groups of people who make the rules and dominate the social construction of the hierarchy of categories" (Boje & Rosile, 1994, p. 16). Such a hierarchy of categories implicitly validates issues of systemic and institutionalized racism, ethnocentrism, and re-mobilized neo-colonialism (which the idealized rhetoric of equality chooses to underplay).

EQUALIZING THEMES
AND POSTRACIST HARMONIZING

In their zeal for harmonizing, the discourses of diversity management exclude radicalized power equations. Instead, they reach out for what one Chicana feminist author called a "postracist' space" (Anzaldua, 1990, p. xxii) that is unreal and unrealistic in the short term. She offered a powerful critique of the neocolonial agenda of appropriating the other:

> Dwelling on "diversity" and multiculturalism (a euphemism for the imperializing and now defunct "melting pot") is a way of avoiding seriously dismantling Racism. . . . We want so badly to move beyond Racism to a "postracist" space, a more comfortable space, but we are only prolonging the pain and leaving unfinished a business that could liberate some of our energies. (Anzaldua, 1990, p. xxii)

The desire of diversity managers to enter a make-believe "postracist sphere" is often fired by an idealistic and sincere zeal to go *beyond race and gender* (e.g., Thomas, 1991, 1996). A similar focus on burying the past, and ignoring the present, in premature moves to "forward thinking," occupies major sections of typically conciliatory diversity management texts:

> If we blame and rage against those who have held power, whatever their color, then we miss the point of the diversity movement. If we are to regain the competitive edge and create not only "kinder and gentler" but also more profitable and productive organizations, then it is time to share power. That means representing everyone in the decision-making process. Previously excluded groups who point their fingers and grind their axes move us backward, as do white males who cry reverse discrimination and resist any but token change. Any diversity effort that fails to extend empathy and understanding full circle will end up polarizing people and creating adversaries. We will all lose. (Gardenswartz & Rowe, 1998, p. 522)

Such an approach, however, simplifies complex social issues and underplays the realities of the dynamics of difference in societies as well as organizations. It does not reflect what Rothenberg (1992) called "the incredible complexity of ways race, gender, and class intersect and interact with each other and with other aspects of experience" (p. iv). In the so-called equal opportunity environments of present day organizations, the history of oppression transforms into calls to curb blaming and raging against those who have held power and start anew. But it is this history of inequality that continues to bestow power on dominant coalitions. In the process, it consolidates the often unseen effects of racism against underprivileged minorities. The absent effects of racism, seemingly invisible to the diversity manager, is powerfully captured by a Mexican American poet's response to the "young white man who asked me how I, an intelligent, well-read person could believe in the war between races" (Cervantes, 1992, p. 225). The dangerous everyday realities and emotional scars that Cervantes has to live with because of the ever present racism are not easily comprehended by those with the in-built privilege of being born in a dominant group. By being part of a self-constructed norm, members of this dominant group enjoy "the trappings of power that reside within society" (Lorde, 1992, p. 402). They talk of egalitarianism but may not implement it if their own positions of privilege are threatened.

An example of this egalitarianism is in the treatment of the Maori language in New Zealand. Although both English and Maori are official languages of the country, Maori language has "remained on the margins of New Zealand society, kept there by those who feel contemptuous about anything Maori" (Jackson, 1999, p. A15). Every time there is a proposal to make the teaching of Maori compulsory in primary schools, there is an outburst of opposition to it. Predictably, in October 1999, there was a major outcry against the minister of Maori affairs' suggestion to make Maori a part of the school curriculum. As always, the objections were ethnocentric: "nobody else in the world speaks that language; children would be better off learning the language of our trading partners; Maori lessons would take up valuable time that could be spent on more useful subjects" (Language to embrace, 1999, p. A14).

The state occupies a similar position by not making any attempt to ensure the teaching of both Maori and English in schools despite the statutory status of Maori as an official language on par with English, the preferred tongue of the European segment of the New Zealand population. In fact, it has so far done little to promote Maori, beyond incorporating Maori translations of names of state institutions. The objections raised to the inclusion of Maori in the fixed curriculum of primary schools signal the continuing race-power nexus that diversity managers attempt to ignore or underplay.

The rhetoric of superficial racial harmony in the discourses of a corporatised homogeneity suppresses ongoing struggles in the contested spaces of race and ethnicity. In diversity management's rhetoric of equality there is nothing that "speaks about racial domination, guilt, and hatred" (Haraway, 1997, p. 264). The drive for homogeneity in organizational norms consolidates the elitist paradigm in organizations. Such a process not only marginalizes the experiences of the other but perpetuates the discrimination of those who refuse to step out of their race, gender, or class identities. To comprehend the paradox of minority groups facing systemic discrimination in diversity-managed multicultural organizations, diversity management theorists will have to look not beyond "*race and gender*" (italics added; Thomas, 1991, 1996) but beyond *racism and sexism*.

In adopting an apparently benevolent frame, diversity management's often latent neo-colonial tendencies have remained largely unchallenged in organizational management, public relations, and the business media. One reason for this lack of adequate challenge is because these fields have not given much attention to scholarly work in areas sensitive to the less benevolent frames of colonialism such as postcolonial, subaltern, feminist, and aboriginal/indigenous studies. There have been some powerful presentations of postcolonial and feminist perspectives in organizational studies (e.g., Hegde, 1998; A. Prasad, 1977; Prasad, Mills, Elmes, & A. Prasad, 1997) but these have been extremely rare.

For the most part, diversity management has been guided by a simplistic, albeit harmonious, celebration of pluralism within a dominant frame that "elides serious political and intellectual engagement with the issues" (Hegde, 1998, p. 271) of power imbalances. To go beyond the mere recitation of hollow mantras of diversity, this chapter endorses Hegde's (1998) exhortation that "scholarship in the multicultural context has to open up theoretical spaces that engage politically with difference and not just confirm it descriptively" (p. 272). In the domain of management, the first step toward such an engagement would be to look at how other fields of study have done it. On the lines of "mapping disciplinary change" suggested by Jagtenberg and McKie (1997, p. 28), I seek to open the jammed shutters of management to view "other" fields of study.

UNDERSTANDING DIFFERENCE:
POSTCOLONIAL APPROACHES TO GLOBAL CULTURE

Postcolonial scholarship does not claim that global exploitation and inequality are the doing of the west alone. What such scholarship does assert, however, is that the impact of the major knowledge traditions of the west look "different from the perspective of the lives of the majority of the world's peoples" than from those of the "lives of advantaged groups in the west and elsewhere" (Harding, 1994, p. 321). In other words, postcolonial criticism challenges the grand narrative of colonialism as the equivalent of universal progress.

In adapting postcolonialist critiques to management, this chapter argues that the dominant discourses of diversity in both management and media are still rooted in colonial ideas of "civilizing" what the neo-colonial elite perceives to be an exotic and grotesquely different other. It also suggests that global management needs to recognize diversity issues not just on moral grounds but on economic grounds as well. After all, demographically, it is the Third World, often a loose synonym for the non-western other, that will make up 90% of the world's population in the 21st century (Mercer, 1998).

From a postcolonial perspective, an understanding of a global culture cannot be based on the "exoticism of multiculturalism" (Bhabha, 1994, p. 38). Management needs to recognize that it is not enough to pick up signifiers of cultural diversity which merely represent a range of separate systems of behavior and values (Ashcroft et al., 1998; Bhabha, 1994). Efforts to structure issues of diversity around "such a framework may even continue to suggest that such differences are merely aberrant or exotic, as was implicit in imperialistic ethnographies" (Ashcroft et al., 1998, p. 60).

These structured oppositions in cultural diversity consolidate the otherness of cultures outside the dominant Eurocentric or Anglo-American frame and are patterned by implicit hierarchies of superiority and inferiority. As Shohat and Stam (1994) demonstrated, these hierarchies talk of "*our* 'nations,' *their* 'tribes'; *our* 'religions,' *their* 'superstitions'; *our* 'culture,' *their* 'folklore'; *our* 'art,' *their* 'artifacts'; *our* 'demonstrations,' *their* 'riots'; *our* 'defense,' *their* 'terrorism'" (p. 2). The distinctions between "us" and "them," that underpinned the colonial era, can still be identified today, even in the most benevolent discussions on managing diversity. In effect, the Eurocentrism of the colonial times has only been remobilized as a discursive accompaniment to western economic expansion or neo-colonization.

Colonial discourses and contemporary discourses of diversity express similar values. Both sets of values express the missionary zeal to "civilize" the other. If colonial advertising "took scenes of empire into every corner" (McClintock, 1995, p. 209) of the world to drive home the benefits of western values, contemporary discourses on managing diversity update the picture of a world unified on western terms. By attempting to unite the world on western terms, texts on managing diversity continue to vest power in the hands of the neo-colonial elite. One expressed goal of managing diversity is to

> minimize or remove performance barriers that result from *diversity-related problems* such as turnover, absenteeism, low productivity, work quality, and group cohesiveness. It is also argued that effective recruitment and management of a diverse workforce can enhance a company's competitive advantage by adding expertise relevant to addressing increasingly diverse markets, expanding creativity in problem solving, and increasing organizational flexibility and goal achievement, and profitability. (Weiss, 1996, p. 15: italics added)

In this definition of managing diversity, the paramount position of the western managerial elite is explicit. Diversity becomes the *cause* of organizational problems and, therefore, needs to be *managed* by the controlling elite for the sake of goal achievement and profitability. This focus on problem solving and profitability is further sharpened by the emphasis on a specific set of training that is required to be imparted to diverse groups:

> The effect of diversity on work outcomes depends greatly on the extent to which the diversity is proactively managed. In one of the classic studies of this type, Harry Triandis and his colleagues compared the problem-solving

> scores of homogeneous groups with those of two types of more diverse
> groups: diverse with training and diverse without training. They found that
> the diverse groups that were not trained in the existence and implications of
> their differences actually produced lower problem-solving scores than
> homogenous groups, whereas the diverse groups that were trained produced
> scores that averaged six times higher than the homogeneous groups. (Cox
> & Beale, 1997, p. 37)

The western organizational emphasis on "training" diverse groups is central
to diversity management's project of control. Through such training, neo-colonial organizations establish a uniform administrative and business culture based
on western norms and standards. This process of ideologically indoctrinating
the other helps organizational elites to project what goes against neo-colonial
business interests as problems. In this way, organizational leaders involve
diverse groups in the goal of solving problems faced by elite groups. These
leaders also retain control over the other by defining problems, including
"diversity-related problems" (Weiss, 1996, p. 15), on their terms.

Thus, the civilizing mission of the diversity industry continues the colonial
strategy of Orientalism which, as defined by Edward Said (1978), is the
"Western style for dominating, restructuring, and having authority over the
Orient" (p. 3). This domination depends on the "positional superiority" of the
west that "puts the westerner in a whole series of relationships with the Orient
without ever losing him [sic] the upper hand" (Said, 1978, p. 7). An example of
this positional superiority can be found in the recent public relations campaign
of a western multinational company, PriceWaterhouseCoopers, which seeks to
project its contribution to the development of Asia. One particular advertise-
ment that forms part of the campaign has a photograph of a group of villagers in
India huddled in front of a community television set (see, e.g., *The New Zealand
Herald*, April 14, 1999, p. B6). The caption accompanying the photograph talks
of the company's role in building "new self-esteem for their people" through
western developmental strategies such as setting up "new management teams"
and privatizing electric power (see e.g., *The New Zealand Herald*, April 14,
1999, p. B6). In constructing an image of these western strategies to be superior
and, therefore, worth aspiring for, the campaign actually attempts to impose
western notions of development on the other.

As well as exposing the self-appointed civilizing mission of a "superior"
colonial elite over a deliberately "inferiorized" other, postcolonial scholarship
also takes colonial discourses to task for creating compartmentalized entities
that leave no room for what Homi Bhabha (1994) called "the articulation of
hybridity" (p. 38). Postcolonial studies, in fact, represent, in Hegde's (1998)
terms, "a global discourse that emphasizes interdependencies and dialectical
interconnections" (p. 283). Studies in management need to recognize this notion
of dialectical interconnections and acknowledge Hegde's distinction between

"heterogeneity and difference that emerge from postcoloniality" and "urbane multiplicity" (p. 283).

The urbane multiplicity espoused by contemporary organizational strategists mirrors what Bhavnani (1999) called the "'saris, steel bands and samosas' approach to multiculturalism." Such superficial multiculturalism is based on predetermined cultural characteristics of diverse groups: the food they eat; the languages they speak; the music they play; the clothes they wear; and so on. As Miyoshi (1997) put it, "in the international bazaar of exportable goods, difference is in style only, as in clothing, cooking, or entertainment" (p. 53). By defining *culture* as something that is fixed and static, this kind of unidimensional multiculturalism loses sight of the dialectical interconnections between various groups and works to maintain ethnocentric superiority. In essence, it attempts to consolidate hierarchical binaries around an exoticized other. It is precisely these binaries that subaltern historiography seeks to dismantle. This historiography offers what Spivak (1988) called a "theory of change" that inaugurates a process of "politicization for the colonized" (p. 3) by giving them the power to represent themselves.

Just as an Oriental other was, and still is, *constructed* by Eurocentric thought processes under such grand projects as *Orientalism* (Said, 1978), the subaltern was, and continues to be, *recruited* "to serve in subordinate positions under a determining and defining established authority" (Hawthorn, 1992, p. 97). The project of subaltern studies in postcolonial scholarship looks at the world from the perspective of these subordinated groups and grants them the agency that is denied to them by dominant western historiography. It defines itself

> as an attempt to allow the "people" finally to speak within the jealous pages of elitist historiography and, in doing so, to speak for, or to sound the muted voices of, the truly oppressed. . . . The complex notion of subalternity is pertinent to any academic enterprise which concerns itself with historically determined relationships of dominance and subordination. (Gandhi, 1998, p. 2)

Adopted by Gramsci (1988) to classify people who were subjected to the hegemony of the ruling elite, the term subaltern represents the other—groups that lie outside the influential inner circle of power. Incorporating the Gramscian thesis that *subaltern* groups were deliberately excluded or marginalized by the elitist texts of a universalized history, scholars of the subaltern studies collective have gone about documenting the sociopolitical complexities, the struggles, and the resistance movements of subaltern groups. A major task of these scholars, as Bhabha (1996) said, has been "to retrieve some trace of the voice" (pp. 14-15) of the subaltern from the state's ventriloquism.

THE RHETORIC OF EQUALITY
AND THE INDIGENOUS EXPERIENCE

For the discourses of management and media to be serious about listening to the voice of the other, they would need to re-examine the insistent rhetoric of equality in western models of managing diversity. One way toward such a re-examination would be to look at the work of indigenous/aboriginal studies scholars who have shown how the "destructive social outcomes of radicalized inequalities and racialised marginality" can be compelling "despite the national rhetoric of multiculturalism and diversity management" (Morris & Cowlishaw, 1997, p. 3). Their scholarship exposes how managing diversity fails to be truly egalitarian because it sets out to tackle racial consciousness and divisions by race rather than by the "racialised effects of social and economic inequality" (Morris & Cowlishaw, 1997, p. 3). Nothing illustrates this better than the emphasis of diversity managers on concepts such as "working with Asian Americans," "working with African Americans," and "working with Latino Americans" (see e.g., Carr-Ruffino, 1996). Such concepts, perhaps unwittingly, consolidate the dominant position of the western elite that is seen to be the pivot around which other marginalized groups are expected to revolve. At a critical level, these ideas appear to make a call for equality but often end up keeping the other in the periphery.

The equality value that diversity management espouses is egalitarian on the surface. However, as in the case of the treatment of indigenous groups, it conceals the radicalized effects of such discourses of equality. Anti-discrimination laws leave "untouched the ubiquitous and mundane forms of injustice and inequity that resonate with cultural difference" (Cowlishaw, 1997, p. 178). As a result, despite the prevailing discourse of equality, indigenous people continue to face sociopolitical marginalization and significantly poorer statistics in areas of education, employment, and health throughout the western world. In orchestrating their harmonious multicultural compositions, the dominant neo-colonial elite projects the other as an equal but simultaneously clings to its power to project. The end result casts the other as an entity without an agency of its own. One typical example of this process in practice is in the celebration of the multicultural character of Santa Fe in the U.S. state of New Mexico. An official tourist brochure of the Palace of the Governors, run by the Museum of New Mexico, describes the Native Americans selling their traditional arts and crafts on the porch of the building as a "living exhibit of the palace" ("Palace walks, history talks," 1999). By reducing the first peoples of the land to the status of "exhibits," the dominant elite effectively retains control in its hands. The other is an "exhibit" of diversity that the dominant elite can flaunt. It is the exotic dimension of a multiculturalism that is packaged but not embraced, let alone internalized.

When equality is defined from the perspective of the dominant majority, minorities are relegated to the margins of power structures. In such a climate of pseudo-equality, even institutions built to safeguard the interests of minorities end up being appropriated. In New Zealand, for instance, a statutory institution to promote and observe race relations was set up to work as a watchdog against discrimination on grounds of race. Ironically, it is the majority community that has made far greater use of the services of this institution than has any minority group.

The Annual Report of the Office of the Race Relations Conciliator (1997) reveals that the office received more complaints from the majority Pakeha (European New Zealander) group than it did from any of the minority groups. In 89% of the complaints received by the office, the ethnic background of the complainants was made available. Of these, as many as 40% of the complainants were Pakeha, whereas only 27% were Maori. The number of complaints made by Pacific Islanders and Asians were even smaller. The statistical break-up of the number of complaints reveals that even institutions that are, in spirit, meant for the use of minority groups get used by the dominant majority although majority groups have standard legal outlets available to them for redressal of grievances.

LAYERS OF GLOBALIZATION: FEMINIST CRITIQUES OF THE ECONOMICS OF MULTICULTURALISM

This kind of continued marginalization of the minorities, in a system that purports to include them, is mirrored in the world of globalizing business and industry. As feminist economists point out, globalization processes are "embedded in, and refracted through, power structures grounded in ethnicity, race, gender, class, and age" (Marchand, 1996, p. 586). In fact, according to Chang and Ling (cited in Marchand, 1996), there exist two distinct, and often polarized, versions of the globalized world: One is the "masculinised high-tech world of global finance, production and technology"; and the other is the "feminized menial economy of sexualized, racialized service" (p. 586).

Feminist analyses of neo-classical economics show how the male point of view invariably guides seemingly gender-neutral notions of market relationships (Bakker, 1994). Workers or entrepreneurs, for example, are overtly gender-neutral terms, but women and men (as indeed members of different cultural groups) have very different experiences as workers or entrepreneurs (Bakker, 1994). In fact, as Elson (cited in Bakker, 1994) pointed out, a worker or an entrepreneur "is most often taken to be a man—creating male bias in both economic analysis and economic policy" (p. 5).

Similar critiques of gender power imbalances inform some organizational studies literature. However, if, as feminist critics argue, inherent social, cultural, and political inequalities reinforce the uneven nature of participation in the market by women—and the evidence is strong (see e.g., Bakker, 1994; Brodie,

1994)—then the social, cultural, and political experiences of minority groups face similar racist and sexist organizational structures and thought processes. As a consequence, both women and non-westerners become unequal partners in the superficially multicultural, and nominally equitable, marketplace.

Just as feminist critiques of globalization show how the "dominant discourse of globalization conceals and excludes gender-specific consequences" (Brodie, 1994, p. 48), the dominant voices in the discourse of managing diversity drown out the voices of those that are "managed." Much is made about the fact that "diverse markets and workplaces are increasingly made up of people from various cultures and subcultures" (Carr-Ruffino, 1996, p. 1), but not much attention is paid to the structural inequities in such markets and workplaces. As Lal (1999a) accurately noted, the market-driven global village of today is "an omnipolis of six billion people with a rigid caste system of its own" (p. 6). That system reinforces the "'generally segregated, unequal, and tenuous place' of women and other minority groups in the labor market" (Bakker, 1994, p. 2). Although organizational policy and planning remains wedded to the goals of a globalization that works to widen the gap between the haves and the have-nots, strategies of managing diversity create illusions of an egalitarian world. In effect, they serve as organizational tools to keep the have-nots quiet. The structural inequalities carry over from economic and political space to cyberspace and cyber networks.

These networks illustrate how the diversity-managed world of globalization has effectively imprisoned the other on the periphery of power. Although electronic networks have given women and other marginalized people easy access to cyberspace, they have consolidated the position of the economically strong west. This is underscored by Spender's (1998) analysis:

> At the moment, most of the forums in which cyber-policy is being made are exclusionary. White, professional, English/American-speaking males have got the floor: and they are focusing primarily on technological issues—or pornography, property, and privacy problems. (A survey of *Wired* indicates that these are the hot topics.) It is easier to talk about the latest "toys" and to defend the concept of "free speech" for the boys, than it is to address the major social and political questions which go with the new technologies. (p. 266)

This west-dominated cyber-revolution, despite its lofty goals of uniting the world, mirrors the existing worldwide division between rich and poor with the cyberspace division between the information-rich and the information-poor. In fact, "poorer countries, painfully aware of the irony of becoming more dependent than before on colonial powers for capital investment, credit, trade, and technology" (Lal, 1999b, p. 25) have more reason to be worried about the pathology of this revolution despite its claims to herald equality among peoples.

MAPS WITHOUT MARGINS: RESISTING
NEO-COLONIAL THEORIZING OF DIVERSITY

Similarly, theories of managing diversity do not challenge but only redraw "the lines and circles that define insider and outsider" (Willett, 1998, p. 13). This redrawing of lines does not effectively fill the gap between the center and the margins. Indeed, even the most inclusive and benevolent of theorizing in diversity management ends up, at best, leaving the other at the margins.

Instead of looking at diversity in terms of equitably shared power and resources, the ideology of diversity management aligns with the ideology of world trade. Largely western developed nations provide aid and loans to the underdeveloped nations—the other—on the condition that they not only buy equipment and services from the west but service the loan debt as well. The advertised mission is to bring equality to the world. In practice, this seeming equality works to the obscenely lopsided advantage of the neocolonial west: As little as "20 percent of the world's people in the highest-income countries," largely in the west, "account for 86 percent of the total private consumption expenditures—the poorest 20 percent a miniscule 1.3 percent" (United Nations Development Programmed [UNDP], 1998, p. 2). Although the policymaking dominant elite in international funding organizations and trade bodies live in luxury, nearly three fifths of the 4.4 billion people in developing countries lack basic sanitation, and one third have no access to clean water (UNDP, 1998).

This chapter contends that just as the rhetorics of aid, development and the globalization of trade actually end up increasing the gap between the haves and the have-nots, the rhetoric of cultural diversity in management translates into greater access for expansionist neo-colonial business elites to wider populations and potential profits without any corresponding payoff for most of the inhabitants of non-western nations. This rhetoric is, essentially, guided by the need of the neo-colonial elites to "capitalize on the opportunities presented by a diverse workforce" to get "bottom-line results and a significant edge over the competition" (Gardenswartz & Rowe, 1998, p. 483). What remains unsaid is that, in the quest for bottom lines and competitive edges, the dominant managerial frame remains ethnocentric. Minority groups, whose efforts are "capitalized" upon, therefore, remain on the fringes. Indeed, the privileging of commercial advantage is an example of what Matustik (1998) called the "cannibalising" (p. 111) of global diversity.

Furthermore, I argue that unless, as the postcolonial physicist Shiva (1993) put it, "diversity is made the logic of production" (p. 146), diversity in the workplace cannot be sustained, nurtured, or preserved. Shiva's perspective is echoed in Cheney's (1998) assertion that unless market-driven organizations stop shaping and directing customers according to the narrowly defined desires of the elite that runs them, they cannot achieve the goals of positive social change. "To temper the sweep of marketization," as Cheney suggested, we may have to "consider new measures of social satisfaction, happiness, and social progress as alternatives to traditional measures of productivity" (p. 40). We also have to redefine the market in terms of people and not just in terms of business opportunities for a dominant neocolonial elite.

In reformatting the market along these lines, western participants would need to encompass the needs of the vast majority of the world's population that continues to live in the peripheries of power. The lopsidedness of the existing market is illustrated by global consumption patterns. Today, for example, "each person in the United States uses 45 barrels of oil annually, compared with one barrel of oil for each Indian citizen" (Porter & Brown, 1996, p. 112). The "market," as understood by the countries of the developed west (or north), primarily relates to economic gain for the minority elite that controls the majority of the world's resources. Champions of a free market in the developed world are often the first to impose barriers when their interests are affected. For instance, as Porter and Brown (1996) pointed out:

> Subsidies to agricultural exporters in the United States and other OECD countries deprive developing country-producers of markets and depress world prices for those goods, exacerbating trade imbalances and developing-country indebtedness. European beef exporters undercut African producers by massive subsidies, for example, and thus dominate African markets. (p. 111)

This domination is consolidated in management discourses on issues of diversity. For the neo-colonial elite, diversity is something that can be marketed and exploited for gain. In this environment of what Martin (1998) called "consumerist multiculturalism" (p. 143), the dominant management paradigm stratifies global society, as indeed global organizations, in tiers that are differently advantaged and disadvantaged. The biggest of these tiers that represent the vast multitude of impoverished "others" remains right at the bottom.

This existing dominant paradigm needs to be challenged by a rainbow coalition of a multiplicity of thought processes. These alternate thought processes can cultivate what Shiva (1997) called the kind of diversity that can restore the "right to self-organise" (p. 120) to those coerced into living by rules scripted by imperializing neo-colonial institutions in trade and business. Parallel to minority groups' right to self-organize in an era of homogenized globalization is what Cheney (1999) calls the employee's "right to self-determination" (p. 160) at the workplace. A movement for diversity that recognizes every employee's right "to have some capacity to affect the conditions and requirements of work" (Cheney, 1999, p. 160) would assist in dismantling the colonising influence of market-driven principles of managerialism.

Shiva's (1997) redefinition of diversity as a conservation and consolidation of "a plurality of knowledge traditions" (p. 123) points the way to making the world not only more egalitarian but more productive as well. As diverse organizations are better equipped to deal with complexity in internal and external relationships (McDaniel & Walls, 1997), organizations with a plurality of administrative practices, and diverse decision-making processes, are better placed to survive in times of rapid change that is international in scope. Similarly, a multidimensional diversity or what Shohat and Stam (1994) called "polycentric multiculturalism" (p. 46) can help break down the historical asymmetries in the configurations of power and cultural and managerial hierarchies.

ACKNOWLEDGMENTS

My academic work has drawn strength, sustenance, and stability from the vision and thoughts of David McKie and George Cheney. I thank them both. I also thank Priya Kurian and Akanksha Khwaish for their intellectual, moral, and emotional support. I am also grateful to all those who provided helpful comments on an earlier version of this chapter which was presented at the International Communication Association (ICA) Conference in San Francisco in 1999.

REFERENCES

Annual Report of the Office of the Race Relations Conciliator. (1997, period ended June 30). Wellington: Office of the Race Relations Conciliator.

Anzaldua, G. (Ed.). (1990). *Making face, making soul: Creative and critical perspectives by women of color.* San Francisco, CA: Aunt Luke Foundation.

Ashcroft, B., Griffiths, G., & Tiffin, H. (1998). *Key concepts in post-colonial studies.* London: Routledge.

Bakker, I. (1994). Introduction: Engendering macro-economic policy reform in the era of global restructuring and adjustment. In I. Bakker (Ed.), *The strategic silence: Gender and economic policy* (pp. 1-29). London: Zed/North-South Institute.

Bhabha, H. (1994). *The location of culture.* London: Routledge.

Bhabha, H. (1996). The voice of the Dom: Retrieving the experience of the once-colonized. *Times Literary Supplement, 4923,* 14-15.

Bhavnani, K. (1999, May 7). Countering racisms: Interconnections and hybridity. Public lecture, The University of Waikato, Hamilton, New Zealand.

Blommaert, J., & Verschueren, J. (1998). *Debating diversity: Analysing the discourse of tolerance.* London: Routledge.

Boje, D., & Rosile, G. (1994). Diversities, differences and authors' voices. *Journal of Organizational Change Management, 7*(6), 8-17.

Brodie, J. (1994). Shifting the boundaries: Gender and the politics of restructuring. In I. Bakker (Ed.), *The strategic silence: Gender and economic policy* (pp. 46-60). London: Zed/North-South Institute.

Brooking, T., & Rabel, R. (1995). Neither British nor Polynesian: A brief history of New Zealand's other immigrants. In S. Greif (Ed.), *Immigration and national identity in New Zealand* (pp. 23-49). Palmerston North, New Zealand: Dunmore Press.

Carr-Ruffino, N. (1996). *Managing diversity: People skills for a multicultural workplace*. Cincinnati, OH: Thomson Executive Press.

Cervantes, L. (1992). Poem for the young white man who asked me how I, an intelligent, well-read person could believe in the war between races. In P. Rothenberg (Ed.), *Race, class, and gender in the United States: An integrated study* (pp. 225-227). New York: St. Martin's Press.

Chen, M. (1993). Discrimination, law, and being a Chinese immigrant woman in New Zealand. *Women's Studies Journal, 9*(2), 1-29.

Cheney, G. (1998). "It's the economy, stupid!": A rhetorical-communicative perspective on today's market. *Australian Journal of Communication, 25*(3), 25-44.

Cheney, G. (1999). *Values at work: Employee participation meets market pressure at Mondragón*. Ithaca, NY: Cornell University Press.

Clegg, S. (1992). Postmodern management. *Journal of Organizational Change Management, 5*(1), 31-49.

Conciliator sees "nose dive" in race relations. (1996, April 8). *The Dominion*, p. 2.

Cowlishaw, G. (1997). Where is racism? In G. Cowlishaw & B. Morris (Eds.), *Race matters* (pp. 177-189). Canberra: Aboriginal Studies Press.

Cox, T., Jr. (1993). *Cultural diversity in organisations*. San Francisco, CA: Berrett-Koehler.

Cox, T., Jr., & Beale, R. (1997). *Developing competency to manage diversity: Readings, cases & activities*. San Francisco, CA: Berrett-Koehler.

Culbertson, H., Jeffers, D., Stone, D., & Terrell, M. (1993). *Social, political, and economic contexts in public relations: Theory and cases*. Hillsdale, NJ: Erlbaum.

Fewer given residence. (1996, October 22). *The Dominion*, p. 3.

Fitzgerald, R. (1996, October 22). Voice of the underclass. *The Bulletin*, pp. 20-22.

Gandhi, L. (1998). *Postcolonial theory: A critical introduction*. Sydney: Allen & Unwin.

Gardenswartz, L., & Rowe, A. (1998). *Managing diversity: A complete desk reference and planning guide*. New York: McGraw-Hill.

Gramsci, A. (1988). *An Antonio Gramsci reader: Selected writings, 1916-1935* (D. Forgacs, Ed.). New York: Schocken Books.

Hall, S. (1992). The west and the rest: Discourse and power. In S. Hall & B. Gieben (Eds.), *The formations of modern society* (pp. 276-331). Oxford: Polity Press.

Hamel, G., & Prahalad, C. (1994). *Competing for the future*. Boston, MA: Harvard Business School Press.

Hames, M. (1996, December 6). Maybe Europeans ought to recolonise in Africa. *The New Zealand Herald*, p. A13.

Haraway, D. (1997). *Modest_witness@second_millennium.femaleman_meets_oncomouse: Feminism and technoscience*. New York: Routledge.

Harding, S. (1994). Is science multicultural? Challenges, resources, opportunities, uncertainties. *Configurations, 2*(2), 301-330.

Hawthorn, J. (1992). *A concise glossary of contemporary literary theory*. London: Edward Arnold.

Hegde, R. (1998). A view from elsewhere: Locating difference and the politics of representation from a transnational feminist perspective. *Communication Theory, 8*(3), 271-297.

Humphries, M., & Grice, S. (1995). Equal employment opportunity and the management of diversity: A global discourse of assimilation? *Journal of Organizational Change Management, 8*(5), 17-32.

Jackson, W. (1999, October 15). Racism behind fury over anthem sung in Maori. *The New Zealand Herald*, p. A15.

Jagtenberg, T., & McKie, D. (1997). *Eco-impacts and the greening of postmodernity: New maps for communication studies, cultural studies, and sociology*. Thousand Oaks, CA: Sage.

Judy, R., & D'Amico, C. (1997). *Workforce 2020: Work and workers in the 21st century*. Indianapolis, IN: Hudson Institute.

Kossek, E., & Lobel, S. (Eds.). (1996). *Managing diversity: Human resource strategies for transforming the workplace*. Cambridge, MA: Blackwell.

Lal, S. (1999a). Globalisation gone berserk. *Biblio: A Review of Books, 4*(9 & 10), 6.

Lal, S. (1999b). Global pariahs. *Biblio: A Review of Books, 4*(1 & 2), 25.

Language to embrace. (1999, October 11). *The New Zealand Herald*, p. A14.

Lorde, A. (1992). Age, race, class, and sex: Women redefining difference. In P. Rothenberg (Ed.), *Race, class, and gender in the United States: An integrated study* (pp. 401-407). New York: St. Martin's Press.

Marchand, M. (1996). Reconceptualising 'gender and development' in an era of globalisation. *Millennium: Journal of International Studies, 25*(3), 577-603.

Martin, B. (1998). Multiculturalism: Consumerist or transformational? In C. Willett (Ed.), *Theorizing multiculturalism: A guide to the current debate* (pp. 100-117). Malden, MA: Blackwell.

Matustik, M. (1998). Ludic, corporate, and imperial multiculturalism: Imposters of democracy and cartographers of the new world order. In C. Willett (Ed.), *Theorizing multiculturalism: A guide to the current debate* (pp. 100-117). Malden, MA: Blackwell.

McClintock, A. (1995). *Imperial leather: Race, gender and sexuality in the colonial contest*. London: Routledge.

McDaniel, R., & Walls, M. (1997). Diversity as a management strategy for organizations: A view through the lenses of chaos and quantum theories. *Journal of Management Inquiry, 6*(4), 363-375.

Mercer, D. (1998). *Future revolutions: Unravelling the uncertainties of life and work in the 21st century*. London: Orion Business Books.

Miyoshi, M. (1997). Sites of resistance in the global economy. In K. Ansell-Pearson, B. Parry, & J. Squires (Eds.), *Cultural readings of imperialism: Edward Said and the gravity of history* (pp. 49-66). London: Lawrence & Wishart.

Morris, B., & Cowlishaw, G. (1997). Cultural racism. In G. Cowlishaw & B. Morris (Eds.), *Race matters* (pp. 1-8). Canberra: Aboriginal Studies Press.

Munshi, D. (1998). Media, politics, and the Asianisation of a polarised immigration debate in New Zealand. *Australian Journal of Communication, 25*(1), 97-110.

Munshi, D. (2000). The business of the other: Representing the non-west in management and media. Unpublished doctoral thesis, The University of Waikato, Hamilton, New Zealand.

Munshi, D., & Kurian, P. (1996, December 20). Western attitudes to Africa hypocritical. *The New Zealand Herald*, p. A13.

Nilakant, V. (1995). New Zealand organisations. In R. McLennan (Ed.), *People and enterprises: Organisational behaviour in New Zealand* (pp. 367-405). Sydney: Harcourt Brace.

Orbe, M. (1998). An outsider within perspective to organizational communication: Explicating the communicative practices of co-cultural group members. *Management Communication Quarterly, 12*(2), 230-279.

Palace walks, history talks. (1999, obtained June 19). Santa Fe: Museum of New Mexico.

Porter, G., & Brown, J. (1996). *Global environmental politics.* Boulder, CO: Westview Press.

Pountney, C. (1999, July 5). Racial harmony: We need different rooms in a common house. *The New Zealand Herald*, p. A13.

Prasad, A. (1997). The colonizing consciousness and representations of the other: A postcolonial critique of the discourse of oil. In P. Prasad, A. Mills, M. Elmes, & A. Prasad (Eds.), *Managing the organizational melting pot: Dilemmas of workplace diversity* (pp. 285-311). Thousand Oaks, CA: Sage.

Prasad, P., Mills, A., Elmes, M., & Prasad, A. (Eds.). (1997). *Managing the organizational melting pot: Dilemmas of workplace diversity.* Thousand Oaks, CA: Sage.

Quaintance, L. (1996, May 15). Doctors turn nurse to stay in profession. *The New Zealand Herald*, p. 1.

Residence approvals show big fall in year. (1996, November 16). *The Dominion*, p. 3.

Riordan, D. (1996, May 26). Fewer Asian migrants "bad for economy." *Sunday Star-Times*, p. D1.

Roger, W. (1996, March 15). NZ reservations for Asian immigrants. *Waikato Times*, p. 6.

Rothenberg, P. (1992). *Race, class, and gender in the United States: An integrated study.* New York: St. Martin's Press.

Said, E. (1978). *Orientalism.* New York: Vintage.

Sen, A. (1992). *Inequality reexamined.* Oxford: Clarendon Press.

Shadow of Dreyfus hangs over assault on the immigrants. (1996, August 28). *The Guardian*, p. 10.

Shiva, V. (1993). *Monocultures of the mind.* London: Zed Books.

Shiva, V. (1997). *Biopiracy: The plunder of nature and knowledge.* Boston, MA: South End Press.

Shohat, E., & Stam, R. (1994). *Unthinking eurocentrism.* London: Routledge.

Spender, D. (1998). Social policy for cyberspace: Access and equity. In R. Holeton (Ed.), *Composing cyberspace: Identity, community, and knowledge in the electronic age* (pp. 266-269). Boston, MA: McGraw-Hill.

Spivak, G. (1988). Subaltern studies: Deconstructing historiography. In R. Guha & G. Spivak (Eds.), *Selected subaltern studies* (pp. 3-32). New York: Oxford University Press.

Thomas, R., Jr. (1991). *Beyond race and gender: Unleashing the power of your total work force by managing diversity.* New York: Amacom.

Thomas, R., Jr. (1996). *Redefining diversity.* New York: Amacom.

Tremaine, M. (1997). Towards the inclusive organisation. In F. Sligo, S. Olsson, & C. Wallace (Eds.), *Perspectives in business communication: Theory and practice* (pp. 283-290). Palmerston North, New Zealand: Software Technology.

United Nations Development Programme [UNDP]. (1998). *Human development report.* New York: UNDP and Oxford University Press.

van Dijk, T. (1995). On propositions, racism, and democracy. *Discourse & Society, 6(*2), 147-148.

Walck, C. (1995). Editor's introduction: Diverse approaches to managing diversity. *Journal of Applied Behavioral Science, 31*(2), 119-123.

Weiss, J. (1996). *Organizational behavior and change: Managing diversity, cross-cultural dynamics, and ethics.* St. Paul, MN: West Publishing.

Willett, C. (1998). *Theorizing multiculturalism: A guide to the current debate.* Malden, MA: Blackwell.

SECTION B

Cross-Cultural Identities and Tensions

3

HOW RELEVANT IS TRUST ANYWAY?

A Cross-Cultural Comparison of Trust in Organizational and Peer Relationships

Deborah A. Cai
University of Maryland

Chun-ju Hung
Hong Kong Baptist University

Trust is an important foundation for relationships. As a concept, trust is used widely to measure the quality of both interpersonal and organizational relationships. In this chapter, we examine the dimensions of trust relevant in three types of relationships (with a close friend, a direct supervisor, and the organization as a whole) across three cultures: China, Taiwan, and the United States. We find that, across relationships, trust consists of five dimensions: affective dependability, cognitive dependability, competence, benevolence, and integrity. However, trust was found to be significantly less relevant in relationships with close friends in China and Taiwan than in the United States. Greater differences were found in the relevance of trust between close friend and supervisor for participants from the United States than from China and Taiwan. For all three cultures, trust with a supervisor was more similar to trust in an organization than trust with a close friend. Significant differences in the relevance of trust were not found between China and Taiwan. Implications and directions for future research are suggested.

Trust is an important foundation for relationships. As a concept, trust is widely used to measure the quality of relationships in both interpersonal and organizational communication (Becerra, 1998; Canary & Cupach, 1988; Fisher & Brown, 1988; Fitchen, Hearth, & Fessenden-Raden, 1987; Grunig & Huang, 2000; Grunig & Hung, 2000; Huang, 1994; Hung, 2002; Johnson-George & Swap, 1982; Krimsky & Plough, 1988; Larzelere & Huston, 1980; Yang, 2001). More specifically, trust has been studied in manager/employee relationships (Cheng, 2001; Lewicki & Bunker, 1998; Whitener, Brodt, Korsgaard, & Werner, 1998), how organizations deal with crisis (Mishra, 1996), how trust enhances close relationships (Powell & Heriot, 2001; Rempel, Holmes, & Zanna, 1985; Wieselquist, Rusbult, Foster, & Agnew, 1999), and trust's role in conflict management and negotiation (Lulofs, 1994; Pruitt & Carnevale, 1993). More recently, Doney, Cannon, and Mullen (1998) conceptualized how national culture influences the development of trust, and Wang's (2001) cross-cultural research on trust in China and Japan concluded that Chinese people, constrained by the tendency to trust more in their close friends and relatives, have lower trust of outsiders than Japanese people. But although trust is used widely to assess relationships, expectations of trust in personal relationships (as with a close friend) and impersonal relationships (as with an organization as a whole) may differ across cultures.

In this chapter, we examine the dimensions of trust relevant in three types of relationships (with a close friend, a direct supervisor, and the organization as a whole) across three cultures: China, Taiwan and the United States. We first consider the variety of definitions and dimensions of trust used in previous research. Next, we discuss the effect that values of individualism/collectivism and public/private self have on trust in different relationships across cultures. Based on this discussion, we hypothesize cross-cultural differences in trust across the three types of relationships. These hypotheses are then tested, followed by a discussion of the results and their implications for future research.

THE CONCEPT OF TRUST

Trust has been found to contribute to many positive aspects of relational development and communication processes, including smoother conflict management (Canary & Cupach, 1988), effectiveness in work teams (Lawler, 1992), long-term organizational relationships (Ring & van de Ven, 1992), willingness to cooperate (Cupach & Canary, 1997; Pruitt & Carnevale, 1993), and increased information sharing and likelihood of agreement in negotiation (Lindskold & Han, 1988). Conversely, low trust can lead to increased use of forcing behaviors (Cupach & Canary, 1997), fear of raising concerns (Cloven & Roloff, 1993), higher levels of competition (Pruitt & Carnevale, 1993), and even a hostile orientation toward the mistrusted other (Omodei & McLennan, 2000).

In an early study of this concept, Rotter (1967) defined trust as "an expectancy held by an individual or a group that the word, promise, verbal or written statement of another individual or group can be relied on" (p. 651). Rotter's emphasis on the reliability of the other party is echoed by researchers who examine organizational relationships. For example, negotiation scholars Pruitt and Carnevale (1993) defined trust as "the expectation that the other party will cooperate in the future" (p. 133). In marketing research, Moorman, Deshpande and Zaltman (1993) characterized trust as "a willingness to rely on an exchange partner in whom one has confidence" (p. 23), and Morgan and Hunt (1994) described trust as the confidence in another's reliability and integrity. In public relations, Grunig and Grunig (1998) defined trust as "the extent to which both management and publics express willingness to make themselves vulnerable to the behavior of the other—confidence that the other party will take its interests into account in making decisions" (p. 4).

The common focus of these definitions is whether the other party in the organizational relationship will behave as expected. In contrast, interpersonal definitions of trust, as with friends or mates, put more emphasis on emotions and motives. Hinde (1981), for example, suggested that "the increased vulnerability which arises with intimacy is tolerable only if accompanied by a belief that the partner will not exploit it" (p. 14). Similarly, Gurtman (1992) emphasized the reliability of the other's sincerity, benevolence, or truthfulness, and Larzelere and Huston (1980) defined trust as the extent to which the other is believed to be honest and benevolent.

Although addressing different types of relationships, these definitions have some common qualities. Becerra (1998), for example, pointed out that the existence of trust is likely to enhance a person's willingness to accept risks and to be vulnerable to the other's actions and behaviors. The risks that we are willing to take, however, are likely to differ depending on the type of relationship. In a relationship with a close friend, vulnerability due to intimacy and disclosure is at stake, but in a relationship with one's supervisor, intimacy and disclosure may be inappropriate. In this case, vulnerability may be related more to the competence and reliability of the supervisor to follow through on promised actions as expected. In this chapter, we examine the dimensions that make up trust in the three types of relationships.

Dimensions of Trust

Hovland, Janis, and Kelley (1953) were the first to look at the multidimensional aspects of trust, contending that a person's expertise and his or her motivation to lie influence others' perceptions of trust in that person. Since the 1950s, more than 20 studies have tested dimensions of trust. The most frequent dimensions used in these studies include integrity or honesty, ability or competence, benevolence or goodwill, and dependability (Becerra, 1998; Butler, 1991; Cook &

Wall, 1980; Deutsch, 1960; Frost, Stimpson, & Maughan, 1978; Good, 1988; Grunig & Hung, 2000; Hung, 2002; Jones, James, & Bruni, 1975; Kee & Knox, 1970; Larzelere & Huston, 1980; Lieberman, 1981; Mayer, Davis, & Schoorman, 1995; Mishra, 1996; Ring & van de Ven, 1992; Rosen & Jerdee, 1977; Sitkin & Roth, 1993; Solomon, 1960; Strickland, 1958). Dimensions of trust in a supervisor or an organization include integrity, competence, and dependability, whereas dimensions of interpersonal trust include these as well as benevolence, honesty, and faith (Becerra, 1998; Canary & Cupach, 1988; Larzelere & Huston, 1980; Mayer et al., 1995; Mishra, 1996; Rempel et al., 1985). In a review of trust in the organizational communication literature, Mishra (1996) identified four components of trust that effectively summarize the emphasis of trust in the preceding definitions. These components include competence, openness, concern, and reliability.

Chen and Gao (1991) found two significant factors in building trust between supervisor and employees among Chinese: the foundation for the relationship (*guanxi*)[1] and the individual's achievements. Cheng (1988) considered the trust between supervisors and employees to be determined by three factors: *guanxi*, loyalty, and competence. Yang and Peng (2001) concluded loyalty and competence is a more specific explanation for what Chen and Gao called individual achievement. In echoing the affect of loyalty on trust, Cheng (2001) found from interviews with Taiwanese companies that, among integrity, benevolence, and loyalty, loyalty stood out as the most salient factor on a supervisor's trust to his or her subordinate.

Given the dimensions suggested by extant research, we propose five dimensions of trust: dependability, faith, competence, benevolence, and integrity. We examine these dimensions across three types of relationships and in three cultures by asking the following:

> RQ1:   Are the dimensions of trust the same in relationships with a
>   close friend, a direct supervisors, and an organization?

Dependability.   McGregor (1967), Ouchi (1981) and Gabarro (1987) argued that inconsistencies in words and behaviors decrease levels of trust. As Rempel et al. (1985) explained, "[A]s relationships progress, there is an inevitable shift in focus away from assessments involving specific behaviors, to an evaluation of the qualities and characteristics attributed to the partner. Thus trust is placed in a person, not their specific action" (p. 96). McAllister (1995) noted that there is an emotional bond related to trust, and that this bond relates specifically to the elements of faith and dependability, both affective and cogni-

---

[1]*Guanxi* is a particular type of social network and relationship building in Chinese society. The application and research of *guanxi* on the influence of trust building should be conducted in a separate study; we do not discuss this concept in detail in this chapter.

tive. We believe this emotional bond is more relevant in the relationship with a close friend or supervisor than with an organization.

H1:   Dependability will be more relevant in relationships with a close friend and a supervisor than with the organization.

Faith.   McAllister (1995) and Rempel et al. (1985) made a distinction between faith and dependability. Rempel et al. noted that even though some behavioral patterns can be predicted, new stresses and forces occur so that people's values and goals change over time. Therefore, in addition to dependability, which is based on past experiences, faith is the confidence one party has in another to face an unknown future. Here, dependability influences faith because past experiences provide the basis to develop faith regarding the future.

H2:   Faith will be more relevant in relationships with a close friend and a supervisor than with the organization.

Competence.   Competence is the ability one has to capably perform his or her duties and obligations. Mayer et al. (1995) and Mishra (1996) pointed out that competence is especially important in organizational relationships, such as relationships between supervisors and their employees. Sako (1992) further argued for the importance of competence in the context of organizational relationships. For example, suppliers need to show their products meet quality standards so buyers will purchase the products and a supervisor's ability to make competent decisions can influence an employee's attitudes toward his or her supervisor.

H3:   Competence will be more relevant in relationships with a supervisor and the organization than with a close friend.

Benevolence.   Mayer et al. (1995) defined benevolence as "the extent to which a trustee is believed to want to do good to the trustor, aside from an egocentric profit motive" (p. 718). Benevolence is evident in communal norms, in which individuals consider the needs and welfare of others (Clark & Mills, 1993; Clark, Powell, & Mills, 1986), and is marked by efforts to be unconditionally constructive (Fisher & Brown, 1988). According to Rempel et al. (1985), benevolence is associated with relational intimacy, but as intimacy increases, so does risk. Consequently, as intimacy and risk increase, the need for benevolence increases. As a result, we believe benevolence will be most relevant in the relationship with a close friend and least relevant in the relationship with the organization.

H4:   Benevolence will be more relevant in relationships with a close friend than with a supervisor and with a supervisor than with organization.

Integrity. Integrity relates to parties' sense of justice and whether the parties' behaviors are consistent with their words (Mayer et al., 1995). This dimension serves as a basic foundation in both interpersonal relationships and organizational relationships (Butler, 1991; Hung, 2002; Lieberman, 1981; Mayer et al., 1995; Ring & van de Ven, 1992). Hung's study of Taiwanese companies in China showed that integrity is the foundation of relationships for many Taiwanese companies.

Because intimacy, disclosure, and risk-taking are more relevant in a relationship with a close friend than in a relationship with a supervisor or an organization, we propose that integrity will be most relevant in a relationship with a close friend.

> H5: Integrity will be more relevant in relationships with a close friend than with a supervisor or the organization.

Relationship Types

LaFollette (1996) described two kinds of relationships in interpersonal communication: personal and impersonal. He further stated that in close relationships, the value of relationship is "more intrinsic than instrumental" (p. 81). In other words, in personal relationships each person is treated as a unique individual, whereas in impersonal relationships the only concern is whether the party is able to fill a role or satisfy a specific need. For example, Boon and Holmes (1991) described three stages of romantic relationships: the romantic love stage, the evaluative stage, and the accommodative stage. In the romantic love stage, parties tend to idealize each other; as a result, both sides' commitment to the relationship tends to overshadow the need for trust. In the evaluative stage, both parties begin to realize the imperfections of the other. Trust begins to develop at this stage as both sides engage in reciprocal self-disclosure to determine each other's genuineness. In the accommodative stage, mutual faith is developed as trust becomes more stable. These stages point to both the intrinsic and affective nature of trust in personal relationships as well as to the progression of trust-building through disclosure, vulnerability, and mutual reliance.

In contrast to romantic relationships, an individual's relationship to an organization is especially impersonal because it is not a relationship between two persons but between a person and a reified entity (Goldhaber, 1993). As a result, trust is dependent on the perceived capability of the organization to satisfy specific needs of the employee. In organizational relationships, low trust can lead to low job satisfaction and higher rates of employee burnout.

Bromiley and Cummings (1992) argued that levels of trust noticeably affect organizational outcomes; therefore they advocate increasing levels of trust to help reduce the cost of transactions. In uncertain or risky situations, Luhman (1988) posited that "a system requires trust as an input condition in order to stimulate supportive activities" (p. 103). Bradach and Eccles (1989) recognized that although prices and authority are powerful organizational control mechanisms, trust is necessary in organizational relationships.

Relationships between supervisors and employees can be categorized as either personal or impersonal. Whitener et al. (1998) used social exchange theory and agency theory to describe motivations for trust between supervisors and their employees. Social exchange theory suggests that trust arises from the repeated exchange of benefits because individuals calculate the potential profit associated with continued exchange with the other party. Agency theory illustrates that self-interest motivates both the principle (the supervisor) and the agent (the employee) to maximize their own benefits and minimize the possible risk in the relationships. From this perspective, one party minimizes risk by monitoring the other party's behavior or by adjusting the compensation the other party will gain from the contracted task. In these two theories, the relationship between supervisor and employee is impersonal; trust is dependent on one's ability to achieve his or her own goals and maximize benefits.

In summary, the basis of trust differs in personal and impersonal relationships. In this chapter, we examine trust with a close friend as a personal relationship and with the organization as an impersonal relationship. Furthermore, we ask whether the relationship between supervisor and employee is necessarily impersonal, based on exchange and task outcomes, or whether this relationship may also include more intrinsic and affective elements.

H6:   For all three cultures, overall trust in a relationship with a direct supervisor will be more similar to overall trust in a relationship with the organization than overall trust with a close friend.

CULTURE AND TRUST

Doney et al. (1998) argued that cultural norms and values facilitate the development of trust. In describing how trust develops, Doney et al. categorized five processes: calculation, prediction, intention, capability, and transference. In the calculation process, individuals develop trust by calculating the maximum rewards. In the prediction process, the other's present or future behaviors are presumed based on past experiences. In the intention process, the development of trust is dependent on whether the trustor can perceive benevolence in the other's motives. In the capability process, trust is based on the other's ability to fulfill obligations or expectations. And in the transference process, trust shifts from a "known entity to an unknown one" (Doney et al., 1998, p. 606), as in putting trust in the friend of a friend. This process is likely to be encouraged in a strong interpersonal network. Doney et al. contended that individualist cultures use more calculation and capability processes to develop trust because instrumental factors such as the potential costs and benefits associated with trusting outweigh relational factors. But in collectivist cultures, trust tends to develop through prediction, intention, and transference processes, because relational factors such as considering motives, intentions and interpersonal ties prevail over instrumental factors. In a cross-cultural comparison of trust in Japan and China, Wang (2001) concluded that building trust is more horizontal (building personal networks) for Chinese and more vertical for Japanese (maintaining loyalty to the organization and supervisor).

As a result of these findings, we expect to find differences in the relevance of trust across relationships between China, Taiwan, and the United States:

> H7:   Overall trust will differ significantly for the three cultures across the three relationships.

Triandis (1995) contended that in a collectivist society, people have few but highly intimate in-groups, whereas in an individualist society, people have many but superficial in-groups. Fukuyama (1995) noted that levels of trust with friends tend to be higher in the United States because historically people faced a "common hostile outside environment" (p. 301). Because relatives are not necessarily the primary in-group members in the United States, trust among friends in the United States is extremely important because friends fulfill the role that family and lineage play in other cultures. As a result, people in individualist societies need to develop more communication skills for maintaining relationships compared to people in collectivist societies. Trust may serve as one of the relationship maintenance skills that enables acceptance into certain groups within individualist societies. As a result, we posit that:

> H7a: In relationships with close friends, the relevance of overall trust will be greater in the United States than in China and Taiwan.

Not only is the relevance of trust likely to differ within friendships, the relational expectations employees have of their organization and supervisor may differ across cultures. Lee and Barnett (1997) examined how national culture influenced organizational culture in Japan, Taiwan, and the United States. Their results indicate that because organizations interact with their environment, characteristics of the national culture are evident in organizations. The dimension of individualism-collectivism partially explains how individuals perceive relationships (Hofstede, 1980; Hui & Triandis, 1986; Hui & Villareal, 1989; Schwartz, 1994; Triandis, 1994, 1995; Triandis, McCusker, & Hui, 1990). The major difference between individualism and collectivism is the "I" versus "we" concept of self (Doney et al., 1998; Ramamoorthy, 1996; Triandis, 1989). Collectivist cultures, which include China and Taiwan, focus on group over individual goals, social harmony, cooperation, and protection of in-group interests (Hofstede, 1980; Hui & Triandis, 1986; Schwartz, 1994). In contrast, individualist cultures, such as the United States, focus more on individual goals, competition, affiliate relationships, and protection of self-interests (Hui & Triandis, 1996).

Triandis (1995) explained that within individualist cultures, the basic social unit is the individual whereas in collectivist cultures the basic social unit is the group. Ramamoorthy (1996) referred to collectivism as "the tendency of people to give up self-identity in favor of the embeddedness of self in the group" (p. 11). As a result, in-group relationships are more important and more highly valued in collectivist cultures than individualist cultures. For example, Trompenaars (1993) reported that 85% of U.S. managers disagreed with the statement that a company is responsible to assist in finding housing for its employees but only 18% of managers from China disagreed with this statement. Similarly, in response to a situation where a boss asks subordinates to help paint the boss' house, 89% of Americans agreed with the response that the subordinate did not have to help because the boss has little authority outside of work. In contrast, only 28% of respondents from China said they would refuse to help their boss. If the workplace is a source of in-group relationships, then we should expect to find greater similarity in the dimensions of trust between close friend and supervisor relationships in collectivist cultures than in individualist cultures:

H7b: The difference in the relevance of overall trust between close friend and direct supervisor will be greater for participants from the United States than for participants from China and Taiwan.

Finally, the differences in individualist and collectivist cultures provide a rationale for expecting variations in trust across China, Taiwan, and the United States. However, few empirical studies make comparisons between the cultures of China and Taiwan. Instead, research on the People's Republic of China tends to be generalized to Taiwan and vice versa. In this chapter, China and Taiwan are compared. We expect differences between the two groups of participants because of the divergent political, economic, and cultural development and influences in China and Taiwan during the past century. Thus, we posit the following:

H7c: Differences will be found between China and Taiwan in the relevance of overall trust across relationships.

SUMMARY OF THE HYPOTHESES

H1:   Dependability will be more relevant in relationships with a close friend and a supervisor than with the organization.

H2:   Faith will be more relevant in relationships with a close friend and a supervisor than with the organization.

H3:   Competence will be more relevant in relationships with a supervisor and the organization than with a close friend.

H4:   Benevolence will be more relevant in relationships with a close friend than with a supervisor and with a supervisor than with organization.

H5:   Integrity will be more relevant in relationships with a close friend than with a supervisor or the organization.

H6:   For all three cultures, overall trust in a relationship with a direct supervisor will be more similar to overall trust in a relationship with the organization than overall trust with a close friend.

H7:   Overall trust will differ significantly for the three cultures across the three relationships.

H7a: In relationships with close friends, the relevance of overall trust will be greater in the United States than in China and Taiwan.

H7b: The difference in the relevance of overall trust between close friend and direct supervisor will be greater for participants from the United States than for participants from China and Taiwan.

H7c: Differences will be found between China and Taiwan in the relevance of overall trust across relationships.

METHOD

Eighty-four participants in the People's Republic of China (females = 19, males = 65, Mean age = 35.13 years), 114 participants in Taiwan (females = 65, males = 49; Mean age = 49 years), and 171 participants in the United States (females = 95, males = 76, Mean age = 24.4 years) took part in the study. Participants were from Yangzhou and Shanghai in China, from Taipei in Taiwan, and from the mid-Atlantic region in the United States. Although every effort was made to achieve equivalent samples, the education level of participants from China ($M = 2.29$, $SD = 2.72$) was significantly less than the education of participants from Taiwan ($M = 3.22$, $SD = 1.24$) $t(193) = -3.22$, $p < .01$, and from the U.S. (*M* = 3.25, *SD* = .95) *t*(252) = 4.12, *p* < .001, on a scale where 1 = *less than high school diploma*, 2 = *high school diploma*, 3 = *some college*, 4 = *bachelor's degree*, 5 = *some graduate or professional school*, and 6 = *professional, master's or doctoral degree*. There was no significant difference between the samples from Taiwan and the United States, *t*(281) = .17, n.s.

The questionnaire used in this study compiled scales measuring characteristics of trust developed by Cummings and Bromiley (1996), De Furia (1997), Garthoeffner, Henry, and Robinson (1993), Johnson-George and Swap (1982), Larzelere and Huston (1980), Mayer et al. (1995), McAllister (1995), and Rempel et al. (1985). Also included were questions on demographic information of the participants. After examining the 81 items from combining the trust scales, we deleted repetitious items and items clearly related only to organizational contexts. The 64 remaining items were constructed so respondents answered for each of the three relationships (see the appendix; e.g., "First, to what extent do you agree with each statement for describing trust in a close interpersonal friend," second, "in a supervisor at work with whom you must work closely [or your advisor]," and third, "in the organization in which you work [or your school]"). All items were responded to using a 7-point scale (1 = *strongly disagree*, 7 = *strongly agree*). In a pilot test of the measures, participants suggested that some items might be irrelevant to trust within one or more of the relationships. As a result, we added the option of responding with "0" along with the 7-point scale so that respondents could indicate items they believed to be irrelevant to trust in any relationship. These items were treated as missing data.

Translation

To ensure the quality of translations into Chinese for use in both China and Taiwan,[2] two participants from both China and Taiwan completed the translated versions and commented on the appropriate wording of questions. This process ensured the comprehensibility of the questionnaires and is effective for eliciting valid responses (van de Vijver & Leung, 1997).

Because of distance, the pilot studies in China and Taiwan were conducted by fax and e-mail. Participants suggested changes via e-mail, fax, and telephone. In the United States, the pilot study was administered directly to participants, followed by a 30-minute interview in which participants were encouraged to identify ambiguous terms and suggest appropriate changes. Changes were made accordingly.

---

[2]Separate versions of the questionnaire were prepared, using simplified Chinese characters for the version used in China and traditional Chinese characters for the version used in Taiwan.

Factor Analyses

Each of the five factors of dependability, faith, competence, benevolence, and integrity was factor-analyzed for each relationship type (i.e., close friend, direct supervisor, and organization) using a principal components analysis. Factors were assessed for internal consistency and parallelism of the dimensions (Hunter, 1980). For each dimension, factors were based on the best fit across all three relationships. For example, if one item fit for two relationship types but not as well for a third, we assessed the relative consistency and parallelism of the item and its effect on scale reliability to determine whether the item should be included or deleted in the scale for all three relationship types. As a result of the factor analyses, scales consisted of items that created single unidimensional factors.

The factor analysis for dependability resulted in two separate unidimensional factors (see the appendix), the first indicating an affective dimension and the second indicating a cognitive factor (see McAllister, 1995). Because the factor analysis of items measuring faith resulted in only two highly correlated items, these items were factor-analyzed with dependability. As noted earlier, faith is conceptually related to dependability because dependability provides the basis for faith in the other person. The factor analysis supported the inclusion of these two faith items in the scale measuring affective dependability. As a result, the affective dependability scale consisted of seven items focusing on emotional elements such as concern, support, and feelings of security. The cognitive dependability scale consisted of eight items focusing on aspects such as dependability in making decisions, influence on goals, and information sharing. Both scales had satisfactory reliabilities. (See Table 3.1 for the alpha reliabilities for all of the factors across relationships, for both the entire sample and within the three groups.)

The factor analysis of competence resulted in a three-item scale with strong reliability as a whole and within cultures, with one exception. The reliability of competence in a close friend relationship for Taiwan was low ($\alpha = .54$); the remaining reliabilities were satisfactory, and no further changes were made to this measure. The measure for benevolence consisted of a five-item scale and the measure for integrity consisted of a 13-item scale.

For each of the five factors, the scale items were summed to create a score for that factor across each of the three relationships. Correlations between the five factors within each relationship type averaged .78 for close friend, .76 for direct supervisor, and .69 for organization. A sum of the five scores across each of the three relationships was used in the analyses that compared the three culture groups on the relevance of overall trust across relationships.

TABLE 3.1   Alpha Reliabilities of Factors Across Relationships and Cultures

| Factor | Culture | RELATIONSHIP | | |
		Close Friend	Supervisor	Organization
Dependability	U.S.	.82	.89	.86
(affective)	China	.86	.81	.80
	Taiwan	.82	.85	.86
	Overall	.87	.87	.86
Dependability	U.S.	.83	.87	.82
(cognitive)	China	.75	.80	.71
	Taiwan	.80	.86	.88
	Overall	.86	.86	.83
Competence	U.S.	.77	.81	.82
	China	.65	.76	.78
	Taiwan	.54	.67	.79
	Overall	.76	.78	.81
Benevolence	U.S.	.83	.89	.84
	China	.69	.78	.75
	Taiwan	.78	.86	.88
	Overall	.86	.87	.84
Integrity	U.S.	.91	.91	.91
	China	.86	.80	.80
	Taiwan	.84	.91	.91
	Overall	.91	.90	.89
Overall Trust	U.S.	.87	.89	.88
	China	.90	.92	.87
	Taiwan	.87	.91	.90
	Overall	.90	.90	.88

RESULTS

Research Question 1

Research Question 1 (RQ1) asks whether the same dimensions of trust are relevant in relationships with a close friend, a direct supervisor and an organization. To test RQ1, the factor scores for each of the dimensions were subjected to factor analysis for each relationship type and found to support a second-order unidimensional measure of trust for all three relationships. The alpha reliabilities of the five dimensions are .90 for close friend, .90 for direct supervisor, and .88 for organization (see Table 3.1). The reliability of the five-item second-order scale suggests that all five dimensions are relevant across the three relationship types.

Hypotheses 1 to 5

Hypotheses 1-5 (H1-H5) propose differences in the relevance of the five dimensions of trust across the three relationships. To test these hypotheses, we performed a series of 3 x 3 repeated measures ANOVAs, with relationship type (close friend vs. direct supervisor vs. organization) as the within-subjects factor, culture (China vs. Taiwan vs. U.S.) as the between-subjects factor, and the relevant dimensions of trust as the dependent measures. Contrast comparisons were also performed to test for differences in the specific relationships (see Table 3.2).

H1 and H2 propose that dependability (H1) and faith (H2) will be more relevant in relationships with a close friend and supervisor than with the organization. As noted earlier, factor analyses supported two scales for dependability (i.e., affective and cognitive), and supported combining faith with affective dependability. The contrast comparisons for both affective and cognitive dependability demonstrate that these dimensions are significantly more relevant in the relationship with a close friend than with a supervisor and with a supervisor than with the organization. These results provide overall support for the predictions of H1 and H2.

H3 posits that competence will be more relevant in impersonal relationships, such as with a supervisor or an organization, than with a close friend. The results of the contrast comparisons for this dimension show an opposite trend: Competence is more relevant with a close friend than with a supervisor or an organization, so H3 was not supported. H4 and H5 predict that benevolence and integrity will be more relevant in a relationship with a close friend than with a supervisor or an organization. The contrast comparisons provide support for both of these hypotheses.

Hypothesis 6

H6 proposes that in all three cultures, overall trust with a direct supervisor will be more similar to trust in the organization than trust with a close friend. To make this comparison, we first subtracted the summed score of overall trust with direct supervisor from the summed score of overall trust with a close friend. We then subtracted the summed score of overall trust with a direct supervisor from the summed score of overall trust in the organization. A paired-sample t test was performed between these two differences, showing that trust in a supervisor is significantly closer to trust in the organization than with a close friend (mean difference between supervisor and close friend, $M = 37.23$, $SD = 32.61$, and supervisor and organization, $M = 17.70$, $SD = 24.47$, $t(146) = 5.40$, $p < .001$), across all three cultures (separate analyses for each culture produced similar results). So H6 is supported.

Hypothesis 7

H7 and its subpoints (i.e., H7a, H7b, H7c), propose cross-cultural differences in the relevance of overall trust. H7 posits that overall trust will differ significantly for the three cultures across the three relationships. To address this hypothesis, we performed a 3 x 3 ANOVA with repeated measures, with relationship type (close friend vs. direct supervisor vs. organization) as a within-subjects factor, culture (China vs. Taiwan vs. U.S.) as a between-subjects factor, and level of overall trust as the dependent measure. The results revealed a significant main effect for relationship, $F(2, 288) = 132.72$, $p < .001$, $eta^2 = .48$, suggesting that the relevance of trust is not the same across the three relationships. Additionally, a significant relationship by culture interaction was also found, $F(4, 288) = 9.42$, $p < .001$, $eta^2 = .12$, suggesting that the relevance of trust differs in the three relationships across the three cultures. The within-subjects contrast shows that the relevance of trust is significantly greater in relationships with a close friend than either a supervisor or an organization and greater in relationships with a supervisor than an organization. Post hoc between-subjects comparisons were performed using Tukey's honestly significant difference test, showing significant differences between the United States and both China and Taiwan but no significant difference between China and Taiwan. Table 3.2 shows within-subjects comparisons across relationships, Table 3.3 provides descriptive statistics, and Table 3.4 shows between-subjects comparisons across cultures. Figure 3.1 demonstrates the relationship by culture comparisons.

TABLE 3.2 Within Subjects Contrasts Comparing Relationship Types on Trust and Dimensions of Trust[a]

	CLOSE FRIEND VS. SUPERVISOR	CLOSE FRIEND VS. ORGANIZATION	SUPERVISOR VS. ORGANIZATION
Overall Trust			
$F(1,144)$ eta^2	110.99 (.44)	195.20 (.58)	41.54 (.22)
Dependability (Affective)			
$F(1, 224)$ eta^2	216.37 (.49)	325.34 (.59)	61.18 (.22)
Dependability (Cognitive)			
$F(1, 233)$ eta^2	185.95 (.44)	298.10 (.56)	54.12 (.19)
Competence			
$F(1, 270)$ eta^2	14.78 (.05)	37.28 (.12)	14.61 (.05)
Benevolence			
$F(1, 234)$ eta^2	155.06 (.40)	313.31 (.57)	66.06 (.22)
Integrity			
$F(1, 200)$ eta^2	117.57 (.37)	218.22 (.52)	36.60 (.16)

[a]All comparisons are significant at $p < .001$.

TABLE 3.3 Descriptive Statistics of Trust and Dimensions of Trust Across Cultures and Relationships[a]

DIMENSION & RELATIONSHIP	CHINA MEAN (SD)	TAIWAN MEAN (SD)	U.S. MEAN (SD)	TOTAL MEAN (SD)
Overall Trust				
Close friend	175.63 (32.03)	182.76 (30.09)	210.29 (27.03)	197.38 (30.09)
Supervisor	151.37 (26.07)	157.47 (32.29)	163.61 (35.33)	160.15 (32.39)
Organization	140.58 (23.16)	142.45 (28.93)	142.41 (32.24)	142.45 (28.93)
Dependability (Affective)				
Close friend	38.03 (7.83)	42.36 (6.39)	47.99 (6.05)	44.57 (7.46)
Supervisor	32.80 (6.77)	35.12 (7.22)	34.42 (9.11)	34.41 (8.19)
Organization	31.69 (6.52)	31.54 (7.46)	28.55 (8.11)	30.04 (7.89)
Dependability (Cognitive)				
Close friend	34.19 (4.86)	36.12 (5.01)	41.70 (5.49)	38.53 (6.12)
Supervisor	30.56 (4.99)	29.87 (6.53)	31.70 (7.73)	30.90 (6.95)
Organization	29.02 (4.66)	26.96 (6.56)	27.35 (7.42)	27.53 (6.73)
Competence				
Close friend	14.55 (2.30)	15.31 (2.12)	17.68 (2.72)	16.33 (2.80)
Supervisor	14.59 (3.04)	14.32 (2.89)	16.23 (3.40)	15.30 (3.29)
Organization	14.27 (3.21)	13.77 (2.95)	15.09 (3.69)	14.50 (3.42)

TABLE 3.3 Descriptive Statistics of Trust and Dimensions of Trust Across Cultures and Relationships[a] *(Continued)*

DIMENSION & RELATIONSHIP	CHINA MEAN (SD)	TAIWAN MEAN (SD)	U.S. MEAN (SD)	TOTAL MEAN (SD)
Benevolence				
Close friend	23.41 (4.51)	25.38 (4.27)	30.80 (4.14)	27.87 (5.22)
Supervisor	20.12 (4.74)	20.66 (5.12)	23.07 (6.56)	21.81 (5.97)
Organization	18.56 (4.69)	18.56 (5.12)	18.80 (5.97)	18.68 (5.49)
Integrity				
Close friend	62.86 (9.20)	69.58 (11.42)	75.15 (11.26)	69.58 (11.42)
Supervisor	57.17 (7.36)	55.59 (11.35)	58.71 (14.99)	57.39 (12.77)
Organization	53.92 (7.84)	51.84 (10.37)	50.88 (12.64)	51.74 (11.18)

[a]Means are based on summed scores of scales.

TABLE 3.4 Main Effects and Post Hoc Comparisons[a] of Cultures on Trust and the Dimensions of Trust

	U.S. vs. CHINA	CHINA vs. TAIWAN	U.S. vs. TAIWAN
Overall Trust			
Culture main effect: $F(2, 144) = 5.44, p < .01$, $eta^2 = .07$			
Mean diff.	16.25	-5.32	10.93
(Std. Error)	(5.99)	(6.44)	(4.36)
sig.	$p < .02$	ns	$p < .04$
Dependability (Affective)			
Culture main effect: $F(2, 224) = 2.98$, ns ($p < .06$), $eta^2 = .03$			
Mean diff.	2.82	-2.17	.65
(Std. Error)	(1.15)	(1.22)	(.88)
sig.	$p < .04$	ns	ns
Dependability (Cognitive)			
Culture main effect: $F(2, 233) = 7.56, p < .001$, $eta^2 = .06$			
Mean diff.	2.33	.27	2.60
(Std. Error)	(.88)	(.95)	(.73)
sig.	$p < .01$	ns	$p < .001$

TABLE 3.4 Main Effects and Post Hoc Comparisons[a] of Cultures on Trust and the Dimensions of Trust *(Continued)*

	U.S. vs. CHINA	CHINA vs. TAIWAN	U.S. vs. TAIWAN
Competence			
Culture main effect: $F(2, 270) = 20.51, p < .001$, $\text{eta}^2 = .13$			
Mean diff.	1.87	.004	1.86
(Std. Error)	(.33)	(.43)	(.40)
sig.	$p < .001$	ns	$p < .001$
Benevolence			
Culture main effect: $F(2, 234) = 14.75, p < .001$, $\text{eta}^2 = .11$			
Mean diff.	3.53	-.84	2.69
(Std. Error)	(.82)	(.86)	(.61)
sig.	$p < .001$	ns	$p < .001$
Integrity			
Culture main effect: $F(2, 200) = 5.03, p < .01$, $\text{eta}^2 = .05$			
Mean diff.	3.60	.50	4.09
(Std. Error)	(1.72)	(1.82)	(1.39)
sig.	ns	ns	$p < .01$

[a] Post-hoc comparisons performed using Tukey honestly significant difference test.

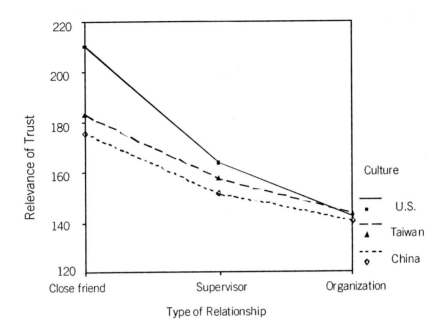

Figure 3.1 Relevance of trust for three types of relationships in China, Taiwan, and the United States.

To examine specific predictions regarding the three relationships across the three cultures, we proposed three subpoints to H7. H7a predicts that in relationships with close friends, the relevance of overall trust will be greater in the United States than in China and Taiwan. Independent sample t tests support significant differences in overall trust in a relationship with a close friend between the United States and China, $t(148) = 6.83$, $p < .001$, and between the United States and Taiwan, $t(182) = 7.24$, $p < .001$, so H7a is supported.

H7b predicts that the difference in the relevance of overall trust between close friend and supervisor will be greater for participants in the United States than in China and Taiwan. To make this comparison, we used the difference between the summed score of overall trust with direct supervisor and the summed score of overall trust with a close friend, computed previously for H6. We then performed independent t tests between the United States and China and between the United States and Taiwan. The results for these tests supported our hypothesis (U.S. vs. China: t [124] = 3.29, $p < .01$; U.S. vs. Taiwan: t [163] = 3.70, $p < .001$).

H7c posits that the relevance of overall trust across relationships will be different in China and Taiwan. The post hoc comparison between China and Taiwan finds that there is no significant difference between the two cultures on trust across all three relationships (see Table 3.4).[3] Thus, H7c is not supported.

Summary

In response to RQ1, we found that trust with a close friend, a direct supervisor, and an organization all consist of the same five dimensions: affective dependability, cognitive dependability, competence, benevolence, and integrity. For predictions about the specific dimensions of trust (H1-H5), all but one of the hypotheses were supported. Only H3, which posited that competence would be more relevant in relationships with a supervisor and an organization than with a close friend, was not supported. In summary, all five dimensions were found to be significantly more important in the relationship with a close friend than with a supervisor and in the relationship with a supervisor than with an organization.

In support of H6, for all three cultures, trust with a supervisor was more similar to trust in an organization than trust with a close friend. For H7, a relationship by culture interaction, along with post hoc comparisons, demonstrated that trust differs across the three relationships and across cultures. In support of H7a, trust with a close friend was greater for participants from the United States than from China or Taiwan. In support of H7b, there was greater difference in trust between close friend and supervisor for participants from the United States than from China and Taiwan. But in contrast to the prediction of H7c, no difference in overall trust was found between China and Taiwan.

DISCUSSION

In this chapter, we tested the dimensions of trust and examined the relevance of trust across three relationships (i.e., a close friend, a direct supervisor, and the organization) within three cultures: China, Taiwan, and the United States. The results demonstrate that five dimensions make up trust, and that these dimensions are relevant within all three relationships. The five dimensions consist of affective dependability (e.g., concern, support, and feelings of security), cognitive dependability (e.g., making decisions, influence on goals, and information sharing), competence, benevolence, and integrity.

Significant differences were found across the three cultures in the relevance of trust in relationships with a close friend, a direct supervisor, and an organiza-

---

[3]Independent t tests for the three types of relationships show a similar lack of difference between the two cultures.

tion as a whole. Because we found relatively little difference between the cultures in their view of trust with an organization (see Figure 3.1), we can rule out the suggestion that our findings are based merely on mean differences in trust across the three groups. Otherwise the pattern of relationships would be the same in all three relationships and across all three cultures.

One of the most notable findings in our study is the high relevance of trust in a relationship with a close friend in the United States compared to the same relationship in China and Taiwan (H7a). In support of this finding, Fukuyama (1995) noted that historically, the radius of trust in Chinese communities often did not extend beyond lineage lines. Similarly, Hui (1990) noted the prevalence of nepotism in Chinese businesses because "as in-group members, their relatives are seen as more trustworthy than others" (p. 200). In China and Taiwan, both considered collectivist, individuals may rely more heavily on familial relationships to provide assistance and support. Yang (1992) proposed social and family orientations to describe Chinese cultural characteristics, arguing that the family orientation, which emphasizes the close relationships with family, is the basis for Western categorizations of Chinese culture as "collectivist." Although close friendships are important in China and Taiwan, there may be less dependence on friends than relatives, so concepts such as dependability, benevolence, competence, and integrity are not important for the role that a friend plays in Eastern cultures.

Chang and Holt (1991) provided further insight into cultural differences in trust with a close friend. They noted that interpersonal relationships for the Chinese are often based on the concept of *yuan*, or "facilitative conditions" for the relationship. *Yuan* results in a willingness to engage in a relationship based on contextual factors rather than on personality compatibility. These researchers further note the implications of such relational differences on communication:

> By resigning themselves to unknown factors that bring association as well as dissociation between people, Chinese feel no need to develop especially communicative strategies to maintain their relationships. By cherishing the chance of association, and by allowing their relationship to develop according to its own course, Chinese are more willing to tolerate a bad relationship or to disengage a relationship without using communicative strategies to do so. (p. 54)

Chang and Holt pointed out that, for the Chinese, communication is not the primary means for determining relationships. This idea is in contrast to the Western focus on building close relationships through the sharing and disclosing of information (Berger & Bradac, 1982; Parks, 1982). As a result of these differences, trust may be less relevant in establishing and maintaining close interpersonal relationships in China and Taiwan than in the United States.

Note, however, that the opposite of trust is not distrust (Lewicki, McAllister, & Bies, 1998; Omodei & McLennan, 2000; Peng, 2001), so that these findings do not suggest that people from China and Taiwan distrust close friends. Instead, our findings suggest that trust is significantly less relevant in relationships with close friends in China and Taiwan than in the United States.

Our findings of cross-cultural differences across relationships have implications for our understanding of trust and for how we manage cross-cultural relationships in international organizational alliances. Frequently, the literature for Americans doing business with the Chinese prescribes the need to "make friends" and "build trust." Yet our results suggest that the role of trust in making friends may be understood differently across cultures. Furthermore, expectations of a supervisor are understood differently across the cultures, with trust in a supervisor more closely related to trust in a friend in China and Taiwan than in the United States (H7b). Our findings provide a challenge to implicit assumptions that trust plays the same role in relationships across cultures. Future research should examine cross-culturally the process of building trust and the role of trust across relationships.

One hypothesis not supported in our study was the prediction that the relevance of trust across relationships would differ in China and Taiwan. Although Table 3.4 shows some differences between the two cultures, these differences were not statistically significant. The lack of difference may be due, in part, to sample size. Our findings suggest that participants in Taiwan have an understanding of trust that is more similar to China than the United States. We note, however, that our findings do not support a general combining of the two cultures in future research. Future research should continue to compare subtle differences between the two cultures.

There are three main limitations to this study. The first limitation is the significant difference in age between the three groups and the significantly lower education level of the participants from China. Comparisons across the culture groups should be understood keeping this caveat in mind. Second, although we found trust in all three relationships consists of the same five dimensions, we did not ask questions about the relevance of vulnerability or intimacy in these relationships. These aspects of relational trust are likely to provide more distinction of what trust means across relationship types and across cultures. Third, we did not ask participants about trust in familial relationships. In hindsight, we believe this would provide an important comparison of trust in relationships between the United States, China, and Taiwan. Much of the explanation for our findings suggests that a primary difference between the two cultures is that people in China and Taiwan are dependent on familial relationships whereas people in the United States are more dependent on the friends they select.

The relevance of trust across relationships has important implications for international organizational communication. In cross-cultural training, the importance of developing trust with international counterparts is often emphasized as part of developing relationships that will make negotiations and doing business easier. For example, Hui (1990) discussed trust in work attitudes and managerial behaviors as

> generally [developing] from authenticity in self-presentation as well as from accuracy of social perception and attribution. Naturally there would be a greater degree of authenticity and accurate perception between good friends than between acquaintances and in an in-group relationship than between two persons who consider each other out-group members. (p. 199)

But our findings suggest that developing trust across cultures is not necessarily the same as making friends, at least as the concept of friend is understood in the United States. Trust appears much less relevant in close friendships in China and Taiwan than in the United States. As a result, being considered a friend in China and Taiwan may not mean that trust has been established. Individuals from Western organizations looking for familiar means of establishing trust as found in close friendships may misunderstand the process of building trust in China or Taiwan. Our research suggests that training seminars, manuals, and guides to international management that promote the importance of trust will need to consider the cross-cultural differences regarding who is likely to be granted trust, how it is built and maintained in relationships, and the role of communication in these processes.

APPENDIX: SCALES FOR DIMENSIONS OF TRUST

Dependability (Affective)

1. I can count on (my friend/my supervisor/the organization) to be concerned about my welfare.
2. Although times may change and the future is uncertain, I know (my friend/my supervisor/the organization) will always be ready and willing to offer me strength and support.
3. I have found that (my friend/my supervisor/the organization) is unusually dependable, especially when it comes to things that are important to me.
4. Whenever we have to make an important decision in a situation we have never encountered before, I know (my friend/my supervisor/the organization) will be concerned about my welfare.
5. I can rely on (my friend/my supervisor/the organization) to react in a positive way when I expose my weaknesses to him/her/it.
6. I would be able to confide in (my friend/my supervisor/the organization) and know that he/she/it would want to listen.

7. When encountering difficult and unfamiliar new circumstances I would not feel worried or threatened by letting (my friend/my supervisor/the organization) do what he/she/it wanted.

8. When I am with (my friend/my supervisor/the organization), I feel secure in facing unknown new situations.

Dependability (Cognitive)

1. I feel that (my friend/my supervisor/the organization) can be counted on to help me.

2. (My friend/My supervisor/The organization) can be relied on to keep his/her/its promises.

3. I believe that (my friend/my supervisor/the organization) takes my opinions into account when making decisions.

4. I influence (my friend/my supervisor/the organization) as much as (my friend/my supervisor/the organization) influences me.

5. (My friend/My supervisor/The organization) influences others in things such as goals, policies, and decisions.

6. Sharing information with (my friend/my supervisor/the organization) is open and easy.

7. (My friend/My supervisor/The organization) encourages me to make my own decisions.

8. (My friend/My supervisor/The organization) encourages others to participate in the establishment of their goals and performance objectives.

Competence

1. I feel very confident about (my friend's/my supervisor's/the organization's) skills.

2. (My friend/My supervisor/The organization) has the ability to accomplish what he/she/it says he/she/it will do.

3. (My friend/My supervisor/The organization) approaches the work to be done with professionalism and dedication.

Benevolence

1. If I told (my friend/my supervisor/the organization) what things I worry about, he/she/it would not think my concerns were silly.

2. I can talk freely about difficulties I am having at work and know that he/she/it will want to listen.

3. (My friend/My supervisor/The organization) is very concerned about my welfare.
4. My needs and desires are very important to (my friend/my supervisor/the organization).
5. (My friend/My supervisor/The organization) will go out of his/her/its way to help.

Integrity

1. I can rely on (my friend/my supervisor/the organization) to keep the promises he/she/it makes to me.
2. (My friend/My supervisor/The organization) treats me fairly and justly.
3. Even when (my friend/my supervisor/the organization) makes excuses that sound rather unlikely, I am confident that he/she/it is telling the truth.
4. (My friend/My supervisor/The organization) is perfectly honest and truthful with me.
5. (My friend/My supervisor/The organization) is truly sincere in his/her/it promises.
6. Sound principles seem to guide (my friend's/my supervisor's/the organization's) actions.
7. (My friend/My supervisor/The organization) does not mislead me.
8. Whenever (my friend/my supervisor/the organization) makes an important decision, I know he/she/it will be concerned about me.
9. I find that I do not need to monitor (my friend/my supervisor/the organization) closely.
10. (My friend/My supervisor/The organization) keeps me informed about what is happening.
11. Others can get what they need from (my friend/my supervisor/the organization) without being discouraged or hampered by rules or procedures.
12. (My friend/My supervisor/The organization) has a strong sense of justice.
13. I never have to worry about whether (my friend/my supervisor/the organization) will stick to his/her/its word.

ACKNOWLEDGEMENTS

The authors wish to thank Drs. Edward L. Fink and George A. Barnett for their thoughtful comments and suggestions. A previous version of this chapter was presented at the annual conference of the International Communication Association in Acapulco, Mexico, June 2000.

REFERENCES

Becerra, M. (1998). Nature, antecedents, and consequences of trust within organizations: A multilevel analysis within the multinational corporation (Doctoral dissertation, University of Maryland, 1998). *Dissertation Abstracts International*, AAT9719808.

Berger, C. R., & Bradac, J. J. (1982). *Language and social knowledge: Uncertainty in interpersonal relations*. London: Edward Arnold.

Boon, S. D., & Holmes, J. G. (1991). The dynamics of interpersonal trust: Resolving uncertainty in the face of risk. In R. A. Hinde & J. Groebel (Eds.), *Cooperation and prosocial behavior* (pp. 190-212). Cambridge, UK: Cambridge University Press.

Bromiley, P., & Cummings, L. L. (1992). *Transactions cost in organizations with trust* (Discussion Paper #128). Minneapolis: University of Minnesota, Strategic Management Research Center.

Butler, J. K. (1991). Toward understanding and measuring conditions of trust: Evolution of a condition of trust inventory. *Journal of Management, 17*, 643-663.

Canary, D. J., & Cupach, W. R. (1988). Relational and episodic characteristics associated with conflict tactics. *Journal of Social and Personal Relationships, 5*, 305-325.

Chang, H. C., & Holt, G. R. (1991). The concept of yuan and Chinese interpersonal relationships. In S. Ting-Toomey & F. Korzenny (Eds.), *Cross-cultural interpersonal communication* (pp. 28-57). Newbury Park, CA: Sage.

Chen, J. X., & Gao, C. X. (1991). Tai wan chi yeh yun juo de she hui ju xu: Ren qing guan xi yu fa lu [The social order of how Taiwanese corporations function: Relationships and laws]. *Dong Hai Journal, 32*, 219-232.

Cheng, B. X. (1988). Jia ju yu lin dao xin wei [Familialism and leadership behaviors]. In C.F. Yang & A. B. Yu (Eds.), *Jong guo ren, Jong guo xin: ren ge yu xe hui pian* (pp. 365-407). Taipei, Taiwan: Yuan Liu.

Cheng, B. X. (2001). Chi ye ju chi zhong xan xia xu de xin ren guan xi [The trust relationship between supervisors and subordinates in a corporation]. In C. F. Yang (Ed.), *Interpersonal relationship, affection and trust of the Chinese: From an interpersonal perspective* (pp. 271-291). Taipei, Taiwan: Yuan Liu.

Clark, M. S., & Mills, J. (1993). The difference between communal and exchange relationships: What it is and is not. *Personality and Social Psychology Bulletin, 19*, 684-691.

Clark, M. S., Powell, M., & Mills, J. (1986). Keeping track of needs in communal and exchange relationships. *Journal of Personality and Social Psychology, 51*, 333-338.

Cloven, D. H., & Roloff, M. E. (1993). The chilling effect of aggressive potential on the expression of complaints in intimate relationships. *Communication Monographs, 60*, 199-219.

Cook, J., & Wall, T. (1980). New work attitude measures of trust, organizational commitment, and personal need nonfulfillment. *Journal of Occupational Psychology, 53*, 39-52.

Cummings, L. L., & Bromiley, P. (1996). The organizational trust inventory (OTI). In R. Kramer & T. Tyler (Eds.), *Trust in organizations: Frontiers of theory and research* (pp. 261-287). Thousand Oaks, CA: Sage.

Cupach, W. R., & Canary, D. J. (1997). *Competence in interpersonal conflict.* New York: McGraw-Hill.

De Furia, G. (1997). *Organizational trust survey.* San Francisco, CA: Jossey-Bass

Deutsch, M. (1960). The effect of motivational orientation upon trust and suspicion. *Human Relations, 13,* 123-140.

Doney, P. M., Cannon, J. P., & Mullen, M. R. (1998). Understanding the influence of national culture on the development of trust. *Academy of Management Review, 23,* 601-620.

Fisher, R., & Brown, S. (1988). *Getting together: Building relationships as we negotiate.* New York: Penguin Group.

Fitchen, J. M., Hearth, J. S., & Fessenden-Raden, J. (1987). Risk perception in community context: A case study. In B. B. Johnson & V. T. Covello (Eds.), *The social and cultural construction of risk* (pp. 31-54). Dordrecht, Holland: D. Reidel.

Frost, T., Stimpson, D. V., & Maughan, M. R. C. (1978). Some correlates of trust. *Journal of Psychology, 99,* 103-108.

Fukuyama, F. (1995). *Trust: The social virtues and the creation of prosperity.* New York: Simon & Schuster.

Gabarro, J. (1987). *The dynamics of taking charge.* Boston: Harvard Business School Press.

Garthoeffner, J., Henry, C., & Robinson, L. (1993). The modified interpersonal relationship scale: Reliability and validity. *Psychological Reports, 73,* 995-1004.

Goldhaber, G. M. (1993). *Organizational communication.* Madison, WI: Brown & Benchmark.

Good, D. (1988). Individuals, interpersonal relations, and trust. In D. Gambetta (Ed.), *Trust: Making and breaking cooperative relations* (pp. 31-48). New York: Basil Blackwell.

Grunig, J. E., & Grunig, L. A. (1998). Does evaluation of PR measure the real value of PR? *Public Relations Reporter, 41,* 4.

Grunig, J. E., & Huang, Y. H. (2000). From organizational effectiveness to relationship indicators: Antecedents of relationships, public relations strategies, and relationship outcomes. In J. A. Ledingham & S. D. Bruning (Eds.), *Relationship management: A relational approach to public relations* (pp. 23-53). Mahwah, NJ: Erlbaum.

Grunig, J., & Hung, C. (2000, June). *Development of indices and an initial study of trust, control mutuality, commitment, satisfaction, and communal and exchange relationships as measures of organization-public relationships.* Paper presented at the annual conference of the International Communication Association, Acapulco, Mexico.

Gurtman, M. (1992). Trust, distrust, and interpersonal problems: A circumplex analysis. *Journal of Personality and Social Psychology, 62,* 989-1002.

Hinde, R. A. (1981). The bases of a science of interpersonal relationships. In S. Duck & R. Gilmour (Eds.), *Personal relationships* (pp. 1-22). New York: Academic Press.

Hofstede, G. (1980). *Culture's consequences.* Newbury Park, CA: Sage.

Hovland, C. I., Janis, I. L., & Kelley, H. H. (1953). *Communication and persuasion.* New Haven, CT: Yale University Press.

Huang, Y. H. (1994). *Technological risk and environmental activism: Case studies of public risk perception in Taiwan.* Taipei, Taiwan: Wu-Nan Publishers.

Hung, C. J. (2002). *The interplays of relationship types, relationship cultivation, and relationship outcomes: A dialectical perspective on how multinational and Taiwanese companies practice public relations and relationship management in China*. Unpublished doctoral dissertation, University of Maryland, College Park.

Hui, C. H. (1990). Work attitudes, leadership styles, and managerial behaviors in different cultures. In R. W. Brislin (Ed.), *Applied cross-cultural psychology* (pp. 186-208). Newbury Park, CA: Sage.

Hui, C. H., & Triandis, H. C. (1986). Individualism-collectivism: A study of cross-cultural researchers. *Journal of Cross-Cultural Psychology, 17*, 225-248.

Hui, C. H., & Villareal, M. J. (1989). Individualism-collectivism and psychological needs: Their relationships in two cultures. *Journal of Cross-Cultural Psychology, 20*, 310-323.

Hunter, J. E. (1980). Factor analysis. In P. R. Monge & J. N. Cappella (Eds.), *Multivariate techniques in human communication research* (pp. 229-257). New York: Academic Press.

Johnson-George, C., & Swap, W. (1982). Measurement of specific interpersonal trust: Construction and validation of a scale to assess trust in a specific other. *Journal of Personality and Social Psychology, 43*, 1306-1317.

Jones, A. P., James, L. R., & Bruni, J. R. (1975). Perceived leadership behavior and employee confidence in the leader as moderated by job involvement. *Journal of Applied Psychology, 60*, 146-149.

Kee, H. W., & Knox, R. E. (1970). Conceptual and methodological considerations in the study of trust. *Journal of Conflict Resolution, 14*, 357-366.

Krimsky, S., & Plough, A. (1988). *Environmental hazards: Communicating risks as a social process*. Westport, CT: Auburn House.

LaFollette, H. (1996). *Personal relationships: Love, identity, and morality*. Cambridge, MA: Blackwell.

Larzelere, R. E., & Huston, T. L. (1980). The dyadic trust scale: Toward understanding interpersonal trust in close relationships. *Journal of Marriage and the Family, 42*, 595-604.

Lawler, E. (1992). *The ultimate advantage: Creating the high-involvement organization*. San Francisco, CA: Jossey-Bass.

Lee, M. H., & Barnett, G. A. (1997). A symbols-and-meaning approach to the organizational cultures of banks in the United States, Japan and Taiwan. *Communication Research, 24*, 394-413.

Lewicki., R. J., & Bunker, B. B. (1998). Developing and maintaining trust in work relationships. In R. M. Kramer & T. R. Tyler (Eds.), *Trust in organizations: Frontiers of theory and research* (pp. 114-130). Thousand Oaks, CA: Sage.

Lewicki, R. J., McAllister, D. J., & Bies, R. J. (1998). Trust and distrust: New relationships and realities. *Academy of Management Review, 23*, 438-458.

Lieberman, J. K. (1981). *The litigious society*. New York: Basic Books.

Lindskold, S., & Han, G. (1988). GRIT as a foundation for integrative bargaining. *Personality and Social Psychology Bulletin, 14*, 335-345.

Luhman, N. (1988). Familiarity, confidence, trust: Problems and alternatives. In D. Gambetta (Ed.), *Trust: Making and breaking cooperative relations* (pp. 94-108). New York: Basil Blackwell.

Lulofs, R. S. (1994). *Conflict: From theory to action*. Scottsdale, AZ: Gorsuch Scarsbrick.

Mayer, R., Davis, J., & Schoorman, F. (1995). An integrative model of organizational trust. *Academy of Management Review, 20*, 709-734.

McAllister, D. (1995). Affect- and cognition-based trust as foundations for interpersonal cooperation in organizations. *Academy of Management Journal, 38*, 24-59.

McGregor, D. (1967). *The professional manager.* New York: McGraw-Hill.

Mishra, A. (1996). Organizational responses to crisis: The centrality of trust. In R. M. Kramer & T. R. Tyler (Eds.), *Trust in organizations* (pp. 261-287). Thousand Oaks, CA: Sage.

Moorman, C., Deshpande, R., & Zaltman, G. (1993). Factors affecting trust in market research relationships. *Journal of Marketing, 57*, 81-101.

Morgan, R. M., & Hunt, S. D. (1994). The commitment-trust theory of relationship marketing. *Journal of Marketing, 58*, 20-38.

Omodei, M. M., & McLennan, J. (2000). Conceptualizing and measuring global interpersonal mistrust-trust. *Journal of Social Psychology, 140*, 279-294.

Ouchi, W. G. (1981). *Theory Z: How American business can meet the Japanese challenge.* Reading, MA: Addison-Wesley.

Parks, M. R. (1982). Ideology of interpersonal communication: Off the couch into the world. In M. Burgoon (Ed.), *Communication yearbook 5* (pp. 79-108). New Brunswick, NJ: Transaction.

Peng, S. C. (2001). Xin ren de jian li ji chi: Guanxi yun juo yu fa ji xou duan [The mechanism on the building of trust: The guanxi implication and legal application]. In C. F. Yang (Ed.), *Interpersonal relationship, affection and trust of the Chinese: From an interactional perspective* (pp. 315-333). Taipei, Taiwan: Yuan Liu.

Powell, C. M., & Heriot, K. C. (2001). The interaction of holistic and dyadic trust in social relationships: An investigative theoretical model. *Journal of Social Behavior and Personality, 15*, 387-398.

Pruitt, D. G., & Carnevale, P. J. (1993). *Negotiation in social conflict.* Pacific Grove, CA: Brooks/Cole.

Ramamoorthy, N. (1996). The influence of individualism-collectivism (I/C) orientations on the administration of and reactions toward performance appraisal and reward systems (Doctoral dissertation, University of Maryland, 1996). *Dissertation Abstracts International,* AAT9908916.

Rempel, J., Holmes, J. & Zanna, M. (1985). Trust in close relationships. *Journal of Personality and Social Psychology, 49*, 95-112.

Ring, S. M., & van de Ven, A. (1992). Structuring cooperative relationships between organizations. *Strategic Management Journal, 13*, 483-498.

Rosen, B., & Jerdee, T. H. (1977). Influence of subordinate characteristics on trust and use of participative decision strategies in a management simulation. *Journal of Applied Psychology, 62*, 628-631.

Rotter, J. (1967). A new scale for the measurement of interpersonal trust. *Journal of Personality, 35*, 651-665.

Sako, M. (1992). *Prices, quality, and trust: Inter-firm relations in Britain & Japan.* New York: Cambridge University Press.

Schwartz, S. H. (1994). Beyond individualism-collectivism: New cultural dimensions of values. In U. Kim, H. C. Triandis, Ç. Kagitcibasi, S. C. Choi, & G. Yoon (Eds.), *Individualism and collectivism: Theory, method, and applications* (pp. 85-119). Thousand Oaks, CA: Sage.

Sitkin, S. B., & Roth, N. L. (1993). Explaining the limited effectiveness of legalistic remedies for trust/distrust. *Organization Science, 4*, 367-392.

Solomon, L. (1960). The influence of some types of power relationships and game strategies upon the development of interpersonal trust. *Journal of Abnormal and Social
Psychology, 61*, 223-230.

Strickland, L. H. (1958). Surveillance and trust. *Journal of Personality, 26*, 200-215.

Triandis, H. C. (1989). Self and social behavior in differing cultural contexts.
Psychological Review, 96, 269-289.

Triandis, H. C. (1994). Theoretical and methodological approaches to the study of collectivism and individualism. In U. Kim, H. C. Triandis, Ç. Kagitcibasi, S. C. Choi,
& G. Yoon (Eds.), *Individualism and collectivism: Theory, method, and applications* (pp. 41-51). Thousand Oaks, CA: Sage.

Triandis, H. C. (1995). *Individualism & collectivism*. Boulder, CO: Westview.

Triandis, H. C., McCusker, C., & Hui, C. H. (1990). Multimethod probes of individualism and collectivism. *Journal of Personality and Social Psychology, 59*, 1006-1020.

Trompenaars, F. (1993). *Riding the waves of culture*. London: Nicholas Brealey.

van de Vijver, F., & Leung, K. (1997). *Methods and data analysis for cross-cultural
research*. Thousand Oaks, CA: Sage.

Wang, F. X. (2001). Gua wen hua bi jiao yu jong guo ren de xin ren yan jiou [A cross-
cultural study comparison and Chinese trust]. In C.F. Yang (Ed.), *Interpersonal
relationship, affection and trust of the Chinese: From an interactional perspective*
(pp. 293-314). Taipei, Taiwan: Yuan Liu.

Wieselquist, J., Rusbult, C. E., Foster, C. A., & Agnew, C. R. (1999). Commitment, pro-
relationship behavior, and trust in close relationships. *Journal of Personality and
Social Psychology, 77*, 942-966.

Whitener, E. M., Brodt, S. E., Korsgaard, M. A., & Werner, J. M. (1998). Managers as
initiators of trust: An exchange relationship framework for understanding managerial trustworthy behavior. *Academy of Management Review, 23*, 513-530.

Yang, C. F. (2001). *Interpersonal relationship, affection and trust of the Chinese: From
an interpersonal perspective*. Taipei: Yuan Liu.

Yang, C. F., & Peng, S. C. (2001). Ren ji xin ren de gai nian hua: Yi ge ren ji guan xi de
guan dian [Conceptualizing interpersonal trust: From the interpersonal relationship
perspective]. In C. F. Yang (Ed.), *Interpersonal relationship, affection and trust of
the Chinese: From an interpersonal perspective* (pp. 371-399). Taipei: Yuan Liu.

Yang, K. S. (1992). Chinese social orientation: From the social interaction perspective.
In K. S. Yang & A. B. Yu (Eds), *Chinese psychology and behavior* (pp. 87-142).
Taipei: Laurel.

4

DATA-DRIVEN DYNAMIC MODELS (3D) FOR INTERCULTURAL COMMUNICATION AND DIVERSITY TRAINING IN ORGANIZATIONS

Catherine Becker
University of Hawaii, Hilo

Intercultural communication researchers and diversity trainers in search of relevant communication theories, models, and methods to guide their efforts need to consider the relationship among communication, variations within cultures, and cultural change over time. Data-driven dynamic models (3D) that incorporate the concepts of co-culture and organizational culture were developed from narrative approaches, neural networks, and Galileo theory. Cultural mapping was used to demonstrate how such models could be used to accommodate for cultural variations within cultures and cultural change over time. Four such approaches to intercultural communication research and diversity training are explained and examined for their contributions and limitations. Examples of applications in organizations are presented.

As a result of accelerated communication throughout the world and the increasing emphasis on the importance of diversity and accountability, organizations that will survive during the new millennium will confront unprecedented intercultural communication challenges. Knowledge about and competence in intercultural communication is no longer an area of interest for just a specialized elite; it has become a requirement for professional and organizational survival. However, it is becoming more difficult to prescribe specific guidelines for successful intercultural communication because intercultural communication competence has come to mean much more than fluency in the language and customs of two or more national groups. Intercultural communication competence requires the ability to address the cultural variations and changes *within* national boundaries and organizations along with the ability to communicate effectively across the lines of culture, class, race, ethnicity, and gender.

This chapter discusses some of the issues confronted by intercultural communication and diversity trainers in search of relevant communication theories, models, and methods to guide their efforts. It discusses the problems related to the construct of culture and suggests that data-driven dynamic (3D) models of intercultural communication training may help to overcome some of these problems. 3D models of intercultural communication training provide organizations with techniques developed from theories and models that accommodate for culture as a communicative process that changes over time and context. Procedures that could be developed for assessing diversity and the effectiveness of diversity training programs, an area where procedures are limited or almost nonexistent (Brinkman, 1997; Chung, 1997), are provided. Four models, the Dialogue Model, 3Cs, Cultural Mapping, and the International Microcultures Approach (IMCs) combined with Cultural Mapping are presented. Examples of how the models have been or could be used in organizations are provided. Each model's potentials and limitations are also considered.

Hall (1959) stated, "culture is communication and communication is culture" (p. 217). If culture is communication then like communication, culture is a process, not a discrete variable that is in the possession of a group. If culture is communication, then culture is something that members of groups *do*, rather than something that they have. Furthermore, organizational members are often confronted with multiple cultural influences and affiliations that may be relevant in some contexts in regard to some tasks and irrelevant in others. As a result, organizational communication in any particular situation may be a result of multiple cultural influences that may not be easily predicted by normative approaches. Models of intercultural communication and diversity training that treat culture as a variable that changes over time, rather than a discrete phenomenon, are needed. These models must accurately address the complex and dynamic nature of culture, diversity, and intercultural communication. To accommodate for cultural variation and change, training models must be data-driven, dynamic, and offer a way to assess their effectiveness. 3D models of intercultural communication and diversity training provide organizations with techniques that have developed from theories and methods that treat culture as a process that changes over time and context.

BACKGROUND

In order to meet the challenge of the increasing need for intercultural communication competence, it is necessary to begin with a definition of *culture* that adequately captures the complexity of the phenomenon. In a review of the intercultural communication literature previous to 1977, Moon (1996) found a lack of consistency in definitions of culture. Definitions of culture varied from "nation-state," to race, social class, and gender identity. After 1978, culture began to be conceived almost entirely in terms of "nation-state," in the form of a variable, used for empirical research throughout the 1980s. As a result, intercultural communication research tended to involve a comparison of cultures, dyadic interaction between members of different cultures, and microanalysis of cultural traits such as nonverbal communication styles (Moon, 1996).

Influenced by the limited definitions of culture used in intercultural communication research after 1978, intercultural communication training in organizations has frequently focused on providing information about cultural tendencies of the "other" in order to enable intercultural communicators to accommodate for specific cultural variations. The problem with training approaches based on culture defined as a nation-state is that they underestimate the cultural variations within any particular nation, they seldom acknowledge that culture is a process that changes over time, and they do not address the notion that individuals, even within a nation-state, may have alliances to more than one culture simultaneously.

Although it has been shown that national culture influences organizational culture (Lee & Barnett, 1991; Lindsley, 1999), what is problematic is that national cultures are comprised of a variety of co-cultures that may exert their influences on organizational culture in different ways. Consider the complexity of defining the culture of the United States. Although many people in the United States share beliefs, behaviors, and communication styles that distinguish them from other cultures around the world, within the United States many crucial differences exist among the various groups who comprise the U.S. population.

Co-culture is a term that may be used to describe the variation in shared experiences, behaviors, perceptions, and expectations that distinguish some groups from the dominant culture and other groups (Orbe, 1996). Although the differences between co-cultures might not be as great as those between national cultures, co-cultures can have a major influence on perception, behavior, and communication. If organizational members are unaware of the ways that co-cultural variation may affect communication, then conflict that inhibits organizational goals may result. Organizational communication can become particularly problematic if organizational members erroneously assume that all people who live a particular nation and speak the same language have the same values, expectations, and meanings. Even within organizational cultures, co-cultures exist based on outside cultural affiliations, or the subcultures of the organizational culture itself, such as departments and/or networks. Furthermore, individuals within a particular culture may choose to act in ways that contrast with the cultural prescriptions for behavior (Gudykunst & Lee, 2001).

Many contemporary training models attempt to teach appropriate behavior for conducting business in specific cultures. Fontaine (1991) claimed that most organizations miss the distinction between cross-cultural training (training in how other cultures do business) and intercultural training (training in how to do business with other cultures). He further suggested that both forms of training have their limitations. Cross-cultural training leads organizational members to attempt to behave "their way." Intercultural training leads organizational members to attempt to compromise, behaving a little "their way" and a little "our way." He said that the problem with either of these approaches is that whether one attempts to accommodate or compromise, it is not feasible or perhaps even possible to learn in a 1-day or 1-week training program what it takes members of specific cultures a lifetime to learn.

Approaches that attempt to teach organizational members the rules for appropriate conduct in regard to particular cultures are referred to as normative approaches. Normative approaches also have been criticized for inadvertently increasing tension between people by perpetuating stereotypes that focus on differences rather than commonalities (Kerston, 1996; Sowell, 1993). Armstrong and Bauman (1993) suggested that normative approaches also contradict mathematical models of cognitive processing and sociolinguistic theory. They said, "it is more productive to look at communication as a process in which social identities are negotiated rather than seeing communication as following a fixed set of norms and rules" (p. 82). Because cultural affiliation is a form of social identity, it is also negotiated rather than fixed. Because they are designed to accommodate cultural change and variation, 3D models provide a way to address cultural processes as negotiable rather than fixed.

The Dialogue Model

The first example of a 3D model is called the Dialogue Model. It may be linked to the Dialogue Approach of Storti (1994) and the Narrative Paradigm (Fisher 1978, 1984). Dialogues are small communication sequences in which there is some type of misunderstanding occurring that can be used in intercultural communication training for role playing and demonstration (Storti, 1994). The Narrative Paradigm is based on the assumption that *Homo Sapiens* should be renamed *Homo narrativis*, storytellers, as humans are first and foremost storytelling creatures (Fisher, 1978). Fisher (1984) said that narratives are meaningful for persons in particular and in general, across communities as well as cultures, across time and place. According to MacIntyre (1981), "Narratives enable us to understand the actions of others because we all live out narratives in our lives and because we understand our own lives in terms of narratives" (p. 197).

Collective stories in organizations form a shared consciousness or what Durkheim (1953) referred to as "the group mind." Collective stories have been used for describing organizational culture (Kramer & Berman, 2001), to change consciousness about the issue of sexual harassment in organizations (Clair, Chapman, & Kunkel, 1996), and in other organizational change efforts (Barnett, 1988).

Gudykunst and Kim (1992) conceptualized effective intercultural communication as the extent that one is able to minimize misunderstandings. The dialogue technique attempts to minimize misunderstandings by making them the focus of the training. Cultural and co-cultural misunderstandings are defined as any incident in which communication with another person led one to feel that the other person is ignorant of the person's or group's point of view or perspective. Cultural misunderstandings may occur when people are communicating with someone of a different race, ethnicity, gender, sexual orientation, age, class, religion, occupation, physical ability, geographical origin, or any other group affiliation. The narratives are used to generate dialogues; the dialogues are constructed to teach training participants the types of misunderstandings that occur and how they may be prevented. They are used for role playing exercises and to generate discussions about the cultural patterns and stereotypes that may exist within the organization.

The Dialogue Model was used in intercultural communication and diversity training sessions conducted at a university in the southwestern United States (Becker, Pirie, & Johnson, 1996). The trainings resulted in 356 narratives about co-cultural misunderstandings being generated. The trainings began with the participants sharing their own cultural and co-cultural affiliations. Next, participants were asked to write narratives about misunderstandings with members of other cultures or co-cultures. Then the narratives were translated into dialogues by the participants. The narrative-to-dialogue phase has also been used successfully in several different intercultural communication and diversity-training contexts where the trainer does the translation (Pirie, 1995). In either instance, the approach is dynamic in that the model allows the cultural themes to emerge from the organizational members themselves rather than having them imposed on the group based on one or more sets of pre-established cultural norms. The model provides a way for relevant co-cultural differences to be identified and then shape the agenda for the training sessions.

Here is an example of a dialogue generated by one of the participants, who changed the names of the parties involved:

Please Make the Salsa (Setting: The Office)

Lorraine: Anna, could you make me some of your fabulous salsa, some of my sisters are coming over for dinner on Sunday night and I would love to be able to turn them on to it.

Anna:	Yes, I am planning on making some tomorrow night.
Sue:	By the way Lorraine, what time should I come over to your house on Sunday?
Lorraine:	Seven.
Anna:	*(Hurt and confused because she was asked to share her salsa, Anna heard Lorraine say she was making dinner for her sisters, wasn't invited to the dinner and then overheard Sue ask what time the she should arrive at Lorraine's.)* I thought you said your sisters were coming over?

Analysis: The confusion here comes from the use of the word sisters. To Anna, who is a married Latina, the word "sisters" is used only for immediate siblings. Anna felt excluded and suspected that it might be because she was married or Latina that she wasn't invited. For Lorraine and Sue, who are gay, the word "sisters" describes their support group comprised of other politically active and socially interdependent lesbians.

A dialogue such as the one above may lead to a discussion of co-cultures and the problems that can result from the assumption that all members of the organization are using similar rules and codes. Dialogues have the potential to open up an unlimited realm of possibilities for exploring cultural patterns and assumptions. They are dynamic in that the cultures and types of misunderstandings that exist in the organization emerge from the narratives themselves rather than from normative templates.

The initial narratives that students told about their cultural affiliations encouraged them to begin to analyze ways that their diverse backgrounds shape their worldview and, subsequently, the ways in which they communicate. Although some students reported being completely unaware of any cultural influences in their lives, others shared their experiences in foreign countries or in traditional ethnic households. These narratives enabled students to establish or confirm their cultural affiliations. They then collected (via interviews with other students and members of the university community) and shared narratives about cultural or co-cultural misunderstandings. The narrative to dialogue phase of the process encouraged them to analyze the potential complexity of inter- or intracultural communication.

Storti (1994) stated that for a dialogue to be successful the following four ingredients must be included:

1. The conversation must sound natural.
2. The difference or mistake must not be obvious.
3. The mistake must not be a result of some esoteric knowledge unfamiliar to the average reader.

4. The conversation should contain clues to the problem (which become apparent when the co-cultural differences are pointed out).

Although many of the dialogues that the students prepared included these four ingredients, many did not. Some of these were missing the third and fourth ingredients due to the fact that the "average" reader was quite unfamiliar with the way that codes and rules may operate in other cultures or groups. This limitation may be overcome by discussing relevant cultural or co-cultural behaviors after the narratives are collected and the groups are identified. This would allow for even the narratives and the dialogues that do not meet Stori's criteria to be heuristically useful, as they still have the potential to expand organizational members' awareness about other cultures and interpretations of behaviors.

The 3C Model

The 3D model discussed here has also been influenced by the Narrative Paradigm. Like the previous model, the 3C model also provides trainers with a way to customize the training sessions based on the needs of a specific organizational culture. The first two sessions of the training are the same as the sessions in the Dialogue Technique in that they begin by having participants discuss their cultural affiliations and share narratives about co-cultural misunderstandings. However, once the narratives are collected, instead of generating dialogues, the trainer chooses a team to code the narratives into categories. The teams, which may be comprised of two or more of the participants, are taught the definitions of the following categories: close calls, clashes, and crashes.

Close calls (misunderstandings) are instances of communication in which the participants attempt to communicate but talk past one another. Communicators describe these interactions as frustrating and requiring a great deal of effort. These interactions are identified by comments such as, "Something didn't go quite right, but I couldn't put my finger on what it was." Close calls usually are usually resolved after the participants are provided relevant cultural information.

Clashes (collisions) are what Barnland (1994) described as a collision, a circumstance in which rules relating to communication conduct (topical appropriateness, customs regulating physical contact, the use of time and space, or strategies for managing conflict) collide with one another. Communicators frequently describe these interactions as causing them to feel that the "other" was "rude," "out of it," or "lacking in manners." Clashes may indicate that the participants in the misunderstanding could be lacking relevant cultural information and/or could benefit by using conflict management techniques.

Crashes (discrimination) are a more serious form of collision in that the behavior of one or more of the participants may be so severe that there could be legal implications. These interactions, whether a result of misunderstandings, cultural difference, or prejudice, can be legally classified as racism or sexism. In these instances, assumptions about the "other" strain the communication severely enough that the situation often requires professional or legal intervention.

The narratives collected for the dialogue training discussed previously were used to test the model. Of the narratives, 178 were classified into one of the three categories by two coders with an agreement of 0.80. The coders seemed to have some difficulty making a distinction between close-calls and collisions (17 cases). This may be attributed to the difficulty in understanding the role culture may play in the misunderstandings and could indicate a need for the further training that focuses specifically on intercultural communication, rather than discrimination or sexual harassment.

Cultural Mapping Model

The third 3D model presented has been influenced by Galileo Theory (Woelfel & Fink, 1980) and the symbols and meaning approach to organizational culture (Barnett, 1998; D'Andrade, 1984). The Cultural Mapping model assumes that culture emerges through communication. Therefore, as an organization's members interact, organizational culture is produced (Barnett, 1988). The way that any particular organizational culture is comprised may be due to the influence of national culture (Lee & Barnett, 1997; Lindsley, 1999), co-cultural affiliations or networks (Alba, 1978; Pirie & Becker, 1995), and/or organizational subcultures (Lont, 1990). Researchers have described the ways that discourse within organizations produces shared patterns and meanings among organizational members (Becker & Levitt, 1999; Becker, Levitt, & Moreman, 1998; Geertz, 1973; Pacanowsky & O'Donnell-Trujillo, 1983; Smircich & Calas, 1987). Organizational culture consists of learned-patterned systems of meaning, communicated through language, or other symbolic systems that have "representational, directive, and affective functions" that are capable of producing particular senses of reality (D'Andrade, 1984, p. 116). Cultural Mapping provides a method to empirically describe the organizational culture and the relationships between the various co-cultures within the organization.

The Cultural Mapping model begins the same way as the two techniques previously discussed. But, rather than translate the narratives into dialogues or code them into categories, the narratives are content-analyzed in order to identify core concepts. Core concepts are the symbols that represent an organization's culture. Core concepts have been used to analyze organizational communication in the Maquiladoras—American-owned assembly plants in Mexico (Lindsley, 1999), in international banks (Lee & Barnett, 1997), and in educational institutions (Becker & Easely, 1993).

The narratives used to test the models discussed in the previous sections were content analyzed for core symbols using CATPAC, a self-organizing artificial neural network that has been optimized for reading text. As a self-organizing artificial neural network, CATPAC attempts to approximate the processes that go on in neurological and cultural systems, in which meanings are recognized as a result of patterns of activation rather than as stored symbolic information. CATPAC uses cluster analysis to identify the most important words in a text and determines their patterns of similarity based on their associations in the text (Doerfel & Barnett, 1996). From this information, it is able to identify the core concepts in the text (Woelfel, 1990, 1993). Armstrong and Bauman (1993) discussed the ways that artificial neural networks may be used in intercultural communication training to generate probabilistic inferences on the basis of incomplete input information while being flexible in novel situations. Woelfel (1993) showed how artificial neural networks such as CATPAC may useful for solving problems with incomplete, partial or contradictory inputs, which is frequently the case in intercultural interactions.

Content analysis of the 178 narratives about cultural misunderstandings that were used to test the previous two models revealed the following core concepts: males (93), Whites (53), women (51), parents (47), Hispanics (39), Mexican Americans (38), Blacks (24). Cluster analysis revealed that the following terms co-occurred frequently: "White male," "mother father," "Mexican American," "Hispanic female," "man woman," "Black guy," and "Spanish culture." The concepts provide the starting place for discussions related to perceptions and assumptions about members of these co-cultural groups. They reveal that in addition to the expected co-cultural differences between the Anglo and the Latino cultures, it may also be important to look at co-cultural communication between students and their parents, across gender, and at the intersection of race and gender. It might also be useful to discuss perceived similarities and differences between "Mexican American" and "Spanish culture." For example, does "Spanish culture" refer to a linguistic community or colonial conception? What are the implications of the term *Mexican American* being used rather than *Chicano*, a term most likely to be used among more politicized students?

Perhaps the largest limitation of each of the models discussed so far is that they tend to focus on misunderstandings, rather than the tasks that need to be accomplished to fulfill the organization's mission. Therefore, an organizational trainer may want to modify the training sessions to focus on the *relationship* between a particular task or the overall mission of the organization, and the co-cultural groups, rather than misunderstandings. This could be achieved by initiating the session with a discussion of co-cultural affiliations and perceptions about the co-cultural affiliations of others and the ways that they might relate to a specific task or the organization's mission. The narratives generated from these discussions could then be analyzed using CATPAC to produce cultural maps that could be used to illustrate the ways that the various co-cultures within the organization and organizational culture might be related.

Cultural maps are generated by attributing a distance to the relationship between each of the core symbols. Each of the core symbols is compared to the others and an arbitrarily set criterion pair. For example, participants might be asked, "If white and grey are 100 units apart, how far apart are 'diversity' and 'the administration." Symbols that occur in close proximity to one another are given a lower number, and are assumed to be more similar. The average for each set of pairs for all participants combined is considered to represent the collective meanings of the symbol set. The averages are submitted to a multidimensional scaling algorithm from which a set of coordinate axes is produced. These coordinates are used to generate a map that represents the culture of the organization at a given point in time (Woefel & Fink, 1980).

In Fig. 4.1, a cultural map was generated using data collected at a private Catholic school that was attempting to adjust to a more diverse student population (Becker & Easley, 1993). The school administrators identified the emergence of two co-cultural groups among the student population due to recent demographic changes in the environment surrounding the area where the school was located. The groups that they were concerned about were a traditionally all "White" population and an increasing number of "Black" students. The mission of the organization was to effectively educate all of its students in an organizational cultural centered around Catholic values.

Other co-cultural groups that emerged from the analysis of the narratives included administrators, teachers, and people of color. The term, *this school* was used to replace the name of the school. The core concepts identified included "discipline," "self-expression," "cultural heritage," "cultural diversity," and "integration." The concepts "yourself" and "good" were included by the researchers to provide additional points of reference to indicate the average ways that individuals in the organization related to the core concepts and to assess the climate of the organization. The size of the circles represents the amount of variance in perceptions regarding each of the core concepts. For example, there is little disagreement about the meaning of the concept "White people," but there is a great degree in variance perceptions about the meaning of "people of color" and "Black people." This may be because groups in power tend to have a more "stable" or uncontested identity (Warren, 2001). Consequently, members of these groups tend to be less conscious of the privileges related to their group affiliation.

A trainer who is working in an organization with co-cultural dynamics similar to those at this school might attempt to find ways to get the Black students or parents more involved with the mission of the school, its discipline policies, and/or the administration. He or she might suggest that the administration and teacher populations be comprised of more Blacks or people of color. He or she might suggest that discipline policies be revised to accommodate cultural differences in self-expression because these data reveal that could be one of the problems. When using Cultural Mapping, the process can be repeated to measure the motion of the symbols that may result from additional communication (Barnett, 1988; Woelfel & Fink, 1980). Therefore, cultural maps such as the

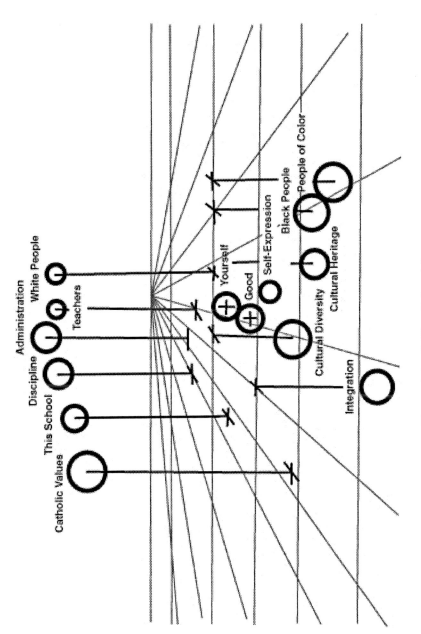

Figure 4.1   Galileo Cultural Space

one presented in Fig. 4.1 not only provide data to drive the training, they also provide a way to assess the training's effectiveness.

International Microcultures Combined with Cultural Mapping

The final 3D approach is a combination of the Cultural Mapping model with what Fontaine (1991) referred to as International Microcultures (IMCs). The IMC model can be linked to Systems Theory because it focuses on the relationship between the environment and the task at hand, rather than any particular culture. The training begins by establishing IMCs within the organization. IMCs are "shared ways of doing business based on the ecology of the tasks that must be completed" (Fontaine, 1991, p. 53). The ecology is comprised of the various systems in which the task takes place such as the cultural, social, and physical environment. It also considers relevant subsystems. For example, the biology of the organizational members would become relevant if they had jet lag or the economic constraints of a department's or project's budget might need to be examined if economic concerns were inhibiting decision making or the implementation of necessary procedures. Within IMCs, organizational members are encouraged to behave in ways that may be different from their normal way of doing things but that are appropriate for the ecology of specific tasks.

Fontaine (1991) provided an example of an IMC that developed in a multicultural classroom within an educational organization in Hawaii. Hawaiian educational organizations are comprised of diverse cultural influences such as Asian, caucasian, and Pacific Islander, all of which have many co-cultural variations. Additionally, variables of gender, class, religion, and political affiliation may also influence the organizational culture. In Fontaine's example, the task is to help all students in multicultural classrooms learn material despite their different expectations and preferences regarding teaching/learning styles:

> Caucasians often expect and prefer a teaching style which allows for direct teacher-student interaction with questioning and discussion and they tend to get bored with more formal lecture-only formats; Asians and Pacific Islanders on the other hand, tend to expect and prefer the lecture format and are uncomfortable and often withdrawn with direct teacher-student interaction in front of the class. (p. 56)

He pointed out that a teacher may be competent in one of these styles and not the other, thereby making it difficult to accommodate some of the students in the class, even if both styles are attempted. What emerges from an IMC is a style that may not be the expected or preferred style of any of the students or the teacher, but nevertheless is appropriate for the ecology of the task of teaching the information in a multicultural classroom. Fontaine broke the students into several small groups, offers mini-lectures, provided the groups opportunities to discuss the material within their groups, and physically moved from group to group to answer questions and provide examples. This creates an IMC in the classroom that allows the Asian and Pacific Islander students to receive some formal lectures, discuss the material in less threatening contexts, and ask the professor questions in front of a few students with whom they have become acquainted, rather than the entire class. Fontaine said that although this method is not unique in educational organizations, it is not likely the expected or the originally preferred style of any of the co-cultural groups in the class. However, it is a successful example of an IMC adapted to the ecology of a task.

Other types of organizations that are attempting to optimize co-cultural dynamics may also generate IMCs that are appropriate to specific tasks. Although some combination of "Their way" and "Our way" may still be appropriate, what is different about IMCs is that the focus is on the *relationship* between the task at hand and the ways that various co-cultural norms may help or hinder the success of accomplishing it (or the organizational mission). IMC training techniques consist of developing an awareness of the task, relevant ecological characteristics, alternative strategies, a selected strategy, and evaluation (Fontaine, 1991).

One limitation that Fontaine discussed is that generating an IMC may be difficult if the facilitator has difficulty being psychologically present or sensitive to the immediate ecological environment. Another possible limitation is that even within IMCs, intercultural misunderstandings are likely to occur unless diverse cultural interpretations of the task at hand and expectations are made explicit. However, these limitations may be reduced through the appropriate selection of facilitators and additional specialized training (Fontaine, 1989; Gudykundst & Hammer, 1984), which may include social skill development (Furhman & Bochner, 1986), improvement of communication skills (Singer, 1987), stress management skills (Barna, 1983), and the increased ability to empathize (Brislin, 1981). Limitations may be further reduced if the IMC model is combined with the Cultural Mapping model. This would involve replacing questions that illicit narratives about cultural misunderstandings with questions that illicit narratives about the ways that co-cultural communication relates to the fulfillment of the organization's mission. *"Given the mission to do A at Organization B, how does communication between members of co-cultures $C_{1,2,3...n}$ in Organization B assist or inhibit Mission A's success?"*

It is important that the trainer does not assume that he or she knows which co-cultures may be relevant to the discussion. Instead, participants are provided with a definition of co-culture and are then asked to discuss any co-cultural affiliations they have that may be relevant to access progress toward a specific organizational mission. The narratives that are generated from this prompt may provide useful information, not only about the co-cultural perceptions and orientations toward a specific mission, but also about co-cultural communication dynamics and diversity within the organization.

For example, diversity was examined at the University of Hawaii, Hilo (UHH), a campus designated as the most diverse public institution in the United States (*U.S. News* and *World Report*, 2002). The mission document of UHH includes the following statement, "Providing an environment that is responsive to the needs of a diverse student population is central to the UHH philosophy." In 2002, 24 faculty members (15% of the UHH faculty) and 78 students (3% of the student population) were read this mission in face-to-face interviews and then asked to discuss what this statement meant to them, reflect on how well the university was succeeding, share stories that illustrated their perspective, and describe any relevant co-cultural affiliations. Each of the interviews lasted approximately 50 minutes and the transcribed text was used to generate maps of the culture of diversity at UHH and identify key groups and issues. Maps for each of the relevant groups' responses were also generated; this included "professors," "students," "Japanese," "Hawaiians," and "Caucasians" (often called *haoles* in Hawaiian). Maps were also generated for Filipino students, because even though they were not identified as a primary group, they are the most underrepresented ethnic group at UHH (-13.22% proportionate to Hawaii county's population).

The maps were generated by transcribing all of the interviews, assigning a neuron to each major word in the text and running the scanning window through the text. The neuron representing a word becomes active when that word appears in window. As in the human brain, the connections between neurons that are simultaneously active are strengthened. The pattern of connections among the neurons forms a representation of the associations among words in the text. The pattern of connections is a complete paired similarities matrix, allowing for statistical analysis (Woelfel, 1998).

It is beyond the scope of this chapter to analyze all of the maps generated, however, the co-cultural map of UHH faculty (see Fig. 4.2) demonstrates the potential of the procedure. The faculty co-cultural map indicates that these faculty members think of diversity primarily in terms of ethnic and cultural diversity. For example, there is no mention of gender, physical ability, or sexual preference issues. Therefore, it may be useful for diversity training to include a discussion of the invisibility or absence of some groups and explore possible reasons and implications.

The map demonstrates that concepts that organizational members may relate to diversity may be different than prespecified categories. For example, many studies provide a category for ethnicity called Asian/Pacific Islander. Yet at UHH these categories contain meaningful co-culture distinctions within them such as Japanese and Hawaiian. In Hawaii, co-cultural affiliations such as Chinese, Japanese, Samoan, Portuguese, and Filipino all carry different meanings. This map, within the category "caucasian," which is typically used by researchers to indicate the ethnicity of anyone descended from northern Europe, has two referents, "caucasian" and haole. More research is needed to see if they

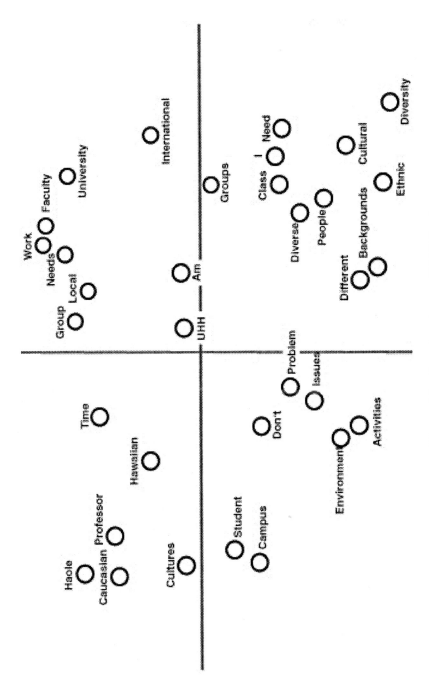

Figure 4.2 Co-cultural map of UHH faculty.

are used interchangeably or if the two terms indicate there are two different meanings attributed to the concepts. For example, some interviewees used the term *haole* with a negative connotation in stories that reflect conflict or frustration with the behavior of the *haole* co-cultural group. Some interviewees used the term along with caucasian to describe their ethnicity; these interviewees usually were not born or raised in Hawaii. Caucasian interviewees who were born or grew up in Hawaii described their primary co-cultural affiliation as "local"; interviewees who were other ethnic groups also used the term *local* to indicate they were born or raised in Hawaii.

The map also indicates that UHH faculty members are primarily caucasian or haole; this perception was verified by demographic data provided by the personnel office (71% of UHH faculty are described as caucasian; 32% of the students are described as caucasian). Furthermore, the map indicates the interviewed faculty members do not consider this a problem and associated the terms *Hawaiian, local, diverse*, and *international* with UHH. Maps such as this one can be used to initiate discussion and dialogue. It is important to remember that the maps are not conclusive or static but that may be used heuristically to generate dialogue regarding their interpretations and the implications these interpretations have for the organization and the co-cultures within it.

CONCLUSION

This chapter has shown several ways that 3D models may be incorporated into intercultural communication and diversity training in organizations. It has provided examples from previous attempts to implement and evaluate the models. It has also examined some of the potentials and limitations of the models and possible directions for future improvements. 3D models for intercultural communication and diversity training provide a method for trainers to use models that acknowledge that cultures and co-cultures are dynamic and changing and that they are comprised of individuals who have multiple identities and alliances. The chapter began by discussing the complexities related to the term *culture* and implications for intercultural communication and diversity training and research. It concludes by considering the limitations of the term *diversity* and the importance of acknowledging the dynamics power of relations when using the models.

Like the term *culture*, the term *diversity* has many possible definitions, all of which have implications for intercultural communication and diversity training and research. Models for intercultural and diversity training in organizations that are data-driven and dynamic do not assume that diversity is a fixed construct that does not change over time. Loden and Rosener (1991) identified two different levels of cultural diversity. They say that first-level identifiers tend to be more stable than second-level identifiers. First-level identifiers include more fixed variables such as age, ethnicity, gender, physical abilities or qualities, race, and sexual or affection orientation. Second-level identifiers include more changeable variables such as education, geographic influences, family status, military experience, religion, professional affiliations, and economic status. Both levels may contribute to an individual's identity, and may be relevant in interactions. However, Loden and Rosener suggested that individuals or groups whom may be oppressed based on identifiers of the first level, have a different type of experience than those whom are oppressed based on identifiers on the second level. Although both may influence communication, the degree to which they become central to group member's self-perception, identity, and subsequent interactions with members of other co-cultures may be less severe for those on the second level. Consequently, there may be implications for co-cultural communication dynamics within the organization that would not be considered if "diversity" is defined merely as "difference."

Orbe (1998) suggested that it is the groups who are on the top of the social hierarchy that determine the communication system. Consequently, groups that are not at the top of the social hierarchy may attempt to overcome communication constraints by devising strategies that allow them to "negotiate" for power. Orbe claims that the ways members of different co-cultures communicate is influenced by the intersection between their preferred outcome for the interaction and the communication approach that is utilized. He referred to the intersection between preference and approach as co-cultural orientation and identifies different communication strategies that could confound intercultural communication or training attempts if a trainer is not aware of how co-cultural orientation and its relation to power dynamics may influence communication. For example, some groups prefer separation rather than assimilation (merging identity). Orbe claimed that when this is a case, communication behaviors may be enacted to maintain barriers, strengthen stereotypes, or even attack or sabotage co-cultural communication efforts. Consequently, it may be necessary to consider the influence of co-cultural orientation and its influence on communication. Issues of power may need to be explicitly addressed.

One way to initiate a discussion of power dynamics would be to include the term *power* as a construct to be measured when using paired comparison technique for generating cultural maps. Including power as a construct to be described via the cultural mapping method may allow potential power dynamics and influences to be assessed and measured over time. This may also provide information necessary for organizational restructuring efforts designed to distribute information and power more equally throughout the organization.

Diversity management requires assessing and often changing an organization's core culture (Brown, Snedeker, & Sykes, 1997). Because they are dynamic and data-driven, 3D intercultural training models do offer intercultural communication trainers a way to address cultural variation, change, and power dynamics without prescribing specific behaviors for successful interactions with members of specific cultures based on preconceived notions of how members of different cultures behave. Instead, 3D approaches provide trainers a way to adapt intercultural communication training to the needs of specific cultures, co-cultures, organizational cultures, and tasks. As organizations are increasingly asked to evaluate the effectiveness of the culture of the organization in terms of diversity, programs, procedures, and processes, 3D approaches may be usefully implemented in organizations that need to use evidence to account for changing or maintaining organizational practices. These models may assist in this effort by producing empirical data that can be used for assessment and continual improvement.

REFERENCES

Alba, R. (1978). Ethnic networks and tolerant attitudes. *Public Opinion Quarterly, 42*(1), 1-16.

Armstrong, G.B., & Bauman, I. (1993). A mathematical model for intercultural interactions: Making connections and increasing harmony. *Journal of Communication, 43*(1), 81-101.

Barna, L.M. (1983). The stress factor in intercultural relations. In D. Landis & R.W. Brislin (Eds.), *Handbook of intercultural training* (Vol. 2, pp. 19-49). New York: Pergamon.

Barnett, G.A. (1988). Communication and organizational culture. In G.M. Goldhaber & G.A. Barnett (Eds.), *Handbook of organizational communication* (pp. 101-130). Norwood, NJ: Ablex.

Becker, C., & Levitt, S. (1999). Women in organizations: Perceptions of power. In P. Salem (Ed.), *Organizational communication and change* (pp. 273-288). Cresskill, NJ: Hampton Press.

Becker, C., Levitt, S., & Moreman, S. (1998). Computers, new information and communication technologies and the status of women in organizations. In G. Barnett & L. Thayer (Eds.), *Organization-communication: Emerging perspectives* (Vol. 6, pp. 117-139). Norwood, NJ: Ablex.

Becker, C., Pirie, B., & Johnson, P. (1996). A narrative approach to successful intercultural navigation. Training session at the Society for Intercultural Education, Training, and Research, Munich, Germany.

Becker, C.B., & Easely, B.A. (1993). Applied communication education: A participatory model. *ERIC Data Base*. Bloomington: Indiana University.

Brinkman, H. (1997). Managing diversity: A review of recommendations for success. In C. Brown, C. Snedeker, & B. Sykes (Eds.), *Conflict and diversity* (pp. 35-50). Cresskill, NJ: Hampton Press.

Brislin, R.W. (1981). *Cross-cultural encounters: Face-to-face interaction.* New York: Pergamon.

Brown, C., Snedeker, C., & Sykes, B. (1997). Defining diversity. In C. Brown, C. Snedeker, & B. Sykes (Eds.), *Conflict and diversity* (pp. 5-15). Cresskill, NJ: Hampton Press.

Chung, W. (1997). Auditing the organizational culture for diversity: A conceptual framework. In C. Brown, C. Snedeker, & B. Sykes (Eds.), *Conflict and diversity* (pp. 63-83). Cresskill, NJ: Hampton Press.

Clair, R.P., Chapman, P.A., & Kunkel, A.W.(1996). Narrative approaches to raising consciousness about sexual harassment: From research to pedagogy and back again. *Journal of Applied Communication Research, 24*(4), 241-249.

D'Andrade, R.G. (1984). Cultural meaning systems. In R. A. Shweder & R.A. LeVine (Eds.), *Cultural theory: Essays on mind, self, and emotion* (pp. 88-119). Cambridge, UK: Cambridge University Press.

Doerfel, M., & Barnett, G.A. (1996). The use of CATPAC for text analysis. *Cultural Anthropology Methods, 8*, 4-7.

Durkheim, E. (1953). *Sociology of philosophy.* Glencoe, IL: The Free Press.

Fisher, W. (1978). Toward a logic of good reasons. *Quarterly Journal of Speech, 64,* 367-384.

Fisher, W. (1984) Narration as human communication paradigm: The case of public moral argument. *Communication Monographs, 51,* 1-22.

Fontaine, G. (1989). *Managing international assignments: The strategy for success.* Englewood Cliffs, NJ: Prentice-Hall.

Fontaine, G. (1991). Managing intercultural effectiveness. *Australian Journal of Communication, 18*(1), 52-66.

Furhman, A., & Bochner, S. (1986). *Culture shock: Psychological reactions to unfamiliar environments.* New York: Methuen.

Geertz, C. (1973). *The interpretation of cultures.* New York: Basic Books.

Gudykunst, W., & Lee, C. (2001). An agenda for studying ethnicity and family communication. *The Journal of Family Communication, 1*(1), 75-85.

Gudykunst, W., & Kim, Y. (1992). *Communicating with strangers: An approach to intercultural communication* (rev. ed.). New York: McGraw-Hill.

Gudykundst, W.B., & Hammer, M.R. (1984). Dimensions of intercultural effectiveness: Culture specific or culture general? *International Journal of Intercultural Relations, 8*(1), 1-10.

Hall, E.T. (1959). *The silent language.* New York: Doubleday.

Kerston, K. (1996, March 11). *The myth of diversity.* Report on All Things Considered, National Public Radio.

Kramer, M., & Berman, J. (2001). Making sense of a university's culture: An examination of undergraduate students' stories. *Southern Communication Journal, 66,* 297-311.

Lee, M., & Barnett, G.A. (1997). A symbols-and-meaning approach to the organizational cultures of banks in the United States, Japan, and Taiwan. *Communication Research, 24(4)*, 394-412.

Lindsley, S.L. (1999). Communication and "The Mexican Way": Stability and trust as core symbols in Maquiladoras. *Western Journal of Communication, 63(1),* 1-31.

Loden, M., & Rosener, J.B. (1991). *Workforce American! Managing employee diversity as a vital resource.* Homewood, IL: Business One Irwin.

Lont, C.M. (1990). Persistence of subcultural organizations: An analysis surrounding the process of subcultural change. *Communication Quarterly, 38(1),* 1-12.

MacIntrye, A. (1981). *After virtue: A study in moral theory.* Notre Dame, IN: University of Notre Dame Press.

Moon, D.G. (1996). Concepts of "culture": Implications for intercultural communication research. *Communication Quarterly, 44*(1), 70-84.

Orbe, M.P. (1996). Laying the foundation for co-cultural theory: An inductive approach to studying "non-dominant" communication strategies and the factors that influence them. *Communication Studies, 47*, 157-176.

Orbe, M.P. (1998). *Constructing co-cultural theory: An explication of culture, power, and communication.* Thousand Oaks, CA: Sage.

Pacanowsky, J., & O'Donnell-Trujillo, N. (1983). Organizational communication as cultural performance. *Communication Monographs, 50*, 126-147.

Pirie, B. (1995, November). People recalling their stories: Local diversity, global connections, communication and culture in business. Training session at the second International Conference on Communication and Culture in the Workplace. Sydney, Australia.

Pirie, B., & Becker, C. (1995). *Dialogues between co-cultures in the United States.* Unpublished manuscript, Pirie Associates, Honolulu, HI.

Singer, M. (1987). *Intercultural communication: A perceptual approach.* Englewood Cliffs, NJ: Prentice-Hall.

Smircich, L., & Calas, M.B. (1987). Organizational culture: A critical assessment. In F.M. Jablin, L.L. Putnam, K.H. Roberts, & L.W. Porter (Eds.), *Handbook of organizational communication* (pp. 228-263). Newbury Park, CA: Sage.

Sowell, T. (1993). Multicultural instruction. *The American Spectator, 26*(4), 47-49.

Storti, C. (1994). *Cross-cultural dialogues: 74 brief encounters with cultural difference.* Yarmouth, ME: Intercultural Press.

U.S. News and World Report. (2002). January 23. www.usnews.com.

Warren, J. (2001). The social drama of a "Rice Burner": A (re)construction of whiteness. *Western Journal of Communication, 65*(2), 184-205.

Woelfel, J. (1990). The Catpac user's manual. In J. Woelfel (Ed.), *Principles of communication.* Buffalo: State University of New York at Buffalo, Department of Communication.

Woelfel, J. (1993). Artificial neural networks in policy research: A current assessment. *Journal of Communication, 43*(1), 63-80.

Woelfel, J. (1998). *Catpac II user's manual.* Ann Arbor, MI: The Galileo Company.

Woelfel, J., & Fink, E.L. (1980). *The Galileo system: A theory of social measurement and its application.* New York: Academic Press.

5

ONE MILLION INITIAL CONDITIONS

At-one-ment as Organizational Coherence

Renée Houston
University of Puget Sound

Mark Lawrence McPhail
Miami University

The emergence of systems thinking in science offers the opportunity to establish a coherent understanding of the relationship between human thought and action. Bohm's (1994) conceptualization of system incorporates both the individual and the institutional, the organism and the organization. That Bohm included organization in his conceptualization of systems is significant because it is through organizing systems that social relations and structures emerge. Furthermore, Bohm suggested that incoherent practices are sustained in systems by a reflexive commitment to necessity, *whereas coherence is made possible by the recognition of* contingency. *This notion of systems as sites of balance between necessity and contingency undergirds our critical intervention into the various logics at work in the social and symbolic systems that circumscribed the Million Man March. Drawing on the work of both Bohm (1994) and Maturana and Varela (1980), we examine how the Million Man March established a set of initial conditions that reveal the transformative potential of intercultural coherence. In this chapter we argue that the March represents a self-organized, autopoietic moment that redefines our understanding of agency and organization, of identity and action.*

The evolution of systems theories from von Bertalanffy's (1968) notion of systems as open which highlights the role of environment to Bohm's (1994) treatise on *Thought as a System* has opened important and provocative spaces for theoretical and critical interventions by communication theorists. The shift from simple to complex explanations of individual agency and institutional structures has established a theoretical trajectory that allows for a rethinking of communicative and organizing practice that exhibits emancipatory and transformative potential. This trajectory runs parallel to a move from correspondence to coherence, a paradigmatic expansion from positivist conceptualizations of phenomena as reflections of an essentially unchanging explicit reality to a constructivist orientation that emphasizes the self-organizational capacities of agencies and agents and their implicate ordering. The evolution of organizational communication theory and practice continues to be significantly influenced by this expanding conceptual universe, its reconstruction of epistemological boundaries, and the challenge it poses for our understanding of human symbolic and institutional action. Like the ancient Chinese symbol for change found in the I Ching, self-organizing systems theory represents danger and opportunity for our discipline; it promises to be both unsettling and exciting in its auguring of a future that may ultimately transform the way we think about organizing, communication, and the relationship between the two.

In particular, we are interested in exploring the intersection between communication and organizing in the context of intercultural communication. Although at first these worlds may seem too far apart to comment on, one important emphasis shared by contemporary intercultural and organizational communication scholars is the relationship between identity and diversity. Intercultural inquiry has long been concerned with how cultural differences influence the symbolic and social dimensions of defining ourselves and others, and organizational theorists are increasingly focusing attention on the complex ways in which identities are negotiated in corporate and institutional contexts. This focus on difference and identity is a relatively recent phenomenon, and has been accompanied by theoretical and methodological shifts of emphasis in both fields, from descriptive conceptualizations of culture and communication that assumed both to be transparent, to perspectives that emphasize the role of discourse in the creation and maintenance of organizations and institutions. Intercultural communication scholarship has expanded beyond its early social scientific emphases to include interpretive and critical theories and methods (Martin & Flores, 1998; Martin & Nakayama, 1999). Similarly, organizational communication appears to have experienced a "paradigm revolution": a shift from operationalist, to interpretive and critical approaches (Taylor, 1993). In both intercultural and organizational communication, the integration of new theoretical and methodological approaches along with the emphasis on identity and difference has led to a renewed appreciation of one the discipline's oldest and most foundational approaches to inquiry: the study of rhetoric.

Rhetorical approaches have enriched both intercultural and organizational scholarship through an emphasis on how both difference and identity are constructed in discourse. In intercultural scholarship, this is reflected in efforts to examine the cultural dimensions of identity and difference. As Martin and Flores (1998) wrote: "Rhetorical scholars, then, might seek to understand the rhetorical strategies used to mask or highlight culture. While they rely on particular tools in their analysis (e.g., identifying metaphors), the do not explicitly predict what they will find. Instead, they are likely to let the findings emerged from the data" (p. 12). Rhetorical approaches to intercultural communication consider how identity and difference are defined within cultural groups instead of examining differences between groups. In organizational communication, rhetorical approaches similarly focus on difference and identity, but also consider how groups interact with external audiences and constituencies as well. For example, Cheney (1991) described organizational rhetoric in terms of "the management of multiple identities, both individual and collective," and suggested that "[a]s a guiding concept, the management of multiple identities can be used to understand and evaluate all types of organizations and rhetorical situations" (p. 21). In both intercultural and organizational studies, then, rhetoric offers a powerful heuristic to understand the complex relationships between self, other, and the social and political contexts within which they are negotiated.

In this chapter we explore one of the opportunities offered by the notion of autopoietic and self-organizing systems theory by drawing on their underlying assumptions and principles to theorize a model of *organizational coherence,* or an alignment of thought and action. Based on Bohm's (1994) conceptualization of thought as a system, we further define organizational coherence as the capacity for achieving symmetry between institutional and attitudinal norms through the discursive alignment of thought and action. It is exemplified by the degree to which an organizing vision or set of values is realized in actual conditions and becomes the catalyst for self-productive and self-reflexive transformation. Using Bohm's (1994) and Maturana and Varela's (1980) systems thinking, we examine mediated interpretations of the Million Man March as an organizing event that also represents a site for intercultural dialogue. We expect our analysis will reveal how the March established a set of initial conditions to reveal the transformative potential of organizational coherence. Our bifocal exploration of the March juxtaposes first, its framing by dominant media with a second reading that illustrates how the March actually created a blurring of boundaries and a reinscription of agency. This second or "coherent" reading of the March resists and reconstructs mainstream attempts to constrain the event to a rendition confined by notions of linearity and correspondence.

The layout of the chapter is as follows: Initially we briefly consider the emergence of systems perspectives in communication theory and their articulation in other disciplines to establish a theoretical framework for analysis. Next, we juxtapose two readings of the March, the first based on notions of correspondence and the other on notions of coherence, to illustrate how the former conceals the intersections between thought and action that are revealed by the latter. Finally, we focus on the autopoietic character of the March as expressed by its participants, its role in reinscribing the dominant conception of difference, identity and diversity, and its potential to establish an alternative set of initial conditions for explicating the impact of gender, race, class, and classification in the establishment of individual and institutional identities. We offer a critical consideration of self-organizing systems theory in order to invigorate communication theory and practice, and to suggest that an understanding of organizations unfettered by mechanistic assumptions will enhance our ability to deal with the complexity of human symbolic and social action, and the transformative potential for unity it presents.

FROM LOGIC TO LOGICS: AUTOPOIESIS AS ORGANIZATIONAL PRACTICE

The emergence of systems thinking in organizational theory and practice has consistently reflected a need to establish a coherent understanding of the relationship between human and material resources. The classical model of organizational theory placed its primary emphasis on the material, which are the structures and functions of organizations, largely divorced from the subjective concerns of human agency. As a response to the classical model, a human relations school emerged that reversed its emphasis, establishing a binary relationship that privileged the individual over the institution. This reversal did little to account for the complex character of organization, and so gave way to a third perspective, what is alternately described in organizational theory as the "social systems" model, and in communication theory as the "human systems" perspective. The systems perspective attempted to account for both the classical school's emphasis on structure and function, and the human relations school's concern with people by assuming they were interrelated. Its "underlying logic" is reflected in the notion of interdependence, or that all parts interact to affect the whole, and that every action reverberates throughout the entire system. The systems school of thought in organizational theory, echoing the concerns of general systems theory (von Bertalanffy, 1968), emphasized change as an agent of stability and focused on the implicate orders of transformation, interdependence, and balance as key concepts for understanding and theorizing the character of organizational life.

These key concepts established a framework for viewing organizations as "open systems," which Buckley (1967) described as, "not simply that it (*the system*) engages in interchanges with the environment, but that this interchange is an essential factor underlying the system's viability" (p. 50, italics added). Katz and Kahn (1966) suggested that a boundary between the system and its environment serves to control the degree of system openness. Because it is open and is able to adapt and change in the face of environmental forces, an open system focuses on the maintenance of its equilibrium to ensure survival through the mechanism of homeostasis. This "steady state" maintains the ratio of energy exchanges as the system receives a continuous inflow of energy from the external environment and continuously exports its own products (Katz & Kahn, 1966). The steady state does not necessarily mean that the system does not change, rather it denotes that the system adapts or expands itself to incorporate environmental influences.

Because open systems are bounded by equilibrium change, its methodological approaches are constrained by deterministic notions (Contractor, 1994). The dissatisfaction with the results yielded by these causal analyses provides evidence for the need of a "methodological pluralist" approach. Pearce, Cronen, and Harris (1982) explained the implications of systems thinking on the methodological approaches in human communication theory as: "(1) a liberation from the limiting reductionist assumption; (2) direct focus on the structure of systems, per se, with the need to discover the logics by which they are organized; and (3) a reintroduction of causality as a topic for concern" (p. 27). These implications signal a move from the foundationist and externalist epistemological concerns of *correspondence* to the holistic and organic emphases of *coherence*. Varela (1987), whose work informs Pearce et al.'s (1982) articulation of human systems theory, explained the implications for a parallel move in the field of biology: "In moving from an adaptationist view to an understanding of evolution as natural drift, we have also moved from a logic of correspondence to a logic of coherence. We have left behind the view of mirroring nature in adaptive terms, for a situation of tinkering with whatever is at hand" (1987, p. 57).

This theoretical tinkering reframes our understanding of identity by juxtaposing a conceptualization of identity as inscribed by an external environment (a correspondent logic) against the idea of self as emergent, as "autopoietic" (a coherent logic). Varela explained:

> My sense of self exists because it gives me an interface with the world. I'm "me" for interactions, but my "I" doesn't substantially exist, in the sense that it can be localized anywhere. (p. 215)

Lacking localization, the self cannot be reduced to a simply biological or cognitive entity, but is seen as a "dynamic pattern" of interdependent, interrelated, and constantly changing "properties" or moments:

> An emergent property, which is produced by an underlying network, is a coherent condition that allows the system in which it exists to interface at that level—that is, with others selves or identities of the same kind. You can never say, "This property is here; it's in this component." In the case of autopoiesis, you can't say that life—the condition of being self produced— is in this molecule, or in the DNA, or in the cellular membrane, or in the protein. Life is in the configuration and the dynamical pattern, which is what embodies it as an emergent property. (pp. 215-216)

Varela introduced the term *autopoieses* (from the Greek for self-production) with Maturana in order to explain how system structure and identity is created and re-created. Jantsch (1980) aptly defined *autopoiesis* as the characteristic of living systems to continuously renew themselves and to regulate this process is such a way that the integrity of their structure is maintained. Through the process of autopoiesis, or self-production, meaning systems are continually self-reproducing in terms of processes from which they are created, not in terms of their relationship with an environment. That is, in order for a system to know itself as a system, it must establish a separate and closed loop of interaction. For this reason, self-producing systems are self-contained—everything necessary is already available to it. Although autopoietic systems are autonomous, there is an interdependence between the system and the environment therefore they are paradoxically "open" and "closed." They are open because they exchange energy within their environment, while at the same time they are closed to information and control because they create meaning through the process of self-reference. Self-reference represents knowledge accumulated by the system about itself that affects its own structure and operations (von Krogh & Roos, 1995). As a result, a property of circularity, or a reflexive loop is involved. This invokes both implicit and explicit relations to cybernetics theory that inquires into circular and recursive processes. More importantly, it invokes a focus on second-order cybernetics (Keeney, 1982; Mead, 1968; von Foerster, 1974, 1981), which as Steier (1992) stated involves, "the observer(s) and responsibilities emanating from any act of observation are reflexively made part of any system of description." Or, as Taylor (1995) noted, "The usual distinction between separating producer from product, and input from output, ceases to have any meaning, since the producer is a product of its own production and reproduction" (p. 8). In this autopoietic process, identity emerges as a re-creation of the dynamic boundaries between agency and the environment that functions to both sustain and subvert "an ontological separation between the self and the nonself, between sense and nonsense" (Christensen & Cheney, 1994, p. 228).

Although Taylor's type of "self-reflexivity" establishes the theoretical possibility of interrogating our "usual distinctions," we are not sure that such possibilities are necessarily translated into praxis. These distinctions are framed by what Bohm (1994) described as two levels of incoherence. The first level of incoherence is characterized by an unconscious acceptance of beliefs, that is, at one time we were aware of the beliefs, but just as once we learned to walk and then never took thought about it again, beliefs become so endemic to our social thought that when they are presented to us, we accept them sine qua non. The second level of incoherence emerges as a defense of the first. This occurs when the first level of incoherence becomes apparent to one's thought, but rather than move toward coherence, one defends the incoherence. So, for example if an individual finds out about communication practices that introduce the possibility of conflict—his or her reaction is to attack the credibility of the report and continue in his or her original course, rather than being self-*reflexive* about one's own thinking and practices. Bohm noted, "the basic sign of incoherence is that you're getting some result which you don't intend and don't want" (pp. 56-57). In other words, incoherence is felt. The oppositionality that occurs at the second level of incoherence is revealed as, "contradiction, and conflict and confusion. Coherence is sensed as harmony, order, beauty, goodness, truth, and all that everybody wants" (p. 60). The relationship between incoherence and coherence is not, however, one of mutually exclusivity: Each is always implicated in the other. The realization of coherence is seen in the capacity to integrate diverse perspectives, which is a reflexive move, and to articulate that integration in action, which is a *reconstructive* move. The process of autopoiesis, as well as self-reflexivity, in this sense not only creates conditions for the production and reproduction of a system, but also introduces the possibility of systemic transformation.

Bohm's (1994) conceptualization of system incorporates both the individual and the institutional, the organism and the organization. "A corporation is organized as a system—it has this department, that department, that department. They don't have any meaning separately; they can only function together. And also the body is a system. Society is a system in some sense. And so on. Similarly, thought is a system" (1994, p. 19). Bohm suggested that incoherence is sustained in systems by a reflexive (in the sense of physiologically reactive) commitment to *necessity*, whereas coherence is made possible by the recognition of *contingency*. Both are always at work in systems and implicated in each other. The possibility of achieving higher levels of coherence and lower levels of incoherence is, for Bohm, determined by one's ability to balance necessity and contingency, determination and agency. The "usual distinctions" that individuals embrace as necessary are thus seen as contingent, and their meanings do not cease to exist, but instead provide insight into the degrees of coherence that individuals might discern in the diverse logics at work in any system.

Bohm's notion of systems as sites of balance between necessity and contingency undergirds critical intervention into the various logics at work in the social and symbolic systems that circumscribed the Million Man March. Following Pearce et al., we assume that the "various logics of differentially complex systems not only mean that different systems can behave differently, but that the nature of the 'necessity' of their behavior is of different *kinds*" (p. 27). The "necessity" assumed by a logic of correspondence conceals a larger system of beliefs sustained in American culture that defines African-American identity in oppositional and contradictory terms. The necessity assumed by a logic of coherence, on the other hand, reveals the contingent character of this system of beliefs, and thus opens the possibility of transformation and reconciliation. By juxtaposing two readings of the March based on these alternative logics, we consider how the March itself represent an example of how organizational coherence evolves out of the incoherence of the larger system of beliefs and institutions that delimited the event. The March embodies "order out of chaos," and represents a spontaneous and self-organized, autopoietic moment that redefines the understanding of agency and organization, of identity and action.

NECESSITY, IDENTITY, AND
THE LOGIC OF CORRESPONDENCE:
THE CASE OF THE MILLION MAN MARCH

In light of the epistemological commitments of a logic of correspondence, reading the Million Man March demands an exploration of the principled and empirical "truths" that are privileged in the system of thought that circumscribes American beliefs about racial difference. Grounded in foundationist and externalist theories of knowledge, the logic of correspondence emphasizes self-evidence, linearity, and causality as explanatory mechanisms, and assumes the existence of essentially distinct identities and a referential reality. The consequences of these assumptions are revealed in the tensions and contradictions of American racial thought and practice, which on the one hand upholds the self-evident truths of equality and individual autonomy yet on the other results in inequitable social conditions and the determination of identity on the basis of hierarchy and separation. And yet the logic of correspondence cannot account for the incoherence of this system of beliefs, and essentially functions as a defense of this incoherence, or the second level of incoherence. This results in the definition of the March as a site of antagonism, an arena of racial struggle between separate and distinct identities and institutions.

This reading of the March reinscribes a number of our "usual distinctions": between leaders and followers, Blacks and Whites, men and women, integration and separation. The prevalence of these dichotomies in American racial thought need not be revisited here, but a consideration of their *necessity* is crucial to understanding the incoherence they create within our conceptual and social systems. Because these distinctions are viewed as necessary, the March becomes bounded by definitions of difference and identity that essentialize and naturalize these distinctions. As a result of this dichotomized thinking, the March can be reduced to one man, Louis Farrakhan, and its participants to static representations of "blackness," "maleness," and their corresponding connotations. Moss and Fields (1995) of *USA Today*, for example, described the March as an event that "puts focus on the problems of black men," and criticized its "organizer" as "controversial": "Louis Farrakhan, who conceived Monday's Million Man March, clearly touched a nerve in African American communities where there's a clamor to solve problems such as chronic poverty, joblessness, underemployment and crime" (p. 1). This reduction serves two purposes: First, it establishes the March as an act of oppositional protest as evidenced by its "leader," and second, it sustains the underlying assumptions of racial separation that juxtapose Black men against the White "system."

This inscription represents a systemic act of self-protection, a defense against the March's potential to expose the underlying incoherence of the American system of beliefs about race, and to reveal how essentialized notions of influence and identity conceal implicature. The American intention of equality, and the country's claim to want a "color blind society," which represent its foundational beliefs, are incongruent with the results that have been obtained, or, its external "realities." In different ways, both Farrakhan and the marchers reveal this tension between intention and result. Farrakhan, although ostensibly a vocal antagonist of the system, reflects the culture's unacknowledged ideological commitment to racial separation and hierarchy. The marchers, often defined by the system as the cause of its incoherence, are also refractions (created/produced by the system) of the material conditions created by the system, and not simply independent entities. Both embody in principle and practice the system's incoherence, its failure to translate intention into result. Although the marchers clearly manifest conditions for self-reflexivity, the logic of correspondence operating in the system observing it (i.e., the media) inscribes a second level of incoherence, or a defense of the current system, rather than an attempt at coherent unity. At its current level of inquiry, this incoherent system undermines the possibility of systemic transformation, essentializing Farrakhan and the marchers as "angry Black males."

Because of his ideological implicature, a correspondent reading of Farrakhan was easy. Many media reports of the March echoed *USA Today*'s criticisms and generalized these concerns to all of white America, "For black men, it was a day of celebration and solidarity," wrote Larry Downing (1995) in *Newsweek*. "But many whites were angered and baffled by Louis Farrakhan's star power. Was the march a step toward black self-help—or a step back to a more divided America?" (p. 28). One day before the March, *The Washington Post* expressed similar sentiments in its headline, "March's Direction: Unifying or Divisive?" Like *USA Today*, the *Post* focused on the event's relationship to Black men and Farrakhan's leadership. "With organizers predicting one of the largest demonstrations ever in the nation's capital, and law enforcement officers preparing for significant disruptions in the city's routine, the march already has focused widespread attention of the concerns of black men and on the event's controversial originator, Nation of Islam leader Louis Farrakhan" (Fletcher & Harris, 1995, p. 1). Another issue circumscribed by the media was the issue of March attendance. Both *USA Today* and the *Post* expressed doubt over whether or not the March would achieve its anticipated attendance.

Within these readings of the March we see the reductionistic and essentializing tendencies of a logic of correspondence which, although subtle, establish a set of boundaries that attempt to diminish the significance of the event. Questions concerning the effectiveness of the March, such as those expressed in *USA Today*'s assertion that "turnout in Washington and participation nation-wide remains in question" (p. A2), and the *Post*'s claim that "much about the event—including how many people will attend remained uncertain yesterday" (p. 1) implied that the event was unlikely to achieve its numerical goals as well as hinted that its ideological objectives might also be in question. The "final" count was estimated by the U.S. Park Police at 400,000 participants. Ironically, after the count was called into question by the Rev. Benjamin F. Chavis, Jr., the March director, the Park Police have instituted a policy of no longer counting crowds. The lack of agreement over the count, although unfortunate, it not as unfortunate as the policy of second-level incoherence that emerged as a result of the March.

The juxtaposition of the organizer's predictions with "law enforcement officers preparing for disruptions" similarly established a subtle opposition between Black men and the legal guardians of the system, anticipating the possibility of chaos interjecting itself into the social order. The binary boundaries of "unity" or "division" also limited the transformative possibilities of the March to the existing constraints that circumscribe racial thinking in America, the same constraints that ultimately implicate Farrakhan in the system he is purported to oppose.

If a logic of correspondence effectively essentialized Farrakhan in opposition to "the system," it failed to achieve a similar reification of African-American male identity. This is precisely because a logic of correspondence does not account for systemic transformations that cannot be traced to linear relationships or anticipated in expected outcomes. Farrakhan's input, although critical, did not define the character of the Million Man March, nor did it provide a representative anecdote for African-American male identity. Instead, he functioned like a strange attractor, a perturbation thought to be responsible for a system's movement from equilibrium to far-from-equilibrium conditions

(Crutchfield, Farmer, Packard, & Shaw, 1986)[1]. Farrakhan's role then served to establish *the potential* for a systemic recognition of implicature, and the possibility of a transformative reinscription of identity and identification. The anticipation of argumentative antagonism, violence, and disorder—of angry Black protest—associated with Farrakhan's leadership never materialized. Instead, the system—America—was given an opportunity, as Lacayo (1995) observed, "to think long and hard about itself" (p. 34).

Lacayo contended that the march was another reminder that race is the inescapable complication of American life. "The Million Man March altered the landscape," said Secretary of Housing and Urban Development Henry Cisneros (1995). "Americans know that things are profoundly wrong. The question now is where do we go from here?" (p. 34). Lacayo suggested that the March opened both a space for re-reading race in America, and an opportunity for the reinscribing of African-American male identity:

> For the black men who where there, it was also a moment of profound psychological vindication. In the most heated political and policy debates of recent years, black men have seen themselves cast sometimes openly, sometimes with a wink and a nod, as the welfare freeloader, the affirmative action hire, the low end of the bell curve, Willie Horton. Even worse than the stereotypes sometimes are the facts. For black men the average life expectancy is 65, eight years less than for white males. For young black men, the major cause of death is murder. Nearly one in every three black men between the age of 20 and 29 years of age is behind bars, on probation or on parole. (p. 34)

Lacayo here succinctly expressed the intuited and empirical "truths" of the American racial belief system and the boundaries of Black male identity that the system sustains. He also suggested that the African-American men who attended the March exposed the incoherence of this belief system. "For a day last week, all that was swept aside by the picture of black males urgently but peacefully demonstrating, in all senses of the word, their strength and capability. It was a mood that even Louis Farrakhan couldn't spoil" (p. 34). Indeed, it was a mood that might best be described as an *autopoietic moment,* not only for the system as a whole, but of those parts purportedly separated from and outside of it: African-American men. The moment they created represents a profoundly self-reflexive understanding of American racial thought and institutions, and opens the way for an enlarged understanding the possibilities offered by organizational coherence.

---

[1] See Svyantek and DeShon (1993) for a discussion of attractors in organizational systems.

CONTINGENCY IN ACTION:
THE LOGIC OF COHERENCE

Despite the attempts by critics and detractors of the Million Man March to bind the event to Louis Farrakhan and the American image of the angry Black male, we argue that the March exemplified the ability of African-American men to establish organizational coherence outside the constraints of traditionally defined institutions. This coherence was revealed not only in the actions of the Marchers, but also in the epistemological assumptions that undergirded those actions. The March exemplified a shift from dialectical to dialogic thought, a breaking out of the boundaries of essential difference that circumscribe American ideologies and institutions, and a rethinking of the possibilities of definition and identification. This shift was accomplished by embracing the very definitions of blackness and maleness that separated African-American men from "the system," revealing their contingency, and using them as the basis for self-reflection and transformation. It was a profound acknowledgment of implicature, a recognition that African-American men had helped to sustain the systemic incoherence of the culture that had defined them as "Others." They used the most powerful manifestation of that incoherence, violence, to establish a trajectory toward coherence.

We find that Bohm's conceptualization of coherence as a transformative epistemic stance is reflected in the self-reflective trajectory of the March, "people in a situation of hate and violence are in a situation connecting them with a lot of energy. And this can transform into another kind, which is friendship and fellowship and love," Bohm (1994) explained. "But that requires that we take this seriously and really sustain the work of communicating—of dialogue—if we are going to be able to do it together" (p. 226). This is precisely the transformation witnessed by the Million Man March, and for Bohm it cannot be reduced to individual agency, either in the form of leadership personal initiative. It is instead, a collective phenomenon that embraces difference and the diverse influences, both positive and negative, that establish our identities:

> Doing it together means that we're communicating, facing all these issues and whatever happens—persisting and sustaining the work even when it becomes difficult and unpleasant. The fact is that we are violent, we have all that. To imagine that we don't have it will be meaningless. So we have to say that we have it. And we have to stay with it. We perceive it. We need to perceive the real meaning of it, which is that we are bound together by this physical thing we call "violence." (p. 226)

Bohm's discussion of the possibilities of coherence almost appears to be an epistemological blueprint for the transformations realized by the Million Man March. African-American men were acutely aware of the ways in which their lives had been symbolically and socially inscribed with violence, and consciously chose to reinscribe this association through both words and deeds.

This reinscription took many forms, all of which were connected to intense self-reflection and evaluation. "It was a day of peace and spontaneous embraces, a day of reflection and self-examination, a day to pause and pray, a day to speak up and speak out against racism, a day for African American men to honor one another," observed Cottman (1995). "A day to remind ourselves that we're not alone" (p. 9). Cottman's account of the March illustrates the collective commitments to peace, inclusivity, and affirmation that bound the actual event, and silenced critics who anticipated a day of violence, exclusivity, and negativity. The diverse voices he chronicled echoed a common commitment to redefining Black male identity by accepting responsibility, rejecting violence, and embracing organized action. And although the event clearly had the political overtones of protest, its larger implications were bounded by spiritual and psychological transformation. "There is no denying that this was not a civil rights march. It was a march for spiritual renewal and psychic uplift," explained Michael Eric Dyson. "It was a cultural ritual of spiritual transformation, a rehabilitation of our image, a way of bonding together to support one another as we endure the pain of Black male existence" (cited in Cottman, 1995, p. 11).

The rehabilitation of the image of the African-American male involved challenging the system of thought that circumscribed both the larger society and the individuals who attended the March. "Society has been so conditioned that when people hear the word 'black' they think negative, so when people heard one million Black men were coming together, these people, who have been preprogrammed, thought negative—but they saw something positive," remarked March participant Tom Feelings (cited in Cottman, 1995, p. 11). Cottman expressed similar sentiments: "African-American men have reached a crossroads in American history where the constant barrage of negative images forced us to prove the skeptics wrong" (p. 24). Cottman explained that the March was not simply an oppositional event, but was a forum for self-reflection and transformation:

> We marched against stereotypes. We marched against a media that continues to portray Black men as criminals. We marched against conservative ideology that is anti-Black. We marched against angry white males who have concocted a myth that Black men are taking jobs away from them through affirmative action. We marched against the contract with America. We marched against Rush Limbaugh, Newt Gingrich, and Jesse Helms. We marched against *The Bell Curve*. We marched to silence the skeptics. But we also marched for ourselves. (p. 25)

Although the oppositional themes of the March were largely implicit in the words of the event's major speakers, the self-reflexive and transformative sentiments of the marchers were largely expressed by individuals. These sentiments were marked by reinscriptions of the image of Black men by participants who "were motivated by high moral purposes," Dyson explained. "To atone for our failures. To take greater responsibility for our own plight. To reconcile with Black women and one another in the fight for dignity and respect" (cited in Sadler, 1996, p. xii). Even in the service of oppositionality, "the fight for dignity and respect," the March focused on self-transformation and was inwardly directed.

This focus was translated into an expanding of the March's boundaries from an event led by Louis Farrakhan and the Nation of Islam to an act of spiritual redefinition. Both Farrakhan and the Nation of Islam were associated with various negative connotations also ascribed to African-American men: patriarchy, anti-White sentiments, homophobia, and so on. But for many of the marchers, these associations were overshadowed, and indeed overcome, by deeper spiritual commitments. "This March was about spiritual oneness for us as a people. Not since the civil rights movement had I witnessed such a sense of unity in the African American community. Christians, Jews, Muslims, and others were all in Washington for one reason," explained Neil James Bullock. "We were there to prove that African American men are not powerless in the country and that we are able to mobilize our collective awareness" (cited in Sadler, 1996, p. 26). In mobilizing that collective awareness, the divisive chasms of race and gender were sutured by a commitment to inclusivity. Seth W. Pickens noted that the "vast majority of women and Caucasians, however, were there to support the spirit of the March. Despite what 'we' think, showing up took a lot of courage on their part. We all tried to make them feel a part" (cited in Sadler, 1996, p. 34). In contrast to the patriarchal and racially exclusive frames that had been imposed on the March by its critics by insinuating these correspondences between the March and Farrakhan's Nation of Islam, the event itself reflected a more coherent and inclusive sense of identity. Cleo Manago recalls coming "upon a 'gay Black' contingency, decked with pink triangles, gay pride placards, and gay rainbow flag cutouts of the African continent. I noticed among them a smattering of White, apparently gay men." In contrast to the dominant depiction of black men as hostile to Whites and homosexuals, a much different sensibility was realized. Manago noted that "the legion of brothers in the vicinity were respectful. Not a harsh word was exchanged" (cited in Sadler, 1996, p. 75).

Indeed, the March was a complete rescripting of the "harsh words" that had been articulated in much contemporary African-American protest, especially that ascribed to Farrakhan and the Nation of Islam. "This March was not about Louis Farrakhan," commented Douglas S. Lee. "This March was not about the Nation of Islam. This March was about one million Black men and one unity" (cited in Sadler, 1996, p. 86). Even Farrakhan contributed significantly to this sensibility. "His usual harsh, cynical, and sometimes bitter words were different this time," recalled James Raymond Reid. "It seemed as though he put his own personal differences aside to deliver a message of peace, unity, and reconciliation for past mistakes, and for men to atone for those mistakes" (cited in Sadler, 1996, p. 122). In contrast to his usual oppositional stance, Farrakhan focused on the importance of self-reflection for the transformation of Black and White America. In calling for a commitment to organized action as a vehicle for social and political change, Farrakhan also established an agenda for this transformation to be realized. "We must become a totally organized people, and the way we can do that is to become a part of some organization that is working for the uplift of our people," he remarked in his speech of October 15, 1995. "Every one of you must go back and join a church, synagogue, temple or mosque that is teaching spiritual and moral uplift" (cited in Cottman, 1995, p. 76). Farrakhan here anticipated the possibility of *organizational coherence*, a possibility realized in what Cottman described as "random acts of blackness."

These acts occurred in the wake of the Million Man March in African-American communities across the nation. In Detroit, Michigan, "Black men jammed Fellowship Temple for a meeting several days after the March and signed up to adopt Black children and mentor teenagers after school." In Philadelphia, Pennsylvania, adult African-American men "spoke with young Black men about their responsibility as fathers and voters." In Indianapolis, Indiana, Charlotte, North Carolina, Long Island, New York, Washington DC, and Trenton, New Jersey, Black men created interfaith coalitions, spoke out against interracial violence, reminded young men of their ethical responsibilities as African Americans, and aided and supported African-American women. Although these random acts may appear to be incoherent, they can also be read as conscious acts of redefinition, reflections of "a burning desire on the part of African-American men to improve the image of how White America view us," and a self-reflexive realization of where transformative action is initiated. "Only we can heal our communities," Cottman concluded. "The answers to our problems are within us; within me, within you" (1995, p. 89). As Steier (1991) put it, "[second-order cybernetics] forces an observer to accept responsibility for his or her observations, descriptions and explanations" (p. 163). We find this move indicative of the self-reflexiveness necessary to develop coherent thought and practice.

CONCLUSION

Our bifocal reading of the March reveals the limitations and potential for two systems of thinking. In the first, our analysis reveals the reinscription of agency and identity in traditional American thinking about ethnicity. The "logic of correspondence" limits our ability to provide alternative explanations for the March based on anything other than race that serves to reinscribe traditional thinking based on ethnicity and perpetuates incoherent systems of race relations. From a systems standpoint, we operate in a closed system that fails to provide the opportunity to learn and grow beyond what we already recognize. The correspondent analysis thus exposes the underlying incoherence in our systems of thought concerning the cultural inscription of race, agency, and identity. On the other hand, our coherent reading of the March offers the opportunity to reflect on our position, recreate our identity and learn from self-reflection in order to improve intercultural communication and race relations. In our analysis, the "random acts of blackness" are an indication of the possibility for the reflexive healing of both communities and self to be successful. Furthermore, the Million Man March provides a powerful model for *organizational coherence*, the transformation of principle into practice born of self-reflexive action. This model suggests important implications for our understanding of organizational communication, because it illustrates the efficacy of reframing our understanding of organizations as discrete entities and communication as a linear process of persuasion and argumentation. It suggests equally important implications for our conceptualization of self-organizing systems theory, because it also indicates the possibility of understanding initial conditions not simply as derived from, but *as becoming* (see Prigogine, 1980). The March established a new set of initial conditions for the transformation of African-American male identity and American identity as well. This model of organizational coherence can be usefully applied to a challenge that today is faced by organizations in particular and society in general, a challenge successfully met by the Million Man March: the challenge of diversity.

ESTABLISHING ORGANIZATIONAL COHERENCE: LESSONS LEARNED FROM THE MILLION MAN MARCH

The challenge of diversity is one of the most important issues now facing contemporary organizational systems, from corporations to social and political institutions. Organizational theorists are acutely aware of the difficulties engendered by managing and valuing diversity in systems that have traditionally been defined by hierarchical relationships and static conceptions of identity. Often, diversity is reduced to issues of race or gender, without a corresponding recognition of its significance for resolving antagonism wedded to class, classification, and morality. This essentializing of diversity reflects a tendency of organizations to sustain incoherence and resist self-reflexivity. As Garmon (1996) suggested, "Corporate positions on issues of cultural, economic, and ethical significance are, perhaps, more clearly visible to the onlooker than the corporation itself" (p. 106). As a result, the need for some form of organizational coherence like that modeled by the Million Man March has become an important preoccupation of inquiries into the character of organizational structure, behavior, and communication.

DIVERSITY AND DIALOGUE

The value of diversity is indicative of Prigogine's (1980) research on "dissipative structures." Prigogine, a Nobel Prize-winning physicist, discovered that points at which discontinuities are exhibited actually indicate where system variables exhibit random behavior yet there is a pattern or order that emerges out of the chaos introduced by the discontinuiuty. When the disorder created by diversity and variation becomes a part of a system, it is said to be self-organizing. Steier (1992) aptly called these type of relations in social situations "cybernetics as mutualling," or a self-organizing process of joint inquiry emerging from what would initially appear to be "disorder." A variety of diverse interactions causes a "creative destruction" of individual inputs and thereby generates a coherent unity. This process of creative destruction emphasizes underlying, nonlinear processes that rely on diversity to produce a self-organized unity.

Senge's (1990) research, which draws on Bohm's work, suggests that coherence, as it is reflected in the practice of dialogue, is central to this inquiry. Following Bohm, Senge explained that dialogue occurs when "a group explores complex difficult issues from many points of view," and "suspend their assumptions but they communicate their assumptions freely" (p. 241). He also noted that dialogue creates spaces for self-reflexivity because it allows individuals "*to become observers of their own thinking*" (p. 242). It is important to note the distinction between this move towards a dialogic approach and consensus, which involves traditional notions of what is thought of as an acceptable outcome. Isaacs (1993) noted that the purpose of consensus is to seek some rational means of delimiting options and finding what the majority of people can live with. Essentially, consensus mutes the voices that need to be heard and gives the illusion of coherence, whereas dialogue holds promise for collective thinking and communication, not negotiation. Drawing the connection between Bohm's work and Senge's, one of the authors of this analysis has suggested the notion of "coherent dialogue" as a way "to establish a new model of interaction within organizations and society that will affirm the democratic impulses of symbolic action and interaction, and enrich the impoverished psyches and spirits of human actors struggling to find a balance between identity and community, self and other, and the one and the many" (McPhail, 1996, p. 232). These are the same struggles that motivated the Million Man March, and their translation into autopoietic practice in that arena provides important directions for organizational theory and practice in other domains.

Those possibilities will entail a rethinking and enlarging of the spaces that presently constrain our definitions of organizational and communicative practices that reflects a shift from the logic of correspondence to that of coherence. This shift invites an interrogation of the theoretical boundaries that circumscribe prevailing notions of autonomy and organizational complexity. It suggests that the seemingly chaotic social and symbolic terrain of difference and identity can be remapped, and that the incoherent resistance to change that undermines the possibility of individual autonomy and collective action can be transformed into a recognition of the implicate order that exists just below the surface of our epistemological and institutional systems. Organizational coherence, in the Million Man March and beyond, exemplifies the transformative possibilities of the process of autopoiesis, self-reflexivity of thought, and the reconstructive potential of dialogue. It leads us to the same question to which both proponents and opponents of the March were ultimately led: and *now what?* The answer to that question will be determined by our willingness to look inward, embrace a new vision of ourselves, and translate that vision into reality. This is the lesson of the Million Man March: that we can all benefit from the act of at-one-ment, regardless of whether it is defined as cultural, spiritual, or intellectual.

ACKNOWLEDGMENT

A previous version of this chapter was presented at the Alta Conference on Communication and Self-Organizing Systems Alta, Utah August 1997.

REFERENCES

Bohm, D. (1994). *Thought as a system.* New York: Routledge.

Buckley, W. (1967). *Sociology and modern systems theory.* Englewood Cliffs, NJ: Prentice-Hall.

Cheney, G. (1991). *Rhetoric in an organizational society: Managing multiple identities.* Columbia: University of South Carolina Press.

Christensen, L.T., & Cheney, G. (1994). Articulating identity in an organizational age. In S. A. Deetz (Ed.), *Communication yearbook 17* (pp. 222-235). Thousand Oaks, CA: Sage.

Contractor, N.S. (1994). Self-organizing systems perspective in organizational communication. In B. Kovacic (Ed.). *New perspectives in organizational communication.* Albany: State University of New York Press.

Cottman, M. (1995). *Million man march.* New York: Crown Trade Paperbacks.

Fletcher, M., & Harris, H. (1995, October 15). March's direction: Unifying or divisive? *The Washington Post,* pp. 1, A25.

Garmon, C. (1996). Expatriate/repatriate training: Corporate advocacy of interculturalism. In J. Hoover (Ed.), *Corporate advocacy: Rhetoric in the information age* (pp. 105-119). Westport, CT: Quorum Books.

Isaacs, W.J. (1993, Autumn). Taking flight: Dialogue, collective thinking, and organizational learning. *Organizational Dynamics*, 24-39.

Jantsch, E. (1980). *The self-organizing universe: Scientific and human implications of the emerging paradigm of evolution.* Ithaca, NY: Cornell University Press.

Katz, D., & Kahn, R.L. (1966). *The social psychology of organizations.* New York: Wiley.

Keeney, B. (1983). *Aesthetics of change.* New York: Guilford.

Lacayo, R. (1995, October 30). I too sing America. *Time,* pp. 34-36.

Martin, J.N., & Flores, L.A. (1998). Colloquy: Challenges in contemporary culture and communication research. *Human Communication Research, 25*(2), 293-299.

Martin, J.N., & Nakayama, T.K. (1999). Thinking dialectically about culture and communication. *Communication Theory, 9*(1), 1-25.

Maturana, H., & Varela, F. (1980). *Autopoiesis and cognition: The realization of the living.* Boston: D. Reidel.

McPhail, M. (1996). "Not worth the money I paid for it": Dialogue, diversity, and the rhetoric of organizational advocacy. In J. Hoover (Ed.), *Corporate advocacy: Rhetoric in the information age* (pp. 220-233). Westport, CT: Quorum Books.

Mead, M. (1968). Cybernetics of cybernetics. In H. von Foerster, J. D. White, L. J. Peterson, & J. K. Russell (Eds.), *Purposive systems: The first annual symposium of the American society for cybernetics.* New York: Spartan.

Moss, D., & Fields, G. (1995, October 13-15). Theme timely, but organizer is controversial. *USA Today,* pp. 1-2.

Pearce, W.B., Cronen, V.E., & Harris, L.M. (1982). Methodological considerations in building human communication theory. In F. E. X. Dance (Ed.), *Human communication theory: Comparative essays.*New York: Harper & Row.

Prigogine, I. (1980). *From being to becoming.* San Francisco, CA: Freeman.

Sadler, K.M. (Ed.). (1996). *Atonement: The million man march.* Cleveland, OH: Pilgrim Press.

Senge, P. (1990). *The fifth discipline: The art & practice of the learning organization.* New York: Doubleday/Currency.

Steier, F. (1991). *Research and reflexivity.* Newbury Park, CA: Sage.

Steier, F. (1992). Cybernetics as mutualing. *Cybernetics and Human Knowing, 1,* 2/3.

Svyantek, D.J., & DeShon, R.P. (1993, Fall). Organizational attractors: A chaos theory explanation of why cultural change efforts often fail. *Public Administration Quarterly,* 337-353.

Taylor, J.R. (1993). *Rethinking the theory of organizational communication: How to read an organization.* Norwood, NJ: Ablex.

Taylor, J.R. (1995). Shifting from a heterotonomous to an autonomous worldview of organizational communication: Communication theory on the cusp. *Communication Theory, 5*(1), 1-35.

Varela, F. (1987). Laying down a path in walking. In W. I. Thompson (Ed.), *Gaia, A way of knowing: Political implications of the new biology* (pp. 48-64). San Francisco: Lindisfarne Associates.

von Bertalanffy, L. (1968). *General system theory: Foundations, development, applications.* New York: George Braziller.

von Foerster, H. (1974). *Cybernetics of cybernetics or the control of control and the communication of communication.* Urbana: Biological Computer Laboratory, University of Illinois.

von Foerster, H. (1981). *Observing systems.* Seaside, CA: Intersystems Publications.

von Krogh, G., & Roos, J. (1995). *Organizational epistemology.* New York: St. Martin's Press.

SECTION C

**Focus on Mexican
Organizations**

6

POSSESSING A "SENSE OF COMMUNITY"

A Study of Employee Perceptions in Selected Work Organizations in Mexico

Héctor R. Díaz-Sáenz
*Instituto Tecnológico y de
Estudios Superiores de Monterrey*

Patricia D. Witherspoon
The University of Texas at El Paso

The importance of "family" and "community" are deeply embedded within the culture of Mexico. In turn, these societal values affect the organizational cultures in work organizations, including the creation and sustenance of community within those cultures.

This chapter reports the results of a study involving 22 focus groups in eleven companies within four Mexican cities. The purpose of the study was to assess employee perspectives on how community is created within their work organizations, and the role communication plays in that process. The chapter reviews relevant literature on the notion of community in general, the creation of community in the workplace more specifically, and the relationship between communication and community. The importance of community in Mexican culture, and the resultant emergence of community creation in work organizations are discussed, as are the research questions that guided the study, the research methods used to implement it, and the findings and conclusions that emerged from the study.

Organization and communication theories are situated in the historical eras in which their creators lived. As these theories bridged the 20th and 21st centuries, they illustrated evolving interests in finding a balance between meeting the goals of an organization and the goals of its individual members, of jointly pursuing organizational efficiency and individual development.

According to Pinchot (1998) and Seiling (1997), the type of organization appropriate for the competitive environment of the 21st century has a communal quality. It promotes cooperative social interactions and strives to attain a balance between the welfare of the organization and the welfare of its members. Put another way, "the most important reason for building a community is that its features meet the needs of a society in transformation. Teamwork, learning. flexibility, caring, a sense of belonging, and gainsharing . . . are qualities to be found in community and they perfectly complement the managerial requirements of the new (business) paradigm" (Nirenberg, 1993, p. 111). For some, however, the notion of community in the workplace is important because Americans appear to have lost community in their personal lives, due to the urbanization of society, the mobility of individuals and families, and technologies that allow us to communicate with other people at a distance, and in increasingly distant relationships. As Reich (1991) said, "in real life, most Americans no longer live in traditional communities. Most commute to work and socialize on some basis other than geographic proximity to where they sleep. And most pick up and move every five years or so to a different neighborhood" (p. 277). Indeed, Nirenberg (1993) observed: "Some who seek community in their workplace have become rootless, estranged by their mobility, and on a demanding career track that allows little time for non-job-related activity" (p. 114).

Not all societies have seen the decline in "community" to the extent witnessed in the United States, although economic globalization has affected many countries. One nation that still values "community" in its cities and towns, its plazas and schools, and its work organizations is Mexico, where the expectation of working and socializing together is a key component of the psychological contracts in Mexican companies, and in some American-owned firms. Mexico is increasingly important to the American economy, due to its border location, its involvement in the North American Free Trade Agreement (NAFTA), and immigration patterns that have increased greatly the Hispanic/Mexican American population in the United States. It is therefore important to study our neighbor to the south, because its influence economically, demographically, and culturally is increasingly significant to American society.

This chapter examines the concept of *community* from the perspective of members of selected Mexican organizations. Its main purpose is to identify the components of community and the ways that communication develops and sustains it in the workplace, according to individuals who live in a country where "community" is an integral part of the national culture. It is not our purpose to compare "community" in Mexican organizations with that which may exist in some American companies. Nor is it our purpose to illustrate that community results in any particular outcome. The people to whom we listened to in this study value community in and of itself, not as a means to an end, not as a strategy or a motivational tool. Workers in Mexican organizations possess an expectation that the opportunity to work as a community will be present in their places of work— it is one component of the psychological contracts under which they labor.

The chapter begins with a review of relevant literature on the notion of community in general, the creation of community in the workplace more specifically, and the relationship between communication and community. The importance of community in Mexican culture, and the resultant emergence of community creation in work organizations are then discussed. The next section of the chapter discusses the research questions that guided the study, and the research methods used to implement it. Our findings, and conclusions that emerged from the study, are then presented.

REVIEW OF RELEVANT LITERATURE

Notions of "Community"

A number of scholars have offered definitions of *community* (Davis & Jasinki, 1993; Etzioni, 1998; Frazer, 1999; Moemeka, 1998; Pinchot, 1998; Pinchot & Pinchot, 1993). Although there is no one best definition of the term, the most basic notion of a *community* is that it is a collective of individuals that has something in common (Davis & Jasinki, 1993; Etzioni, 1998; Frazer, 1999; Moemeka, 1998; Pinchot, 1998; Pinchot & Pinchot, 1993), or is "aligned around a common interest" (Barksdale, 1998, p. 93). Among the elements that community members have in common are goals, principles, laws, meanings, goods, and structures (Frazer, 1999). However, a community is more than shared goals and values, which is characteristic of any organizational culture. A community is formed by sets of relationships, which are the core of life in such settings (Etzioni, 1998; Frazer, 1999; Moemeka, 1998). It is, as Buber (1958) wrote, a "living togetherness, constantly renewing itself," and it attends to strengthening "the immediacy of relationships" (pp. 135-136). In the past, he observed, "common affairs were deliberated and decided not through representatives but in gatherings in the market-place; and the unity that was felt in public permeated all personal contacts" (pp. 135-136). Community cannot be forced (Arnett, 1986); it must emerge among "a group of people who have committed themselves to a process of ever-deepening levels of communication. Such a group becomes capable of learning, self-reflective behavior, and the capacity to balance individual and group needs. Building community is a process, not a place, a feeling, or a particular type of organizational structure" (Gozdz, 1993, p. 111).

In 18th- and 19th-century America, community was created in the kitchens and town squares of a growing nation. It emerged in immigrant neighborhoods on the stoops of New York City and the streets-turned-ball parks of Chicago and Boston. It was a "living togetherness" seen in the mom and pop stores, the front porches, and the barn-raisings of rural America. Then, in the 20th century, Americans in large numbers began to change where and how they lived and worked. They moved to cities, and increasingly worked in formal, hierarchical organizations.

As a result, Buber wrote, the community of the past "has gone irrevocably and forever. . . . The pressure of numbers and the forms of organization have destroyed any real togetherness. Work forges other personal links than does leisure. . . . The collectivity is not a warm, friendly gathering but a great link-up of economic and political forces" (cited in Arnett, 1986, p. 79).

Community In The Workplace

The notion and importance of "community" in work organizations is a concept that has received very little empirical attention in the field of organization studies, or practical attention within organizations themselves. Work life in much of the 20th century, at least in Western societies, was influenced by Weber's writings on the worth of organizational bureaucracy. From a sociological point of view, the main contribution of bureaucracy was the regulation of social interactions in the workplace. Prior to the Industrial Revolution, family feeling or friendship influenced the type of social interactions in organizations, primarily because these organizations were small, craft-based, and/or family-owned and operated. The bureaucratic organization, characterized by its rules, procedures, and formal, hierarchical structure, was considered a great innovation as larger, production-focused, multifunctional organizations developed (Pinchot & Pinchot, 1993). Such organizations offered a division of labor, a chain of command, distinct functional units, and a rule-ordered environment that brought order to social interactions in order to achieve higher production levels (Albrecht & Bach, 1997; Pinchot & Pinchot, 1993). In these organizations, position descriptions were used "to establish limits to involvement and responsibility, instructing members to 'Keep ideas to yourself'" (Seiling, 1997, p. 188).

At the beginning of the 21st century, however, new production and information technologies, the globalization of markets, and better educated workers have increased the complexity of the business environment and workers' expectations of how they should be valued and treated in that environment. New ways of working encourage cooperation, even collaboration, across hierarchical levels and functions. Pinchot (1998) suggested that a strong sense of community in contemporary organizations will lower the barriers that impede collaboration across organizational boundaries and achieve the productivity required for the information age. It will foster the intensive cross-functional communication and continual peer-level coordination required for the complexity of the current business environment (Pinchot & Pinchot, 1993). However, the purpose of creating a community is not solely to improve production. It is also needed to enhance the quality of life in the places where many of us spend much of our time. As Nirenberg (1993) observed:

> many middle and upper managers are finding themselves putting in long hours which also includes time at the in-house gymnasium and spending time in corporate sponsored social activities. Many singles committed to the organization are finding after-hours times an important opportunity to mingle and catch up on reading while still at the workplace. For some workaholics long days allow the pleasure of missing time at home with their families. The corporation is increasingly providing around-the-clock access to families and after-hours amenities for those who stay on. (p. 115)

Consequently, the workplace "provides a natural place for modern workers to search for some sense of community, especially for those who have difficulty finding it in other areas" (Gossett & Tompkins, 2001, p. 115).

Although the work ethic in the United States historically has valued "rugged individualism," the world of work has changed to value cooperation and collaboration in the workplace. When organization members have a choice of whether to belong to a community, they are motivated by their interest to be part of a social entity that has a purpose or a goal aligned with that of other members (Moemeka, 1998; Seiling, 1997). Thus, for the notion of community to succeed in an organization it is fundamental that its people find an intersection of their self-interest and the interest for the whole (Pinchot, 1993). "Community is established when the bulk of the people take responsibility for working together to design a better system, a better environment for everyone" (p. 56).

There are several characteristics shared by an organizational community that emerge from relevant research literature. Moemeka (1998) suggested the following features: a defined boundary, close affinity, common interest, and social control. Commonly held beliefs, norms, and symbols also are central to community life in work organizations. Other characteristics include a common goal, integration of members, voluntary membership, interdependent relationships, member participation, and shared values (Davis & Jasinki, 1993; Etzioni, 1998; Frazer, 1999; Moemeka, 1998; Pinchot, 1998; Pinchot & Pinchot, 1993). However, a workplace community is more than commonality. Before an organization, or a group within it, can become a community, a strong commitment by its members is needed—a commitment to each other and to share information, time, tasks, and support. Sharing implies individuals' willingness to sacrifice something of value. Members reciprocate out of respect and concern for one another, and it is through this willingness to share and to develop interdependent, caring relationships that communities evolve. As Frazer (1999) explained: "A firm might become a community if employees and employers began to interact with each other in multiplex relations—adding to the economic exchange of work for wages, cultural exchanges for sociability, shared leisure, participation in the locality, the organization of voluntary work, education, etc." (p. 73). Stamps (1997) stated that working and learning are social activities, and workers are looking for such opportunities. "They develop a common way of thinking and talking about their work. Eventually they come to share a sort of mutual identity—a single understanding of who they are and what their relationship is to the larger organization" (p. 34). One perspective of workplace communities, however, emphasizes their role as sources of organizational control (Barker, 1993; Gossett & Tompkins, 2001; Tompkins & Cheney, 1985), whose relationships are based on "trust, allegiance, fealty, and responsibility" and whose benefits include "open communication, productivity, identification, control, and security" (Gossett & Tompkins, 2001, p. 131). This perspective may be culture-specific, according to our research. In some cultures, where people do not live to work, where work is a social activity as much as an economic one, is community a source of control or cooperation? Is it a source of embedded power or social sustenance? According to Pinchot (1998), community at work is essential to happiness at work, as well as to organizational loyalty and intraorganizational cooperation.

How do communities evolve? How are they sustained amid the myriad intrapersonal, interpersonal and organizational forces that exist to undermine and destroy them? As the sociologists at The Chicago School observed as they studied immigrant communities of Chicago in the early part of the 20th century: "Once everything had been removed—homeland, tradition, structure, institutions, norms—communities still managed to develop. The only principle of explanation left was communication" (Depew & Peters, 2001, p. 19).

Communication and Community

Depew and Peters (2001) remind us that the French theories of why communication creates community emphasize that communication plays this role because "it ignores, marginalizes, privatizes, or even suppresses individuality in the normal sense" (p. 10). However, Philipsen's (1989) notion of "the communal function of communication" better informs a study of workplace communities in a society that values Buber's notion of "living togetherness" in their workplaces and their social lives (p. 79). In this function, Philipsen stated, communication is "a means for linking individuals into communities of shared identity" (p. 79.) As Carbaugh (1996) wrote, communication serves to unite, not divide individuals, through "common symbols, forms and meanings" that "provide the basic communicative ingredients for 'membering' or for 'realizing' a shared identity" (p. 201). Indeed, communication creates "webs of social relations" that develop and sustain community (Etzioni, 1998, p. xiii).

In work organizations, Nirenberg (1993) emphasizes, the main task of community "is knowledge based: the sensing, gathering, interpretation, processing and reevaluations of information, concepts and ideas. The operative environment that is established is inclusive, responsive, created and recreated by its members for the purpose of doing their work effectively but also in order to develop a high quality of 'work life' for its own sake" (p. 111). Indeed, he stated: "Community means inclusion, acceptance, efficacy, freedom of expression and having social as well as organizational goals legitimated. It also means being able to communicate openly and freely" (p. 118). Arnett (1986) drew a parallel between the characteristics of community-creating communication and Makay and Brown's (1972) characteristics of ethical communication. Such characteristics include:

1. Human involvement from a felt need to communicate.
2. An atmosphere of openness, freedom, and responsibility.
3. Dealing with the real issues and ideas relevant to the communicator.
4. Appreciation of individual differences and uniqueness.
5. Acceptance of disagreement and conflict with the desire to resolve them.
6. Effective feedback and the use of feedback.
7. Mutual respect and, hopefully, trust.
8. Sincerity and honesty in attitudes toward communication.
9. A positive attitude for understanding and learning.
10. A willingness to admit error and allow persuasion. (cited in Arnett, 1986, p. 96)

These characteristics are certainly important in the discourse of contemporary organizations who desire to create and sustain community.

A postmodern perspective of the world focuses on the production of meaning within communities and on the negotiation of meaning between communities (Davis & Jasinki, 1993). The relationships experienced in a community allow members to develop a mental map of the whole to which they are emotionally bonded. The use of symbols and narratives allow individuals to experience both the boundaries of their community and its virtual center, which "holds" community members together (Frazer, 1999). Rituals and other communication forms used in a community coordinate experiences and induce common perceptions of the social world (Davis & Jasinki, 1993). In communities, there are a variety of metaphors that describe the importance of communication—the glue that holds the organization together, the web that connects individuals to one another, the thread that weaves a tapestry of different groups and individuals together. Shepherd (2001) referred to communication as a gift in communities: "As such, it requires volition. We cannot communicate without giving of ourselves; nor can we communicate if not served by the gifts of other selves. This requires action on our part, and faith in that of others" (pp. 33-34).

The characteristics of a workplace community, and its communication practices, are affected by the environment(s) in which it lives, that is, by the regional and/or national culture of its people. Such is particularly the case in Mexico.

THE INFLUENCE OF CULTURE
ON MEXICAN ORGANIZATIONS

The culture of Mexico greatly influences the cultures of its social and work organizations, and the evolution of communities within them. Devotion to family, and participation in religious and national celebrations, are integral components of Mexican society. Indeed, the family is the cell, the foundation, of Mexican society.

Importance of the Family

One's "family" in Mexico includes multiple generations and relational links (e.g., grandparents, cousins, nieces, and nephews). Festivities in the life of a family, one's church, or the nation, are shared with relatives. The Mexican family is, in itself, a community, and family ties often make job mobility emotionally difficult.

An important aspect of familial life in Mexico is the support offered among family members. This support is not limited to financial help, but it is manifested in diverse forms of caring. For instance, a family member may fulfill babysitting needs. In some cases, when a brother or a sister and his or her family has economic problems, they are invited to move into a family member's home. This show of support provides stability that makes it easier to recover from difficult times. Additionally, in many instances, when grandparents reach a certain age they move in with one of their sons or daughters, instead of going to a nursing home. This is why several generations sometimes live in Mexican homes.

Importance of Celebrations

Mexico is a festive nation, and individuals celebrate a variety of special occasions with their families. Religious holidays, such as Christmas, are commonly celebrated with a family reunion. Other important events, such as wedding anniversaries, are celebrated with a mass. Baptisms and first communions are also special occasions in which family participation is meaningful. Furthermore, it is common to have a relative as a godfather or godmother during baptism or first communion. In this case, family members become "padrino" and "madrina" for children, and assume spiritual responsibilities for them. Finally, birthdays are major celebrations within families. In all these instances, the show of affection, care, and support among family members reflects the notion of "community."

Elements of Culture in the Workplace

In Mexico, the family is highly influential in the workplace. "Mexican employees base their job decisions and expectations on the needs of their families, who are central to their lives" (Diaz-Saenz & Witherspoon, 2000, p. 159). As opposed to an American employee, a Mexican employee views work as secondary in importance after the family (Alducin-Abitia, 1993; Kras, 1986). This priority of the family is a well-honored assumption to the extent that in some companies a phone call from a family member is a sufficient reason to leave a meeting. Additionally, companies invite employees and their families to parties and celebrations. Organizations also take into consideration the families of their employees when considering work benefits. For instance, some large corporations in Mexico build recreational facilities for employees and their families to enjoy. These facilities may include swimming pools, soccer and baseball fields, basketball and tennis courts, and places for artistic and cultural activities. Additionally, health and educational support is provided in these types of facilities. Such facilities reflect the importance of spending weekends with family, not at the office.

For Mexicans, the workplace is an important social setting (Gutierrez-Vivo, 1998), and social interaction and friendship is very important within it (Diaz-Saenz & Witherspoon, 2000). Personal respect and recognition are basic motivations in a working relationship, and Mexican employees are often more loyal to their supervisor than to their company (Flynn, 1984). When executives move to another company, it is not uncommon for some of their subordinates to go with them. The importance of the workplace as the scene of cooperation, not competition, is also an important concept in Mexico (Alducin-Abitia, 1986).

> It's much more important for a Mexican person to have a congenial working environment than it is to make more money. There have been cases where very good workers, ones who have performed well and received pay recognition for that have left the company because they felt ostracized by their co-workers. (Flynn, 1984, p. 44)

Considering the culture of Mexico, which values "community" throughout its society, and the increasing interest in workplace communities as they may, or may not, exist in different countries, the lead author undertook a study of how Mexican workers in selected organizations view the notion of community, and its relationship to organizational communication. The next section of the chapter describes the research questions that guided the study, and the research methods that implemented it.

THE STUDY

Research Questions

Considering the importance of community in Mexican culture, and the strong cultural influences on Mexican work organizations, one research question (RQ) critical to this study was:

RQ 1:   *What does the word community mean* within *Mexican organizations?*

For members of an organization to have a sense of community, their workplace should possess the characteristics of a community. Such characteristics include the sharing of goals, goods, interdependence, and a common fate, and the submission of individual interests for the social entity as a whole. The second research question guiding this study emerged as:

RQ 2:   *What are the factors that make an organization a "community" in Mexican organizations?*

Communication is the process through which community is created and maintained. It is through communication that individuals understand and value their community, and initiate and sustain the integrative relationships that perpetuate the community. Accordingly, the third research question on which this study was based is:

RQ 3:   *How is "community" created through communication in Mexican organizations?*

Research Participants and Procedures

To answer the research questions, the lead author sought to conduct a study in selected Mexican work organizations. Working with a professor at a Mexican university, he contacted human resources managers in several organizations to include their companies in the study. Ironically, "community" is a taken-for-granted concept in some Mexican organizations, and some managers chose not to include their companies in the study for that reason. Ultimately, however, 11 companies in four different Mexican cities did participate. Personal contacts with organizations developed through the lead author and the Mexican professor facilitated their participation, as well as their belief that the research would provide valuable information to their organizations.

To elicit rich data from respondents, focus group interviews were used—a research method that yields answers through the process of discussion. Such a method seemed appropriate in a study of "community." The lead author did not share existing conceptual information about "community" with participants, because the importance of the study resided in capturing definitions of community, and related concepts, from the point of view of the participants.

Twenty-two focus groups were created, comprised of 149 Mexican individuals from different hierarchical levels in the companies. Of those participants, 79 were male and 70 were female. Two groups in each of the 11 firms were formed, one comprised of individuals working at high levels of the organizations ($n = 69$), and one comprised of individuals working at the lower levels of each company ($n = 80$). Higher level positions included marketing and sales manager, exports manager, human resources manager, store manager, and operations manager. Lower level positions included secretary, maintenance worker, and clerk. There were six or seven individuals in each focus group. Educational attainment was predominantly at the middle school level or less for the groups of lower level employees, although some participants had technical or baccalaureate degrees. Most higher level employees had bachelor degrees. Some of them had master's degrees; a few had only high school degrees.

Only one of the companies was a public organization—the others were private corporations. The only public organization also was the only American company. However, the company prided itself on its commitment to be managed as a Mexican organization. This was the only participating company that had grandparents, parents, and grandchildren employed at the same time. Many of the Mexican traditions are followed, and it has built a large shrine to the Virgen de Guadalupe in front of its building, a structure that emphasizes Mexican architecture. (Executives have instructed Mexican managers to preserve Mexican traditions to please the workforce.)

All companies in the study had between 130 and 2,280 employees. A wide range of industries were represented, including pharmaceutical, construction, textile, education, retail, automotive, and manufacturing industries. Participants were invited to voluntarily attend focus group sessions by a contact in their organizations, usually one from the company's human resources department. Subjects did not receive detailed information prior to the focus group sessions to prevent undue influence on their attitudes and participation in the process. Indeed, the only information released to organizational contacts concerned the topic of the session. After several focus group sessions, the lead researcher learned that most contact persons did not share what little information they had about the research project. As a result, most of the participants did not know the purpose of the sessions, although a few were told they were attending training meetings.

A semi-structured questionnaire consisting of 10 questions was used to initiate and direct focus group discussions (see the appendix). The first two questions sought opinions about the notion of "community" in general. The next three questions asked about the concept of "community" in an organizational context. Question 6 asked how a sense of community can be created through communication. Question 7 asked about the importance of having a sense of community in a work organization. Questions 8 and 9 sought opinions about the relationship between "community" and Mexican culture. Question 10 sought opinions about the effect of community on organizational commitment, identification, and satisfaction.

Data Analysis

All focus group sessions were audiotaped and the tapes were then transcribed. The sessions were conducted in Spanish and the transcripts remained in the same language. The transcripts were analyzed using some themes prevalent in the research literature, including voluntary membership, member support, interdependency, collaboration, social control, collectivistic behavior, defined boundary, common fate, shared meanings, shared values, and participation. The order of the questions varied little during the focus group sessions, which made comparisons of the answers in all transcripts relatively easy, as suggested by Morgan (1988). The themes were used as codes to keep track of how frequently those themes appeared in each group's responses. Additionally, other ideas or issues that emerged as important to the participants were coded and checked for recurrence as well as how those ideas or issues related to the main themes. Comparisons also were made among hierarchical levels and between cities looking for differences and similarities among them. Finally, findings were translated into English.

FINDINGS

The following findings emerged from an analysis of focus group discussions.

What Constitutes a "Community."   Contrary to initial expectations, respondents, regardless of organizational position or geographical location, shared similar conceptualizations about what constitutes a "community" in society at large and within organizations. Participants were asked to think about an organization in general, not their own. However, the tendency of all groups was to develop the ideal definition of "community" and discuss their respective organizations in terms of how they fit the definition. Many of the participants indicated that their organizations were communities. However, a few individuals, those at both higher and lower organizational levels, expressed with some bitterness their wish to have that quality in their organizations. The lack of community in a few organizations was associated with a leader's lack of interest in creating community. Almost all of the companies in the study were family-owned. In such companies, the leader/owner often exercises a directive leadership style. Groups in one such organization indicated that a sense of community in their organization was lost when the next generation of owners, educated in a U.S. university, took control of their organization. The former generation of owners was known to have more warmth and personal contact with their employees than the new executives. All groups but one expressed the importance of having a sense of community in their organizations. Participants suggested that when community does not exist it is because management is not taking action to create it, particularly through communication practices.

Definition of Community Within Organizations.   Community within organizations was defined as a group of people working together toward a common goal. As one participant stated *"Community is defined as everybody working towards a common end, that is, everybody going in the same direction."* Interdependence exists among community members to accomplish a common goal. The members of a community share rules, norms, rights and obligations, traditions and customs, values and beliefs. Also, community was defined as people with something in common, such as race or religion. It was suggested that individuals may belong to different communities at the same time (e.g., at work, church, and in a neighborhood).

Voluntary Membership in a Community.   If an individual does not accept the rules, values, and beliefs predominant in that organization, he or she moves to another community, where people share the same values and beliefs. *"That is right, you can withdraw because you do not fit in that community because maybe they do not have your customs, your values in that community and what do you do? Well you withdraw, don't you?"*

Organizational Community and Emotional Bonding.   If an organization has a sense of community, members develop an emotional bonding that makes it very painful to leave the organization. Belonging to an organization with a sense of community is much more than a place to work. It is also a social "place" where people feel positive about being part of it. An expression that emerged often to indicate the feeling among individuals that emerges if there is a sense of community was, "a gusto" (e.g., "as one likes it").

Role of Family.   An unexpected finding in this study was the role of the family in influencing a sense of community. The desire to belong in a community emerges from the family. Thus, many Mexicans may expect to find a sense of community in their work organizations. Participants said that the worst thing that could happen to anyone is being socially isolated in their workplace. *"We spend more time in our work than in our house but the sense of family or community we have is deep-rooted . . . and I believe that those values, that way of life we bring to the firm."* Another participant said: *"When the family is strong, very united, then communities develop similar to them."* In other words, organizational members take their talents and experience in creating strong familial relations into the workplace with them, and attempt to develop similar webs of supporting relationships there.

Participants indicated that a sense of community within organizations is a reflection of what happens in the family. At the same time, organizations also influence the family. Training and work experience allow members to develop and improve their work, so employees become an example to their families and they share with them what they have learned.

The importance of family was a core value mentioned in every group. Furthermore, the mother was identified as the key individual that promotes a sense of community within a family. Mothers in Mexico make sure that family members are well, and check on their children even when they become adults. Some groups mentioned that when a sense of community evolves, love and appreciation for the community also develops.

Social Interactions and Community.   A sense of community in Mexican organizations develops from social interactions, which facilitate bonding among individuals. Communication was the most important component of community named by all focus groups. As one group explains, *"Well, I think that communication is a very important factor, very important for the development of every economic, informational, and religious aspect* [of the community]."

The opinions of several groups are reflected by one individual who emphasized that *"Constantly talking to people, without losing communication with them, being in touch with people, promoting any type of reunions, gatherings, work talks, this way the community will be maintained."* The growth of a company and the way it operates may negatively affect communication with employees. One participant commented sarcastically:

> *Supposedly the purpose of the company's magazine is to precisely inform the community, but . . . how wonderful that the company has become so big that we feel isolated because we never appear in the magazine. This city is never in the magazine. Now they are going to distribute it [laughs], they distribute it through Internet, but what is going to happen? Since we do not appear in it, we are not going to print it or we are not going to deliver it [referring to local employees]. Why? Because there is a lack of communi-*

cation from a magazine that does not acknowledge us. . . . So we are isolated, we end up knowing that something happened in our company through rumors.

Leadership and Community.   Leadership emerged as the critical agent that influences an organization's sense of community and the corporate policy to support it. The relevance of leaders is illustrated by the following comment:

I had the opportunity to see in an occasion that a director of a company said to the other directors, "I need you to care for each other because we are in the same organization. I would not expect you to believe that your best friends are here. But I would expect that you are concerned for each other as persons and to show support for each other."

Another comment was: *"As long as people on top have a sense of community, the rest . . . observe and thus it permeates down. In fact, it is easier for people on lower levels to work as a community than it is for upper level people."* Most of the time, the leadership figure was identified as a top-level leader, often the company's owner. Some participants said that top executives do not know their employees, and should have a greater presence in their organizational work areas. Immediate superiors were also identified as another set of leaders, however, without as much influence as the owners of the company. Additionally, participants observed that leaders emerge in every group and/or level. Cascading information flow (from upper levels of the organization throughout the other hierarchical levels) is critical in an organizational community, so that all organizational members receive the same messages. As it was explained in one group, in every company information should flow from

the strategic level . . . to the tactical level . . . to the operative levels. I mean, as it was mentioned by my colleague, in every company there is a leader. If the leader has a sense of community, sense of communion, sense of values that is compatible with the mission, with the vision of the company, then he can generate . . . activities that fortify that sense of community to include everybody . . . including the janitor. Right?

Leadership communication facilitates a sense of community in an organization, and may create a sense of an overarching community instead of many small ones. One example of this is illustrated in the following comment:

when there is a boss that believes in one-way communication, that is, 'I command, you don't count,' then I will not feel in a community. But when you have a boss that knows that communication is . . . both ways, most of all, that he listens . . . it's not that he only hears you. . . . You understand

what I'm trying to say, even when you don't agree with what I'm telling
you, but you understand me, you understand what I'm really saying.

In addition to disseminating information, leaders' visits to various organizational units were described as being important to creating community in
Mexican organizations—because such visits communicate consideration, even
if they do not include conversations with the leader(s). Participants also
expressed the need for all organizational members' involvement in creating and
maintaining a sense of community. Focus group members indicated that self-
interest prevents a sense of community in organizations. This type of attitude
was labeled as the "*yo-yo*" syndrome, which is Spanish for I–I or me–me.

Fulfilling Needs of Members.   Fulfilling the needs of members was another
identified characteristic of a sense of community. This is related not only to
material prosperity but also to wisdom, capabilities, and personal growth. A
related factor is the disposition to teach colleagues, as well as to learn from
them. As one individual stated:

> *Look after the needs of that community, the achievements of that community*
> *. . . if one individual grows, the rest should grow at the same rate and I am*
> *not talking only material growth but in wisdom, knowledge, capabilities*
> *and everything that involves growth. I cannot think of a community in*
> *which I am the only one with prosperity. What do I do? Against whom am I*
> *going to compare? With the one who knows nothing? With the one I have*
> *not taught to do anything?*

Member Integration.   This also was mentioned as a characteristic of a community, that is, when people put aside self-interest (*yo-yo*) to work cooperative-
ly with different people. Members share the same desired goals and everyone
participates to achieve them. This integration nurtures a collective sense of
well-being as well as mutual respect.

> *When I belong to an organization, I identify with it. When I put its t-shirt on*
> *and I embark in the same direction with my peers when I am in purchasing,*
> *when I am in sales—or at least I have a notion of what it is to be in purchas-*
> *ing and to recover the investment. Then I have an idea and that makes me*
> *put on the t-shirt and to belong to the organizational community, if not I end*
> *up outside. Well, not in the strict sense but I mean that I would see myself*
> *not participating with the rest of my peers for the common end [goal].*

One participant indicated that is important to have a sense of community to
encourage unity and communication, thus the attitude of each individual needs
to be oriented to integrate him or herself into the community.

A time ago someone told me, or I might have read it somewhere, "if you don't find the job you like, make yourself like the job you found." And it is true. If you are in an organization . . . you already are part of a community after all. In a contrary situation you become like an appendage that at the end will be cut and sent somewhere else. Right? You should integrate yourself, but as a person, to that community. That is why it is important . . . as I am telling you, you need to arrive with this mindset to "be part of" (the group), not that the whole group must join to you.

Face-to-face Communication   This was identified as the primary way to develop a sense of community within Mexican work organizations. Written communication was second in importance, seen as a support channel for face-to-face communication. Some groups stressed the importance of sequencing face-to-face communication and written communication. Written communication via memo gives support and permanence to what is said orally. Other media such as newsletters, Lotus Notes and bulletin boards support the development of a sense of community. People desire face-to-face communication because it includes multiple (verbal and nonverbal) cues. It was discussed as the most expressive medium to use in organizations, and the best one to communicate the values of the organization and motivate organizational members to share them. To have a face-to-face dialogue with a superior in Mexico is very motivating. Receiving feedback in regard to performance is perceived as very rewarding. A lack of communication makes people feel isolated from the community; it takes away the sense of belonging. Some participants stressed the importance of avoiding autocratic leadership. They wished for a type of communicative leadership that uses face-to-face conversation with subordinates to build a relationship. Focus group members expressed a need for superiors to know them better, to know what their needs are.

Special Events As Community-Creating Activities.   Some focus groups mentioned company conventions held every year. They were highlighted as important social gatherings where members of different departments or regions meet and share experiences. It is a context where face-to-face communication has a significant impact on the development of a sense of community.

Orientation and Training Programs.   Orientation and training programs were mentioned as contexts through which to create community among individuals from different departments. The training context is not only an environment in which people may learn collectively—they also share information and socialize during breaks.

Recognition as Community-Creating Activity.   Recognition of individual achievements in company ceremonies was identified as a community-creating activity, in part because such ceremonies can bridge hierarchical levels in the organization. Additionally, communicating feedback in one-on-one sessions also was seen as a community-creating activity—one person at a time. The communication of empathy by superiors during evaluation sessions was a related activity mentioned.

Traditions and Religion. Traditions and religion are embedded in events offered by the work organizations we studied to promote a sense of community. There was agreement among the focus groups that social events help to bring organizational members together. The event most mentioned was the *posada* celebrated during Christmas time. This is a festivity that commemorates Joseph and Mary's search for a place to stay before Jesus was born. *Posadas* are offered by organizations every year. This is a very traditional event in which family members of employees participate, and Mexican employees greatly value activities that involve their families. As one group mentioned: *"We have* posadas *for the children, so the whole family gets together there."*

Another religious event is the pilgrimage to visit the shrine of the Virgen de Guadalupe around December 12th. This is an event that commemorates the appearance of the Virgin Mary in Mexico. Employees in one focus group mentioned that this event is also celebrated with a mass inside the company's facilities. This tradition is so important that the whole family participates in the celebration.

> *Here in the company there is a tradition that takes place year after year; it is December the 12th, which is the feast day of the Guadalupe Virgin. So here inside the company a mass takes place to celebrate weddings, first communions. Here in the firm's patio, everybody in the organization comes . . . to attend mass and to celebrate . . . as do the families of each one of our work mates.*

In most of the companies represented in the focus groups, there is also a special place within the company's physical setting dedicated to the Virgen de Guadalupe, the patron saint of Mexico, where people may congregate to visit or honor the saint quietly.

Celebrations and Community. Finally, the anniversary of the organization is a celebratory event in some companies. This type of event engenders a feeling of camaraderie and community in the organization. As the focus group discussions illustrated, Mexicans enjoy festivities as an opportunity for social get-togethers. As mentioned earlier, celebrating with others is part of the Mexican spirit and social gatherings are an inherent part of the Mexican culture. Often a birthday or a similar occasion is used as an "excuse" to convene employees. On these occasions, Mexican workers enjoy grilled meat or cake—or some type of festive food.

One of the groups discussed a recreational facility that an organization offers for employees and their families to enjoy, which helps develop a sense of community.

> *It is the company's recreational park for the members of the organization. They can attend with their family and also they can ask for a pass to cele-brate a mass for the daughter's 15th birthday celebration and other family gatherings. [A daughter's 15th birthday is a special celebration in Mexico, a* quinceañera.*] There are recreational activities, movies, art; they offer several types of courses such as crafts, computation, Tae Kwan Do, gym, football [soccer] for children. That is, there is a gym, and . . . sport fields. Over there families get together very often.*

In general, the focus group discussions emphasized the role of communica-tion in creating community through activities that implement the expectations Mexicans have of "living together" in their work organizations. Such activities predominantly facilitate face-to-face interaction, and emphasize the role of the family as well as national and religious traditions and practices.

Limitations and Observations about the Data-Gathering Process

One of the main limitations of this study may be that focus group participants were not randomly selected. However, the number of groups as well as the inclusion of 11 organizations from four different cities help compensate for this problem. Furthermore, the qualitative nature of this study facilitated the acquisi-tion of rich data. Because few, if any, similar studies situated in Mexico have been conducted, the findings of this study can be used as a foundation for future research.

Participation in this study's focus groups was greater among those individu-als employed at higher organizational levels in their companies. Although there was consistency in their responses across all groups, it was noticeable that most of the time participants from higher levels engaged in longer discussions than lower lever participants. Perhaps the organizational positions, educational level, and training experiences of these individuals facilitated their being more com-fortable about articulating their opinions.

All of the groups mentioned that the notion of "community" in organiza-tions is taken for granted in Mexico, and some expressed surprise that it was a topic for research. However, most of the groups appreciated the opportunity to discuss the topic with their co-workers. They viewed the focus group sessions as learning opportunities, and were quite enthusiastic and motivated during their discussions. They invested more time in the sessions than what was requested. Indeed, there was only one group whose discussion was very brief. The mem-bers of this one group responded to all questions, but with short responses. They mentioned that they were not accustomed to being asked for their opinions, but were pleased to have the opportunity to offer them. This group had the fewest years of formal education, and members are never invited to attend meetings or take training courses in the organization.

There was only one group that could not agree on the majority of their responses. Although some members' opinions were consistent with those of the other groups, other group members had opposite views. This was a group comprised of employees at lower organizational levels and sales people. The group had the longest session among the focus groups and did not finish answering all questions on the semi-structured schedule. They focused on the general notion of "community" in their discussion, and could not agree on the concept as it applies to organizations.

Our research did not address the perceptions of community among members of transnational firms in Mexico. Thus, several questions remained unanswered in this regard. For instance, are there differences about the notion of "community" between members of Mexican-owned companies and those of transnational organizations? How have transnational organizations influenced the notion of community among their Mexican employees? Have transnational organizations been forced to adapt to the Mexican notion of community in order to be successful? Future research in Mexico should include studies of community in transnational organizations.

CONCLUSIONS

In reviewing the findings of the study, the following conclusions emerge. The organizations that are a community, according to their employees, have the following:

- Activities that encourage at least some degree of member integration. For instance, their members participate in courses or conventions that promote interaction among people from different departments.
- Some inclusion of family members in company benefits.
- Traditional social activities such as *posadas* or company celebrations.
- Collaborative work, where organizational members are connected to each other to accomplish company goals. The one group that could not agree with the concept of community inside the organization was the only group composed of sales people. For those individuals, their incentives tend to be more individualistic—the greater their individual effort, the better their individual benefits. The performance of their peers do not necessarily have an effect on them.

The groups that said their organizations were not communities had the following attributes:

- Few activities to promote social integration. For instance, the *posada* in one organization was cancelled by management due to financial concerns, which upset employees at all levels. This was seen as a breach of a psychological contract, because it was an expected and valued activity, suddenly eliminated without discussion.
- Poor communication with top management. They felt forgotten by top-level management. It was clear that those employees closer to their headquarters or to top-level management were better taken care of. When the organizational units are geographically dispersed, even in the same city, leaders were portrayed as unaware of their employees' needs and concerns.

Do high-level professionals experience more community in organizations than workers at lower organizational levels? Do they experience it differently? Based on focus group responses, it appears that professionals have an advantage, because of their formal education, to be located closer to where policy-making is conducted. As a result, they are able to influence top-level management or they are more visible to top level management so they may receive more attention. However, this does not mean that they experience "more community" than their colleagues at other organizational levels.

These questions are just a few that deserve research attention. Others include the following:

- What are the messages of community creation? That is, what are the topics discussed and what is the tone of interpersonal interaction in community creation?
- How do organizations identify channels/media for creating and sustaining community?
- How does the culture in which the organization is situated, and the organizational culture itself, affect the communication processes involved in creating community?

It is evident in this study, as indicated by Conrad and Poole (1998), that the way people make sense of their actions is influenced by core societal values and beliefs. In the Mexican context, culture influences the social interactions that take place within organizations. This study illustrates the meaning of "community" in an environmental context in which being part of a collective is appreciated. The organizations with a sense of community as described by Pinchot (1998) and Seiling (1997) pursue the same goal as other organizations, which is to make organizations competitive. Nevertheless, how people understand, value, and use the elements that develop a sense of community within organizations is unique from region to region.

As this study illustrates, creating community in Mexico is situated in both interpersonal and public communication contexts. It emerges in celebrations and during the accomplishment of day-to-day tasks. It emerges from recreation and work, influenced by a societal dedication to family, religion, and the commemoration of political independence.

In the Mexican organizations we have studied, and among the employees we have heard, there is great interest and concern in retaining a sense of community and becoming a more competitive economic power. Some larger Mexican organizations are endeavoring to create facilities where employees and their families can continue to celebrate life, albeit in areas devoted to work. As Nirenberg (1993) noted:

> Community is in effect an organism, not a given way of being but an evolving way of being that must be ever vigilant to meet the current needs of its members. It is therefore important that the process of connecting with one another be continuously reinforced and attended to. Not only must the work be the focus of building relationships but there must be time for celebration, for play, for refreshing one's mental and physical energy, and time to think, to share ideas with one another outside of the formal forums and representative bodies but still during official time. (p. 166)

And what is the role of communication in this evolution? It is "both a phenomenon of community, and the primary means of its sustenance," and because life in organizations, especially community, "is not made up of discrete moments and events" but "meaningfully integrated experiences . . . communication is often used to enact, construct, or encourage that integration" (Rothenbuhler, 2001, p. 172). According to Arnett (1986):

> If we are left with voluntary commitment to community and recognition of the importance of a center out of which community can emerge, then narration or communication must carry the essence of our center. For a community to survive, it must have a story. That story must be one that individuals can relate to, feel a part of, and affirm. It is a communicative vision of where we are going and why that keeps a community vibrant and healthy. Time is needed for people to tell their stories and to retell them. If we become too efficient in time use, we may close the door to a sense of community within our group and our organization. (p. 173)

Mexico is attempting to find a balance between efficiency and effectiveness, between economic concerns and social priorities, and between becoming a "first-world" economy without losing its commitment to community in its families, its cities, and its workplaces. As we reviewed the transcripts in this study, the changes affecting Mondragón, the 45-year old, highly successful industrial cooperative in Spain came to mind. There, too, in a work culture that is both individualistic and collaborative (Cheney, 2001), changes are underway within its two corporations in order for them to be competitive in a global market. Created within the Basque culture, this cooperative was founded on the importance of Basque workers' "commitment to one another as well as their connections to the land and the region in which they live" (Cheney, p. 139). This *solaridad* is changing—not all workers are Basques, and according to Cheney, "much of the actual growth of the cooperatives in recent years has been outside their well-spring communities and beyond the borders of the Basque Country" (2001, p. 149).

Throughout the history of Mexico, the town plaza has been the center of economic and social community. It is where news was shared from foreign places. It is where young men and women talked and courted under chaperones' watchful eyes. It is where friendships began, and fiestas were organized and implemented. At least two questions are prompted by our findings: Where is the plaza in 21st century Mexico and what are its functions? What can American work organizations learn from Mexican companies, as both attempt to achieve the quality of work and the quality of life that their multiple constituencies are seeking? There are two findings important to the authors. First, "community" in Mexico, even in Mexican work organizations, is akin to Buber's notion of "living togetherness." Early American colonist John Winthrop also once described this notion in his hope for a "city on the hill" in a new land: "We must delight in one another, make others' conditions our own, rejoice together, mourn together, labor . . . together, always having before our eyes our community as members of the same body" (cited in Bellah, Madsen, Sullivan, Swidler, & Tipton, 1985, p. 28). Second, "community" in one country may not be similar to "community" in another country, even a neighboring country. "Community" in Mexico and its workplaces may be very different from those that may exist in the United States. This does not mean that U.S. companies cannot learn from such places and their people. The United States is not the only country that can teach scholars and practitioners something about living, working, and communicating, in organizations. Indeed, there are important lessons to be learned from our neighbor to the south.

APPENDIX:
FOCUS GROUP QUESTIONS

1. What is the meaning of the word *community*?
2. What are the elements or factors that influence the development of a sense of community?
3. What is the meaning of the word *community* within Mexican organizations? What is the difference between this definition and the one already defined?

4. What makes an organization a community in Mexican organizations?
5. What are the factors or elements that make an organization a community, in Mexican organizations?
6. How could the sense of community be created by communication, in Mexican organizations?
7. Is it important or not, for you, to have a sense of community within an organization? Why or why not?
8. Do you consider sense of community to have a special meaning in Mexican culture? Why or why not?
9. Do you believe that Mexican culture facilitate or promote activities or events that promote the sense of community in organizations? Why or why not
10. Do you consider that a sense of community generates a sense of commitment, identification, or satisfaction with the organization? Why or why not?

ACKNOWLEDGMENTS

We wish to thank Jaime Diaz-Sáenz, director of the Academic Business Administration Department at ITESM Campus Laguna, for his assistance during the data collection phase of this study, and George Cheney, for his comments in the early stages of the project.

REFERENCES

Albrecht, T.L., & Bach, B.W. (1997). *Communication in complex organizations: A relational approach*. Fort Worth, TX: Harcourt Brace & Company.

Alducin-Abitia, E. (1986). *Los valores de los Mexicanos: México entre la tradición y la modernidad* [The values of the Mexicans: Mexico between tradition and modernity] (Vol. 1). Mexico: Fomento Cultural Banamex.

Alducin-Abitia, E. (1993). *Los valores de los Mexicanos: en busca de una esencia* [The values of the Mexicans: In search of an essence] (Vol. 3). México: Fomento Cultural BANAMEX.

Arnett, R. (1986). *Communication and community: Implications of Martin Buber's dialogue*. Carbondale: Southern Illinois University Press.

Barker, J.R., (1993). Tightening the iron cage: Concertive control in self-managing teams. *Administrative Science Quarterly, 38*, 408-437.

Barksdale, J. (1998). Communications technology in dynamic organizational communities. In F. Hesselbein, Goldsmith, M., Beckhard, R., & Schubert, R. F. (Eds.), *The community of the future* (pp. 93-100). San Francisco, CA: Jossey-Bass.

Bellah, R., Madsen, R., Sullivan, W., Swidler, A., & Tipton, S. (1985). *Habits of the heart*. Berkeley: University of California Press.

Buber, M. (1958). *Paths in utopia*. Boston: Beacon Press.

Carbaugh, D. (1996). *Situating selves*. Albany: State University of New York Press.

Cheney, G. (2001). Forms of connection and "severance" in and around the Mondragón worker-cooperative complex. In G. Shepherd & E. Rothenbuhler (Eds.) *Communication and community* (pp. 135-155). Mahwah, NJ: Erlbaum.

Conrad, C., & Poole, M.S. (1998). *Strategic organizational communication into the twenty-first century*. Fort Worth, TX: Harcourt Brace College.

Davis, D.K., & Jasinki, J. (1993). Beyond the culture wars: An agenda for research on communication and culture. *Journal of Communication, 43*(3), 141-149.

Depew, D., & Peters, J. (2001). Community and communication: The conceptual background. In G. Shepherd & E. Rothenbuhler (Eds.), *Communication and community* (pp. 3-21). Mahwah, NJ: Erlbaum.

Diaz-Saenz, H.R., & Witherspoon, P.D. (2000). Psychological contracts in Mexico: Historical, familial, and contemporary influences on work relationships. In D. M. Rousseau & R. Schalk (Eds.), *Psychological contracts in employment: Cross-national perspectives* (pp. 158-175). Thousand Oaks, CA: Sage.

Etzioni, A. (1998). *The essential communitarian reader*. Lanham, MD: Rowman & Littlefield.

Flynn, G. (1984). HR in Mexico: What you should know. *Personnel Journal, 73*(8), 34-41.

Frazer, E. (1999). *The problems of communitarian politics: Unity and conflict*. Oxford: Oxford University Press.

Gossett, L., & Tompkins, P. (2001). Community as a means of organizational control. In G. Shepherd & E. Rothenbuhler (Eds.), *Communication and community* (pp. 111-133). Mahwah, NJ: Erlbaum.

Gozdz, K. (1993). Building community as a leadership discipline. In M. Ray & A. Rinzler (Eds.), *The new paradigm in business* (pp. 107-119). New York: Jeremy P. Tarcher/Perigee.

Gutiérrez-Vivó, J. (1998). *El otro yo del Mexicano*. [The other self of the Mexican]. México: Editorial Oceano.

Kras, E.S. (1986). *Cultura gerencial: México-Estados Unidos*. Guadalajara, Jalisco, Mexico: Impresora Analco.

Makay, J., & Brown, W. (1972). *The rhetorical dialogue*. Dubuque, IA: William C. Brown.

Moemeka, A.A. (1998). Communalism as a fundamental dimension of culture. *Journal of Communication, 48*(4), 118-141.

Morgan, D.L. (1988). *Focus groups as qualitative research*. Newbury Park, CA: Sage.

Nirenberg, J. (1993). *The living organization*. Homewood, IL: Business One Irwin.

Philipsen, G. (1989). Speech and the communal function in four cultures. *International and Intercultural Communication Annual, 13*, 79-92.

Pinchot, G. (1998). Building community in the work place. In F. Hesselbein, M. Goldsmith, R. Beckhard, & R. F. Schubert (Eds.), *The community of the future* (pp. 125-137). San Francisco, CA: Jossey-Bass.

Pinchot, G., & Pinchot, E. (1993). *The end of the bureaucracy & the rise of the intelligent organization*. San Francisco, CA: Berrett-Koehler.

Reich, R. (1991). *The work of nations*. New York: Knopf.

Rothenbuhler, E. (2001). Revising communication research for working on community. In G. Shepherd & E. Rothenbuhler (Eds.), *Communication and community* (pp. 159-179). Mahwah, NJ: Erlbaum.

Seiling, J.G. (1997). *The membership organization: Achieving top performance through the new workplace community*. Palo Alto, CA: Davies-Black.

Shepherd, G. (2001). Community and the interpersonal accomplishment of communication. In G. Shepherd & E. Rothenbuhler (Eds.), *Communication and community* (pp. 25-35). Mahwah, NJ: Erlbaum.

Stamps, D. (1997). Communities of practice: Learning and work as social activities. *Training, 34*(2), 34.

7

AN INTERPRETIVE STUDY OF THE FORMAL ORGANIZATIONAL MESSAGES AND ORGANIZATIONAL CULTURE IN A MEXICAN MULTINATIONAL COMPANY

Mariela Pérez Chavarría
Instituto Tecnológico y de Estudios Superiores de Monterrey

This chapter examines the corporate rhetoric of CEMEX, a Mexican construction company that only recently became a multinational corporation. Using a variety of data sources—including a corporate video, annual reports, and observations—I identify key themes in the corporation's public messages. Then, I make speculative linkages with the corporate culture internal to the organization. The case is especially interesting because the company is fast becoming recognized in the world market. We can glimpse the tension in the corporate public rhetoric between a Mexican identity and "global" image, although the latter is fast overtaking the former in the image-making efforts of the organization.

INTRODUCTION

In the dynamic context of globalization, where the mergers, joint ventures, and networks of multinational corporations are commonplace, research about organizational culture takes on special importance and new challenges. Of course, organizational culture deals not only with the specific activities of a company but also its values, identities, norms, distinctive rituals and other practices. For purposes of this chapter, the narratives or stories that an organization tells about itself deserve careful attention, even though those messages may not be reflective of the totality of experience within an organization. I make this claim simply because of the need on the part of multinational corporations (as for all transnational organizations) to express themselves publicly in an environment of multiple and conflicting values. This challenge is as pertinent to public relations and identity management as it is to advertising and marketing.

Despite the prevalence of complex interfirm relations today, very little research has been conducted on communication and culture in the domain of multinational corporations, their cultures, and their "positioning" of themselves. Specific to my concerns here, there is practically no research on how multinational corporations express their own values and cultural commitments within the wider arena of global commerce. In fact, very few studies of organizational culture even refer to multinationals. And, extant work in this area has focused on (a) interpersonal communication, formal and informal, in the process of socialization or enculturation (Falcione & Wilson, 1988; Pacanowsky & O'Donnell-Trujillo, 1983); (b) the preservation of culture within multinationals (Gundry & Rousseau, 1994; Harrison & Carroll, 1991); and (c) the transmission of culture through face-to-face communication, especially by leaders (Brown & Starkey, 1994; Moran, Harris, & Stripp, 1993).

In the domain of organizational culture research, narratives and organizational histories stand out as the most available and one of the most important indicators of the "official story" of an organization's culture and how organizational leaders seek to position the organization with respect to various audiences, both internal and external (cf. Barnett, 1988; Brown & Starkey, 1994; Feldman, 1990; Hansen & Kahnweiler, 1993).

It is evident that when companies globalize their operations, organizational communication and its relations with national cultures become very complex. Best known in the research of multinational corporations and culture is the program by Hofstede, Neuijen, Ohayv, & Sanders (1990), who studied and compared the organizational cultures in 20 units of 10 different organizations in Denmark and the Netherlands using a quantitative survey methodology. Among other things, they found that values represent the core of organizational culture and the differences in organizational units fundamentally lie in the practices and perceptions of their members.

Hofstede et al. (1990) took as a starting point the hypothesis that organizational culture is determined by the nationality, regional culture, the type of industry, and the tasks performed by the organization, among other factors. Through their analysis, Hofstede and his colleagues contributed to strengthening the notion of organizational culture as a common element of theory and practice for administrators, recognizing that national culture and organizational culture are two different phenomena. Although this work has been heavily criticized for simplicity of measurement and conceptual reductionism, it has drawn our attention to the multidimensional relationships between the cultures of organizations and those of host or represented countries.

Hence, the process of organizational cultural expression within multinationals is not well understood. What we have are studies conducted chiefly in companies from the United States, Japan, and Western Europe. These companies and their subsidiaries are usually investigated with questionnaire methodologies that attempt to discern the "average" or most widely held commitments of leaders and employees. There are virtually no research reports on organizational culture or rhetoric for Latin American multinationals; however, this is understandable in light of the fact that Latin American-*based* multinationals appeared only a few years ago.

THEORETICAL FRAMEWORK
AND MODEL FOR THE ANALYSIS

This chapter begins with the premise that *organizations are cultures*. With this in mind, the operative methodological perspective for this study is interpretive. According to Morgan (1991), Smircich and Calás (1992), Kersten (1986), Pacanowsky and O'Donnell-Trujillo (1982), Bormann (1983), Putman (1983), and Bantz (1993), among others, this perspective seems to be the most appropriate focus for understanding organizations as cultures. The interpretive perspective allows the researcher to come close to an "insider's view" of organizational reality by adopting a native understanding of the communicative function of certain cultural symbols.

Interpretive analysis starts from the premise that organizations are dynamic, lively places where individuals contribute to a "social construction, symbolically constituted and reproduced through interactions" (Smircich, 1983). This perspective endeavors to understand—as Pacanowsky and O'Donnell-Trujillo (1982) argued—how organizational life is largely created through communication: "through the sending and use of messages in organizations, culture is mutually constructed, maintained and transformed" (Bantz, 1993, p. 109).

At the same time, Geertz (1987) proposed that *culture* be defined as a web of shared meanings, or "the total structure of communications" (Hall, 1978, p. 46). Culture is understood as the context or the referential framework in which messages are comprehended or decoded. The framework or web is "woven" by certain stories, ways of speaking, and by peculiarities that give substance and sense to that which in another way would be a insensate behavior. From this interpretive standpoint, a specific goal of the researcher is to understand how certain organizational messages are produced and interpreted by organizational members, and especially how some messages come to take on greater significance than others, sometimes by design and sometimes without intention. For the mission statement of any organization, as well as for concepts such as efficiency, redesign of processes, re-engineering, and so on, meanings are established and maintained as the members of a group or organization co-construct them, as they use terms in different contexts and situations, and as certain stories are repeated. In this way, meanings are confirmed or transformed by the community. Culture thus acts as a frame of reference in which meaning is negotiated, defined, and established.

OBJECTIVES OF THE STUDY

The central purpose of this work is to conduct an exploratory study of formal communication and the organizational culture within a multinational company of Mexican origin. A qualitative investigation was based in the analysis of formal communication documents, especially those documents directed toward the internal audiences (employees or members of the company around the world), but also toward the external audiences that have access to annual reports, such as stockholders, the government, competitors, and so forth. The analysis presented here is intended to illuminate the official expression of the organization's culture, especially as expressed in important internal and external corporate messages.

Hence, this study falls into the tradition of the study of organizational rhetoric (see Cheney, 1983), in that it uses key public corporate documents to infer aspects of an organization's "cultural positioning" within its market and with respect to the larger society. By *rhetoric*, in this study, I mean the deliberate, strategic, and carefully crafted messages that serve in one way or another to represent the organization in the public realm. Because of my desire to make inferences about organizational culture, statements of values and principles are among the aspects of the documents most closely examined.

RESEARCH QUESTIONS
AND RESEARCH METHODOLOGY

This chapter specifically explores and infers the organizational culture of a multinational corporation of Mexican origin, through the analysis of formal communication documents or public corporate texts, such as the corporation's annual reports, a corporate video, and the speeches of the CEO. These documents constitute only a part of the great quantity of what is known as corporate public discourse, and, as Cheney and Frenette (1993) pointed out, have been little appreciated by specialists but that nevertheless reflect the identity of the corporation and have important rhetorical and persuasive functions. Among the advantages of utilizing this method of analysis, several stand out:

- Organizational processes are not interrupted (unobtrusive method) (Cassell & Symon, 1995).
- Data and derived interpretations can be easily checked because they are recorded or printed (McMillan, 1986).
- Key documents are valuable evidence because they contain a registration of facts and history of organizations (i.e., the organization's official story).
- The organization may be studied longitudinally (throughout its life).
- Formal messages represent key means by which the organization presents itself to various audiences, both internal and external (Cheney, 1991).

Although the use of these formal documents has been criticized as lacking adequate detail for analysis, the messages contained in them are representative of how the organization pictures itself. Because of this, and the fact that such documents are widely used, they are a part of the official organizational communication and constitute a resource that the corporation uses to create, negotiate, and maintain meanings with its different audiences.

There are several common objections to this type of analysis, which I address here. These are summarized by Cheney and Frenette (1993) in their analysis of internal (house organs) and external (annual reports) corporate documents. Specifically, the making of inferences about values and other aspects of corporate culture from formal organizational "texts" can be problematic because (a) particular corporate documents may not be read by particular audiences and therefore may or may not be considered as corporate communication, and (b) even though a certain audience might read the documents, this audience might not be persuaded by them. The most important objection to this type of analysis is that the values found in the corporate documents, whether explicit or implicit, may not reflect the actual organizational values.

Despite what has been mentioned previously, the advantages just described constitute a solid support for analysis. Additionally, the words are permanent and, as Schein (1999) expressed, language is a primary manifestation of culture. Consequently, what an organization expresses in writing or through particular images reflects what that organization—in the form of its policymakers and key spokespersons—believes and values, and therefore forms part of its permanent history.

For data collection, a "grand tour" was made of the corporation (Spradley, 1979). The purpose of this tour was to identify, among accessible and available documents, those that had the greatest diffusion and use. In this way, I obtained nine annual reports (1988–1996), a commemorative video of the 90th anniversary of the corporation (1996), and two important speeches of the CEO (given at the opening and closing of the second Executive Annual Conference in 1996 (an event for executives of all the offices and subsidiaries of the corporation). I chose these specific messages precisely for the frequency with which they appeared and the importance they were given in the company. When I asked organization members about the significance of these messages they told me that for them these messages represented the confirmation or the consolidation of the company. So, for example, the video is important because it both celebrated the corporation's 90th anniversary and marked the company's expansion into the international arena, which happened four years before, in 1992. This set of diverse messages reveals important features of the corporate culture, at least as officially presented, by presenting values and assumptions with which the corporation intends to persuade its public.

The *primary research questions* (RQ) that guided this study were as follows:

RQ1:   To what extent does this set of messages speak to issues of organizational culture?

RQ2:   What specific aspects of organizational culture, as officially presented, can be inferred from this set of messages?

RQ3:   What values and principles are most prominently represented in this set of messages?

Beyond these questions are the following *secondary and more speculative queries*:

RQ4:   What role do the annual reports and the stories in the corporate video potentially play in the transmission of the culture?

RQ5:   Would it be possible to find in these messages elements that contribute to the development of organizational culture or the shared interpretation of reality?

Because so complex and dynamic a concept as organizational culture cannot be simply measured or definitively classified, this work is a case study from an interpretive perspective. This study does not pretend to prove or demonstrate any hypothesis; rather it explores the emergent organizational culture in a very young Mexican-based multinational whose history is rich and fascinating.

The data for this investigation are the messages contained in formal, organizational texts, including a video. Some investigators, such as Barr, Stimpert, and Huff (1992), concluded that these types of documents are similar to communication from a public relations (PR) department designed to create "positive face" for the organization. In the context of market globalization and with the pressure on organizations of all types to assert themselves through a variety of forms of communication, messages such as the ones being examined here take on even greater importance than before. It is not that all such messages are influential or even carefully attended to by their intended audiences. Rather, all large organizations (and in particular, multinational corporations) are compelled to participate in a broader discourse that features not only products and services but in addition values, principles, visions, and so on (see Cheney & Christensen, 2000). For example, the Mattel company and its subsidiaries in Mexico launched an unusual PR campaign called *la cruz rosa* (the pink cross), alluding to the Red Cross. This consisted of asking young girls who had several "Barbie" dolls to donate one or more of them, and Mattel would agree to repair them completely and offer them, along with the name of the donor, to girls from underprivileged neighborhoods or orphanages during the Christmas season.

Framework for the Analysis

To conduct this analysis, a model was developed from the ideas of Harrison and Beyer (1993) and Bantz (1993). The first component of the model was based on the proposals that culture consists of two forms: *substance* and *cultural forms*. Substance refers to the essence, ideology, assumptions, and values that are not visible but that nevertheless have an impact on the behavior of the members of the organization. Cultural forms are the concrete manifestations or observable expressions of the substance; for example, language and stories. Of course, this distinction is not a "clean" one in that, for example, certain symbols can be powerful encapsulations of entire ideologies (McGee, 1980). For a specific framework for analysis, I turn to Bantz's methodology, Organizational Communication Culture (OCC), based on the analysis of systematic organizational messages. Bantz proposed taking into account the following dimensions: where the messages come from, the way in which they are structured, the vocabulary used, metaphors, the values they reflect, themes, meanings, and so on. In this way, combining the ideas of the three authors, we can identify these elements:

1. *Sources*: external descriptions, relative to the nature of the document being analyzed. For example, a video and its characteristics, or characteristics of annual reports (number of pages, photos, etc.).
2. *Specific Forms or Manifestations of the Culture*, including the following:
   • Language (vocabulary, slang or argot, adjectives, pronouns, and metaphors). Dimensions include everyday words, specialized words, rare words or words unique to the organization. Some terms,

for instance, like cement, vertical mill, hydraulic concrete, or clinker, are industry-specific.
- Fundamental themes (topics of the messages). For example, there are recurrent themes, such as quality or commitment to clients.
- Narratives or identifiable stories.
3. *Substance or Ideology—values and beliefs or assumptions*: the concepts that seem more fundamental to a particular group and that to some extent, determine the conduct of its members; for example, honesty, punctuality, or loyalty.
4. *Organizational Meanings*: These represent in some way the collective character of an organization; they may be inferred in from the analysis of messages and organizational expectations.

Each of the last two levels of analysis just mentioned demands a substantial degree of inference, although such inferences should ultimately be tied to the content of the text. Table 1 (based on Bantz's, 1993 OCC model) organizes the aforementioned points that are the basis of the model:

TABLE 7.1   Scheme for the Analysis of the Culture based on Corporate Texts

LEVEL 1: Sources ("Texts")	LEVEL 2: Manifestations of Culture	LEVEL 3: Substance or Ideology	LEVEL 4: Inference of Organizational Meanings
Official reports	Language: vocabulary (e.g.,adjectives, pronouns,and specialized nouns: argot)	Stated and Implied Values	Underlying ideas and ideologies regarding the company, the market, and success
Corporate promotional video	Proverbs and slogans	Stated and Implied beliefs	
Speeches by the CEO	Metaphors		
	Key themes		
	Narratives		

RESULTS: ANALYSES AND INTERPRETATIONS

Summarizing a qualitative investigation is usually complicated by the sheer amount of data the researcher has collected. Here, I offer a synthesis of this particular analysis of formal organizational messages as they relate to organizational culture. My analysis is structured according to the categories and steps advanced by Bantz (1993) and Harrison and Beyer (1993). The coding of data was performed as follows:

1. *Description of the basic characteristics of messages.* For example, the number of pages of the annual reports, number of sections or parts they are divided into, titles of documents, illustrations, and the type of paper used. The sources and possible receivers of these messages were identified, for the purpose of conceptualizing and classifying each document better.

2. *Analysis of messages considered as cultural forms.* For this, a detailed analysis was carried out to characterize word choice, including vernacular versus professional terms, and uses of adjectives and pronouns. Next, metaphors, slogans, and proverbs that reflect beliefs were identified and analyzed. Then the central themes or organizing topics, which emerged from the previous analyses and were identified. Finally, stories and myths were isolated.

3. *Inference about substance or ideology: values and beliefs.* In this part of the analysis, I looked across the various texts for important patterns, taking pains to crosscheck what appeared to be organizing themes.

4. *Based on this, an inference was made as to what were the interpretations or global ideas that seemed to emphasize the collective character of the organization,* at least as presented in the formal messages.

Sources ("Texts")

The annual reports and the video both can be considered the official "voice" of the corporation. For McMillan (1986), these types of documents reveal the corporate persona, created and sustained through the public messages. From this perspective, it is possible to conceive the organization as a sender, owner of a speech that identifies and distinguishes it from other similar organizations. Both include the properties particular to their genre, and are representative of formal communication (e.g., PR) intended to spread an image of the organization. Their communicative purposes are clear—to inform and persuade various audiences to behave and form opinions that support organizational interests. Thus, support versus nonsupport is the key dimension along which most formal organizational messages should be considered, especially when profit and growth are at stake.

In contrast, the CEO's speeches deserve a special place as sources of messages for three reasons: (a) they are speeches made by the CEO in the opening and closing of the Executive Conference of 1996; (b) the sender has a name, a voice, a body and speaks as both an individual and a representative of the company; and (c) the audience that hears the messages is select: only high-level executives. Finally, the purpose of these speeches is to motivate and persuade the recipients to seek integration within the company.

Cultural Forms

Language and Vocabulary.   The organizational vocabulary showed terms specific to the cement industry as well as that common to a broader, business-world argot. The shift in usage between the cement industry vocabulary and a more generalized business vocabulary indicates changes in company concerns at moments in its history. For example, national leadership, diversification, and modernization in 1988 to 1990 annual reports, are transformed to growth, globalization, and multinational expansion, in 1996.

The same CEO mentions in his final speech: "Last year, for some reason I closed in English and everyone could understand me without the necessity of simultaneous translators; today I am going to do it again." And at the end of his interventions, he expresses, "I am very pleased that now we can all share the same language." By invoking the concept of a shared language, the CEO alludes to larger shared interests. The CEO thus suggests that "We've made it" into the broader domain of international commerce, recognition, and communication.

Metaphors offer an important reflection of the corporate culture. Although obvious metaphors are not found in many of the texts examined here, their use reflects an organizational personality, voice, history, and other characteristics. Metaphors are present in the three types of documents, but it is in the video where they appear most frequently, above all through the use of personification. For example: "I was born when cities had just begun dressing in concrete . . ." is a clear reference to the year (1906) the company originated, or in the annual reports: "concrete is our inseparable and silent companion." In this way, the company is elevated to the status of a personal agent and its chief product is valorized and romanticized.

In the speeches, the CEO also uses personification when he speaks about "Young CEMEX," or when he says, "the new CEMEX needs new blood infusions." When he speaks about the clients he points out: "CEMEX treasures the clients." In another paragraph of the same speech, when he alludes to a necessity for change, he says: "Tradition is the guardian of bureaucracy and at the same time enemy number one of change, flexibility and speed," emphasizing innovation as a constant of the corporation.

Despite their relative scarcity of use, slogans—identifiable exhortations deliberately invented by someone with the intention to persuade others to do something—(Harrison & Beyer, 1993) are important means of communicating ideas about what an organization is and what an organization values. These slogans especially stand out: "world-class company" and being "proactive." The phrase "in harmony with nature," expressed for the first time in the 1991 annual report, becomes more prominent and reflects the company's preoccupation with the environment. Already by 1993, the phrase was one of the central slogans of the company.

Several other slogans are repeated in the last three reports. These include "low costs of operations, competent administration, state of the art technology, market leader, solid financial structure" (Annual Report, 1994). These slogans reflect images of organizational strength that the organization would like to instill within their audiences.

Central Themes. The following organizing themes emerge through a careful analysis of the various texts:

- *The evolution of the company*: where its achievements are exalted. In 1988, CEMEX was reborn with a new identity (the company actually dates to 1906). In 1990, it was a "solid Mexican group." In 1992, it was the fourth largest cement producer in the world and leader in the Mexican and Spanish markets. In 1994, it became one of the largest producers in the world and leader in Latin America. In 1996, it was one of the three most important cement companies in the world.
- *Corporate strategies*: growth, acquisitions, and geographic diversification.
- *The human being*: but as an essential factor in the growth; as a "permanent value."
- *The environment*: with frequent mention of anticontaminant equipment, energy saving, international standards compliance, recycling programs, and respect for the environment.

From the data it is clear that most of the content of the corporation's public messages are self-promotional, designed for external audiences but at the same time intended to be self-reinforcing. The corporation is exalted, its values are celebrated, its history revered, stressing its orientation toward growth and the future.

I would also mention secondary, or less prominent themes, such as Mexico and its development, international pressures, and technology. Importantly, I found few internal contradictions within the texts I examined, especially because the abstract appeals to growth and internationalism seemed to envelope other concerns.

Narratives. Finally, the analysis of the manifestations ends with narratives, considered as one of the forms that best reflect the tie between culture and communication. Narratives are symbolic forms *par excellence* that order the otherwise chaotic organizational reality (Boyce, 1995; Brown, 1986; Hansen & Kahnweiler, 1993). In the opinion of experts such as Feldman (1990), narratives have not received yet sufficient attention in spite of their power in transmitting meanings and values to individuals in a given community. In the case of CEMEX, at first glance, one may not expect to find a unifying story. But within the annual reports a thematic story whose hero is a "character" called CEMEX emerges. The story of CEMEX reinforces what appears to be the only story worth telling in this organization: the company's own unified and seamless narrative.

The central story in the video begins in 1906: "When constructors saw cement was the indispensable material to bind their dreams . . . I was born in that specific moment when cities were just starting to dress in concrete . . . slowly I started to define my identity. I wanted to stand out in what I liked." In 1931, the cement company joined with another local cement company and remained static until 1970, when "I decided to know other places and other people" (regional expansion). "Then the most interesting competition started . . . I allowed myself to dream of a better future. . . . First, I decided to strengthen myself." In the 1970s, expansion continued and at the end of the decade of the 1980s, CEMEX was "the number one in the Mexican market, one of the biggest in the world." "I can't deny the path was hard and with pride I recognize that I never abandoned my ideals . . . so accomplished was I, that I decided to participate in the international competition." This happened around 1992, and when the video was made in 1996, the hero said: "And here I am now, with pride, for having reached all the major achievements, but with the responsibility of giving an endless, immense, and passionate leap of continuous growth."

Using the rhetorical device of anthropomorphism, the story personifies this singular "hero" that, in the first person, relates his life and achievements, from its birth in 1906 up to 1996. The story of CEMEX, as the central character of the narrative, is that of a winner whose achievements remind us of the epics of Homer, with a hero similar to Ulysses. He (CEMEX) appears not to age, or at least not to be affected by time. As it happens in the Homeric stories, the central character only develops fortitude, cleverness, decisiveness, combativeness and wisdom, among other qualities. Thus, such a cultural manifestation with its peculiar narrative form (there are three voices in the dialogue), appears to contribute in an important way to the creation and diffusion of a base of shared meanings between members of the company. The fictional hero embodies the defining values of the organization and acts according to them. He represents the prototype of the ideal behavior for the members of the company and contributes to the creation of a myth about the company.

Another version of the same narrative was found in the annual reports. The annual reports describe the historical narrative in different terms and more detail. It is true that only the good things are being pointed out, but some slips and mistakes were reported. For example, the reader learns that in 1988

CEMEX announced its incursion in other areas as a strategy of diversification; but with the exception of a small investment in tourism, the plans never took place. The company also faced accusations for illegal dumping and reduced personnel through the closing of inefficient plants and job elimination. Despite the negative implications of these actions, the company seemed to surmount all obstacles. Far from blurring the company's success, the reports show how the company learned and rectified its earlier mistakes.

A minor tale that belongs to the huge history of CEMEX is in the 1989 annual report. The report explains how, facing globalization and possible pressure from the market, CEMEX changed the strategy of growth and decided to concentrate on its main businesses: production and sales of cement and concrete. Confronting the menace of becoming vulnerable because of the foreign market and being relegated to a medium-sized regional company, CEMEX took a risk to purchase the second producer of cement in the country. In their judgment, this was one of the "most important and far-reaching" decisions in company history.

CEMEX is clearly trying to present itself as a protagonist in its industry, within the business world of Mexico, and in the larger domain of international commerce. Narratives, such as those found in CEMEX's video, are intended to influence the members of an organization because they present an important feats narrative in a simple form that is easily understood by audiences. Today's multinational corporations try hard to present a univocal organizational identity because that, in itself, connotes confidence, certainty, and strength.

The Central Values Expressed within and Inferred from the Texts

Probing deeper into the organizational messages, we can detect the less visible components of a culture, such as basic values and beliefs. For both of these dimensions, of course, I focus primarily on how the corporation is projecting itself, although we may expect that "official story" to reveal something important about the managerial culture of the company. Whether these professed values and beliefs actually represent those of a broad band of employees is a matter of speculation here and a compelling questions for further study (see Harrison & Beyer, 1993).

To Ireland and Hitt (1992) and Pearce and David (1987), the mission is one of the central documents of an organization because it contains its definition, tasks, essence, and the direction the company will follow. In the case of CEMEX, the first version of its mission statement was published in 1995. This means that by 1996, the year of the last report studied here, CEMEX had only 12 months since the message was emitted, but in the 1992 report it can be read:

> We have imposed the mission of being prepared to operate in a fast and systematic way, investing in our country and taking plenty advantage of the opportunities that the international market presents. (p. 2)

The relatively late emergence of the mission statement does not mean in any way that the corporation previously had no announced definition, values, and beliefs. Rather, it simply shows that before it did not perceive the need to print these in a document. By the mid-1990s, of course, corporate fashion dictated that all large firms have vision, mission, and strategic goals statements. The global growth that occurs after 1992 sparked the official declaration of an organizational mission.

Pearce and David (1987) suggested that a mission statement suggests in large part what a company *wants* to be. In the case of CEMEX, this is "the most competent multinational cement organization in the world." The mission includes a statement about products: "cement, pre-mixed concrete, and aggregates"; identifies its goals: "emergent markets with high potential for growth"; reveals its strategies for survival: "focus in the medullar markets, reduce costs and maximize efficiency and profitability, revise and analyze operations and diversify to emergent markets"; and enumerates its competitive advantages: "experience, structure, low costs, state of the art technology, solid financial structure and a leader in the market."

Two central themes stand out in the mission statement: satisfy the construction needs of its clients; and create value for its shareholders, employees, and other audiences. From these themes it is possible to infer that people are most important to the company, but a hierarchy of values exists for the company. Clients or customers occupy the first place, followed by the shareholders, the employees and "other audiences." The phrase "create value" is richly ambiguous, in that each individual can give it the meaning he desires. However, it seems that profitability is the not-so-buried subtext of this expression. As shown in the letter to the shareholders, part of the 1995 annual report, where the company declares through its CEO:

> This ability to surpass the actual economic conditions of Mexico, with *profitability*, to confront the crises of the past and the future, and to *sustain* our growth and *profitability* on the long term, is *a tribute* to our clients, our personnel, our suppliers and shareholders. (Italics added)

Two more details merit attention in this document: I did not find any specific references to the importance of employees to the company (even such this was manifest in other texts) or to the significance of the environment (despite its relevance for an organization of its type). The corporation's strategic philosophy was never elaborated. In fact, the only mention is of a "World-class philosophy," offered without further comment.

Certain other values are reflected in the texts. These include the concept of a "foundation of all our constructive efforts," and a source of "permanent values" (1989 report); an emphasis on "resources for growth" (1992 report); the clients: "our most prized associates" (CEO's speech); "Our environment demands from our people the highest level of productivity and efficiency" (1991 report); and continuous improvement: "We have a compromise with continuous improvement in our performance" (1994 report). It also stands out in the report from 1992, the reference to the environment when the organization defines itself as "a company that aggressively promotes respect for ecology." Although more values are evident, this case is not focused solely on locating values, but on detecting those values that seem to ground the ideology of the company. Finally, values are frequently discussed as giving the company a competitive advantage. In this way, the notion of "value" has a dual orientation for the corporation: abstract commitment and profitability (an "added value").

From another point of view, it is interesting to find that CEMEX's dominant values are parallel to those associated with North American companies (see Cheney & Frenette, 1993). That is the case for productivity, growth, competition, efficiency, and a broad invocation of success. A desire for success is related to profitability and shows an ideological correspondence to U.S. society strongly oriented toward productivity, individual achievement, and consumption. Given that CEMEX was born in a collectivist culture, it is surprising that traditional Mexican and Latin values like family, religion, friendship, and interpersonal relations are not stressed in any of the texts I scrutinized.

In numerous ways the organization stresses prestige and reputation. This is consistent with Archer and Fitch's (1990) argument that in Latin American community's membership in a prestigious organization is a sign of success. From this point of view, it is clear that CEMEX seeks to boost its prestige and reputation through what Cheney and Frenette called the "firstness" value. This means being the first one, the best, the leader. This value is repeated in the three documents: "CEMEX is the most competent and profitable multinational cement organization in the world" (Mission Statement, 1996), an "unquestionable leader" (video).

Like most contemporary corporations, CEMEX elevates the value of change. The company stresses its adaptability: "change, velocity and flexibility are characteristics that have taken us to where we are now" (CEO's speech). "We believe that it is essential to take advantage of opportunities" (1995 report).

It may be said that CEMEX presents a strong, masculine image that is largely achievement-oriented. The corporate texts overwhelmingly emphasize profit, competitiveness, and expansion. The company shows interest in social responsibility to the larger community, except insofar as the company stresses environmental awareness.

All this does not mean, however, that the company does not possess an interest in human relations; it simply shows that these values do not appear in the final official speech or in the analyzed documents. Thus, from this analysis, the concepts laid down in Table 7.2 emerge as the central values of CEMEX. Obviously, there are more values for the company than these. However, a more

TABLE 7.2   Emergent Values

VALUE	MEANING
People	Valuable asset Foundation of its effort (of the company) Permanent value
Environment	Resource Respect Protection Defense
Clients	Associates
Productivity and efficiency	As constant commitments in the company
Added value	Profitability, service, and information

comprehensive analysis of values must take into account policy decisions and daily practices (Collins & Porras, 1995).

SPECULATIONS ABOUT ORGANIZATIONAL CULTURE

With messages whose apparent end is to transmit the annual results of the company, there is embedded an ideology, a vision of the market and the world, a conception of success. Above all, there prevails in them an idea that appears carefully planned and maybe was conceived to generate a consensus in the audience: the creation of an identity and image of CEMEX focusing on the company's greatness, success, innovation, high technology, dependability, efficiency, and productivity.

In this way, the image of CEMEX is promoted, and at the same time the larger identity of the company is consolidated. Through formal communication a company with a strong, consistent, and heroic personality can be perceived, capable of dealing with the rules of the game imposed by the world market. The company displays values such as production, growth, and efficiency, values associated with North American culture (see Cheney & Frenette, 1993).

The company's various texts focus on producing messages that emphasize successes, results, and outstanding achievement, thereby building the company's image: aggressive, self-confident, eager to conquer, and dominate. So, CEMEX appears to be a "person" who is focused on business and productivity, visionary and competent, but with a discourse that is out of balance where human and social matters are concerned: there is no room for modesty and moderation—only confident assertions of success.

With respect to this, Cheney and Christensen (2000) pointed out that these messages, which are communicated inside as well as outside the organization, display a common concern: identity. A strong and mythic personality like CEMEX's can motivate and inspire employees and at the same time generate confidence in stockholders, consumers, and the general public. Additionally, through this form of communication, independent of whether or not the organization manages to convince its audiences with its messages, the company enters into a process of communication with itself (see Cheney & Christensen, 2000). What this means is that the company communicates with itself to tell its story, reinforce its values and beliefs and elaborate its own myth of greatness. In this process, the external public, besides being the receiver of the message, represents a kind of ideal "mirror" inasmuch as it helps the organization to identify how it wants to be viewed by others (see Cheney & Christensen, 2000).

On the other hand, if in the annual reports and the video, all evidence appears to lead toward forging this successful personality or identity, the messages of the CEO project very opposing ideas such as: "we have to *continue learning*, we have to *be flexible*, we have to *be humble* so that we can continuously learn" (closure speech). While in the opening speech he says: "*complacency* and *arrogance are the ruin of success*" (italics added).

These words reveal the complementarity of two messages: one public (in the videos and annual reports), the other private (in the speeches), where the CEO, face to face with his collaborators, asks them to assume a different attitude in order to learn. He asks them to forget the power games and support each other. He also proclaims that working at CEMEX is like competing in a marathon in which only the best competitors are present. This analogy shows without a doubt the high competitiveness of the company, but also reveals a furious *internal* competition, together with the idea of speed and urgency for all those who work in the organization.

It is no wonder that the same words and associated meanings of the CEO are not found in other documents.. The public discourse is permanent and is part of the memory of the company, while the oral message has an ephemeral quality—unless it is transcribed in writing and preserved. In all, despite the probable tension or contradiction between these messages, for certain groups that have access only to the public document, it is possible that the notion of a successful image prevails that may be reinforced with other actions and new formal messages.

This way, it seems that the different organizational meanings such as success, greatness, efficiency, productivity and service, among others, revolve around the idea of the *good name* of CEMEX.

Finally, from another perspective and taking into account the complete set of documents, we can identify at least four different dimensions of messages or discourses:

1. Facts: referring to data, achievements, strategies, investments, and so on.
2. Function or activity: referring to what CEMEX does and how does it does it.
3. Values and beliefs: as expressed primarily in the form of a mission.
4. Personality: as conveyed by the company's spirit and its attitude.

The four converge in a global identity discourse carefully prepared, with which the organization seeks unity, acceptance and good reputation. As Weil (1992) said, the four reinforce the continuity of the company.

CONCLUSIONS

The primary purpose of this research was to carry out an exploratory study of the organizational culture of a multinational corporation, through the analysis of formal communication texts in which the language used served as a basis for examining the image of the company and making inferences about its company culture. Through the study, I considered a variety of features of organizational messages, including uses of pronouns and adjectives, metaphors, and personification, explicit and implicit values.

This study explored several aspects of the communication and culture of a multinational corporation. The global context demands both greater intensity and quantity of messages directed at making the identity of the company known while adapting to different audiences (see Cheney & Christensen, 2000). Therefore, from the analysis developed here, we can consider how the formal communication of big corporations aims to spread the official culture of the company; including ideas of "who we are" and "what we value," and "the way we think in this organization."

As a result, official corporate texts, such as annual reports, commemorative videos, and CEO speeches, can be considered valuable sources of information in making exploratory studies of the company culture, because here the organization introduces itself, tells its own story, and seeks to make salient a story which it wants others to tell.

The major dilemma of formal organizational image-making is how to appear strong and consistent, presenting a coherent and univocal message, while at the same time adapting to multiple audiences, especially in different countries. The overwhelming bias of corporate identity management is on the side of "univocality," yet significant pressures exist for message adaptation (Leitch & Motion, 2000). This tension is ripe for investigation in future studies of CEMEX and other multinational corporations.

The corporation clearly is attempting to foster a broad symbolic alliance with its external audiences, especially clients and investors, with its stress on "added value," "efficiency," and globalization. While being vague, these rhetorical appeals nevertheless situate the company in a league of multinational success stories. An interesting follow-up study would involve interviews with both actual and prospective investors, asking them to react to CEMEX's image. Additionally, the corporation is communicating with itself. "Auto-communication" in this way can include not only the effects which ostensibly external message may have on internal audiences (employees) but also a kind of self-persuasion for the crafters of the public messages and top management. Thus, it would be interesting to interview members of all three segments of the internal audience: message creators, policymakers, and general employees.

In terms of value orientations, it seems that CEMEX, independent of its Mexican origin, identifies more with the values that are common to international companies—especially U.S.-based multinational companies. Perhaps owing to its desire to globalize, the corporation places a higher value on these kinds of "world-class" companies. Additionally, this allows the company to create the image of prestige and success that it needs to be a part of the big world market. Likewise, this strategy seems to help it to strengthen the identity and sense of belonging of its employees around the world, because the values that could identify it as a Latin or Mexican company are intentionally obscured. In this way, the company promotes a global, multinational image: a corporation from everywhere and nowhere. At the same time, it is interesting to note that in all of the organizational discourse, very little attention is given to the human dimension and multicultural dimensions of work. The company claims to be multinational and by implication multicultural, but that character trait never appears in its documents. Instead, the company shows us a strong, aggressive, expansive personality, interested in success and dominance.

An analysis such as the one presented here shows only one face of the organization, although it also opens up the possibility of other types of studies that can help us to discover additional facets of the organization. If there does exist a great distance between the rhetorical, symbolic reality of the company discourse, and the day-to-day reality of the people who make up the company, the documents that have been studied do permit the discovery of the official elements of organizational culture. The official public image would no doubt be an important point of reference for employees, even when they reject that image. Thus, we should pursue audience reception studies of corporate identities and images (Christensen & Cheney, 2000).

For future research, the analysis also suggests the need to study, by other methods, the congruence between various messages and actions, recognizing that power relations and other aspects of the organization's functioning can only be fully appreciated through a more comprehensive, multilevel analysis.

Additionally, the analysis opens the way for the incorporation of other methods, such as interviews with message recipients, observations, and employment of different corporate texts, in order to enrich the findings. And this study, which has no pretense of intercultural generalizability, encourages us to consider other possible "readings" of official corporate documents in the future. But one of the most important implications of the research presented here, without a doubt, is that it leaves us with the challenge of widening the study to other Mexican or Latin corporations, promoting with this other alternatives for the analysis of company culture in virtually unexplored territory.

REFERENCES

Bantz, C. (1993). *Understanding organizations: Interpreting organizational communications cultures.* Columbia: University of South Carolina Press.

Barnett, G. (1988). Communication and organizational culture. In G. M. Goldhaber & G. A. Barnett (Eds.), *Handbook of organizational communication* (pp. 101-130). Norwood, NJ: Ablex.

Barr, P., Stimpert, J., & Huff, A. (1992). Cognitive change, strategic action, and organizational renewal. *Strategic Management Journal, 13,* 15-36.

Bormann, E. (1983). Symbolic convergence. In L. Putnam & M. Pacanowsky (Eds.), *Communication and organizations. An interpretative approach* (pp. 99-123). Beverly Hills, CA: Sage.

Boyce, M. (1995). Collective centering and collective sense-making in the stories and storytelling of one organization. *Organization Studies, 16*(1), 107-137.

Brown, M. (1986). Sense making and narrative forms: Reality constructions in organizations. In L. Thayer (Ed.), *Organization—communication: Emerging perspectives* (Vol 1, pp. 71-84). Norwood, NJ: Ablex.

Brown, A., & Starkey, K. (1994). The effect of organizational culture on communication and information. *Journal of Management Studies, 31,* 807-827

Cassell, C., & Symon, G. (Eds.). (1995). *Qualitative methods in organizational research.* Thousand Oaks, CA: Sage.

Cheney, G. (1983). The rhetoric of identification and the study of organizational communication. *Quarterly Journal of Speech, 69,* 143-158.

Cheney, G. (1991). *Rhetoric in an organizational society: Managing multiple identities.* Columbia: University of South Carolina Press.

Cheney, G., & Christensen, L.T. (2000). Organizational identity: Linkages between internal and external communication. In F.M. Jablin & L.L. Putnam (Eds.), *The new handbook of organizational communication* (pp. 231-269). Thousand Oaks, CA: Sage.

Cheney, G., & Frenette, G. (1993). Persuasion and organization: Values, logics, and accounts in contemporary corporate public discourse. In C. Conrad (Ed.), *The ethical nexus* (pp. 49-72). Norwood, NJ: Ablex.

Collins, J., & Porras, J. (1995) *Empresas que perduran: Principios exitosos de compañías triunfadoras* [Build to last: Successful habits of visionary companies]. Bogotá, Colombia: Norma, S.A.

Falcione, R.L., & Wilson, C.E. (1988). Socialization processes in organizations. In G.M. Goldhaber & G.A. Barnett (Eds.), *Handbook of organizational communication* (pp. 151-169). Norwood, NJ: Ablex.

Feldman, S. (1990). Stories of cultural creativity: On the relation between symbolism and politics in organizational change. *Human Relations, 43*(8), 809-828

Geertz, C. (1987). *La interpretación de las culturas* [The interpretation of cultures]. Barcelona: Gedisa.

Gundry, L., & Rousseau, D. (1994). Critical incidents in communicating culture to newcomers: The meaning is the message. *Human Relations, 47*(9), 1063-1087.

Hall, E. (1978). *Más allá de la cultura* [Beyond the culture]. Barcelona, España: Gustavo Gili.

Hansen, C., & Kahnweiler, W. (1993). Storytellings: An instrument for understanding the dynamics of corporate relationships. *Human Relations, 46*(12), 1391-1409.

Harrison, M.T., & Beyer, J. (1993). *The cultures of work organizations.* Upper Saddle River, NJ: Prentice-Hall.

Harrison, R., & Carroll, G. (1991) Keeping the faith: A model of culture transmission in formal organizations. *Administrative Science Quarterly, 36,* 552.

Hofstede, G., Neuijen, B., Ohayv, D., & Sanders, G. (1990). Measuring organizational cultures: A qualitative and quantitative study across twenty cases. *Administrative Science Quarterly, 35,* 286-316.

Ireland, R.D., & Hitt, M. (1992). Mission statements: Importance, challenge, and recommendations for development. *Business Horizons,* 34-42.

Kersten, A. (1986). A critical-interpretative approach to the study of organizational communication: Bringing communication back into the field. In L. Thayer (Ed.), *Organization—communication: Emerging perspectives* (Vol. 1, pp.133-150). Norwood, NJ: Ablex.

Leitch, S., & Motion, J. (2000). *A Foucaultian critique of organizational identity.* Working paper, The University of Waikato, Hamilton, New Zealand.

McGee, M.C. (1980). The ideograph: A link between rhetoric and ideology. *Quarterly Journal of Speech, 66,* 1-16.

McMillan, J. (1986). In search of the organizational persona: A rationale for studying organizations rhetorically. In L. Thayer (Ed.), *Organization—communication: Emerging perspectives* (Vol. 2, pp. 21-45). Norwood, NJ: Ablex.

Moran, R.T., Harris, P.R., & Stripp, W.G. (1993). *Developing the global organization.* Houston, TX: Gulf.

Morgan, G. (1991). *Imágenes de la organización* [Organizational images]. México: Ediciones Alfaomega.

Pacanowsky, M.E., & O'Donnell-Trujillo, N. (1982). Communication and organization. *The Western Journal of Speech Communication, 46,* 115-130.

Pacanowsky, M., & O'Donnell-Trujillo, N. (1983). Organizational communication as a cultural performance. *Communication Monographs, 50,* 127-147.

Pearce, J., II, & David, F. (1987). Corporate mission statements: The bottom line. *Academy of Management Executive, 1*(2), 109-116.

Putnam, L. (1983). The interpretative perspective. In L. Putnam & M. Pacanowsky (Eds.), *Communication and organizations. An interpretative approach* (pp. 31-53). Beverly Hills, CA: Sage.

Schein, E. (1999). *The corporate culture. Survival guide* (1st ed.). San Francisco: Jossey-Bass.

Smircich, L. (1983). Concepts of culture and organizational analysis. *Administrative Science Quarterly, 28*, 339-358.

Smircich, L., & Calás, M. (1987). Organizational culture: A critical assessment. In F.M. Jablin, L. Putman, K.H. Roberts, & L.W. Porter (Eds.), *Handbook of organizational communication: An interdisciplinary perspective.* (pp. 228-263). Newbury Park, CA: Sage.

Spradley, J. (1979). *The ethnographic interview.* Austin, TX: Harcourt Brace Jovanovich College Publishers.

Weil, P. (1992). *La comunicación global* [Global communication]. Barcelona: Paidós.

SECTION D

Studies in a Global Perspective

8

THE MYTH OF THE NONGOVERNMENTAL ORGANIZATION

Governmentality and Transnationalism in an Indian NGO

Shiv Ganesh
The University of Montana

This chapter uses the Foucaultian concept of governmentality *to analyze the transnational characteristics of "sustainable development" discourse in an Indian nongovernment organization (NGO), the manner in which it is linked with market-oriented forces, and its relationship with the Indian State. An ethnographic study of the NGO reveals that the discourse of "sustainable development" serves to governmentalize the NGO and align it with the ethos of transnational capital. This governmentalization occurs by way of the development of shared vocabularies and structures that reinforce rather than resist the economizing tendencies of the market, thereby producing and reproducing an ideology of entrepreneurialism. All this serves to ensure that the notion of an independently functioning "nongovernmental" organization is a mythical one. Still, given the role that the Indian State plays in the everyday activity of the NGO, this "myth" is clearly necessary.*

Two characteristics of politics between the "first" and "third" worlds stand out in the decades after World War II. The first is the centrality of the issue of "development" both in international politics and as the raison d'être of nation-states in the third world. *Development* has been a controversial issue, to say the least. Although some claim that the very meaning of the category has changed radically from a narrowly defined economistic vision to a more wholesome, broad definition that encompasses proactive social and political change (Goldthorpe, 1996), others have radically interrogated the historical relationship between development and democratic social change (Chatterjee, 1993; Kaviraj, 1992). In the last few decades, the most important hallmark in the discursive evolution of "development" has been the emergence of the discourse of "sustainable development." The upsurge in such discourse is an indication of the centrality of environmental conflict in international politics (Peterson, 1997). The predominance of sustainable development discourse has foregrounded strains between ecology-first and market-first approaches to contemporary environmental crises. In particular, the eco-friendly credentials of sustainable development discourse have become more and more suspect. Several scholars have argued that in its attempt to promote the market over the environment, "sustainable development" discourse reveals itself as part of the nexus between "global" capitalism and the developmentalist apparatus (Escobar, 1995; Gupta, 1998; Imber, 1996; Stephens, 1992).

The second feature that has characterized political relationships between the first and third worlds is the proliferation of nongovernmental, "alternative" structures to deal with the issue of development and underdevelopment. Relationships between states and markets have shifted on a worldwide scale, especially since the advent of economic deregulation and the conversion of formerly closed economies into liberalized markets (Cheney, 1999; McMichael, 1996). As this has occurred, the roles that "global" nongovernment organizations (NGOs) play in the international developmental apparatus have become more prominent. Some see NGO work as a response to the crisis of the state or as a response to the environmental crises caused by the rapid proliferation of markets (Chambers, 1987; Halliday, 2000; McMichael, 1996; Spiro, 1994). Given this, it becomes important to study this "response" and ask whether NGOs are in fact the solution to the crisis of the state and the market, or whether they are indicative of another set of problems altogether.

Moreover, given that sustainable development is increasingly central to development discourse in general and NGOs are becoming increasingly important in its deployment (Welling-Hall, 1994), critical examinations of how NGOs strategize the idea of sustainable development are pertinent. This chapter attempts to address this need by using Foucault's concept of *governmentality* to analyze and gain understanding of three issues: the transnational character of sustainable development discourse in an Indian NGO, the manner in which the NGO is linked with market-oriented forces, and the relationship of the NGO with the Indian state. In the first section, I engage in a theoretical discussion of the concept of governmentality as it is used in this chapter, emphasizing its transnational character. In the second section, I move on to an ethnographic analysis of how the notion of sustainable development, as it is deployed by the NGO, produces and reinforces a transnational neoliberal ideology. In the last section, I examine the ways in which the activity of the NGO, despite its formal renunciation of a relationship with the state, is actively engaged with it. I conclude the chapter with a discussion of its limitations and outline two contributions that governmentality studies can make to organizational communication and transnational communication scholarship.

THEORIES OF GOVERNMENTALITY

In this section, I introduce the notion of *governmentality* as it is sketched out by Foucault, drawing attention to the continuity, diversity and diffuseness that characterize the concept. Following this, I discuss the notion of *governing at a distance* and its relationship with transnational neoliberal ideology. I then present three shifts in contemporary modes of governmentality that serve to frame the subsequent ethnographic analysis of an Indian NGO.

The concept of *governmentality* crept into popular academic discourse in the early 1990s with the publication of *The Foucault Effect: Studies in Governmentality* (Burchell, Gordon, & Miller, 1991). The book represented the coming of age of a body of secondary literature on Foucault, largely British, that attempted to explain changes in the state, economy, and civil society in Britain (Barry, Osborne, & Rose, 1996; Burchell et al., 1991; Miller & Rose, 1990; Rose & Miller, 1992; Stenson & Watt, 1999). Since then, the literature on what has come to be known as "governmentality studies" has grown significantly in terms of volume and contexts. A glance at the Social Science and Humanities Citation Index reveals that more than 90 academic articles and a number of books have been published on the subject in a variety of journals in the last decade. Moreover, one third of those articles were published in the 1998-1999 time period. The contexts for governmentality studies have widened dramatically as well. Scholars have begun focusing on manifestations of governmentality in other nations such as Canada (Blake, 1999; Braun, 2000), China (Ng & Tang, 1999), France (Donzelot, 1991), India (Gupta, 1998), Malaysia (Brosius, 1999), Mexico (McDonald, 1999; Stern, 1999), New Zealand (Larner, 1997, 1998), South Africa (Durrheim & Foster, 1999), Sri Lanka (Scott, 1999), and the United States (Graham, 1997). As this has occurred, the concept has been applied to a widening array of issues and subjects such as accounting (Radcliffe, 1999), citizenship and participation (Purvis & Hunt, 1999; Tully, 1999), education (Beck, 1999), emotion (Watson, 1999), empire (Gupta, 1998; Malpas & Wickham, 1997; Scott, 1999), environmentalism (Bennett, 1999;

Brosius, 1999; Gupta, 1998), globalization (Dalby, 1999), health (Hughes & Griffiths, 1999; Scambler & Higgs, 1998; Stern, 1999), journalism (Eide & Knight, 1999), labor movements (Manning, 1999), library studies (Joyce, 1999), police studies (Watson, 1999), television (Ouellette, 1999), territoriality (Braun, 2000), and tourism (Hollinshead, 1999).

Foucault first introduced the neologism *governmentality* during a lecture he delivered at the College de France in February 1978. Foucault's work on the concept has been read as his response to critics who state that his preoccupation with the specifics of disciplinarity in everyday communicative practices failed to explain international politics and articulate a theory of interests (Gordon, 1991; Spivak, 1988). The English translation of "governmentality" appears as chapter 4 of *The Foucault Effect*. In the essay, Foucault (1991) said of governmentality:

> It is the ensemble formed by the institutions, procedures, analyses and reflections, the calculations and tactics that allow the exercise of this very specific, albeit complex form of power, which has as its target population, as it principle form of knowledge political economy, and as its essential technical means apparatuses of security. (p. 102)

Foucault's concern in the essay was to establish how the invention of government during the 16th century and its expression in the 18th century in the form of liberalism, produced an upward and downward continuity between the individual and the state. This discursive and regulative continuity, said Foucault, puts an end to the notion of Machiavellian sovereignty where subjects directly obey the will of the sovereign. This is because

> upward continuity means that a person who wishes to govern the state well must first learn how to govern himself, his goods and his patrimony, after which he will be successful in governing the state . . . we also have a downward continuity in the sense that, when a state is well run, the head of the family will know how to look after his family, his goods and his patrimony, which means that individuals will, in turn, behave as they should . . . the central term of this continuity is the government of the family, termed *economy*. (pp. 91-92)

In the last decade or so, the governmentality studies tradition has built on this basic formulation. In an early article on the subject, P. Miller and Rose (1990) stated the following:

> The notion of government draws attention to the diversity of forces and groups that have, in heterogeneous ways, sought to regulate the lives of individuals and the conditions within particular national territories in pursuit of various goals. (p. 3)

Taken as such, the state is conceived of as a *product* of governmentality, rather than as its *producer*. Miller and Rose stipulated that traditional theoretical dualisms such as "state versus civil society" or "public versus private" cease to be of central conceptual importance in governmentality studies, given the diversity and diffuseness of the relationships that are made visible via the notion of governmentality. Government is seen to operate in a range of social sites, not just in the offices of state agencies. Pushed further, this thesis results in the counterintuitive position that the state itself is fictitious. As Rose and Miller (1992) said:

> To speak of the "power" of a Government, a Department of State, a local authority, a military commander or a manager in an enterprise is to substantialize that which arises from an assemblage of forces by which particular objectives and injunctions can shape the actions and calculations of others. (p. 184)

Of course, to say that the state is "fictitious" is not to say that the state is incidental or transparent. On the contrary, Rose and Miller stipulated that the fiction of the state is essential for governmental control to occur. However, the notions of continuity, diversity, and diffuseness that characterize governmental control entail that it is exercised not via direct coercion, but via distantiation. Miller and Rose referred to this form of control as "government at a distance," and relate the idea to Latour's (1987) concept of "action at a distance." For Latour, the production of knowledge by a "center" about remote places and events resulted in the center's ability to dominate that which was distant from it (Latour, 1987). For Miller and Rose, governmentality works similarly, via loosely aligned networks that produce a dominant "center." They say that

> language . . . plays a key role in establishing these loosely aligned networks and in enabling rule to be brought about in an indirect manner. It is, in part, through adopting shared vocabularies, theories and explanations, that loose and flexible associations may be established between agents across time and space . . . whilst each remains, to a greater or lesser extent, constitutionally distinct and formally independent. (Miller & Rose, 1990, p. 10)

This phenomenon is epitomized in neoliberal states that conduct governance via such strategies as public contracting. For example, it is an eminently governmental strategy for the state to ensure that the "private" development of telecommunications in general and new information technology in particular occurs within a framework controlled by the state.

Governmentality studies has been particularly concerned with the form of political rationality constituted by neoliberal ideology, and it is this form of "governmental" rationality that forms the core of the concept of "transnationalism" as it is used in this chapter. The field of intercultural/international communication recently witnessed the publication of several books all of which theorize the notion of *transnationalism* in similar terms (Martin & Nakayama, 1997; Mohammadi, 1997; Mowlana, 1996; Nakayama & Martin, 1999). The idea of transnationalism here, loosely speaking, can be referred to as "the activity of migrating across the borders of one or more nation-states" (Nakayama & Martin, 1999, p. 346). Such a definition is useful first because it allows us to retain space for the nation-state in our theoretical formulations about "new" social formations. Second, it is useful because it addresses the multiplicity of contexts in which we can locate the transnational (Hegde, 1998). Given this, it is important to stipulate that this chapter is concerned with the specific manifestations of the transnational in the context of the phenomenon of governmentality and *liberalization*.

Liberalization, the driving force behind worldwide economic change since the 1980s, is the central policy prescription of the neo-liberal model of "global" economic growth supported by such agencies as the World Bank and the International Monetary Fund. In its current avatar, *liberalization* refers to a shift away from "structuralism" or state-sponsored development to market-driven capitalism (Castells, 1996). It entails a move away from structuralist ideas, specifically with reference to its advocacy of shifts from import substitution to export orientations and its encouragement of foreign (or international) capital investments. Moreover, it encourages the control and ownership of industry by private capital rather than by the state (Heeks, 1996). The predominance of liberalization policies in the third world today marks the pervasiveness of transnational capitalist modernity, that set of widespread historical developments that mark the triumph of the market in all spheres of life (Rajagopal, 2001; Tomlinson, 1991).

That governmentality research has begun to examine what I refer to as the *transnational* manifestations of neoliberal ideologies is hardly surprising given Foucault's emphasis that liberalism is not so much an historical epoch but the *ethos* of governmentality itself (Burchell, 1996). Whereas traditional accounts of neoliberalism equate it with the phenomenon of "globalization," within governmentality studies the term carries much more meaning. It refers not only to the regulation of economic life, but the production of the category of "economy" itself, by way of intellectual technologies, practical activity, and expert authority in all realms of social life (Miller & Rose, 1990; Tully, 1999). Accordingly, rather than conceive of worldwide neoliberal economic reforms such as privatization, tariff reduction, or downsizing in terms of a state willfully abandoning civil society to the capriciousness of the market (Castells, 1996), governmentality studies conceive of it in terms of the reorganization and interpenetration of an extant principle—that of "governing at a distance." In other words, governmentality studies conceive of worldwide shifts in political economy over the last several decades in *additive* terms. In addition to the continuity between the individual and the nation-state, continuities between local forms of organization and an increasingly deterritorialized market become established not so much in terms of direct institutional isomorphism, but in terms of a governmental *ethos*.

In particular, Rose (1996) sketched out three shifts that he associated with "advanced" liberalism:

1. A new relation between expertise and politics where expert knowledge is "responsibilized" (or simply, made responsible) in relation to claims that are overtly independent from its own criteria of truth and competence. This is exemplified by phenomena such as marketization or monetarization and the demand that knowledge be both "efficient" and "applicable."
2. A new pluralization of "social" technologies, where the center detaches itself from the unified network it sought to assemble (epitomized by the welfare system) and instead links itself more heterogeneously to a variety of autonomous entities—enterprises, communities and individuals.
3. A new specification of the subject of government, where active individuals are increasingly urged to "enterprise" themselves and maximize their life through acts of choice.

These three shifts are highlighted in the following examination of an NGO that I call Different Visions (DV). In the analysis, I show that the concern with deploying the concept of sustainable development entails that the organization develop structures and practices that produce and reinforce a transnational neoliberal ideology while simultaneously maintaining a relationship with the state. I begin the analysis by providing a history of the organization in order to demonstrate its significant transnational connections. I then move on to a discussion of organizational ideology, focusing specifically on the manner in which DV deploys sustainable development in terms of its advocacy of an "independent" sector, its organizational structure, and its emphasis on entrepreneurialism. In the next section, I turn to a discussion of the relationship of the NGO and the state in terms of their informal collaboration, concluding that far from developing a disinterested relationship with the Government of India, the NGO, and the state are actively engaged in enacting the phenomena governmentality studies scholars call *governing at a distance*.

A brief note on methodology is warranted at this point. I characterize my research approach in terms of an extended case method—one where ethnographic and historiographic approaches are combined at a "microlevel" in order to give substance and depth to "macrolevel" analysis (Burawoy, 1991, 1998). The bulk of my evidence was collected in 1999 during a month-long stint at the organization, although some of the documents that I have used were collected during earlier visits. In this chapter, although I have used a fair amount of evidence obtained from direct interviews, a substantial portion of the case I build is based on several different kinds of organizational documents—annual reports, research proposals, funding proposals, progress reports, studies, internal memos, and public relations pamphlets. However, the documents I used were not selected at random, but as a result of the interviews themselves. As part of each interview, I asked respondents to identify organizational documents that they felt were most pertinent to their work and that would give me a better understanding of the work-related themes that they had been discussing with me. I have italicized quotations from respondents in order to allow the reader to distinguish between documented material and the words of respondents themselves.

GOVERNMENTALITY AND DIFFERENT VISIONS

In this section, I discuss the governmentalization of DV and its alignment with market forces. In order to do so, I first provide a brief history of DV. Following this, I discuss the ideology and orientation of DV with reference to the way in which sustainable development serves as a "core value" for the organization. I then move on to discuss the manner in which DV positions itself as part of an "independent sector" and the covert market bias of such positioning. Following this, I analyze the ideology of entrepreneurialism as it is manifested at DV. I do so in two ways. First, I focus on the relationship between DV's organizational structure and its marketing activities. Second, I discuss the manner in which DV constructs its "clientele." In the process, I provide an example of DV's activity in the form of its initiation and development of micro-concrete roofing projects. I conclude the section with a discussion of how the overall governmentalization of DV relates to Rose's (1996) formulation of three "shifts" in governmentality under late capitalism.

HISTORY

DV, founded in 1983, would not have grown or even have been formed if not for its significant transnational connections. Its founder and president, Dr. Amit Kapoor, formed the agency after working for several decades on an appointment and consultancy basis with various branches of the Indian government, as well as with various international development agencies. His significant contacts, developed over decades, include relationships with international development organizations such as the United Nations Development Programme (UNDP), various U.S. universities, branches of the Indian government, especially the Ministry of Human Resources, and individuals in other international environmental organizations such as the Worldwide Fund for Nature. These linkages meant that the fledgling organization, based in a major north Indian city, boasted an impressive array of credentials from the very outset. This ensured that it became a NGO with an audible voice in international developmentalist discourse. As importantly, it ensured that the new organization, formed during significant worldwide economic shifts toward liberalization and privatization, had access to funds from the UN, international funding agencies, multinational corporations, and several Western governments. Some in the organization see these connections as essential. Said one senior member:

> *There are plenty of challenges if you're working in the Indian setup. There are institutional constraints, recruitment issues, pay, constraints in the industrial environment, government, corruption, red tape . . . this is why you need high level people in the organization.*

DV is now an organization headquartered in a major Indian city with activities in various parts of the country. It is a large organization by Indian NGO standards, as it employs nearly 200 people. These linkages have done more than provide impetus to the growth of the organization; they are in many ways constitutive of it and deeply affect the organization's structure and ideology.

Ideology and Orientation

The last page of every report generated by DV contains a summary of the "aims and objectives" of the NGO. The very first sentence of the page reads:

> DV is an organization dedicated to devising and promoting better approaches for the Development of India.

On one hand, this broadly construed mandate serves as an interesting example of strategic ambiguity (Eisenberg, 1984; Markham, 1996) that allows the organization to potentially develop and execute virtually any set of activities in the name of "development." On the other hand, the visible discourse of its members as well as the discourse of organizational documents are fairly specific about where DV positions itself with reference to large development apparatuses, including the Government of India and international development organizations. At a presentation that DV members delivered at an international conference on development, DV was described as "a non-profit corporate organization with a mission to promote sustainable development through appropriate technology, institutional design and environmental management."

This makes it clear at many levels just what DV is all about: "appropriate technology," "institutional design," and "sustainable development" (in the form of environmental management). How these themes play themselves out in DV's organizational structure is addressed below.

Of the three terms, *sustainable development* is key to DV's ideological positioning in the development apparatus. There was an extremely high degree of consensus, both on the part of people I interviewed as well as in organizational documents, that all DV's activity fell under the umbrella term *sustainable development.* There was, however, some dissensus with reference to the definition of sustainable development itself and the manner of its deployment. This took the form of an interesting difference between documented material and verbal responses as to what constitutes sustainable development. Whereas the former are much more specific about how sustainable policies are to be operationalized, the latter are more ambivalent about the specifics of the term. This ambivalence was visible in a comment by one of DV's senior scientists about the deployment of "sustainable development." He said:

> *In many ways, sustainable development is an empty term. Anyone with any kind of scientific integrity would not say that they "do" sustainable development. But they contribute to it indirectly.*

The statement that "anyone with scientific integrity would not say that they 'do' 'sustainable development'" is telling because it acknowledges that science as a body of knowledge should not be colonized by an external technology, in this case, the technology of sustainable development. Yet, the scientist goes on to say "but they contribute to it indirectly." This, too, is telling because it points toward the fact that regardless of the ambiguity that individuals might feel about "doing" science for "sustainable development," ultimately, all organizational activity is subsumed under the "sustainable development" umbrella. Thus, it emerges as an explicit "core" value that underlies and rationalizes all organizational activity at DV.

There are two ways in which this "core value" affects DV's organizational structure. The first is centered on the manner in which it positions itself as an "independent sector" and the second has to do with its internal and external advocacy of the notion of entrepreneurialism.

DV as Part of an Independent Sector

That DV positions itself as part of an independent sector working in the area of development is evident in a number of research proposals, studies, and pamphlets, as well as from interviews with a number of respondents. One such document, to which a few respondents made specific reference, is titled "Independent Sector Organizing and the Earth Summit," authored by the head of the organization. The document was part of DV's preparation for the "Global

Forum" at Rio de Janeiro in 1992, the "parallel" conference held by global NGOs at the same time as the United Nations Conference on the Environment and Development (UNCED) that June. This position paper advocates enacting sustainable development in terms of a move away from state-sponsored development toward independent-sector aided development:

> Sustainable development is too complex a problem and too urgent a need to be left entirely in the hands of the government or international agencies . . . a growing body of opinion places a major responsibility on the *independent sectors* for achieving the specific objectives of a more rational and just form of socio-economic development. Development requires a large scale, decentralized but coherent effort for the delivery of goods and services aimed at fulfilling human needs and thereby enhancing management. (italics added)

Not only does the document advocate a move away from state-managed development, it also stipulates that this new managerialism is to be staged by virtually any kind of organization but the state. This is glaringly apparent in the very definition of the *independent sector:*

> . . . over the last few years the definition of the independent sector has grown from the original NGO or voluntary agency to a wide variety of organizations concerned with women's issues, youth and students, workers unions, corporate sector associations, religious groups, professional bodies and others.

The document also outlines an institutional design required to enact sustainable development: a design often referred to in many other project proposals, research reports, and position papers produced by the organization in subsequent years. The paper characterizes contemporary approaches to development as being determined by a "conventional institutional design." Conventional institutional design involves the duplication of "development" related activities by governments, company cooperatives, NGOs and other voluntary agencies. In advocating a "new" institutional design, the paper stipulates that the invention of an "independent" sector would yoke together the most effective and efficient aspects of "conventional" institutional design. In this scheme, specific roles are assigned to each institutional sector. Governments, it says, should restrict themselves to determining broad social objectives; NGOs are to provide motivation; the "private sector" must become the "multiplier" of development; and the job of the citizenry is to "participate." The advocacy of this vision of society is not shy of interpreting history as having borne witness to its success:

> voluntary effort provided a large part of the impetus for the freedom struggle and the independence movement throughout the first half of the 20th

century . . . the formal systems of government introduced by the Moghuls
and later refined by the British were relatively isolated phenomena . . . a
large part of the subcontinent's social and political activities were based for
much of its history on more informal, community-based or religion-based
organizations.

The document sums up its critique of current social arrangements and its
advocacy of an independent sector as follows:

Conventional institutional design has been unable to keep up with the
changing needs of society . . . largely invented more than a hundred years
ago to satisfy feudal and colonial imperatives, these legal frameworks
severely limit the capacity of present day institutions to respond to the
wholly new requirements of sustainable development. . . . The requirements
of sustainable development now make it essential to develop entirely new
institutional concepts which multiply the strengths and minimize the weaknesses of previous institutions. The independent sector appears to have
great potential for dealing with . . . the best of each previous type of institution. An organization in the independent sector must have the capacity to
think globally and act locally, link R&D to the realities of production and
marketing, and close the gap between innovation and production.

Thus advocated, the independent sector appears to fuse the gap between
public and private forms of organization, and indeed several documents at DV
specify as such. The organization, therefore, uses the rhetoric of sustainable
development and the independent sector to delimit the role that the state should
play in "development," thereby enabling a better power balance between different agents involved in the development process.

Underlying such "fusion," however, is an implicit move toward entrepreneurialism as a necessary prerequisite for the enactment of sustainable development. Take the following paragraph from the 1995 annual report:

The independent sector must synthesize the dialectical elements of three
important dimensions in its goals and structure—the private and the public
(it has to employ the organizational methods and motivational devices of
the private sector and have the social, developmental purposes of the public
sector), the big and the small (it has to combine the responsiveness of the
local, small-scale facilities for innovation, manufacturing and marketing
with the financial and technical power of a larger backup system), the old
and the new (it must derive maximum advantage from both traditional
knowledge and the opportunities offered by modern science).

To say that the motivation for social change must come from the private sector
(read business), to advocate direct linkages between local economies and large

markets and to take an eminently instrumental approach toward "traditional knowledge" is to privilege private entrepreneurship over public forms of social action. As will be shown in the next section, this move toward entrepreneurialism is not an add-on to DV's work but is constitutive of the structure of the organization itself and provides a means by which individuals identify with the organization.

The Ideology of Entrepreneurialism and DV's Organizational Structure

The rhetoric of sustainable development and the role that it plays in constituting DV itself allows the ideology of entrepreneurialism to saturate the organization. Entrepreneurialism is often quoted as a major strategy, if not *the* strategy that will further the goals of sustainable development. The ideology of entrepreneurialism is visible at two levels: the first is in the way it has shaped the internal organizational structure itself, and the second is in the manner in which the organization constructs its "clientele."[1]

The concept that social change needs to be market-driven is highlighted not only in formal organizational documents, but in everyday interaction itself. From the outset, DV has conceived of itself as a "matrix" organization: one where labor is cross-divided and individual organizational units are affiliated with at least two organizational level functional "networks." In DV's case, in addition to the development of such organizational units as the Environmental Systems Branch, Technology Systems Branch, Administration, and the Center for Global Climate Change, each unit is affiliated with "innovation," "production," and "marketing" networks that criss-cross the entire organization. The very first reference to these three networks that I detected was made in the 1982 project proposal for the organization itself, where the "matrix" structure was recommended as an efficient structure for an NGO by NASA administrators, among others. The three networks remain integral to DV's functioning and are much touted in various annual reports and research proposals. The matrix metaphor is also evident in DV's day-to-day functioning. It is especially visible in the organization of meetings at DV. In addition to weekly intra-unit meetings that deal largely with administrative matters, there are regular "innovation" meetings, "production" meetings, and "marketing" meetings that are attended

---

[1]It is true that the distinctions made in organizational studies between "internal" and "external" organizational communication serve to reinforce the container metaphor of organization and the conduit metaphor of communication, both of which have been subject to much critique. Still, as Cheney and Christensen (2000) argued, what is at stake in the distinction between "internal" and "external" organizational communication practices is not that they are inherently different or that one crosses more boundaries than the other. What is interesting is the manner in which organizations integrate their identities and their ideologies by explicitly constructing internal structures and external audiences. That DV does so is clearly evident in the deployment of the ideology of entrepreneurialism.

by affiliated individuals in each unit. At an organizational level, in addition to regular meetings between unit heads, units and networks deliver monthly presentations of their work to each other. Each unit is affiliated with various networks in varying degrees. For instance, the Technology Systems Branch, which characterized itself as the "heart" of the "innovation" network in its 1998 annual report, is also engaged in "outreach and action" by way of marketing its designs in kilns, ferrocement roofing and earth block technology to various corporate and nonprofit customers. The idea of "innovation" that organizes the Technology Systems Branch in particular, bears testimony to DV's role as a producer of "new" knowledge. As this chapter eventually demonstrates, such knowledge is cast as "expert" and made "applicable" to the problems of the rural market in India.

It is also interesting to note that the idea of innovation seemed to be central to individual identification with the organization. Several of the people I conversed with were at pain to point out to me the value of DV's "innovative" approach. The notion that "we do it differently" emerged as a source of pride and identification. Said one respondent:

> *I'm not sure I could work anywhere else. We take such a different approach from the government . . . we are always talking with each other. There is no hierarchy here. I can go into Amit's office anytime I want to if I have a problem. It's very rewarding.*

Another member, even though she professed a dislike of the constant meetings and presentations, admitted that it was important for the organization.

> *We keep on having meetings for this and meetings for that. It makes it difficult to spend as much time on my project as I want . . . but I know that if not for everyone else doing what they do, I would not have had my project in the first place.*

These three terms, *innovation, production*, and *marketing*, in addition to providing a source for individual identification and organizing the structure of DV, also reflect a largely economistic approach to issues of social change. Such economism is highly consonant with the economizing tendencies associated with neoliberalist ideologies (Imber, 1996). It is in the notion of marketing that the ideology of entrepreneurialism is most clearly visible. Of the three networks, the marketing network appears to be the most extensive. Attention to marketing is paid by the Technology Systems group, the Environmental Systems group, as well as by administration. That the concern with marketing is central to DV is clearly evident by the founding of Marketing and Rural Technology (MART) in the mid-1980s. MART was initiated in order for DV to further its franchising activities. In the words of one respondent:

DV provides the technology and know-how, and MART brings our clientele directly into our network by collaborating with them in order to make sure that our products are manufactured according to brand specifications.

Products that are developed at DV and marketed by MART in order for them to be produced on a larger scale by other organizations include stoves, pollution kits, and micro-concrete roofing technology.

The emphasis on marketing as a central organizational activity at DV is visible in many position papers, annual reports, and research reports. Two sets of documents especially reflect this emphasis. The first is a set of documents produced between 1986 and 1988 that argue for the necessity of marketing itself, and the second set, produced between 1994 and 1998 focuses on the approach spelled out by earlier papers onto the issue of technology transfer.

The most common justification visible for marketing at DV is its applicability to rural India. The conversion of rural India into a market is seen as the solution to centuries of rural problems. A 1987 position paper titled "Alternative Strategies for Rural Marketing" produced by the marketing network says:

> that there has been a catastrophic failure of the market in rural India is unquestionable. It is self-evident that there exists a great range of unfulfilled needs, yet there appears to be no demand. On the other hand, there exists a vast number of technologies and products which can meet these needs, and yet there is no supply. . . . Programmes based solely on government initiative for developing the rural economy are limited . . . in their ability to reach the large numbers involved. . . . Any solution to the problems of the rural poor must lie in the establishment of commercially viable mechanisms which enable the demand and supply of rural products to jump to much higher levels than exist today.

In a 1988 position paper, Amit Kapoor builds on this formulation and goes on to identify a networked approach as most appropriate for the rural market given its variability and decentralization, and stresses the importance of evolving an appropriate "product range" for the rural market. Consequently, it is especially important to engage in "corporate R&D:"

> . . . the principles of which are well understood by successful multinational corporations but not adequately followed in the third world. For a product to be marketable, it must pay someone to make it, it must pay someone to market it, it must pay someone to maintain it, and above all, it must be of sufficient benefit to the end-client and inexpensive enough to be within his [*sic*] purchasing power for him [*sic*] to be willing to buy it.

Interestingly enough, these early papers also contain a critique of the role of multinational corporations, namely their involvement exclusively in urban, organized markets, and their refusal to venture into rural markets. Yet, as is clearly visible above, the papers also endorse the overall approach of multinational corporations to product development, production and marketing, while being staunchly critical of government-sponsored endeavors. The effort to be distinct from the government is visible in later reports and papers as well. The distinction is especially evident in DV's advocacy of "alternative" approaches to technology transfer. A paper written in 1994 by a senior DV architect says:

> mechanisms set up for technology transfer (so far) have been inadequately designed (by the government). We have relied on demonstration projects, model programmes, training schemes and more. . . . These mechanisms have limited themselves to the scheme based supply of houses through construction agencies such as housing boards and do not have multipliers built into the project that can catalyze the use of demonstrated technology by local builders. Basically, initiatives in the transfer of shelter technology have failed to make an impact because their objectives have been limited to display of technology and house construction.

Another similar paper goes on to argue that:

> in line with the concept of sustainable development and AGENDA 21, the primary objective of any technology transfer exercise must be redefined as the creation of economically and ecologically sustainable livelihoods (which) can be found in the form of micro-enterprises . . . rather than in the disbursement of technology by the government.

ILLUSTRATION:
MICRO-CONCRETE ROOFING SYSTEMS AT DV

A good example of DV's "strategic vision" in action can be found in its development of micro concrete roofing systems. In this case, the innovation, production, and marketing system found expression in terms of (a) an initial needs assessment, (b) the design and development of the product, and (c) the dissemination and institutionalization of the technology.

According to a 1994 report on micro-concrete roofing systems (MCR), such systems were developed at DV because:

> there was a clear need for a roofing technology priced mid-way between thatch and reinforced cement concrete and more durable than the former . . . sloping roofs in most parts of India are of either thatch or baked clay tiles, at the lower end of the class structure.

On the other hand:

> more durable material such as Asbestos and GI sheets or RCC roofs are
> affordable only by the fairly well-off. In the southern parts of India baked
> clay tiles are becoming expensive to manufacture; on the other hand, good
> quality thatch is becoming scarce in the northern parts. There was thus need
> for a roofing system which is more durable, cost effective and easily acces-
> sible to people in small towns and villages.

Accordingly, DV's scientists developed a MCR machine (called a vibrator)
that was to be sold to various villages in south India. The available technology
for the vibrator was imported by DV from the industrial sector (specifically, a
multinational company in Bombay). DV adapted it for a more rural market by
developing and producing a version that did not require the use of electricity,
and that used sand, stone grit and cement to produce the tiles, instead of clay or
asbestos.

The final step according to the overall strategy was the "dissemination" of
the product, and as highlighted earlier, this is where the marketing orientation of
DV is most clearly visible. One early report on MCR says:

> There is a low success rate in the transition from the design and develop-
> ment phase to the dissemination phase. The reasons are not difficult to
> find—the "need" for MCR does not easily get translated into a "demand"
> for it, resulting in market failure conditions. The multivariate objectives
> which MCR are expected to fulfill also lead to varying degrees of success.
> Apart from these internal factors, lack of well-recognized and clearly artic-
> ulated business plans have thwarted their take-off. Needless to say, whatev-
> er be the "noble" objectives, unless they are business successes, these lofty
> objectives cannot be fulfilled. Thus, business and commercial viability
> should be duly recognized as the bottomline of future strategies of MCR
> promotion.

After advocating that market forces should be the center of the plan, the
report goes on to make a recommendation:

> To enable the production of MCR, it is important to have in place a pack-
> age of measures. Financial, market and institutional linkages have, for a
> long time, been regarded as essentials only for private business interests . . .
> the technology package of the MCR tiles includes the vibrator equipment,
> instructions manual and quality control kit. Moreover, the whole process is
> demonstrated on site to the buyer by skilled staff. A complete production
> package for manufacture of the vibrator has also been developed (by
> MART).

After casting its initial foray into MCR as a failure, DV's overall approach to MCR technology in the 1990s became more market-oriented, in line with its overall redefinition of technology transfer. The 1996 report reflects this shift:

> The entire MCR programme at DV underwent a strategic shift from R&D to market development and marketing. This shift has proved critical to the success of MART MCR in different parts of India . . . franchisees in different parts of the country have been running successful businesses through this technology.

In 1994, there were 30 franchisees of DV's MCR technology, and that number has since tripled. DV now considers the project at least a moderate success. All in all, this illustrates the centrality that is accorded market forces at DV today.

DV'S "CLIENTELE": THE "RURAL POOR"

DV's preoccupation with conceiving of social change in terms of market development serves to compose an explicit image of its "clientele" as potential consumers. This composition constitutes the second way in which DV's entrepreneurial ideology is manifested. The object of "sustainable development" as enacted by the "independent" sector is constructed specifically as the "rural poor": "the size, spread and poverty of the rural population . . . must now comprise the primary target of any effort aimed at sustainable development" says the 1998 annual report.

In addition to defining its target as "the poor," DV positions itself as experts acting on their behalf. As evidenced in the MCR example it speaks authoritatively about their needs and the manner in which these needs are to be met. As also evidenced in this example, the needs of the "poor" are to be met with technology:

> the poor have many basic needs—food, water, energy, shelter, clothing, transport, health care, education and productive employment. Almost all these needs have a close relationship with environmental values, and all have largely been unmet by past development strategies. The cycle of poverty is made more vicious by the lack of access of the poor to capital, technology or know-how—not to mention the riches of the resource base. With the evolution of societal perceptions, aspirations and conditions . . . and with recent developments in science, design, new materials and production processes, technological innovation is becoming increasingly important for solving the problems of poverty. New products and technologies, many with significant, positive social and environmental spinoffs, are now possi-

ble for mass distribution as a result of the application of sophisticated scientific and technological knowledge.

On one hand, any effort at improving the economic lot of underprivileged groups is an admirable one. On the other hand, describing the "poor" as a monolithic target to be acted upon is problematic. If the only lens through which "rural India" is viewed involves the two terms "market" and "poor," then important social differences become obscured (especially in terms of caste, gender, and status) within the social groups that comprise the "target population" of DV's initiatives. I have no direct evidence that DV's work actually contributes to reinforcing inequality in its narrowly defined "target population." However, it is telling that although DV produces data on a yearly basis to provide evidence of how its work serves to alleviate poverty, there is an absence of reports and studies that detail precisely how DV works to reduce social inequalities as distinct from working to increase economic activity.

THE GOVERNMENTALIZATION OF DV

Eventually, it can be said that the deployment of sustainable development at DV serves to align it with the political rationality of neoliberalism. This is evident in the way DV conceives of itself as an "independent" sector, its advocacy of a new "institutional design," its organizational structure, its reliance on the rhetoric of entrepreneurialism, and its role as an "expert" on the poor. These factors make it possible to read DV's work as an attempt to insert the organization into the current market-driven system of capitalist production, consumption and exchange, rather than a reaction, or a response, to the "evils" of capitalism itself.

It is also evident, moreover, that DV is clearly aligned with Rose's formulation of the three shifts associated with late economic liberalism. For one, the notion that all DV's work and research is subsumed under the umbrella of sustainable development also implies that it "responsibilizes" all its innovation and production (its "knowledge" related activity) in terms of the logic of the market. Second, its activity, focused as it is upon "marketing" can be read as an attempt to link up various communities and institutions in rural India to a transnational capitalist system using the rhetoric of environmental friendliness and sustainable development. And finally, the construction of its clientele in terms of the "rural poor" cast them as bodies of potential consumers serving, in Rose's (1996) terms, to *enterprise* them through their participation in a market.

It is the adoption of such strategies and vocabularies that "governmentalize" the organization and render its "nongovernmental" notion of itself as mythical. If DV is eminently governmental then the center that "governs" DV can be located with reference to the international development apparatus and eventually transnational capital. Certainly, the extensively critiqued ideological biases of sustainable development point us toward this interpretation.

Although the overt vocabulary of the organization that is aligned directly with the interests of transnational capital illustrates the phenomenon of governing at a distance, it does not provide a complete picture of the process by which this takes place. It is not just in the sharing of an abstracted vocabulary that the idea of governing at a distance makes itself evident. It is when one examines the daily activity of the organization that one emerges with a clearer picture of how the phenomenon is enacted. This allows us to further extend Rose's formulation with reference to the connections that the organization develops and maintains as part of its daily work. As a systems manager at DV said:

> we are what we are because of the people we know. If you don't maintain your connections, you won't be able to make any kind of impact on issues you care about.

It is when one examines significant connections that DV maintains in order to conduct work that the role of the state, hitherto unseen, becomes visible.

DV AND THE STATE

Despite its overt rhetoric of separatism and its critique of the "excesses" of the state, DV's relationship with the state is visible in its day-to-day activity in two forms. The first is its dependency on the state, and the second is its active collusion with the state.

Dependence

DV is dependent on the goodwill of government ministers and bureaucrats in order to "get the job done" and DV's members admit this freely. One respondent said:

> zoning permits, funding, travel . . . for all these, we need to maintain a good relationship with the government. When a minister calls, we jump. Just the other day, a minister called . . . because we are dependent on him for information about crop output in [his constituency], we have to cooperate with him. He had a scheme [under Jawahar Rozgar Yojna, an agricultural development program] that we agreed to implement.

The idea, never apparent in any formal documents, that the initiation of programs by DV might occur for reasons other than their inherent scientific and technological superiority, was articulated fairly frequently by various members of the organization in their conversations with me. Said one senior advisor firmly:

> *This organization was built because of our connections. If Amit hadn't worked in the Ministry, then working with the government now would be twice as difficult. A lot of us work pretty hard at keeping our contacts up. I like to think of the government as an enabler—we are not working against them but we have to be cohesive with them.*

Collusion

The second aspect of DV's relationship with the state lies in the way its informal emphasis on "collaboration" results in an active collusion with the developmental interests of the state. DV has strong ties with several organizations that are affiliated with the government. Senior members of the organization have initiated several research projects with the National Institute for Science and Technology in Development, for instance. In producing their pollution kits and housing programs, DV has also worked extensively with the Central Pollution Control Board, the Housing Board, and the Ministry of Human Resource Development.

The initiation of several programs at DV has occurred not because of their centrality to the concept of sustainable development, but because of the situational confluence of resources and the need to keep powerful state agents happy. The City Environmental Action Network (CEAN), part of the Environmental Systems Branch, is a case in point. CEAN was launched in 1996, and is a program that mobilizes school children to conduct environmental tests in various areas in the city using equipment designed by DV and produced by MART. According to the coordinator of CEAN:

> *CEAN was not set up because it was automatically the best thing to do. Someone from the Rajiv Gandhi Foundation called up and said that they would donate a bus/mobile lab to us if we would take on this project. That's why we did it—it was important to keep them happy.*

The Rajiv Gandhi Foundation is an organization initiated in 1991 after the death of former Prime Minister Rajiv Gandhi. It is a nongovernmental funding organization with strong ties to the Congress Party and the Ministry of Human Resource Development.

Another good example of DV's overall collusion with the state is its study of plains tribes in Assam. This study, which involved 21 researchers and took more than 2 years to complete, was initiated by DV to gauge the need for "technological innovation" among tribal groups in north-east India. DV constituted an advisory group of high-ranking members of academic institutions and state organizations such as the National Planning Commission. Their contacts enabled DV to employ researchers from local universities in the north-east, contact officials of the state government and the Census Bureau, and collect data using the machinery of state bureaucracy in the form of assistance from district and block-level officials. Although DV was formally responsible for the study, its execution would not have been possible without the active collaboration of government officials and agencies. Some organizational members actually went so far as to say that there was pressure on them to "get involved." Said one advisor:

> *Expansion decisions are getting increasingly difficult to make. There are many pressures on us [from the government] to get involved. In fact, institutional discipline is required not to expand. This makes maintaining our connections a constant balancing act.*

In summary, we have here what initially appears to be a contradiction. On one hand, DV formally distances itself from the state. On the other hand, it is informally dependent on it and actively collaborates with it. A closer look reveals that this contradiction is, in fact, part of the logic of "governing at a distance." Governmentalization in a neoliberal state entails that the state actively identify domains that are formally outside it and manage it without destroying its autonomy (Rose & Miller, 1992). This is precisely what DV's relationship with the Indian State highlights. In order for governmentalization to occur, DV must *necessarily* formally distance itself from both the state and the multinational corporation on one hand, and informally engage with them on the other. It is in this sense, ultimately, that although the notion of an NGO working in an independent sector is mythical, it is also a necessary myth.

CONCLUSION

In summary, this chapter has established that the discourse of sustainable development serves to governmentalize DV and align it with the ethos of transnational neoliberal ideology. This occurs by way of developing shared vocabularies and organizational structures that reinforce rather than resist the economizing tendency of the market, thereby producing and reproducing an ideology of entrepreneurialism. Eventually, this serves to ensure that the notion of an independently functioning NGO in this instance becomes a mythical one. The formal distinctions that DV seeks to make between itself and the state are repudiated by their ongoing interaction with state agents, and the importance of these agents in determining the flow of work at DV. In terms of the principle of governing at a distance, such formal distantiation is in fact required for governmentalization to occur, and this renders the "mythical" nature of DV as an NGO an entirely necessary myth.

This chapter has focused on issues of continuities rather than discontinuities. In other words, it has focused on the reproduction of transnational neoliberal ideology via the principle of governmentality, rather than resistance to governmental practices. It should be evident why this is the case—it is crucial for critical scholars, especially those in organizational communication, to constantly examine and re-examine the heterogeneous modes of domination by which the "rules" of our collective engagement with late capitalism are expressed. Nevertheless, as has been said repeatedly by critical scholars in the field (Mumby, 1997), it is important to be able to identify equally heterogeneous spaces of resistance and action that social collectives carve out in everyday practice, not least because it allows scholarly work to remain vigilant about late capitalist modernity, rather than taking its effects for granted.

It is in this sense that this study is incomplete. Further work in the area should, while focusing on the diversity of locations and mechanisms of governmentality, also work to theorize how governmentality as a process is "incomplete," never achieving complete disciplinarity. This is theoretically implicit in Foucault's own work (Miller, 1993) but its modalities need to be researched.

Finally, there are two areas in which governmentality studies can make a contribution to transnational communication scholarship in general, and those scholars concerned with the study of organizational communication in particular. First, the concept of governmentality provides a valuable lens through which scholars can examine the ideological micro-workings of transnational capital. In this sense, governmentality is an eminently "organizational" term because it draws attention to aspects of discursive practices and organizational strategies and structures that produce and reinforce such capitalist logic.

Second, governmentality studies help reconfigure the nation-state in the concept of the transnational. Unlike the received notion of *globalization* which effaces the impact of the nation-state to the point of absence, the very term *transnationalism* implies that the nation-state still plays an important role in the "global" economy—and this is the reason that I have used it throughout this chapter. Urging us to reconsider the received view of globalization, Manuel Castells (1996) asks us to understand it in terms of an interaction between increasingly deterritorialized economic agents and historically rooted political systems. The focus on informal activity that the notion of governing at a distance entails allows us to do precisely this. Eventually, it results in more tempered insights about the "newness" of the cultural phenomena that form late capitalist modernity. This chapter is, I hope, a small contribution in that direction.

ACKNOWLEDGEMENT

This chapter was conducted as part of my dissertation research at the Department of Communication, Purdue University. An earlier version of this chapter was presented at the National Communication Association's Summer Conference in Iowa City, June 2000. I thank Dennis Mumby, Arvind Rajagopal, Mary Keehner, and John Pomery for their help and support. Thanks are also due to the editors of this volume and the anonymous reviewers for their advice and recommendations.

REFERENCES

Barry, A., Osborne, T., & Rose, N. (1996). *Foucault and political reason: Liberalism, neo-liberalism and rationalities of government.* Chicago: University of Chicago Press.

Beck, J. (1999). Makeover or takeover? The strange death of educational autonomy in neo-liberal England. *British Journal of Sociology of Education, 20*(2), 223-238.

Bennett, P. (1999). Governing environmental risk: Regulation, insurance and moral economy. *Progress in Human Geography, 23*(2), 189-208.

Blake, L. (1999). Pastoral power, governmentality and cultures of order in nineteenth-century British Columbia. *Transactions, 24*(1), 79-93.

Braun, B. (2000). Producing vertical territory: Geology and governmentality in late victorian Canada. *Ecumene, 7*(1), 7-46.

Brosius, P. (1999). Green dots, pink hearts: Displacing politics from the Malaysian rain forest. *American Anthropologist, 101*(1), 36-57.

Burawoy, M. (1991). The extended case method. In M. Burawoy, A. Burton, A. A. Ferguson, K. J. Fox, J. Gamson, N. Gartrell, L. Hurst, C. Kurzman, L. Salzinger, J. Schiffman, & S. Ui (Eds.), *Ethnography unbound: Power and resistance in the modern metropolis* (pp. 271-287). Berkeley: University of California Press.

Burawoy, M. (1998). The extended case method. *Sociological Theory, 16*(1), 4-33.

Burchell, G. (1996). Liberal government and techniques of the self. In A. Barry, T. Osborne, & N. Rose (Eds.), *Foucault and political reason: Liberalism, neo-liberalism and rationalities of government* (pp. 19-36). Chicago: University of Chicago Press.

Burchell, G., Gordon, C., & Miller, P. (1991). *The Foucault effect: Studies in governmentality.* Chicago: University of Chicago Press.

Castells, M. (1996). *The rise of the network society.* Oxford, UK: Blackwell.

Chambers, R. (1987, May 2). Thinking about NGO priorities. *IDS Mimeo,* 1-8.

Chatterjee, P. (1993). *The nation and its fragments.* Princeton, NJ: Princeton University Press.

Cheney, G. (1999). *Values at work: Employee participation meets market pressure at Mondragón.* Ithaca, NY: Cornell University Press.

Cheney, G., & Christensen, L. (2000). Identity at issue: Linkages between "internal" and "external" organizational communication. In F. Jablin & L. Putnam (Eds.), *New handbook of organizational communication* (pp. 231-269). Newbury Park, CA: Sage.

Dalby, S. (1999). Against "globalization from above": Critical geopolitics and the World Order Models Project. *Environment and Planning D: Society and Space, 17*, 181-200.

Donzelot, J. (1991). Pleasure in work. In G. Burchell, C. Gordon, & P. Miller (Eds.), *The Foucault effect: Studies in governmentality* (pp. 251-280). Chicago: University of Chicago Press.

Durrheim, K., & Foster, D. (1999). Technologies of social control: Crowd management in liberal democracy. *Economy and Society, 28*(1), 56-74.

Eide, M., & Knight, G. (1999). Public/private service: Service journalism and the problems of everyday life. *European Journal of Communication, 14*(4), 525-547.

Eisenberg, E. (1984). Ambiguity as strategy in organizational communication. *Communication Monographs, 51*(2), 227-242.

Escobar, A. (1995). *Encountering development: The making and unmaking of the third world.* Princeton, NJ: Princeton University Press.

Foucault, M. (1991). Governmentality. In G. Burchell, C. Gordon, & P. Miller (Eds.), *The Foucault effect: Studies in governmentality* (pp. 87-104). London: Harvester/Wheatsheaf.

Goldthorpe, J.E. (1996). *The sociology of post-colonial societies: Economic disparity, cultural diversity and development.* Cambridge, UK: Cambridge University Press.

Gordon, C. (1991). Government rationality: An introduction. In G. Burchell, C. Gordon, & P. Miller (Eds.), *The Foucault effect: Studies in governmentality* (pp. 1-51). Chicago: University of Chicago Press.

Graham, L. (1997). Beyond manipulation: Lillian Gilbreth's industrial psychology and the governmentality of women consumers. *The Sociological Quarterly, 38*(4), 539-565.

Gupta, A. (1998). *Postcolonial developments: Agriculture in the making of a modern India.* London: Duke University Press.

Halliday, F. (2000). Global governance: Prospects and problems. *Citizenship Studies, 4*(1), 19-34.

Heeks, R. (1996). *India's software industry: State policy, liberalization and industrial development.* Thousand Oaks, CA: Sage.

Hegde, R. (1998). A view from elsewhere: Locating difference and the politics of representation from a transnational feminist perspective. *Communication Theory, 8*(3), 271-297.

Hollinshead, K. (1999). Surveillance of the worlds of tourism: Foucault and the eye-of-power. *Tourism Management, 20*(1), 7-23.

Hughes, D., & Griffiths, L. (1999). On penalties and the Patients Charter: Centralism v de-centralised governance in the NHS. *Sociology of Health and Illness, 21*(1), 71-94.

Imber, M.F. (1996). The environment and the United Nations. In J. Vogler & M. F. Imber (Eds.), *The environment and international relations* (pp. 138-154). London: Routledge.

Joyce, P. (1999). The politics of the liberal archive. *History of the Human Sciences, 12*(2), 35-49.

Kaviraj, S. (1992). On state, society and discourse in India. *Institute for Development Studies Bulletin, 21*(4), 12-15.

Larner, W. (1997). A means to an end: Neoliberalism and state processes in New Zealand. *Studies in Political Economy, 52*(1), 7-38.

Larner, W. (1998). The discourse of restructuring: Employment in the New Zealand telecommunications industry. *Journal of Sociology, 34*(3), 264-280.

Latour, B. (1987). *Science in action.* Milton Keynes: Open University Press.

Malpas, J., & Wickham, G. (1997). Governance and the world: From Joe DiMaggio to Michel Foucault. *UTS Review, 3*(2), 91-108.

Manning, P. (1999). Categories of knowledge and information flows: Reasons for the decline of the British Labour and Industrial Correspondent's Group. *Media, Culture and Society, 21*(3), 313-336.

Markham, A. (1996). Designing discourse: A critical analysis of strategic ambiguity and workplace control. *Management Communication Quarterly, 9*(3), 389-421.

Martin, J., & Nakayama, T. (Eds.). (1997). *Intercultural communication in contexts.* Mountain View, CA: Mayfield.

McDonald, J. (1999). The neoliberal project and governmentality in rural Mexico: Emergent farmer organizations in the Michoacan highlands. *Human Organization, 58*(3), 274-284.

McMichael, P. (1996). *Development and social change: A global perspective.* Thousand Oaks, CA: Pine Forge Press.

Miller, J. (1993). *The passion of Michel Foucault.* New York: Simon and Schuster.

Miller, P., & Rose, N. (1990). Governing economic life. *Economy and Society, 19*(1), 1-31.

Mohammadi, A. (Ed.). (1997). *International communication and globalization.* Thousand Oaks, CA: Sage.

Mowlana, H. (1996). *Global communication in transition: The end of diversity?* Thousand Oaks, CA: Sage.

Mumby, D. (1997). The problem of hegemony: Rereading Gramsci for organizational studies. *Western Journal of Communication, 61*(4), 343-375.

Nakayama, T., & Martin, J. (Eds.). (1999). *Whiteness: The communication of social identity.* Thousand Oaks, CA: Sage.

Ng, M.K., & Tang, W.S. (1999). Urban system planning in China: A case study of the Pearl River delta. *Urban Geography, 20*(7), 591-616.

Ouellette, L. (1999). TV viewing as good citizenship? Political rationality, enlightened democracy and PBS. *Cultural Studies, 13*(1), 62-90.

Peterson, T.R. (1997). *Sharing the earth: The rhetoric of sustainable development.* Columbia: University of South Carolina Press.

Purvis, T., & Hunt, A. (1999). Identity versus citizenship: Transformations in the discourses and practices of citizenship. *Social and Legal Studies, 8*(4), 457-482.

Radcliffe, V.S. (1999). Knowing efficiency: The enactment of efficiency in efficiency auditing. *Accounting, Organizations and Society, 24*, 333-362.

Rajagopal, A. (2001). *Politics after television: Religious nationalism and the reshaping of the Indian public.* Cambridge, UK: Cambridge University Press.

Rose, N. (1996). Governing "advanced" liberal societies. In A. Barry, T. Osborne, & N. Rose (Eds.), *Foucault and political reason: Liberalism, neo-liberalism and rationalities of government* (pp. 37-64). Chicago: University of Chicago Press.

Rose, N., & Miller, P. (1992). Political power beyond the state: Problematics of government. *British Journal of Sociology, 43*(2), 173-205.

Scambler, G., & Higgs, P. (Eds.). (1998). *Modernity, medicine and health: Medical sociology towards 2000.* London: Routledge.

Scott, D. (1999). *Refashioning futures: Criticism after postcoloniality*. Princeton, NJ: Princeton University Press.

Spiro, P.J. (1994). New global communities: Nongovernmental organizations in international decision-making institutions. *The Washington Quarterly, 18*(1), 45-56.

Spivak, G.C. (1988). Can the subaltern speak? In C. Nelson & L. Grossberg (Eds.), *Marxism and the interpretation of cultures* (pp. 271-313). Urbana: University of Illinois Press.

Stenson, K., & Watt, P. (1999). Governmentality and "the death of the social"?: A discourse analysis of local government texts in south-east England. *Urban Studies, 36*(1), 189-201.

Stephens, S. (1992). *"And a little child shall lead them:" Children and images of children at the UN Conference on environment and development*. Dragvoll, Norway: Norwegian Center for Child Research.

Stern, A.M. (1999). Responsible mothers and normal children: Eugenics, nationalism and welfare in post-revolutionary Mexico. *Journal of Historical Sociology, 12*(4), 369-397.

Tomlinson, J. (1991). *Cultural imperialism: A critical introduction*. Baltimore, MD: Johns Hopkins University.

Tully, J. (1999). The agonic freedom of citizens. *Economy and Society, 28*(2), 161-182.

Watson, S. (1999). Policing the affective society: Beyond governmentality in the theory of social control. *Social and Legal Studies, 8*(2), 227-251.

Welling-Hall, B. (1994). Information technology and global learning for sustainable development: Promises and problems. *Alternatives, 19*, 99-132.

ORGANIZATIONAL COMMUNICATION AND GLOBALLY DISPLACED PERIMETER POPULATIONS

A Neglected Challenge for Intercultural Communication Training

Phyllis Bo-yuen Ngai
The University of Montana

Peter H. Koehn
The University of Montana

This chapter applies the open-systems perspective on organizational communication to the neglected international and multicultural not-for-profit interorganizational domain—with specific reference to displaced populations living in camp situations. The discussion highlights the strategic centrality of intergroup and interorganizational communication that occurs beyond formal boundaries and in interfaces with humanitarian assistance agencies. The proposed intercultural communication training begins with critical interactions among perimeter populations and progresses inward via the intercultural mediator program and the aid-project-participant program. Each program incorporates awareness raising, attitude change, new skill development, and stress coping. The discussion shows that frameworks for analyzing organizational communication need to treat diversity inclusively by incorporating the per-

spective of perimeter stakeholders. The conditions and objectives
that prevail in large-scale humanitarian assistance situations also
challenge the view that training should move from the culture-gen-
eral to the culture-specific. Transnational and indigenous organi-
zations possess the capacity for promoting intercultural communi-
cation and cooperation among displaced persons and their hosts.
Extending the vision of organizational communication to encom-
pass perimeter communities constitutes a prerequisite for realizing
this potential.

The world's expanding displaced population includes some 20 million victims of persecution and/or armed conflict seeking refuge outside their country of origin (*refugees*), another 20 to 25 million men, women, and children forced to abandon their homes as a result of (or in order to avoid the effects of) violent political upheaval and/or systematic violations of human rights who have not crossed a nation-state border (internally displaced persons) (Cohen & Deng, 1998; Crossette, 2000b; Ogata, 2000), and countless others dislocated by deliberate alterations in land or water use (see Cernea, 1990), mismanaged environmental impacts (see Suhrke, 1994), environmental warfare (Martin, 1993; also see Castles, 2002), or by natural calamity. Displaced persons present special challenges for organizational communication. The human needs that result from the experience of forced and involuntary dislocation simultaneously are of an emergency and long-term nature. Concomitantly, the assistance context often is characterized by extreme cultural diversity—in terms of numbers of cultures drawn into contact as well as the cultural distance that often separates them—and heightened "potential for *mis*communication" (Cargile & Giles, 1996, p. 385; also see Koehn, 2002). Even when the displaced are culturally homogeneous, the preferred approach to addressing needs in resource-scarce situations requires equal attention to their culturally different hosts.

Furthermore, the agencies responding to the needs of displaced persons—including international nongovernmental organizations (NGOs) such as Doctors Without Borders (Warpinski, 2001), international organizations (IOs) such as the UN High Commission for Refugees (UNHCR), national ministries in countries of asylum, and domestic NGOs such as the Population Development Association of Thailand (Anderson, 1998)—typically encompass multiple nationalities and emphasize linkages across organizational boundaries. In such settings, "intercultural communication constitutes the organizing process that permeates all levels of activity and interpretation" (Stohl, 1993, p. 381). The especially demanding and complex conditions faced when working with displaced and host populations challenge the imagination, highlight the importance of intercultural communication training, and suggest that viable approaches must build on insights from international relations and development management, refugee studies, interorganizational studies, communication studies, and cross-cultural psychology.

This chapter aims to extend and apply the open-systems perspective on organizational communication by calling attention to the neglected international and multicultural not-for-profit interorganizational domain (see Hardy, 1994; Stohl, 1993) and by suggesting ways—with specific reference to refugee camp situations—that intercultural communication training can address this gap. The centrality of the environment-organization interface in studies of contemporary organizational communication and the importance of shifting from the "metaphor of the organization as 'container' of communication" to a more expansive perspective that treats "communication phenomena as central processes of organizing" have been reaffirmed by comprehensive critical reviews of recent research (see Cheney et al., 1998; Taylor, Flanagin, Cheney, & Seibold, 2001). We attempt to demonstrate here that the container metaphor not only is inadequate for understanding organizational communication, but that researchers and practitioners often need to cast a far wider net in order fully to account for critical dimensions of the complex interactions that are taking place.

In an age of permeable and fluid boundaries among organizations, local as well as transnationally networked societies, and multiorganizational action,[1] we would like to move students (and practitioners) of organizational communication out into the community and the world beyond. Through the wedge of intercultural communication training for transnational humanitarian assistance, we aim to highlight the strategic centrality of intergroup and interorganizational relations that occur beyond formal boundaries and in interfaces with the focal unit. In contrast to promoting intercultural communication skills for the purpose of selling more products or negotiating profitable business deals, much is at stake in terms of compelling human needs if intercultural communication fails or succeeds in the context selected for this discussion.

INTERCULTURAL COMMUNICATION TRAINING FOR DISLOCATED PERSONS

In this chapter, we are particularly interested in a critical dimension of training that tends to be overlooked in the wake of human displacement; that is, devel-

---

[1]Hanf and O'Toole (1992) pointed out that "there are very few social problems that still can be dealt with, let alone solved, within or by one or a few organizations working alone. In both making and carrying out all kinds of policy measures, decision makers are dependent on conglomerates of organizations in which the public and private spheres are more or less coupled with one another" (pp. 164-166).

oping the intercultural communication skills of the surviving subjects of dislocation.[2] In the interests of efficiency and empowerment, approaches to refugee health care increasingly rely on community members. The concomitant emphasis on enhancing indigenous human potential underscores the importance of involving displaced persons in intercultural communication training.

When communication is not viewed as a unidirectional process, then skill enhancements among *all* stakeholders, certainly including impacted populations, are understood to exert an important impact on intergroup and interorganizational relations as well as on assistance outcomes. Specifically, the enhancement of intercultural communication competence can be expected to increase the effectiveness of organizational members and intended beneficiaries in the collaborative and culturally complex undertaking of providing appropriate crisis management, conflict resolution, emergency relief, mental health, and sustainable development assistance among displaced populations and the surrounding hosts (see Koehn & Ngai, 2001).

Nevertheless, communication training of all types has not been available to perimeter stakeholder populations in development and relief situations. Perusal of the *Humanitarian Assistance Training Inventory* (http://www.reliefweb.int/training), which encompasses activities and materials offered by UN, donor, international governmental and nongovernmental, and academic/training agencies, confirms the absence, as of December 2002, of specific communication training programs for indigenous populations (as well as programs explicitly focused on intercultural communication). Indeed, although the needs and opportunities are manifold (see e.g., Sollis, 1994), especially given the eager, idle, and largely unskilled audience, camp populations frequently lack access to *any* organized forms of training. Most program funders focus on providing food, safe water, shelter, and rudimentary health care and fail to view education and training (particularly for women, female children, and the disabled) as a priority—even though it is the latter that (re)kindles hope for the future among displaced persons. Consequently, even basic education often is treated as a luxury and only one out of every nine primary school-age refugee children attends school (see Koehn, 1994a; Ruiz, 1994).

Concern over the scope and recurrence of missed opportunities to develop useful skills and abilities among the victims of forced dislocation led one of the authors to organize an international symposium, in collaboration with a major donor—the Japan International Cooperation Agency (JICA)—that focused on training refugees for voluntary repatriation and for effective participation in development activity. The assembled experts—including representatives from

---

[2]Elsewhere, in a complementary essay (see Ngai & Koehn, 2001), the authors discuss an intercultural communication training program that principally is focused on the expatriate managers of refugee-assistance programs (also see Maynard, 1999).

UNHCR, the U.S. Department of State's Bureau of Refugee Affairs, the U.S. Agency for International Development, JICA, the U.S. Committee for Refugees, and NGOs operating around the world—adopted 18 priority recommendations that generally are refugee-empowering and suggest important advances in prevailing approaches to basic and health education and to practical, development-oriented training. However, none of the 18 recommendations explicitly addresses the pervasive intercultural communication challenges that increasingly confront transnational and domestic agencies involved in providing humanitarian assistance to dispossessed populations (see Koehn, 1994a).

In contrast to the neglect of indigenous populations by researchers and training programs, the literature on preparing expatriate professionals for intercultural communication situations overseas is voluminous (see e.g., Harrison, 1994; Kealey, 1990; Kealey & Protheroe, 1996; and the entire Summer/Fall 2000 issue of *Human Resource Management*). Some of the lessons and findings reported in this literature possess broad application and we draw on them where appropriate. However, it is important to make explicit at the outset that our approach differs fundamentally from the prevailing perspective in both focus and direction. Although expatriate studies revolve around a peculiar type of organizational member and, when they extend beyond relations with counterparts, are concerned, at most, with that actor's (inner-to-outer and typically downward) hierarchical communication linkages and interactions with other organizations and/or "clients" in its environment, we start with the organization's perimeter stakeholders and primarily are interested in intergroup (horizontal and perimeter) communication and stakeholder-to-formal-organization (outer-to-inner and typically upward) interfaces. Our distinct approach, and the specific types of horizontal and outer-to-inner organizational boundary-spanning interfaces we identify as important, are elaborated in the discussion that follows.

The chapter proceeds by first orienting readers to the environmental context that frames our discussion of organizational communication; that is, organized settlements ("camps") and their host communities. Then, we introduce the three components of a proposed "progressive" intercultural communication training program that starts with critical interactions among perimeter populations and builds inward to interface with organizations responsible for providing humanitarian assistance to the victims of forced dislocation. These three components— we refer to them as the *camp population-host community program*, the *intercultural-mediator program*, and the *aid-project-participant program*—are developed in terms of (a) the unique environmental constraints, resources, and interactions that affect each case; (b) the specific intercultural communication skills required by each group of perimeter stakeholders; (c) insights from intercultural communication training with organizational members that lend themselves to adaptation with perimeter participants; and, finally, (d) the specific, sequential dimensions of each training program—linked to appropriate and promising training approaches.

ORGANIZED SETTLEMENTS: A GLOBAL PHENOMENON

Refugees and internally displaced persons generally can be distinguished according to the physical surroundings in which they find themselves. Our principal interest here is with dislocated persons who reside in organized settlements (mainly camps), although the insights presented can be adapted to situations involving individuals and families who spontaneously settle among the local population.

Although too numerous to enumerate (see Cohen & Deng, 1998), illustrative situations include the 1 million Azerbaijanis from Nagorno-Karabakh scattered across 40 camps in Azerbaijan (Frantz, 2000); South Ossetians inhabiting squalid collective centers in their native Georgia (*Refugees* 117, 1999); Bosnians, Croatians, ethnic Serbs, and Roma who fled from Kosovo in Serbia (*Refugees* 118, 2000); more than 300,000 refugees from Rwanda, Burundi, and Democratic Republic of Congo occupying organized settlements in the Kagera and Kigoma regions of western Tanzania (Whitaker, 1999); the quarter of a million internally displaced Tamils living in 500 "welfare centers" in Sri Lanka (Cohen & Deng, 1998); and the 240,000 "stranded Pakistanis," referred to locally as Biharis, spread across 66 camps in Bangladesh (*The New York Times*, May 13, 2000, p. A1). Camp populations are more likely than persons who settle among the local population to receive assistance from external sources. Nevertheless, organized settlements require enormous resource-mobilization efforts[3] and involve complex logistical challenges (see Sorenson, 1994). One or more cultural groups can be receiving assistance within a single settlement; for instance, Qoriooley in Somalia "contained two ethnic groups, Oromo and Somali " (Waldron & Hasci, 1995, p. 46) and the refugee population of Qala en Nahal in Sudan included Muslims and Christians, sizeable numbers of people from five ethnic and language groups within Eritrea, and small clusters from seven other ethnic groups (Woodrow, 1998b).

Host Community Impacts

Displaced persons on the move easily overwhelm settlement areas—vastly outnumbering subsistence local populations, overburdening the existing infrastructure, and diverting resources intended for local development (Whitaker, 1999), and wrecking havoc with fragile natural resources by engaging in unsustainable

---

[3]Refugees in Azerbaijan, for instance, "live without running water, electricity or medical care in railroad cars, tents, temporary prefabricated houses and holes in the ground, surviving on a few dollars a month, on handouts and heartache" (Frantz, 2000, pp. A1, 4). In contrast, the Kakuma and Dadaab camps gradually turned into city-like enclaves in sparsely populated and underdeveloped northern Kenya (see de Montclose & Kagwanja, 2000).

use practices (see Cohen & Deng, 1998; Koehn, 1994b; Sorenson, 1994; Waldron & Hasci, 1995; Whitaker, 1999).[4] In order to minimize resentment and avoid animosity on the part of receiving societies, donors and international NGOs are encouraged to provide similar "impacted-area" assistance to host as well as dislocated communities (see Harrell-Bond, 1989; Koehn, 1991; Sorenson, 1994).[5]

Impacted-area Assistance and Intercultural Communication

The impacted-area approach underscores the importance of intercultural communication because relations among affected groups and community cohesion rebuilding efforts can occur in a context of insecurity, fear, exploitation, competition over scarce resources (see Whitaker, 1999), "guarded restraint" (Waldron & Hasci, 1995), destroyed trust, hatred, and/or violence.[6] In the post-Cold War era, population displacements most frequently result from brutal local "identity conflicts" that engulf noncombatants and produce extreme polarization and heightened animosity among neighbors with differing characteristics. Given that "identity conflicts are fought at the community level and among former associates of all kinds, every citizen is a potential victim and a potential combatant" (Maynard, 1999, p. 38).

Moreover, displaced persons frequently inhabit organized settlements for decades, and sometimes for lifetimes. In short, their relations with the members of surrounding host communities are critically important. Yet, the limited (usually technically focused) training programs that exist focus on NGO and agency personnel and neglect members of locally impacted communities—even individuals drawn from the latter who provide essential assistance to outside experts.[7] One intended contribution of this chapter, therefore, is to set forth an approach to intercultural communication competency building that is tailored to the members of perimeter dislocated populations and their hosts.

---

[4]Population influxes exert a differential impact on various segments of local society. For some hosts, particularly the wealthy, new arrivals can be assets "because of their labour power and skills, and because they provide a broader market and generate demands for certain goods" (Sorenson, 1994, p. 180; also see Chambers, 1993; Whitaker, 1999). Others, especially women, the elderly, and those already disadvantaged in terms of access to wealth and power, suffer further marginalization (see Whitaker, 1999). Thus, Chambers (1993) concluded that "the deprivations, needs, and capabilities of the weaker hosts as well as those of the refugees deserve to be taken into account" (p. 43).

[5]In western Tanzania, donors and international and indigenous NGOs "initiated development projects for host communities in water, health, education, natural resources, and infrastructure." For details, see Whitaker (1999, p. 9).

[6]In Djibouti, for instance, "an influx of Issa refugees exacerbated existing ethnic tensions and provoked increased violence from the rival Afar group" (Sorenson, 1994, pp. 181-182).

[7]In an exceptional situation, the Nansen Group offers conflict-management training to Kosovo citizens (see Maynard, 1999, p. 184).

THE PROGRESSIVE TRAINING PROGRAM

A common initial impression is that the challenges of meeting the intercultural communication needs of dislocated and host populations are nearly overwhelming. We intend to demonstrate, however, that by devoting careful attention to local conditions, involving all of the impacted populations that engage in daily intercultural encounters according to the intensity (i.e., the frequency, importance, and specific nature) of their interactions (see Black & Mendenhall, 1989), learning from past intercultural communication skill-building efforts, and making maximum use of available resources through innovative adaptations, it is possible to design and to succeed in implementing feasible training programs in such situations. The training framework set forth here calls for three distinct programs arranged in progressive fashion.

The presence of large populations of needy strangers in the midst of impoverished community members who are deeply attached to the sheltering territory constitutes a recipe for tension, miscommunication, and potential conflict. The initial *camp population-host community training program* is directed toward facilitating communication between *all* members of the displaced population and their culturally distinct hosts.

Whether the presence of the dislocated population be temporary or long-term, the *leaders* of both types of perimeter communities can perform their representative and peace-making roles far more effectively if they are trained in intercultural communication. Our label for this second component is the *intercultural-mediator training program*. One important objective of the intercultural-mediator training component is to develop skills in building trust in interpersonal relationships with members of "stranger" communities and complementary skills in forging trust in jointly articulated covenants and bridging institutions. Once trusting relationships among the core groups of initial instigators and representatives of diverse voices in each community underlie bridging efforts, prospects for sustained intercultural dialogue and collaborative action are greatly improved (Daubon & Saunders, 2002).

The final component (the *aid-project-participant training program*) is designed to address the specific intercultural communication needs of professional and semi-professional *staff* who are recruited locally for positions at all levels of transnational organization operations or, less frequently, within domestic government agencies—such as the model Refugee Health Unit of the former government of Somalia, under which "expatriates as 'advisors and trainers' worked side by side with the Somali doctors, health workers and refugees" (Waldron & Hasci, 1995, p. 47). Hundreds of hosts and displaced persons fill these salaried positions in each impacted area—including the agency driver and guard, the translator who works alongside an expatriate medical doctor, the nurse and dispenser, the public health educator, the community organizer, the supervisor of clerical and/or laboring staff, the individual hired to help an NGO liaise with government officials, the accountant, the computer programmer, and the agent responsible for purchasing local supplies. In 1990, for instance, the Eastern Sudan Refugee Program employed some 700 personnel—about one third of whom were refugees (Sterkenburg, Kirkby, & O'Keefe, 1994; see also Maynard, 1999). In the Dadaad complex of camps in northern Kenya, CARE employs more than 1,000 refugees. Staff drawn from the local host population comprise one fifth of CARE's full-time employees. High-level jobs with superior wages typically are filled by "expatriates or by Kenyans who are not from the province." In Kakuma, NGOs prefer to hire refugees because they work for much less than a Kenyan's salary. Thus, clinics employ "ten refugees to assist one Kenyan" and the camp hospital's staff includes 78 refugees and 21 Kenyans (de Montclose & Kagwanja, 2000, p. 218). Even when the expatriate NGO and donor experts with whom they are working in partnership already have received relevant training, locally hired staff need to develop their own skills in intercultural communication in order to interface effectively with the multicultural workplace that characterizes contemporary relief and sustainable development efforts.

Expected Conditions

An effective training program must take into account the prevailing opportunities and constraints that shape the communication context confronted by trainees. Although many parallel conditions affect training needs for members of dislocated and host communities, important differences also exist. Thus, the next sections briefly identify the most relevant resources and challenges that trainers are likely to encounter among camp and host-community populations in developing countries—where the vast majority of displaced persons have resettled. Given that the pertinent conditions vary both in terms of participants and objectives, they will be identified separately for each type of training program.

Camp Population-Host Community Training Program

Camp Populations. Most available reports on refugee camp populations are not grounded in systematic research. Given the foreign assistance benefits that can be realized by inflating refugee counts, some governments have resisted or even undermined research intended to generate reliable census enumerations (see Kibreab, 1994; Rogge, 1993; Waldron & Hasci, 1995). Furthermore, organized settlements vary in land area, population size and composition, available resources, organizational presence, and types of conflicts. Nevertheless, based primarily on agency field reports and anthropological observations, it is possible to identify some common features.

Dislocated persons living in camp situations typically have lost or become separated from family members, have forfeited all personal possessions and assets and exhausted any resources of monetary value (see Cohen & Deng, 1998), and have been cut off from essential social and economic support networks (see Cernea, 1990; Hansen, 1979). Although one finds islands of resilience and determination, many dislocated men, women, and children have been traumatized by the experiences of oppression, war, rape, torture, the murder of loved ones, homelessness, and/or flight, and suffer from serious illness, injury, malnutrition, and/or continual fear of abuse, depression, and/or posttraumatic stress disorder (see e.g., Maynard, 1999; Woodrow, 1998a). They often are without means of protecting and supporting themselves (Cohen & Deng, 1998; Cuny, 1979; Hansen, 1979; Maynard, 1999; Musisi, 2002) and are prone to prolong cross-group distrust and hostility (Maynard, 1999). Malnutrition can be widespread and death rates in newly established organized settlements can be "up to 40 times higher than normal" (Waldron & Hasci, 1995). Children typically predominate among refugee camp populations. Girls frequently drop out of school because they are expected to help with child care and with daily living requirements (Ahearn, Loughrey, & Ager, 1999). The bulk of the adult population can be expected to possess some primary education; substantial minorities will be illiterate and have some secondary education (see IRC and SCF, 1981). In summary, the required communication training program will encompass large numbers of trainees who possess enormous and diverse short- and long-term needs. Most likely, it will need to rely extensively on the limited availability of external funding.

In many camps, refugees and internally displaced persons must co-exist with strangers of diverse ethnicity who speak an incomprehensible language or dialect and, increasingly, are encouraged to use intraculturally congruent ways of dealing with challenges (Miller, 1999). Encounters among people with different cultural backgrounds occur daily in a variety of expected (e.g., shared water source) and unpredictable (e.g., quarrels over petty theft) circumstances. Refugees also must interact with camp authorities and with those who provide essential services (shelter, food, clothing, medical attention, education, etc.). Additionally, whenever they venture outside of camp boundaries (e.g., in search of firewood, water, trade, employment, or entertainment), they come in contact with other (frequently suspicious or even overtly hostile) strangers (Cernea, 1990)—this time, members of the culturally different host community(ies). Displaced/host community interactions can include socializing together, intermarriage, prostitution, theft, and violence (see Whitaker, 1999).

The first rows of Table 9.*1* highlight contacts with members of different cultures that displaced persons are likely to experience on a weekly basis by the frequency of each encounter category. Among all members of this group, interactions with authorities and assistance providers occur less often than with other camp populations of different cultural backgrounds (if any) and with hosts. Moreover, although the former communication situations are important, it is not cost effective to train the wider populations involved for them because members can be assisted by community representatives and employees when interactions with authorities and assistance providers are required.

In summary, all refugees and displaced persons resettled in camps are likely to be involved in encounters with *one or two different cultures* that arise on an immediate and urgent basis. Intercultural communication training can be partic-

TABLE 9.1 Weekly Intercultural Contacts Encountered by Each Camp Population, Each Host Population, Camp Leaders, and Host Community Leaders: By Likely Frequency of Face-to-Face Interaction

EXTENSIVE	MODERATE	OCCASIONAL
1. *Camp Population(s)*		
Other camp populations(s)	Camp authorities	
Host(s)	Assistance providers	
2. *Host Population(s)*		
Camp population(s)	Assistance providers	Local govt.
Other host population(s)		authorities
3. *Camp Leaders*		
Other camp populations	Local govt. authorities	
Leaders/other camp populations		
Host population(s)/leaders		
Camp authorities		
Assistance providers		
4. *Host Community Leaders*		
Camp population(s)	Camp authorities	
Camp-population(s) leaders		
Other host community leaders		
Other host populations		
Assistance providers		
Local govt authorities		
5. *Indigenous Staff Drawn from Displaced and Host Populations*		
Camp or host population(s)	Expatriate staff of other IOs, international NGOs, bilateral donors	
Expatriate staff/own agency		
Host govt. agencies' staff	Culturally different members of indigenous NGOs	
Culturally different members of own agency		
Camp and local govt. authorities		

ularly useful if, as a result, camp populations manage to eliminate or reduce miscommunication and conflicts with their hosts. For instance, in western Tanzania, refugees "failed to respect the cultural importance of certain local trees which were used to mark gravesites and boundaries, for medicinal purposes, or as aphrodisiacs. . . . This further fueled the struggle between refugees and villagers for control over natural resources" (Whitaker, 1999, p. 5). Minimizing such conflicts allows humanitarian assistance organizations to concentrate their energy and resources on addressing urgent needs and providing development opportunities for the victims of dislocation and their hosts.

Host Communities.   In most developing country contexts, host communities barely are distinguishable from the displaced populations found in their midst in terms of vulnerable economic status (marginal subsistence), nutritional status (undernourished and malnourished),[8] rudimentary level of educational attainment, and health status (widespread infectious disease, low level of immunizations, low life expectancy). They differ, however, in that they may not have been exposed directly to the commitment of atrocities or other traumatic circumstances, they are familiar with local customs/practices and environmental conditions, and, most importantly, in their continued access to land, some personal possessions, and basic support systems. Again, any communication training program would need to provide for large numbers of host community trainees and to rely on limited external funding.

The second part of Table 9.1 addresses the intercultural contacts that host community members are likely to experience on a weekly basis. Interactions with local authorities and assistance providers tend to occur less frequently than with camp members. Again, although the former are important, it is not necessary to train the large populations involved for these types of communication situations because members can be assisted by community representatives and employees when interactions with authorities and assistance providers are required. Among hosts, therefore, vital communication interaction situations are likely to involve *one different cultural encounter*—with camp members. The most useful cross-cultural communication training for the vast numbers involved would involve learning how to avoid or minimize miscommunication.

Intercultural-Mediator Training Program

The second component of the overall training program focuses on the leaders of displaced and host populations. The critical conditions defining each group of intermediaries are basically similar, although slight differences exist.

---

[8]In Ngara District of western Tanzania, for instance, malnutrition rates were up to five times higher in villages surveyed in 1996 than in a refugee camp (see Whitaker, 1999).

Camp Mediators. Among camp populations, community representatives are likely to possess leadership qualities and conversational ability in at least one second language. They are likely to have completed, at most, secondary school. Members of this core group act as cultural mediators between the host and displaced populations by defusing tensions, building trust, resolving conflicts, negotiating agreements, and forging effective and sustainable networks. Their responsibilities include attempting to serve people whose material base for survival is threatened, people who have lost their support networks, people with serious health and nutrition problems, and people subject to continued life-threatening hostility from inside and outside the camp/community, as well as endeavoring to defuse potentially volatile confrontations and to promote collaborative relations among hosts and displaced persons.

Community leaders need intercultural communication skills for roles that involve mediation and conflict-management interactions with the representatives of culturally different camp populations, with diverse voices within their own community, with the leaders of host communities, and with the culturally diverse government authorities who are responsible for maintaining law and order and for overall decision making within the camp. They are likely to perceive the training opportunity as socially meaningful in terms of protecting and promoting the interests of their compatriots or subgroups within their community and to be motivated in personal terms by the enhanced prospects provided for economic survival, family well-being, and improving one's future life through the acquisition of portable skills.

The third section of *Table 9.1* deals with the intercultural communication contacts that camp community leaders are likely to encounter on a weekly basis. In addition to the situations they experience as a camp population member (Part 1), these individuals frequently are called on to interact with the leaders of other camp and host community populations as well as with camp authorities and assistance providers. If only one culturally different population is resident in the organized settlement, camp mediators are likely to be involved in *a minimum of three encounters with different cultures.*

Host Community Mediators. The representatives selected by host communities are likely to possess leadership qualities and conversational ability in at least one second language. They are likely to have completed, at most, primary school. Their responsibilities as leaders will include attempting to serve people whose material base for survival is threatened and people with serious health problems as well as endeavoring to defuse potentially volatile confrontations and to promote collaborative relations between hosts and displaced persons. These leaders will be expected to act as cultural mediators between the host and displaced populations by defusing tensions, building trust, managing conflicts, negotiating agreements, and forging effective and sustainable networks. They will need intercultural communication skills for roles that require mediation, interface, and coordination with camp populations, with diverse voices within their own community, and possibly with culturally different members of government agencies. They are likely to perceive the training opportunity as socially meaningful in terms of protecting and promoting the interests of their compatriots and to be motivated in personal terms by the enhanced prospects provided for economic survival, family well-being, and improving one's future life.

The fourth part of Table 9.1 highlights the likely intercultural communication contacts of host community representatives. In addition to the situations they encounter as a host community population member (Part 2), these individuals frequently are called on to interact with the leaders of camp populations as well as with local government authorities and assistance providers. If only two culturally different populations are resident in the organized settlement and camp and local government authorities are drawn from their cultural group, host community mediators are likely to be involved in *a minimum of three encounters with different cultures*.

Aid-Project-Participant Training Program

Participants in this training program are expected to be personnel recruited by agencies that are assisting refugees and displaced persons from the professional and semi-professional members of the camp population and from the better-educated ranks of rural host community populations. Initially, in many cases, their economic, nutritional, health, and psychological status will not differ markedly from the wider populations they live among. At most, the camp population and host community employees are likely to have completed secondary school and some additional technical, teacher-training, or university-level education. Most locally recruited employees are expected to possess conversational ability in at least one foreign language (the language used most often in internal organizational communication) and to be fluent in at least one other indigenous language. Both groups are likely to perceive the opportunity to assist external agents in a paid semi-professional or professional capacity as socially meaningful in terms of providing vital services to their needy compatriots and to be motivated in personal terms by the enhanced prospects provided for economic survival, family well-being, and improving one's future life through the acquisition of portable skills.

Locally recruited staff often experience patronizing treatment at the hands of expatriates (see Mazur, 1988). In some situations, they are granted only limited access to resources and decision-making processes. Nevertheless, they are expected to act as cultural brokers between the external expert and the local population, to educate outsiders regarding indigenous cultural values and practices as well as local situations (see Maynard, 1999), and to participate in multicultural project teams. In practice, they become embedded in pivotal overlapping relationships inside and beyond the employing organization and provide much of the vital interface between the indigenous society they belong to and the exogenous humanitarian-assistance agencies. Locally recruited personnel also are called on to facilitate communication and coordination with multiple domestic and foreign agencies operating in a turbulent interorganizational field (see e.g., Zetter, 1995). On behalf of the wider community to which they are linked, their primary responsibilities involve proposing, selecting, mobilizing resources for, facilitating and implementing, coordinating, and evaluating projects and strategies designed to benefit people that suffer from trauma and despair, people who have lost all their material belongings and their support networks, people with serious health problems and nutrition needs, and people subject to continued life-threatening hostility both inside and outside the camp. Projects will range from emergency food supply and housing to education and agricultural production. Their work environment is likely to be characterized by a lack of basic material resources, supplies, and equipment. Without appropriate training, problems of interstaff and interorganizational communication are likely to command an inordinate amount of time and effort and to deflect the humanitarian assistance agency from pursuing its principal service objectives (see e.g., Anderson, 1998).

The final rows of Table 9.1 reveal the extent of the intercultural communication challenge that faces both groups of indigenous assistants. They will need additional intercultural communication skills for roles that require intraorganizational interaction with resident expatriates and headquarters nationals from other countries and compatriots from other regions (see e.g., Whitaker, 1999; Woodrow, 1998a) as well as for interface and coordination with a multiplicity of culturally diverse members of other organizations who can facilitate or constrain the completion of their assigned tasks. Given that transnational assistance agencies usually recruit local semi-professional staff from all displaced and host communities, intercultural communication training also is important for interactions among the culturally diverse local recruits.

Thus, for indigenous assistance personnel, communication interaction situations are likely to involve a *minimum of six different critical cultural encounters* and could easily involve urgent and sustained communication with persons from as many as 20 different cultural backgrounds. From the indigenous staff's perspective, cultural distance tends to be particularly vast with the expatriate personnel of IOs, external donors, and transnational NGOs.

REQUIRED PERIMETER STAKEHOLDER SKILLS

An effective intercultural communication training program in refugee camp settings necessitates that differential attention be devoted to six target groups of perimeter stakeholders. Unique programs need to be designed and implemented for camp and host community populations as a whole, their representatives, and, finally, for the professional and semi-professional staff of assistance agencies drawn from each community. The emphasis and nature of each program should be based on assessments of the primary communication skills required by each group of stakeholders. Based on the preceding analysis of the conditions each group commonly confronts and the frequency of the interactions they are called upon to engage in, the following sections outline these skill requirements.

Camp and Host Community Populations

Camp and host community populations require basic intercultural communication skills in order to ensure individual and community preservation and to fashion cooperative, mutually productive intergroup relations in a potentially volatile context where large numbers of outsiders have been resettled in the midst of impoverished long-term residents. Such skills are especially useful for forcibly dislocated populations—who typically resettle for a long stay in a culturally alien location and encounter initial hostility from threatened local inhabitants. It is particularly important that camp and host populations avoid communication misunderstandings that would inflame relations either between two camp populations with different cultural backgrounds (and a possible history of intergroup conflict) or between camp and host populations.

Representatives of Camp and Host Populations

The principal intercultural communication skills required of the leaders or representatives of camp and host community populations relate to their responsibilities for building trust, managing conflicts, intervening on behalf of individual and group needs, and engaging the widest possible range of community members in "collaborative, mutually reinforcing actions" that strengthen bridging agreements and institutions and promote sustained intercultural dialogue (Daubon & Saunders, 2002, p. 184). Tensions always are present in camp-community relations and conflicts frequently arise over such issues as land use, forest depletion, access to safe water, allegations of theft, employment, and terms of trade. Camp populations of different ethnic or religious backgrounds might be at odds over perceived inequities in access to scarce resources or over cultural practices that clash. Conflicts arise with camp authorities over such matters as the failure of inhabitants to adhere to health and safety regulations or due to violations of basic human rights by abusive "security" forces. The daily occurrence of these and other disputes requires that community representatives possess intercultural conflict-resolution skills.

Additionally, the extent to which government agencies and external assistance providers respond to the needs of host and camp communities will depend to a considerable extent on the ability of their interorganizational entrepreneurs to articulate interests, determine priorities, and negotiate effectively across cultural boundaries. Developing competence in intercultural-conflict resolution and negotiation will serve community mediators well in long-term-settlement situations, or on repatriation or third-country resettlement, in terms of personal survival, employment prospects, and future leadership roles.

Professional and Semi-Professional Staff

Intercultural communication competency will be useful to staff members in performing virtually all of their job responsibilities, in teamwork and social interaction with co-workers from diverse and even distant cultural backgrounds, and in terms of advancement prospects (see Bell & Harrison, 1996). The primary culture-broker functions (see Shaffer, 1998) of these indigenous employees are to transfer information and insights between assistance providers and the local (displaced or host) community members and to assist in participatory needs and vulnerabilities assessment, resource identification and mobilization, and project selection, monitoring, and evaluation. Also, they frequently are called upon to serve as cultural interpreters between their agency's expatriate personnel and administrators (some foreign, some from diverse domestic cultures) employed by national and local government agencies, indigenous and international NGOs, IOs, and bilateral donors. Their interpretations—which involve policy issues, security matters, resource allocations, coordination, and logistical arrangements (see Koehn & Ngai, 2001), and human resource matters (see Harvey et al., 1999)—often enrich the manger's portfolio of strategic choices and are of crucial importance for the success of the assistance effort. For this reason, the intercultural communication training approaches set forth below should be an integral part of the specific job-related training programs offered to newly recruited refugees and hosts.

The progressive design of the overall program envisioned here calls for locally recruited staff to participate in all three programs and for community leaders to be involved in the first two programs. Additionally, the program provides for competence building among all parties participating in intercultural encounters. Intercultural communication is presented as a basic skill, mastery of which provides an important personal, organizational, and community asset in circumstances involving involuntary population dislocation.

Now that the participants and their special training needs have been identified, it is appropriate to consider how to construct an effective intercultural communication training program for the context selected here. In the interest of promoting effectiveness in program delivery, we seek to present a comprehensive design. Nevertheless, we caution readers to recognize that limited resources typically require the selective application of training approaches based on locally determined priorities and that the model developed here still requires considerable adaptation given the diversity that characterizes camp conditions around the world and the vastly different environment-organization interfaces that

occur among refugees and internally displaced persons who spontaneously settle among local populations.

ADAPTABLE INSIGHTS FROM INTERCULTURAL-COMMUNICATION TRAINING EXPERIENCE

On the one hand, the complex situation faced by perimeter populations requires
tailored-made training programs that accommodate their unique emergency and
long-term needs. On the other hand, many of the cultural and intergroup conditions they confront resemble those encountered by other types of intercultural
communication trainees. Thus, a review of training theories, methodologies, and
outcomes can provide valuable insights for designing appropriate and effective
intercultural communication programs for the populations of concern in this
chapter.

Comparable Conditions

The conditions that characterize perimeter community members are similar in
certain important ways to those encountered by most intercultural communication trainees. The most relevant of these comparable conditions are as follows:

- Social support is scarce because friends and family may not be in
  close proximity (Brislin, Landis, & Brandt, 1983).
- Many problems encountered are beyond one's own ability to solve
  and, hence, frequently produce low self-confidence (Brislin et al.,
  1983).
- Conflicts that spring from ingroup-outgroup relationships lower the
  productivity of the parties involved (Brislin et al., 1983).
- Intercultural interactions frequently occur at the intergroup rather
  than the interpersonal level (Cargile & Giles, 1996).
- The long-term effectiveness of training will be mediated by intergroup dynamics—especially interactions with hosts (Cargile &
  Giles, 1996).

These comparable training conditions, together with the specific considerations
concerning displaced populations and their host communities described previously, set the context for the training programs designed and presented in this
chapter.

Appropriate Approaches

Cargile and Giles' (1996) *Generalized Model of Intercultural Training as Currently Practiced* offers a helpful menu for designing intercultural communication training programs. On the basis of Gudykunst and Hammer's (1983) categorization of training approaches, Cargile and Giles identified immediate training outcomes and subsequent intercultural interaction outcomes. The four currently practiced training approaches include: experiential culture-general, experiential culture-specific, didactic culture-general, and didactic culture-specific.

The Cargile and Giles' model clarifies that the choice for training content is between a culture-general and a culture-specific approach; the choice for instructional technique is between an experiential and a didactic approach. Although both the experiential/culture-general and the experiential/culture-specific approaches involve the use of simulation games and role plays (see Gudykunst & Hammer, 1983), the former aims to help trainees come to the realization that people from different cultures operate differently and the latter aims to assist trainees in developing the verbal and nonverbal communication skills required for specific intercultural situations. Although both the didactic/culture-general and the didactic/culture-specific approaches rely on traditional lecture format and culture assimilators (see Brislin, Cushner, Cherrie, & Yong, 1986; Gudykunst & Hammer, 1983), the former aims to provide trainees with "an understanding of the general interactional and attributional dynamics involved in cross-cultural communication" (Cargile & Giles, 1996, p. 390) and the latter aims to inform trainees of "facts" about particular cultural groups and their behaviors (Cargile & Giles, 1996). All four approaches ultimately aim to bring about communication competence, adjustment, and task effectiveness.

From Culture-Specific to Culture-General

Gudykunst and Hammer (1983) and Brislin and Yoshida (1994) addressed the question of what techniques should be used in combination, and in what order. The three-stage training model proposed by Gudykunst and Hammer flows from culture-general training to culture-specific training (see Gudykunst & Hammer, 1983). Brislin and Yoshida (1994) recommended a similar progression—from training in general intercultural behavior to training in behavior appropriate in specific cultural contexts. This training design—for a program that runs longer than 3 days—is appropriate for beneficiaries who can afford the time and the ensuing costs. In emergency humanitarian assistance settings, where time and money are in short supply, training programs need to focus on the skills each set of participants requires for fulfilling their paramount roles. Thus, we suggest that training with displaced populations and host communities start out as culture-specific and move on to culture-general approaches for trainees employed in multicultural assistance contexts.

In order to design an effective intercultural training program for the populations of concern in this chapter, moreover, five important "intergroup" and "interaction" factors must be taken into consideration. These considerations are as follow:

1. Trainee attitudes toward and beliefs or stereotypes about the cultural group in question.
2. The larger sociostructural and historical context and the immediate social situation.
3. Interpersonal or intergroup identities or self-concepts in cross-cultural encounters.
4. Well-learned, automatic, unintentional responses.
5. Interaction processes (Cargile & Giles, 1996, pp. 398-399, 404, 407).

Training Stages and Strategies

To develop in trainees the ability to communicate effectively with people from other cultures is the ultimate goal of an intercultural communication training program (Seidel, 1981). This general goal has been approached through three common training strategies: awareness raising, attitude change, and new skill development (Gudykunst & Hammer, 1983; Milhouse, 1996; Seidel, 1981). The training programs proposed here operationalize these three strategies in distinct and sequential stages. Additionally, we introduce a fourth strategy— stress coping—designed to address the emotional state encountered by the intended beneficiaries of training.

Awareness Raising.   During the first stage—awareness raising—trainees are introduced to the following:

1. The subject of culture.
2. The key historical experiences and values of the group(s) with which they are interacting (Maynard, 1999).
3. Problems of communication that have occurred in interactions among the local groups involved and, in general, when members of diverse cultures interact.
4. The extent to which individual behavior is culturally determined (Gallois & Callan, 1997; Gudykunst & Hammer, 1983).
5. The individual uniqueness that is encountered among members of other cultural groups that they interact with on a daily basis (Cargile & Giles, 1996).

Understanding how attitudes, education, and the process of socialization affect actions and patterns of behavior (Paige & Martin, 1983; Seidel, 1981) constitutes a key component of overall intercultural communication competency (Baxter, 1983).

Attitude Change. A positive attitude toward diversity and multiculturalism is the second key element required for effective intercultural communication. Trainees holding "negative attitudes" or stereotypes about the targeted interaction community are prone to avoid "attending to and processing information dissonant with their own attitudes, stereotypes, and feelings" (Cargile & Giles, 1996, p. 401). The challenges here are to "change trainees' stereotypes about the target host group" (Cargile & Giles, 1996, p. 403) and to rebuild trust across identity lines (Maynard, 1999). In some cases, the task is complicated by fixed adversarial perceptions rooted in an historical context of extreme intergroup conflict that continues to be played out in global, regional, or local political events and power applications that induce extensive human suffering and deprivation (see Erlanger, 2000; Maynard, 1999).

There are two keys to bringing about the requisite perspective transformation in such challenging circumstances. First, emphasis should be placed on interactions across cultures that occur on an interindividual and/or interfamily (rather than an intergroup) basis (see Cargile & Giles, 1996). Furthermore, and most importantly, perspective transformation needs to be linked explicitly to personal skill development and to asset building on an individual and community basis. This linkage provides the crucial (and often missing) motivational basis for trainee willingness to accept and even embrace attitudinal change (Cargile & Giles, 1996).

When developing or enhancing culture-general skills is at stake, trainers also need to help trainees "to accept and to be tolerant of values, beliefs, attitudes, and behavior patterns that might be quite different from their own" (Seidel, 1981, p. 190). Additionally, this level of training should aim at developing "the ability to tolerate ambiguity, empathy, the ability to withhold judgment, reduction of ethnocentrism, a culturally relativistic world view, an appreciation of other values and belief systems, personal flexibility, [and] a willingness to acquire new patterns of behavior and belief" (Paige & Martin, 1983, p. 44; Baxter, 1983).

New Skill Development. Skill-building constitutes the third, and most time-consuming, stage of the proposed training program. The type and number of intercultural communication skills of relevance for organizational communication will vary according to institutional mission as well as trainee roles and responsibilities. Examples include the following:

- Interpreting and using cultural nonverbal cues.
- Interacting effectively with members of diverse cultures.
- Accessing the multicultural organizational communication network.

- Reaching agreements in intercultural contexts.
- Managing intercultural conflicts (Ngai & Koehn, 2001).
- Mastering techniques that facilitate continued learning during cross-cultural encounters (Seidel, 1981).
- Developing observational skills that allow learning from the subtleties of the new culture (Seidel, 1981).

Stress Coping. In general, stress-induced anxiety constrains "the type of processing needed in intercultural encounters," encourages "reliance on well-learned stereotypes" (Cargile & Giles, 1996, p. 408), and impairs intercultural functioning by magnifying "the severity of possible threats and worry about things that rarely happen" (Bandura, 1995, p. 8). Thus, the last stage of the proposed training program is especially relevant for the humanitarian assistance organizations and perimeter populations considered in this chapter. The debilitating stress faced by the dislocated and their disrupted hosts is rooted in multiple sources (e.g., starvation, death of loved ones, economic destitution, the psychological consequences of rape and torture, multiple illnesses and injuries, lost property, threats to physical security and identity, and intercultural uncertainty and conflict).

Addressing all sources of stress is beyond the scope of an intercultural communication training program. We suggest that the proposed program focus on helping trainees deal with anxiety-induced stress caused by intercultural communication failure. One effective common strategy would be to encourage the acquisition of pro-active communication techniques that facilitate the formation of mixed-identity friendships.

An Integrated Approach. Woven together, the four stages of awareness raising, attitude change, new skill development, and stress coping encompass cognitive, affective, behavioral (see Milhouse, 1996), and emotional learning. By incorporating all four dimensions, the three training programs elaborated here are able to integrate common training objectives and strategies with specific content derived from the unique conditions faced by each displaced population and its host community(ies). An essential first step, however, is to undertake a thorough preprogram assessment that will provide vital information for tailoring each stage of training to local conditions.

Preprogram Assessment

A comprehensive analysis of the trainees' specific living conditions, their immediate and future needs, and the intergroup communicative context constitutes an essential component of the preprogram assessment process required for tailored programming. All participants should be invited to take part in a needs-

and capabilities-identification exercise in advance of training.[9] Each group of prospective trainees should be surveyed separately. The survey should emphasize encounters with previous intercultural communication problems and approaches to cross-cultural adaptability as well as participant awareness, knowledge, stereotypes, concerns, expertise, experience, and desired skills (also see Pedersen, 1994). It also should identify "cultural-based learning strategies" (Gudykunst & Hammer, 1983, p. 146; Harvey, Speier, & Novicevic, 1999).

Based on the results of this elicited exercise, trainers prepare an inventory that will guide them in tailoring the complete program to the specific backgrounds and needs of each group of trainees. In preparation for program sessions, trainers should integrate trainee doubts, questions, irritations, and delights (see Bond, 1992) into anonymous and hypothetical incidents and situations for analysis and small-group discussion. For instance, if potential trainees mention in the survey that certain types of intercultural conflicts have presented difficult problems to deal with, trainers can design directly relevant conflict-management training sessions. Trainers should aim at addressing trainee concerns and interests by offering practical advice throughout the training program. Moreover, program coordinators should use the survey results to identify trainees whose practical experiences, knowledge, and adaptability skills will enable them to serve as valuable resource persons; those who can provide external trainers with valuable information regarding local communicative practices; and the core-group leaders and aid-project participants who will be invited to participate in further training (see also Anderson & Woodrow, 1989).

PROGRAM FRAMEWORK

Level 1 of our proposed intercultural communication training program for perimeter displaced populations and host communities targets the organized set-

---

[9]This exercise could be carried out in a participatory manner by "spending time with people under their conditions, talking with them, and listening to them" (Waldron & Hasci, 1995, p. 28). The importance of refugee participation and consultation in all stages of decision making regarding their training constituted a recurring emphasis among participants at a 1994 international symposium dedicated to refugee training. The experienced practitioners and other experts in attendance agreed that refugee needs, identified through careful assessments that involve refugees themselves (specifically including women and the elderly), should drive the implementation of training programs (Koehn, 1994a). Specific recommendations included (1) "training should be a community-based process of learning, empowerment, and enhancing self-esteem which takes place within a planning/learning/change spiral where all are teachers and learners" (p. 70); (2) "in order to be sustainable, training in administration and management should be future-oriented and participatory, accommodating people-oriented planning with involvement of all players at all stages . . ." (pp. 69-70); (3) training needs should "reflect the socio-economic, cultural, as well as human-resource needs of the country of origin and the refugees themselves" (p. 72); and (4) "appropriate training should include the incorporation and modification of traditional practices" (p. 68).

tlement population and local residents. In most cases, the mass-based training provided will be relatively brief and will focus on one or two specific cultures. The objective is for trainees to develop the basic intercultural communication competence required for avoiding misunderstanding among members of the interacting cultures.

Community leaders, indigenous peace-makers (see Maynard, 1999), and aid-project staff members drawn from the camp and the host community move on to the next level of training. At this second level of training, the program introduces one additional culture (that of the local authorities) and will address expected local situations, issues, and/or problems. The emphasis here is on enabling trainees to develop sufficient intercultural communication competence to act as effective community mediators through interorganizational networks consisting of camp resident and of the host community representatives, national and local government authorities, and indigenous and international NGO personnel (see e.g., Forrest, 2000).

The next level of training only will involve the aid-project participants who work with people from diverse, multiple, unpredictable, and changing cultural backgrounds. At this third level, therefore, trainers will introduce general differences across communication cultures. Level 3, the most extensive training program, will emphasize developing participants' multicultural or transnational organizational communication competency (see Koehn & Rosenau, 2002).

With progression from one level of training to the next, the range of trainees narrows and the number of trainees decreases while the scope of training expands. The rationale for this integrated design and progressive arrangement is to maximize the limited amount of time and resources available in emergency humanitarian assistance situations. In such situations, effective training results from adherence to the following program design principles: (a) be culture-specific and focus on basic and preventative skills with the broader population; (b) introduce additional content and skills progressively and only as needed in light of the principal roles performed by each group of intended beneficiaries; and (c) reserve cultural-general training for beneficiaries who engage extensively in interaction with persons from an unpredictable multiplicity of cultures.

Each level of training consists of four sequential components: awareness raising, attitude change, skill development, and stress coping (see Tables 9.2–9.4). The particular component(s) emphasized will vary across the three program levels depending, in part, on the needs identified by the trainer together with participating trainees. In each case, intercultural communication skill training should be approached as adding to participants' repertoire of assets rather than as a substitute for intracultural communication and one's own "way" (see Bond, 1992; Kealey & Protheroe, 1996). Additionally, the training approaches utilized in pursuing each component at various levels should be selected on the basis of the educational backgrounds and culturally based learning styles of the majority of trainees and the amount of time and human resources available for particular training sessions. For instance, didactic approaches used for large groups demand less active involvement from trainees and require less training time and human resources. On the other hand, experiential approaches used in small groups work especially well with trainees who are used to interactive, informal learning.

Given that pre-existing training materials concerning specific cultures are not likely to be available on short notice, the appropriate approaches to use in emergency situations should be flexible and open-ended enough to allow for the spontaneous integration of cultural specifics elicited through preassessment and provided by trainees during participatory training activities. Moreover, all training activities adopted should require minimal reliance on printed materials, which are likely to be in short supply, and should be based on simple instructions in order to minimize confusion among trainees.[10] The Level 3 program should be incorporated as an integral part of wider agency-initiated training for locally recruited staff (e.g., basic health worker training), or a single interorganizational program can be designed and delivered for all qualified humanitarian assistance project personnel in the region. Delivering the Level 2 and Level 3 programs in several sessions separated by substantial intervals of time would "allow for practice in real life social situations" and "provide repeated opportunities for corrective feedback and consolidation of learning" (Mak, Westwood, Ishiyama, & Barker, 1999, p. 87). Lessons from the Level 1 program can be reinforced by trained practitioners in conjunction with the provision of basic services to members of displaced and impacted communities (e.g., food distribution, health care, and/or education).

Members of the host community(ies) and the dislocated population are expected to speak different languages. Given the language differences and the preprogram tensions that are likely to exist among the intended beneficiaries, training should be conducted separately for each group at Levels 1 and 2. At Level 2, trainers can bring both groups together for joint activities and interactive exercises that facilitate practice with newly learned mediation and negotiation skills across two or more cultures (Schoenhaus, 2000). Furthermore, joint programming facilitates the organization of sessions in which "members of each cultural group teach skills to the other. *Because the skills are useful to participants, resistance is undercut*" (Bond, 1992, p. 405; italics added). At Level 3, training will be conducted in the language (e.g., English, Spanish, Arabic, French, Swahili) that functions as the *lingua franca* in the region. In this case, aid-project staff hired from both the host community and the camp population can participate in a common training program. In Level 3 training, moreover, "it is particularly important that the subordinate cultural group [locally recruited staff] be given an opportunity to teach the dominant cultural group [expatriate

---

[10]Also see the important practical suggestions set forth in Bond (1992).

personnel]. Such teaching *reverses* the normal organizational pattern of top-down technical instruction, a pattern that reinforces the tendency of the dominant group to consider itself right on nontechnical issues in the organizations" (Bond, 1992, p. 405).

Level 1 Program: Camp Population—Host Community Training

The Level 1 training program (see Table 9.2) primarily aims to increase understanding about specific differences and similarities in beliefs, value systems, customs, lifestyles, and communication styles, and to remove stereotypes with regard to the host community and camp populations, in order to avoid (further) intercultural misunderstanding and conflict (see Dinges, 1983).[11] It proceeds through presentations, actual cases, storytelling, structured discussion, locally created and performed dramas,[12] and/or drawings (see Melkote, 1991; Pedersen, 1994), and can usefully involve intercultural sensitizers who concentrate on key differences between the two relevant cultures (Albert, 1983) and on reducing intercultural uncertainty and unpredictability (Kim, 1988). This program also presents sensitizing background on the displaced/host populations, including the factors responsible for, and consequences associated with, dislocation/resettlement. It is important that these presentations balance discussions of migrant vulnerability with "appreciation of the common resilience of refugee communities, and the considerable resources within them" (Ager, 1999, p. 13). The specific content conveyed through the Level 1 training program will include references to particular cultural sensitivities (e.g., sacred trees) that need to be respected in order to avoid conflicts with members of the other group(s). An emphasis on actual and/or hypothetical daily-life incidents is likely to be particularly effective in this connection (see Kealey & Protheroe, 1996).

Given that the groups involved speak different languages, nonverbal communication constitutes an important intercultural communication channel. As Pedersen (1994) pointed out, "persons from another culture may grossly misinterpret a simple gesture, expression, or implied attitude owing to a different cultural viewpoint. Hints, clues, understatements, and appropriate omissions are some of the more subtle tools of communication that present barriers to multicultural communication" (p. 91; see also Ngai, 2001). Role-playing, demonstra-

---

[11]Cargile and Giles (1996) recommend that "if it is found that most trainees have intense negative feelings about the target host group, those feelings should be addressed and not glossed over" (p. 414).

[12]For instance, "in Croatia and Bosnia, CARE uses theater and dance to help schoolchildren integrate emotional and conceptual understanding of the regional conflict. By acting out a hypothetical dispute and eventually transforming it to a state of peace, the children experience both the emotions of conflict and the process and satisfaction of resolution" (Maynard, 1999, pp. 184-185).

TABLE 9.2   Level 1 Training Program

Target beneficiaries: Camp population(s) and host community(ies)

Main Objective: Develop sufficient intercultural communication competence to avoid cross-cultural misunderstanding among the specific groups involved in training.

		TRAINING PROGRAM	
Sequence	Component	Focus	Training Approaches
1	Awareness raising	Specific cultures—camp population and host community.	- Presentations - Structured group discussion
2	Attitude change	Removing stereotypes that camp population and host community members have of each other.	- Storytelling - Drawing - Local dramas
3	Skill development	Verbal and nonverbal intercultural-communication skills that promote cross-cultural understanding and prevent conflicts and human-rights abuses. Conflict avoidance by selecting the appropriate communication channels.	- Role play - Peer reactions and coaching - Demonstrations and modeling/ practice - Participatory video
4	Stress coping	Relieve stress caused by living side-by–side with members of another group.	- Cooperative projects - Stress-coping rituals - Witness testimony

tions, symbolic and participative modeling of effective cross-cultural communication, together with peer and trainer reactions (see Kealey & Protheroe, 1996) and coaching, can be used to sensitize trainees to their own and others' cultural nonverbal cues and to help them adjust their communication approaches for intercultural encounters. These approaches will work best by arranging the trainees in small groups.

Regarding the verbal aspect, teaching each group important greeting expressions in the language spoken by the other community(ies) would allow program graduates to express goodwill and friendliness during intercultural encounters.

Demonstrations and practice in linguistic initiation and response for daily encounters and in the effective use of nonthreatening questions also would help trainees develop pro-active intercultural communication skills. Beyond this, trainers should emphasize the importance of avoiding premature and inade-quately informed attributions of unexpected behavior and incidents involving members of the other community. Instead, given the language barriers that impede direct communication, they should be encouraged to seek out explana-tions from their group's cultural mediators. This communicative approach can be reinforced by modeling of "proper" intercultural conflict-avoidance behavior when confronting possible incidents involving displaced community members and hosts, and through the use of participatory video (see Stuart & Bery, 1996).

Finally, the program would demonstrate that stress caused by living side-by-side with a culturally different community can be reduced by lowering or removing hostility, uncertainty, and lack of cooperation. While working through conflicts satisfactorily constitutes the most effective strategy for reducing stress in the long run, it would introduce unacceptable risks if applied to untrained populations in volatile circumstances. Thus, we suggest that conflict avoidance and minimizing offensive behavior provide the principal framework for dealing with intercultural suspicion and hostility among total populations until the trust-building process has advanced (Maynard, 1999) and inner and outer resources allow the direct negotiation of more complex understandings. Through small-group training, therefore, participants would be shown how taking the initiative to communicate a friendly and culturally sensitive attitude toward another group avoids intercultural clashes and, thereby, reduces stress in one's daily encoun-ters. They also would practice using conflict-avoiding discourse and labels along with culturally sensitive nonverbal cues, and would learn to turn to their trained intercultural mediators in the resolution of any conflicts that do arise.[13]

Over the long term, Level 1 training can fruitfully involve continuous inter-cultural interaction on small-scale cooperative projects and in areas (such as trade) deemed appropriate for cross-identity contact. Experience in collabora-tively addressing problems that threaten each group and in advancing shared interests is likely to overcome fear and prevailing stereotypes, to generate or rebuild mutual trust (Maynard, 1999), and to build or reinforce confidence in the effectiveness of collective action in uncertain and challenging situations (Bandura, 1995).

Intercultural communication training is particularly relevant and vital in cases involving trauma stemming from the experience and consequences of forced dislocation. Culturally sensitive training for individual and community psychological rehabilitation "generally covers the causes of psychological dis-

---

[13]These recommendations are consistent with the primary goal of third-party nonviolent interven-tion, that is, "a general lowering of hostilities that will create a breathing space for further change to occur safely" (Schoenhaus, 2001, p. 27).

turbance, . . . the typical symptoms and nature of the disorder, . . . the role of specific individuals in the care process" (Maynard, 1999, p. 190), and the importance of resuming, even if in somewhat altered form, disrupted practices and rituals that traditionally are activated in order to cope with stress, extreme hardship, or threatening circumstances—for instance, being able to mourn the death of a loved one properly (Miller, 1999; Mollica, Lavelle, Tor, & Elias, 1989; Musisi, 2002). An essential part of the initial healing process involves "sharing traumatic experiences, perceptions, resulting emotions, and responses" through "storytelling in an atmosphere of compassion, encouragement, and support" (Maynard, 1999, pp. 134-135). Additionally, *witness testimony*, guided by trained mental-health professionals who possess "skills of nuanced interviewing and listening," facilitates civic dialogue, genuine reconciliation, (re)building inter-community trust, and the fashioning of a sound multi-ethnic community (see Maynard, 1999; Weine, 1996).[14]

Level 2 Program: Intercultural Mediator Training

The Level 2 training program (see Table 9.3) emphasizes cultivating empathy for camp populations (for one's own group as well as all others) and for the host community(ies) and aims to develop competence in intercultural conflict resolution. It focuses on intercultural mediators drawn from the camp population(s) and host community(ies).

The Level 2 program builds on what has been covered during Level 1 training. Furthermore, it introduces one additional culture—that of the local authorities—that intermediaries from both the host community and the camp population(s) must deal with.

Storytelling, the presentation of contentious issues from various points of view (Maynard, 1999), and small-group discussion can be especially effective in cultivating among community representatives the empathy required to succeed in the role of mediator for the host or the camp population. Yarbrough and Wilmot (1995) pointed out that:

> a mediator must have a full spectrum of "soft," receptive skills and "hard," directive skills. The mediation process begins with a soft, receptive approach, characterized by listening, exploration, and empathy. As people are heard and understood, as problems are analyzed, and as negotiation begins, the mediator moves . . . to . . . using . . . more directive approaches. (p. 8)

---

[14]Despite the benefits that accrue to refugee populations from such proactive intercultural-communication training approaches, projects such as Filmaid International's projections of Tom and Jerry cartoons and "hopeful" feature films intended to distract children and adults who are bored by the tedium of camp life and to dull the psychological impact of armed conflict and dislocation receive substantially greater donor financial support (see McKinley, 2000).

TABLE 9.3   Level 2 Training Program

Target beneficiaries: Representatives from camp population(s) and host community

Main Objective: Develop intercultural-communication competence for conflict resolution and mediation.

TRAINING PROGRAM

Sequence	Component	Focus	Training Approaches
1	Awareness raising	Specific cultures—camp population and host community; plus one addi tional culture—local authorities.	Elicit problems through: -Trainee presentations - Storytelling - Case-study analysis
2	Attitude change	Developing empathy for "stranger" camp population(s) and host community.	Applications of human-rights principles
3	Skill development	Negotiation and conflict manage-ment/mediation skills, local trust and capacity building, information gathering and sharing skills, pro-moting collaborative relations among community members.	Group & intergroup discussion Modeling of effec-tive intercultural conflict manage-ment & mediation techniques
4	Stress coping	Relieve stress caused by being involved in resolving serious con-flicts and crises among members of two/three cultures.	Role play with feed-back from train-ers & collective reflection among trainees Ample time to practice

To serve in an effective intercultural mediator capacity, trainees need to develop cognitively and behaviorally to rehearse active listening, alternative perspective assessing, trust-building, mutual disclosing, underlying problem identifying, creative alternative generating, negotiating, conflict management, and persuad-ing skills (see Chen & Starosta, 1996; Daubon & Saunders, 2002; Hocker & Wilmot, 1995; Mezirow, 1991; Yarbrough & Wilmot, 1996) through case-study analysis, modeling, and local situation-specific role-playing with feedback from trainers and trainees (Black & Mendenhall, 1989).[15] In this connection, Mak et al. (1999) pointed out that "observing successful . . . performances by others similar to oneself . . . enhances the trainees perceived self-efficacy . . . which in turn increases the chance of attempting and mastering that task . . . ." (p. 83). Another potentially useful approach is to suggest alternative negotiation/mediation frameworks and elicit opinions on which would be more and less culturally appropriate and effective (Schoenhaus, 2001).

In order to perform effectively in mediating roles, the representatives of dislocated populations and host communities also need to be able to gather or share information and to thrash out ideas among themselves and with the broader membership of their group. Presentations on networking techniques, case-study analysis regarding appropriate intercultural information delivering and receiving strategies, relevant applications of human rights principles, and training on techniques for locating and consulting useful and reliable oral and written sources of current information regarding the other contact culture(s), perspectives on past cross-identity conflict (see Maynard, 1999), and overcoming structural impediments to peaceful interactions can be helpful in this part of the program. Another potentially useful approach is to suggest alternative negotiation/mediation frameworks and elicit opinions on which would be more and less culturally appropriate and effective (Schoenhaus, 2001).

In addition to responding to conflicts that occur among members of their own and another culture (see Koehn, 1994a), cultural group leaders can be proactive in building sustainable local capacity for conflict management among the camp population and the host community. For instance, they can be encouraged to create or revitalize valued participatory linkages—such as peace committees and sustained dialogues—that span cultures (see e.g., Maynard, 1999; Philips, 1993), to expand intercultural rapport and acculturation skills (Bemak, Chung, & Bornemann, 1996), and to arrange public forums that consider differences, contentious issues, common interests, and cooperative arrangements in a safe and constructive setting for cross-identity interaction (Daubon & Saunders, 2002; Maynard, 1999). Training programs that emphasize building self-esteem and stakeholder empowerment through, for instance, participatory rural appraisal (see Chambers, 1994; Eade & Williams, 1995), enhance the voice of perimeter communities and expand democratic forms of participation in dealing with assistance organizations and camp authorities.

The challenges involved in intercultural mediation—along with the heavy burden of responsibilities this group of trainees must assume in terms of the potential seriousness of conflicts, emotional attachment to those involved, and the urgency that often accompanies the need to defuse crisis situations—

---

[15]On the advantages of role-playing as a tool for developing intercultural competency, see Mak et al. (1999) and Thomas (1998).

combine to produce exceptionally high levels of stress. Level 2 training, therefore, should including building skills in setting attainable subgoals when dealing with troublesome situations in order to instill a resilient sense of efficacy (Bandura, 1995) and in recognizing the need for support systems and developing them among counterparts from their own and other cultural backgrounds. Furthermore, continuous pro-active efforts to sharpen the conflict-management skills of community members will enable cultural mediators to reduce their case load and, in the long run, will promote community-wide involvement in conflict-resolution approaches that require sophisticated and creative intercultural understanding.

Level 3 Program: Aid-Project-Participant Training

The third (culture-general) level of training (see Table 9.4) covers differences in communicative styles and organizational approaches across a range of intercultural situations—including field office/headquarters, leader/member, technical/nontechnical, and power-differentiated (Brislin et al., 1983). Such awareness raising is intended to develop in aid-project participants the communicative flexibility that will enable them to adapt to and to make effective connections in the multicultural and nonstandardized workplace (see Edwards, 1997). This training includes mastery of cultural-continuum identification and placement, sociocultural map construction, opening and revising culturally specific communication data files in one's mind, and cultural adjustment action planning (see Ngai & Koehn, 2001).

The cultural continuums placement exercise serves as a useful tool for comparing various cultures. Along each continuum, the cultures at issue are at a par with one another in the sense that no culture is superior or more central than the other. This perspective allows trainees to see how diverse cultures complement one another and, hence, to develop respect and appreciation for all cultures and diversity in general. Such attitudes facilitate the generation of cross-cultural synergy in the multicultural workplace.

In identifying issues of relevance to intercultural communication in multicultural organizations, Bond's (1992) experience suggests that *process* is a "powerful illustrator of context . . . " (p. 398). For purposes of awareness-building and attitude unfreezing, Bond focused on the "resistance to the potential for change" that the training process itself tends to activate. Ultimately, this discussion reveals the potential for assuming powerful gate-keeping roles and that "cross-cultural training will enhance everybody's skills . . ." (Bond, 1992, pp. 400-401).

The skill-development part of Level 3 training aims at the following:

- Provide trainees with a range of multicultural organizational communication skills.

- Equip locally recruited staff for participation as a partner in interculturally sensitive planning and for reaching agreements that are shaped by the unique cultures and customs of the involved displaced and host communities.
- Ensure that graduates come away with a lifelong capacity to learn how to learn (see Kealey & Protheroe, 1996).

TABLE 9.4   Level 3 Training Program

Target beneficiaries: Aid-project participants

Main Objective: Develop intercultural-communication competence for working within and across multicultural organizations and with semi-professionals and professionals from diverse, changing, and unpredictable cultural backgrounds.

TRAINING PROGRAM			
Sequence	Component	Focus	Training Approaches
1	Awareness raising	Full range of cultural dimensions.	- Cultural-continuum-placement exercise
2	Attitude	Develop appreciation for working with people of diverse cultural backgrounds.	- Presentations - Role plays
3	Skill development	Multicultural organization communication skills such as team building and teamwork, partnering, problem resolution, making meetings work, networking, negotiation, cross-cultural logistics, participatory appraisals and evaluations, business correspondence, and functioning as an effective voice in mobilizing resources.	- Interactive simulations - Writing exercises - Discussion and sharing - Action plans - Mentoring
4	Stress coping	Relieve stress caused by working with multiple organizational and cultural systems in an emergency situation.	

Trainees develop skills in assessing organizational cultures, trust-building (see Bennett, Aston, & Colquhoun, 2000), and communicating across and within multicultural intraorganizational groups and teams. Additionally, trainers introduce the importance of intercultural competence when one is engaged in processes of network construction and maintenance, joint exchanges and decision making, shared risk-taking, interest articulation, and the identification of major stakeholder groups and their interests, power bases, and limitations (see Kealey & Protheroe, 1996; Siegel, 1985).

As the expatriates they work with increasingly adopt participative management, locally recruited staff will need to be prepared with corresponding partnership skills (see Kealey, 1990; Kealey & Protheroe, 1996). Training also needs to be provided in communication strategies for effective leadership in multicultural and multiorganizational relief and development settings—including participatory rural appraisal and evaluation, project identification and selection (see Hyden, Koehn, & Saleh, 1996), team-building and teamwork, logistical problem resolution, making meetings work, networking, negotiation, providing an effective voice for mobilizing resources from community, government, and donor sources, and integrating diverse constituents into a common organizational culture (Harrison, 1994). Appropriate training approaches include case-study analysis and small-group discussion of organizational communication problems in the multicultural workplace, presentations on effective strategies, action training using actual or simulated policy dilemmas and intercultural communication barriers, and role-playing intercultural negotiations and multicultural meetings. This training session also emphasizes mastery of effective business-writing skills in the *lingua franca*. Trainers should provide guidance in the concise and unambiguous drafting of documents such as situation reports (see Eade & Williams, 1995), grant applications, budget requests, news releases, contracts, other legal documents, and interinstitutional agreements (see Siegel, 1985). Finally, participants should be encouraged to prepare action plans that will guide implementation in their multicultural work environment.

The skill development component of Level 3 training requires receptiveness and commitment on the part of participants to ongoing learning through practice. Trainer follow-up usually is effective in reinforcing such commitment.[16] At periodic intervals over the course of several years, therefore, trainers should visit program graduates at their work sites to answer questions, offer insights, and suggest approaches to handling specific intercultural-communication challenges and promising adaptations in light of observed workplace conditions and

---

[16]Bond's (1992) experience indicates that "knowing that postmeasures will be taken, participants pay better attention during the seminar and are motivated to connect the seminar experience and content to their work situation" (pp. 408-409).

practices (see Xiao, 1996). These visits also can be used to review participants' progress in implementing the action plans they prepared during the Level 3 program, to provide assistance with the further implementation of their action plans, to reinforce efficacy-building experiences, and to develop and sustain an effective mentor system (see Ptak, Cooper, & Breslin, 1995).

Emergency and crisis situations ensure that humanitarian assistance personnel operate in a stressful and rest-deprived work environment. Local staff may witness immense suffering and experience feelings of "helplessness, guilt, or anger . . . ." (Eade & Williams, 1995, p. 973). Service in a multicultural work environment with minimal headquarters and government support and protection (see e.g., Crossette, 2000a; Minear & Guillot, 1996; Summerfield, 1999) adds to the extreme and prolonged level of emotional stress that aid-project participants encounter in the field. One important dimension of the Level 3 program, therefore, should be to help trainees develop skills for coping with the tensions, interpersonal and identity conflicts, disproportionate-influence perceptions, and "other surprises" that will arise (Salk, 1996, p. 49); for expressing their concerns through responsive communication channels; and for eliciting support from co-workers who are prone to use different communicative approaches when dealing with personal emotions (see also Ngai & Koehn, 2001; Planalp, 1999). It is likely to prove valuable in this training context, therefore, to include experienced field personnel when demonstrating the stress-coping utility of group discussions and sharing sessions as well as individual efficacy-building techniques that support perseverance in the face of difficulties (Bandura, 1995).

The Inclusive, Progressive Program

The four sequential components embedded within each program and the three progressive program levels together constitute an integral, holistic training model. Each component provides the foundation for the next one in the sequence; each program level is built on the previous level in progression. Thus, any omission would greatly diminish the effectiveness of the proposed training model. Moreover, the more community members who participate at each level, the greater the prospects for improved intercultural communication outcomes in an impacted area (see also Maynard, 1999). However, if resources for training purposes are scarce and it is impossible to deliver a complete training program to every involved constituent, we suggest that trainers limit the number of perimeter participants rather than compromise the integrity of the program by cutting an entire part. In other words, priority should be placed on quality over quantity. Furthermore, participants in a complete program are more capable than semi-trained graduates would be to assume the role of trainers who can spread the benefits of training among others who are similarly situated.

CONCLUSION

In resource-stricken humanitarian assistance situations, approaches to organizational communication are required to address the paramount needs of dislocated and disrupted populations in a timely and resource-efficient manner. Improvements in the intercultural-communication skills of perimeter stakeholders promise to enhance a wide range of vital communicative processes. This outcome requires a training framework that differs in important ways from conventional models while building upon proven strategies and approaches. In particular, intercultural communication training needs to incorporate the participatory energy and synergy of indigenous beneficiaries (see also Stohl, 1993). Our proposed progressive threefold framework, which involves an outer-to-inner approach that builds from a culture-specific to a culture-general program, is designed to meet the pressing communicative challenges that confront humanitarian assistance agencies in transnational and multicultural settings.

Relevance of a Progressive Framework for Resource-scarce Training Situations

In emergency situations involving externally and internally displaced populations, the top communication training priorities involve addressing the immediate needs of the dislocated and their hosts and the avoidance of further conflict. For this reason, the three-tier progressive training framework set forth here starts off with community-based programs that deal with the specific and immediate cultural environment. In this way, camp populations and their host community(ies) can be equipped with applicable basic and preventative intercultural communication skills within days or a few weeks in a cost-effective manner. Additionally, the first level of training forms the basis for further skill development among community leaders and aid-project participants. As a result, many basics have already been covered when selected leaders and assistance workers move on to the Level 2 program, which focuses on intercultural mediation and conflict-resolution skills.[17] The comparatively time-consuming and costly Level 3 training program, which deals with general cross-cultural differences and relatively sophisticated multicultural organization communication skills, can be restricted to participants who have found employment with transnational aid agencies and can be incorporated and supported as a fundamental part of existing staff-training efforts.

---

[17]Maynard (1999) noted that "conflict management skills training usually spans no more than several days and may be repeated or continued in several sessions" (p. 183).

IMPLICATIONS

By placing the often neglected subjects of population displacement at the center of attention, this chapter's enlarged and multidisciplinary perspective on organizational communication suggests important implications for theory, methodology, and practice. First, frameworks for analyzing organizational communication need to treat diversity inclusively by incorporating the point of view of perimeter stakeholders. In this connection, it is fruitful to extend the concept of participation to encompass the involvement of impacted populations in processes of conflict-management, human-service provision, and education/training. The conditions and objectives that prevail in large-scale humanitarian-assistance situations also challenge the prevailing wisdom, based on social-learning theory (see Harrison, 1994), that training should move from the culture-general to the culture-specific (see Brislin & Yoshida, 1994; Gudykunst & Hammer, 1983). Furthermore, the link between skill-acquisition as a motivator and willingness to accept attitudinal changes illuminates the theoretical nexus between intercultural communication training outcomes and intergroup interactions (see Cargile & Giles, 1996).

Progressive intercultural communication training methodologies that begin with mass-based preventative approaches that emphasize the avoidance of miscommunication promise to yield important payoffs in terms of reducing the demands and stresses placed on participants in programs designed to facilitate conflict resolution and service provision. The key to success in this regard is involving all perimeter communities that are party to intercultural encounters in similar and simultaneous Level 1 training so that the communicative skills they have learned will be reinforced by subsequent intergroup interactions and reactions (see Cargile & Giles, 1996). The refugee and displaced person context also reveals the utility of incorporating stress-coping strategies into the standard methodology for intercultural communication training.

In terms of practice, a major implication of the program elaborated in this chapter is that transnational organizations no longer can use cost considerations as justification for ignoring the potential benefits that accrue from intercultural communication training for impacted persons, communities, and multicultural assistance agencies. The enhanced verbal and nonverbal competence, mediation approaches, and local networking and capacity-building skills acquired through intercultural communication training offer dislocated persons and their new neighbors the prospect of living in harmonious and mutually productive relationship with one another. Furthermore, multicultural organization communication competency allows selected individuals who are members of the impacted populations to provide effective community assistance in the relief and development work conducted by transnational organizations, to acquire valuable and portable professional skills, and to assume powerful cultural-broker and partner roles.

Through complex networks of interorganizational linkages and activities, transnational and indigenous organizations possess the potential capacity for cooperation and problem resolution when confronted with challenging humanitarian-assistance situations. The case of refugees and other displaced persons suggests that extending the vision of organizational communication to encompass perimeter communities constitutes a prerequisite for realizing this potential.

ACKNOWLEDGMENTS

The authors acknowledge with gratitude the helpful comments and suggestions they received from George Cheney and the anonymous reviewers.

REFERENCES

Ager, A. (1999). Perspectives on the refugee experience. In A. Ager (Ed.), *Refugees: Perspectives on the experience of forced migration* (pp. 1-23). London: Pinter.

Ahearn, F., Loughrey, M., & Ager, A. (1999). The experience of refugee children. In A. Ager (Ed.), *Refugees: Perspectives on the experience of forced migration* (pp. 215-236). London: Pinter.

Albert, R.D. (1983). The intercultural sensitizer or culture assimilator: A cognitive approach. In D. Landis & R. W. Brislin (Eds.), *Handbook of intercultural training, vol. II: Issues in training methodology* (pp. 186-217). New York: Pergamon.

Anderson, M.B. (1998). Northeast Thailand project. In M. B. Anderson & P. J. Woodrow (Eds.), *Rising from the ashes: Development strategies in times of disaster* (pp. 315-328). Boulder, CO: Westview

Anderson, M.B., & Woodrow, P. J. (1989). *Rising from the ashes: Development strategies in times of disaster*. Boulder, CO: Westview.

Bandura, A. (1995). Exercise of personal and collective efficacy in changing societies. In A. Bandura (Ed.), *Self-efficacy in changing societies* (pp. 1-45). Cambridge, UK: Cambridge University Press.

Baxter, J. (1983). English for intercultural competence: An approach to intercultural communication training. In D. Landis & R. W. Brislin (Eds.), *Handbook of intercultural training, Vol. II: Issues in training methodology* (pp. 290-324). New York: Pergamon.

Bell, M.P., & Harrison, D.A. (1996). Using intra-national diversity for international assignments: A model of bicultural competence and expatriate adjustment. *Human Resource Management Review, 6*(1), 47-74.

Bemak, F., Chung, R.C., & Bornemann, T.H. (1996). Counseling and psychotherapy with refugees. In P.B. Pedersen, J.G. Draguns, W. J. Lonner, & J. E. Trimble (Eds.), *Counseling across cultures* (4th ed., pp. 243-265). Thousand Oaks: Sage.

Bennett, R., Aston, A., & Colquhoun, T. (2000). Cross-cultural training: A critical step in ensuring the success of international assignments. *Human Resource Managment, 39*(2/3), 239-250.

Black, J.S., & Mendenhall, M. (1989). A practical but theory-based framework for selecting cross-cultural training methods. *Human Resource Management, 28*(4), 511-539.

Bond, M.H. (1992). The process of enhancing cross-cultural competence in Hong Kong organizations. *International Journal of Intercultural Relations, 16,* 395-412.

Brislin, R.W., Cushner, K., Cherrie, C., & Yong, M. (1986). *Intercultural interactions: A practical guide.* Beverly Hills, CA: Sage.

Brislin, R.W., Landis, D., & Brandt, M.E. (1983). Conceptualizations of intercultural behavior and training. In D. Landis & R. W. Brislin (Eds.), *Handbook of intercultural training, vol. I: Issues in theory and design* (pp. 1-27). New York: Pergamon.

Brislin, R., & Yoshida, T. (1994). *Intercultural communication training: An introduction.* Thousand Oaks, CA: Sage.

Cargile, A.C., & Giles, H. (1996). Intercultural communication training: Review, critique, and a new theoretical framework. *Communication yearbook, 19,* 385-423.

Castles, S. (2002, October). *Environmental change and forced migration: Making sense of the debate* (New Issues in Refugee Research Working Paper No. 70). Geneva: UNHCR, Evaluation & Policy Unit.

Cernea, M.M. (1990). Internal refugee flows and development-induced population displacement. *Journal of Refugee Studies, 3*(4), 369-401.

Chambers, R. (1993). Hidden losers? The impact of rural refugees and refugee programs on poorer hosts. In R. F. Gorman (Ed.), *Refugee aid and development: Theory and practice* (pp. 29-43). Westport, CT: Greenwood Press.

Chambers, R. (1994). Participatory rural appraisal (PRA): Challenges, potentials, and paradigms. *World Development, 22*(10), 1437-1454.

Chen, G., & Starosta, W. (1996). Intercultural communication competence: A synthesis. *Communication yearbook, 19*(3), 363-383.

Cheney, G., Straub, J., Speirs-Glebe, L., Stohl, C., DeGooyer, D., Whalen, S., Garvin-Doxas, K., & Carlone, D. (1998). Democracy, participation, and communication at work: A multidisciplinary review. In W. B. Gudykunst (Ed.), *Communication yearbook 21* (pp. 35-91). Thousand Oaks, CA: Sage.

Cohen, R., & Deng, F.M. (1998). *Masses in flight: The global crisis of internal displacement.* Washington, DC: Brookings Institution.

Crossette, B. (2000a, July 24). Aid halted in West Timor after attack on U.N. staff. *The New York Times,* p. A10.

Crossette, B. (2000b, July 24). A new crisis over refugees adrift in their own lands: U.N. seeks ways to help a forgotten group. *The New York Times,* p. A4.

Cuny, F.C. (1979). Viewpoints: Research, planning and refugees. *Disasters, 3*(4), 339-240.

Daubon, R.E., & Saunders, H.H. (2002). Operationalizing social capital: A strategy to enhance communities' "capacity to concert." *International Studies Perspectives, 3*(2), 176-191.

de Montclose, M.P., & Kagwanja, P.M. (2000). Refugee camps or cities? The socio-economic dynamics of the Dadaab and Kakuma camps in northern Kenya. *Journal of Refugee Studies, 13*(2), 205-222.

Dinges, N. (1983). Intercultural competence. In D. Landis & R. W. Brislin (Eds.), *Handbook of intercultural training* (Vol. 2, pp. 176-202). New York: Pergamon.

Eade, D., & Williams, S. (1995). *The Oxfam handbook of development and relief (Vols 1 and 2).* Oxford: Oxfam.

Edwards, M. (1997). Organizational learning in non-governmental organization: What have we learned? *Public Administration and Development, 17,* 235-250.

Erlanger, S. (2000, July 3). U.N. official warns of losing the peace in Kosovo. *The New York Times,* p. A3.

Forrest, J.B. (2000). The drought policy bureaucracy, decentralization, and policy networks in post-apartheid Namibia. *American Review of Public Administration, 30*(3), 307-333.

Frantz, D. (2000, July 24). Hope erodes for Azerbaijan's sea of refugees. *The New York Times,* pp. A1, A4.

Gallois, C., & Callan, V.J. (1997). *Communication and culture: A guide for practice.* New York: Wiley.

Gudykunst, W.B., & Hammer, M. R. (1983). Basic training design: Approaches to inter-cultural training. In D. Landis & R.W. Brislin (Eds.), *Handbook of intercultural training vol. I: Issues in theory and design* (pp. 118-154). New York: Pergamon.

Hanf, K., & O'Toole, L.J., Jr. (1992). Revisiting old friends: Networks, implementation structures and the management of inter-organizational relations. *European Journal of Political Research, 21,* 163-180.

Hansen, A. (1979). Once the running stops: Assimilation of Angolan refugees into Zambian border villages. *Disasters, 3*(4), 369-374.

Hardy, C. (1994). Underorganized interorganizational domains: The case of refugee systems. *Journal of Applied Behavioral Science, 30*(3), 278-296.

Harrell-Bond, B.E. (1989). Repatriation: Under what conditions is it the most desirable solution for refugees? An agenda for research. *African Studies Review, 32*(1), 40-60.

Harrison, J.K. (1994). Developing successful expatriate managers: A framework for the structural design and strategic alignment of cross-cultural training programs. *Human Resource Planning, 17*(3), 17-35.

Harvey, M.G., Speier, C., & Novicevic, M.M. (1999). The role of inpatriates in a global-ization strategy and challenges associated with the inpatriation process. *Human Resource Planning, 22*(1), 38-50.

Hocker, J.L., & Wilmot, W. (1995). *Interpersonal conflict (4th ed.).* Madison, WI: Brown & Benchmark.

Hyden, G., Koehn, P., & Saleh, T. (1996). The challenges of decentralization in Eritrea. *Journal of African Policy Studies, 11*(1), 31-51.

International Rescue Committee and Save the Children Fund (IRC and SCF). (1981). *Tawawa survey results.* Gedaref, Sudan: Author.

Kealey, D.J. (1990). *Cross-cultural effectiveness: A study of Canadian technical advisors overseas.* Hull, Quebec: Canadian International Development Agency.

Kealey, D.J., & Protheroe, D.R. (1996). The effectiveness of cross-cultural training for expatriates: An assessment of the literature on the issue. *International Journal of Intercultural Relations, 20*(2), 141-165.

Kibreab, G. (1994). Refugees in the Sudan: Unresolved issues. In H. Adelman & J. Sorenson (Eds.), *African refugees: Development aid and repatriation* (pp. 45-68). Boulder, CO: Westview.

Kim, Y.Y. (1988). *Communication and cross-cultural adaptation: An integrative theory.* Clevedon, UK: Multilingual Matters.

Koehn, P.H. (1991). *Refugees from revolution.* Boulder, CO: Westview.

Koehn, P. (Ed.). (1994a). *Final report of the international symposium "Refugees and development assistance: Training for voluntary repatriation."* Missoula: Office of International Programs, The University of Montana-Missoula.

Koehn, P.H. (1994b). Refugee settlement and repatriation in Africa: Development prospects and constraints. In H. Adelman & J. Sorenson (Eds.), *African refugees: Development aid and repatriation* (pp. 97-116). Boulder, CO: Westview.

Koehn, P.H. (2002, November). *Transnational competence and migrant marginality: Hidden perspectives on health/illness, health-care outcomes, adherence, ethnocultural practices, and mental-health needs.* Paper presented at the Fulbright New Century Scholars Final Plenary Session, Airlie House, VA.

Koehn, P., & Ngai, P.B. (2001). Managing refugee-assistance crises in the twenty-first century: The intercultural-communication factor. In A. Farazmand (Ed.), *Handbook of crisis and emergency management* (pp. 737-765). New York: Marcel Dekker.

Koehn, P.H., & Rosenau, J.N. (2002). Transnational competence in an emergent epoch. *International Studies Perspectives, 3*(2), 105-127.

Mak, A.S., Westwood, M.J., Ishiyama, F.I., & Barker, M.C. (1999). Optimising conditions for learning sociocultural competencies for success. *International Journal of Intercultural Relations, 23*(1), 77-90.

Martin, S.F. (1993). The inhospitable earth. *Refugees, 89,* 12-16.

Maynard, K.A. (1999). *Healing communities in conflict: International assistance in complex emergencies.* New York: Columbia University Press.

Mazur, R.E. (1998). Refugees in Africa: The role of sociological analysis and praxis. *Current Sociology, 36*(2), 50-65.

McKinley, J. (2000, July 4). Fantasyland of American movies as a tonic for refugee children. *The New York Times,* pp. B1, B3.

Melkote, S.R. (1991). *Communication for development in the third world: Theory and practice.* Newbury Park, CA: Sage.

Mezirow, J. (1991). *Transformative dimensions of adult learning.* San Francisco, CA: Jossey-Bass.

Milhouse, V.H. (1996). Intercultural communication education and training goals, content, and methods. *International Journal of Intercultural Relations, 20*(1), 69-95.

Miller, K.E. (1999). Rethinking a familiar model: Psychotherapy and the mental health of refugees. *Journal of Contemporary Psychotherapy, 29*(4), 282-306.

Minear, L., & Guillot, P. (1996). *Soldiers to the rescue: Humanitarian lessons from Rwanda.* Paris: Organization for Economic Co-operation and Development.

Mollica, R.F., Lavelle, J., Tor, S., & Elias, C. (1989). *Turning point in Khmer mental health: Immediate steps to resolve the mental health crisis in the Khmer border camps.* Cambridge: Committee on Refugees and Migrants, World Federation for Mental Health.

Musisi, S. (2002, November). *Mental health problems of mass trauma in Africa: A study of three countries which experienced war.* Paper presented at the Fulbright New Century Scholars Final Plenary Session, Airlie House, VA.

Ngai, P.B. (2001). Nonverbal communication behavior in intercultural negotiations: Insights and applications based on findings from Ethiopia, Tanzania, Hong Kong, and the China Mainland. *World Communication, 29*(4), 3-35.

Ngai, P.B., & Koehn, P. (2001). Preparing for diversity in the midst of adversity: An intercultural-communication training program for refugee assistance crisis management. In A. Farazmand (Ed.), *Handbook of crisis and emergency management* (pp. 23-37). New York: Marcel Dekker.

Ogata, S. (2000). From refugees to global migration management. *New Perspectives Quarterly, 17*(4), 40-41.

Paige, R.M., & Martin, J.N. (1983). Ethical issues and ethics in cross-cultural training. In D. Landis & R. W. Brislin (Eds.), *Handbook of intercultural training, vol. II: Issues in training methodology* (pp. 36-60). New York: Pergamon.

Pedersen, P. (1983). Intercultural training of mental-health providers. In D. Landis & R. W. Brislin (Eds.), *Handbook of intercultural training, vol. II: Issues in training methodology* (pp. 325-352). New York: Pergamon.

Pedersen, P. (1994). *A handbook for developing multicultural awareness* (2nd ed.). Alexandria: American Counseling Association.

Phillips, B.D. (1993). Cultural diversity in disasters: Sheltering, housing, and long term recovery. *International Journal of Mass Emergencies and Disasters, 11*(1), 99-110.

Planalp, S. (1999). *Communicating emotion: Social, moral, and cultural processes.* New York/Paris: Cambridge University Press.

Ptak, C.L., Cooper, J., & Brislin, R. (1995). Cross cultural training programs: Advice and insights from experienced trainers. *International Journal of Intercultural Relations, 19*(3), 425-452.

Rogge, J. (1993). The challenges of changing dimensions among the South's refugees: Illustrations from Somalia. *International Journal of Refugee Law, 5*(1), 12-30.

Ruiz, H.A. (1994). Training for voluntary repatriation: Challenges and opportunities. In P. Koehn (Ed.), *Refugees and development assistance: Training for voluntary repatriation* (pp. 47-62). Missoula: The University of Montana.

Salk, J. (1996). Partners and other strangers: Cultural boundaries and cross-cultural encounters in international joint venture teams. *International Studies of Management and Organizations, 26*(4), 48-72.

Schoenhaus, R.M. (2000). *Conflict management training: Advancing best practices.* Washington, DC: United States Institute of Peace.

Seidel, G. (1981). Cross-cultural training procedures: Their theoretical framework and evaluation. In S. Bochner (Ed.), *The mediating person: Bridges between cultures.* Cambridge, MA: Schenkman.

Shaffer, L.S. (1998). Maximizing human capital by developing multicultural competence. *NACADA Journal, 18*(2), 21-27.

Siegel, G.B. (1985). Human resource development for emergency management. *Public Administration Review, 45*(2), 107-117.

Sollis, P. (1994). The relief-development continuum: Some notes on rethinking assistance for civilian victims of conflict. *Journal of International Affairs, 47*(2), 451-469.

Sorenson, J. (1994). An overview: Refugees and development. In H. Adelman & J. Sorenson (Eds.), *African refugees: Development aid and repatriation* (pp. 175-190). Boulder, CO: Westview.

Sterkenburg, J., Kirkby, J., & O'Keefe, P. (1994). Refugees and rural development: A comparative analysis of project aid in Sudan and Tanzania. In H. Adelman & J. Sorenson (Eds.), *African refugees: Development aid and repatriation* (pp. 191-208). Boulder, CO: Westview.

Stohl, C. (1993). International organizing and organizational communication. *Journal of Applied Communication Research, 21*, 377-384.

Stuart, S., & Bery, R. (1996). Powerful grass-roots women communicators: Participatory video in Bangladesh. In D. Allen, R. R. Rush, & S. J. Kaufman (Eds.), *Women transforming communications: Global intersections for the 21st century.* Thousand Oaks, CA: Sage.

Suhrke, A. (1994). Environmental degeneration and population flows. *Journal of International Affairs, 47*(2), 473-496.

Summerfield, D. (1999). Sociocultural dimensions of war, conflict and displacement. In A. Ager (Ed.), *Refugees: Perspectives on the experience of forced migration* (pp. 111-135). London: Pinter.

Taylor, J.R., Flanagin, A.J., Cheney, G., & Seibold, D.R. (2001). Organizational communication: Key moments, central concerns, and future challenges. In W. B. Gudykunst (Ed.), *Communication yearbook 24* (pp. 99-137). Thousand Oaks, CA: Sage.

The New York Times (2000, May 13). p. A1.

Thomas, A. (1998). Scientific and practical aspects of cross-cultural cooperation and management in the context of European integration. *Studia Psychologica, 40*(1-2), 69-77.

Waldron, S., & Hasci, N.A. (1995). *Somali refugees in the horn of Africa: State of the art literature review* (Studies on Emergencies and Disaster Relief Report No. 3). Sweden: Nordiska Afrikainstitutet.

Warpinski, A. (2001). *MSF activity report 2000-2001.* Brussells: Médecins sans Frontiéres, International Office.

Weine, S.M. (1996). Bosnian refugees: Memories, witnessing, and history after Dayton. *World Refugee Survey, 1996,* 28-34.

Whitaker, B.E. (1999). *Changing opportunities: Refugee and host communities in western Tanzania* (New Issues in Refugee Research Working Paper No. 11). Geneva, Switzerland: Centre for Documentation and Research, UNHCR.

Woodrow, P.J. (1998a). Promotion of health care among Khmer refugees in Greenhill Site B. In M.B. Anderson & P.J. Woodrow (Eds.), *Rising from the ashes: Development strategies in times of disaster* (pp. 301-314). Boulder, CO: Westview.

Woodrow, P.J. (1998b). Qala en Nahal refugee settlement project: Eastern Sudan. In M. B. Anderson & P. J. Woodrow (Eds.). *Rising from the ashes: Development strategies in times of disaster* (pp. 259-278). Boulder, CO: Westview.

Xiao, J. (1996). The relationship between organizational factors and the transfer of training in the electronics industry in Shenzhen, China. *Human Resource Development Quarterly, 7*(1), 55-73.

Yarbrough, E. & Wilmot, W. (1995). *Artful mediation constructive conflict at work.* Boulder, CO: Cairns.

Zetter, R. (1995). Incorporation and exclusion: The life cycle of Malawi's refuge assistance program. *World Development, 23*(10), 1653-1667.

CONTRIBUTORS

George A. Barnett (PhD Michigan State University, 1976) is currently a professor of communication at the State University of New York at Buffalo. He has written extensively on organizational, mass, international and intercultural, and political communication, as well as the diffusion of innovations. His current research focuses on international telecommunications and its role on social and economic development and globalization. He has served as chair of the Communication and Technology Division of the International Communication Association.

Catherine Becker (PhD, State University of New York at Buffalo, 1993) is associate professor and chair communication at the University of Hawaii, Hilo. Her areas of expertise include intercultural and organizational communication and public relations. Her published research focuses on the relationship between communication, culture, and symbols and their implications for identity, empowerment, community, and sustainable systems.

Deborah A. Cai (PhD, Michigan State University, 1994) is associate professor in the Department of Communication at the University of Maryland. As an international researcher with ties to China, she specializes in intercultural communication, persuasion, and conflict management. In particular, her research examines the effects of culture on cognitive processes related to decision making, perceptions of conflict, and planning in negotiation. Her research has been present-ed at national and international conferences and is published in journals such as *Communication Monographs*, *Communication Yearbook*, *Human Communication Research*, *Journal of Applied Communication*, and the *Asian Journal of Communication*.

George Cheney (PhD, Purdue University, 1985) is professor in the Department of Communication at the University of Utah. He is also adjunct professor in the Department of Management Communication, The University of Waikato, Hamilton, New Zealand. Previously, he taught at the universities of Illinois, Colorado, and Montana. Cheney's teaching and research interests include iden-tity and power in the modern organization, corporate public discourse, quality of work life, employee participation, business ethics, the "marketization" of society, issues of sustainability and globalization, and the rhetoric of war. He has authored or co-authored more than 75 journal articles, book chapters, reviews, and editorials. He has published three other books. Recognized for both teaching and research, Cheney has lectured in Denmark, The Netherlands, Spain, Mexico, and Colombia, in addition to North America and Australasia. He is an advocate of uniting theory and practice and a supporter of such pedagogi-cal strategies as service learning. He believes that the social sciences and humanities have a primary responsibility to encourage reflection about the taken-for-granted assumptions in our world.

Héctor R. Díaz-Sáenz (PhD, University of Texas at Austin, 2003) is an associ-ate professor in organizational communication in the Graduate School of Business Administration and Leadership of ITESM, Campus Monterrey (Monterrey Institute of Technology). His areas of interest are organizational culture and leadership, with a focus on change and the usage of internal com-munication practices in organizations established in Mexico. He co-authored a recent chapter in a book on psychological contracts in employment. He has pub-lished articles as an author and co-author in *COMARI*, the Mexican Confederation of Industrial Relations magazine, in the electronic magazine *Hypermarketing.com* and co-authored an article in *Management Communication Quarterly*. He is a member of the Monterrey (Mexico) chapter of Executives of Industrial Relations Association.

Shiv Ganesh (PhD, Purdue University, 2000) is associate professor in the Department of Communication Studies, University of Montana, Missoula. He studies issues of communication, modernity, and technology from a critical, qualitative perspective. Within this broad framework, he has conducted and published research on the relationships among global sustainable development discourse, information technology, and nongovernment organizations in the South Asian context. He has also conducted and published research on the relationships among corporations, computer-mediated communication, and public discourse. Additionally, he is interested in service learning, conflict resolution, and mediation in organizations as a means of integrating theory and practice.

Susan Hafen (PhD, Ohio University, 1995) is associate professor in the Department of Communication at Weber State University, Ogden, Utah. Her eclectic research interests include diversity training, organizational emotions and gossip, animal–human communication, ethnography, and feminist criticism. Her publications have appeared in *Communication Yearbook* and *Journal of Wisconsin Communication Association*. Prior to her academic life, Hafen worked as human resource manager and/or trainer for Kimberly Clark Corporation in Utah, Mobil Oil in Wyoming, and Potomac Electric Power Company in Washington, DC.

Renée Houston (PhD, Florida State University, 1996) is an assistant professor of communication at the University of Puget Sound where she teaches organizational communication, computer-mediated communication in organizations, business and professional communication, and group communication. Her research interests include organizational communication, technology adoption in developing nations, social effects of computer-mediated communication, collaboration and computer supported cooperative work, and technology and gender. Houston has consulted with organizations in a variety of capacities and industries including public transit, hospitals, U.S. Air Force, and libraries. For her work with the Utah Transit Authority she won top paper honors from the International Association of Business Communications.

Chun-ju Hung (PhD, University of Maryland, 2002) conducts research in public relations, intercultural communication, conflict resolution, and organizational communication. For three years in a row (1999, 2000, and 2001), she won the Inez Kaiser Award from the Association for Education in Journalism and Mass Communication. Recently, she received the Outstanding Graduate Scholar Award from the Department of Communication at the University of Maryland and was awarded the Ketchum 2001 Walter K. Lindenmann Scholarship from the Institute for Public Relations.

Peter Koehn (PhD, University of Colorado–Boulder, 1973) is professor of political science at The University of Montana–Missoula. In 2001-2002, he was named a Fulbright New Century Scholar in the Inaugural Challenges to Health in a Borderless World program. His research and teaching interests include global migration, transnational competence, migrant health care, development administration, U.S.–China relations, and African politics. He is the author of two books, author or co-editor of five additional books and 12 monographs, and author or co-author of 68 articles and chapters, including a piece co-authored with James N. Rosenau in the May 2002 issue of *International Studies Perspectives*. He has taught at universities in Ethiopia, Nigeria, Eritrea, Namibia, China, and Hong Kong, and consulted for UNICEF and with the Japan International Cooperation Agency. From 1987 to 1996, Koehn served as the University of Montana's founding director of international programs.

Mark Lawrence McPhail (PhD, University of Massachusetts, 1987) is professor of interdisciplinary studies at Miami University in Oxford Ohio. He is the author of two books on racism. His work has been published in *The Quarterly Journal of Speech, Critical Studies in Media Communication, the Howard Journal of Communications*, and the *American Literary Review*. His research interests include rhetorical epistemology, language and race relations, and Eastern philosophy and spirituality.

Debashish Munshi (PhD, The University of Waikato, 2000) is a senior lecturer in management communication at The University of Waikato, Hamilton, New Zealand. Munshi is a journalist-turned-academic, and his research interests lie in the intersections of media, management, politics, and culture. He is also passionate about issues of diversity in the workplace. As someone who loves writing, Munshi spends a lot of his time juggling letters on the keyboard to compose a variety of work that includes epistles to friends and family, newspaper and magazine commentaries, and, of late, scholarly articles.

Phyllis Bo-yuen Ngai (EdD, University of Montana–Missoula, 2004) teaches business communication in the School of Education at The University of Montana-Missoula. Her research and teaching interests include cross-cultural communication, intercultural communication training, and bilingual and multi-cultural education. She is the author or co-author of two chapters and one monograph on intercultural communication training and five articles in professional journals, including *World Communication, World Executive's Digest, Journal of Studies in International Education*, and the *Bilingual Research Journal*. She has conducted intercultural communication training with professionals in Hong Kong, Macau, and Shanghai.

Mariela Pérez-Chavarría (LABD, Universidad de Málaga) is professor of organizational communication and public relationships at the Monterrey Tech University (ITESM), Monterrey Campus, in Mexico. Her research and teaching interests include language, corporate identity, and intercultural and organizational communication. She has published articles, essays, and two books. She is a member of the Mexican Association of Organizational Communicators and the International Communication Association.

Patricia D. Witherspoon (PhD, University of Texas at Austin, 1977) is professor and chair of the Department of Communication Studies at The University of Texas at El Paso, and founding director of its Center for Communication Studies. Her research and teaching interests are in organizational leadership, the leadership of organizational change, communication processes in knowledge organizations, and the effect of culture on organizational communication in Mexico. She has published two books and another one is in press, and she is the author of several book chapters and journal articles in the areas of political communication and organizational communication.

AUTHOR INDEX

SUBJECT INDEX

285

Printed in the United States
41640LVS00002B/211-213

9 781572 735491